Keeping the Peace

UN Peace Operations and their Effectiveness: An Assessment

KEEPING THE PEACE

UN PEACE OPERATIONS AND THEIR EFFECTIVENESS: AN ASSESSMENT

Major General (Dr.) Apurba Kumar Bardalai, PhD

Retired, Indian Army

PENTAGON PRESS LLP

KEEPING THE PEACE: UN Peace Operations and their Effectiveness: An Assessment

Major General (Dr.) Apurba Kumar Bardalai, PhD

First Published in 2022

ISBN 978-93-90095-66-7

Disclaimer: The views and opinions expressed in the book are the individual assertion of the Author in his personal capacity and do not have any official endorsement. Moreover the Publisher does not take any responsibility for the same in any manner whatsoever. Attributability of the contents lies purely with Author.

Published by
PENTAGON PRESS LLP
206, Peacock Lane, Shahpur Jat
New Delhi-110049
Phones: 011-64706243, 26491568
Telefax: 011-26490600
email: rajan@pentagonpress.in
website: www.pentagonpress.in

Printed at Aegean Offset Printers, Greater Noida, U.P.

CONTENTS

Foreword

Despite its long history, the results of UN peace operations are mixed. The monumental failures in places like Rwanda, Somalia, or former Yugoslavia, bring UN peacekeeping under criticism. In the process, the brickbats are more for what it has not been able to achieve, and no bouquets are reserved for its contribution to global conflict management. To enhance the effectiveness of the UN peace operations, the UN has tried to introduce several reforms over the last 30 years. Measuring performance remains a key to any successful reforms. Opinions on the methods and evaluation parameters vary, as each peace operation is different in context and scope. In the absence of any standard method of evaluation of UN peace operations, efforts to develop an evaluation framework are the need of the day and praiseworthy.

This book is all about establishing assessment criteria for UN peace operations and then applying them to assess the performance of the United Nations Interim Force in Lebanon (UNIFIL). It is based on the author's PhD thesis on *United Nations Interim Force in Lebanon: Assessment and The Way Forward* from Tilburg University, the Netherlands. I was the author's first Supervisor for the research for over six years. The award of the PhD was based on the author's meeting the primary objectives of his research: *one*, to identify important organizational and conflict-specific factors/variables, with a direct influence on peace operations; *two*, to identify indicators that can be used to assess the success or failure of a peace operation and *three*, to evaluate the outcome of UNIFIL, as a case study and confirming the scales of investigation.

To determine widely-accepted success criteria, the identification of a conceptual framework for the evaluation of peace operations is a prerequisite. The available scholarly works on the development of such criteria have been based on the studies of different UN peace operations, which were generally established to resolve intra-state conflicts. Initially, the book develops a conceptual framework and identification of a standard set of criteria for the evaluation of peace operations. Later, it applies them to assess the performance of a traditional UN peace operation. The author uses UNIFIL as a case study to analyse the effectiveness of traditional UN peace operations using empirical data, supported by perceptions and practical experiences of peacekeepers and 'subject matter experts' at both operational and tactical levels. UNIFIL was used as a case study because even though it is a traditional peacekeeping mission, the mission is unique in several ways. The mission is deployed in a geopolitically sensitive area and has witnessed the recurrence of violence and major conflicts between Israel and Lebanon. If a new inter-state conflict was to occur again in this region, the scope of the violence is likely to expand beyond the geographic region of the Middle East. Secondly, UNIFIL is the only traditional peacekeeping mission where peacekeepers and formed units from a few European nations are participating. These peacekeepers are equipped with advanced weapons and equipment including main battle tanks and artillery guns, which are rare in a traditional peace operation mandated under Chapter VI of the UN Charter. Despite the prevailing security situation of the region and the delicate bilateral relations between Israel and Lebanon, there has not been any major conflict between Israel and Lebanon for close to three decades, after the deployment of the UNIFIL-II post the war in 2006. These complexities make UNIFIL an exclusive case to develop and test a reliable set of criteria to assess a peace operation's outcomes.

The book ends with the author concluding that UNIFIL has hitherto been successful in preventing bloodshed since the 2006 war and has contributed effectively towards the maintenance of peace and tranquillity in the geopolitically sensitive region of the Middle East. Therefore, UNIFIL can be assessed to be a satisfactorily successful UN peace operation. The book has implications for both practitioners and academicians to apply the criterion and further develop it for multi-dimensional peace operations.

Prof. Dr. Joseph Soeters
Tilburg University, the Netherlands

FOREWORD

The UN has a long history of participation in peacekeeping. However, despite the available statistics about its positive contribution to conflict management, it often comes under criticism because of its inability to implement the mandate in several earlier missions. But it is unfair to blame the peacekeeping missions for their inability to implement the mandate as the reasons for failures are always not under the control of the missions. As such the assessment of the UN peace operation has not been easy. In absence of a standard framework for evaluation, opinions of the scholars, practitioners and member states vary on the performance of peace operations. Besides, most writings on peace operations are based on Western literature and lack input from the field.

India has been participating in peace operations for several decades and can boast of fielding its peacekeepers in some of the most complex peace operations, contributing to senior leadership positions and making supreme sacrifices. However, India's intellectual and scholarly contribution to the UN peace operations needs to be enhanced. *Keeping the Peace: UN Peace Operations and their Effectiveness: An Assessment* is the first of its kind by an Indian author. Combining his experiences as a peacekeeper at different levels with his academic credentials, and using qualitative and quantitative analysis, Major General (Dr) AK Bardalai, a veteran of the Indian Army has put forward a conceptual framework for the evaluation of traditional UN peace operations.

The major takeaways and recommendations of the author would provide valuable inputs for the assessment of the current and future UN peace operations. USI of India compliments the author and takes pride in publishing *Keeping the Peace: UN Peace Operations and their Effectiveness: An Assessment* along with Pentagon Press LLP.

Major General BK Sharma (Retired)
Director United Services Institution of India

ACKNOWLEDGEMENTS

This book is based on my PhD research on "United Nations Interim Force in Lebanon: An Assessment and Way Forward". Hence, first and foremost, I am extremely grateful to both my supervisors—Prof. Dr. Joseph Soeters and Prof. Dr. Patricia Shields—for their constant guidance and encouragement in my research. Both had gone out of their way and walked the extra mile to share their ideas on the subject. But for their indulgence, it would not have been possible for me to achieve whatever I have been able to do so far. My meetings and discussions with Professor Soeters and participation in his seminars had always boosted my morale. Out of many PhD theses that he has supervised until now, my thesis was possibly the most challenging because of my academic limitations. Prof. Soeters not only had to take extra care to see that I cross the finishing line, but he continues to guide me in my endeavour to pursue my academic studies. As for Professor Shields, she not only never hesitated, but also was rather prompt in responding to all my queries with new ideas such as the use of pillar questions rather than hypotheses. I am immensely grateful for the support of Professors Soeters and Shields. My words would not be enough to thank them. I also acknowledge the initial motivation that I received from Dr. Jan van der Meulen, the then Professor of Civil-Military Relations, Leiden University, the Netherlands. Both Dr. Meulen and Professor Soeters were confident that I could research UNIFIL.

I would also like to express my sincere gratitude to the members of the PhD review committee—Prof. Dr. J. Goedee, Prof. Dr. T.B.F.M. Brinkel, Prof. Dr. J. Hoffenaar, Dr. C.H. Ruffa and Dr. V.F. Newby for their painstaking efforts to go through the dissertation and offer valuable suggestions. Their suggestions have indeed made my work better and richer.

The process of research was rather challenging, and I always had to fall back on someone in India, who could correctly guide me on the methodology as well as related topics on UN peacekeeping. This help promptly came from Dr. K.K. Sharma (Colonel, retired, Indian Army), a former peacekeeper, my colleague and a Professor at Chitkara University, Punjab, in India. Colonel Sharma, an experienced peacekeeper himself, guided me at every stage. My sincere gratitude to him for the support he extended to his colleague. I am also immensely thankful to Colonel B.S. Negi for his painstaking effort in creating the graphic analyses of important statistical data. In addition, I would like to convey my sincere appreciation to the USI of India, and Pentagon Press LLP for getting the book published.

One of the limitations of the research was to find former peacekeepers who were or are still, affiliated with UNIFIL. These included experts from Lebanon and Israel. Given the current security situation in the Middle East, it was rather difficult to convince subject matter experts to find time to respond to my interviews. With some difficulty, I could interview 25 peacekeeping/subject matter experts. They found time amidst their remarkably busy schedules to answer my questions. I am immensely thankful to them for sharing their valuable time.

Finally, I am extremely thankful to my wife, Meeta, our daughter Nikita, our grandson Reuelkibitu and our son-in-law, Colonel Jonathan Varun Benjamin, for being patient with me and constantly encouraging me in the pursuit of my goal. I sincerely hope that this book will be of some help to our peacekeepers and scholars in understanding the nuances of peacekeeping when they look at it beyond the tactical level.

LIST OF ABBREVIATIONS

ADF	Arab Deterrent Force
AMO	Area of Maritime Operations
AO	Area of Operations
APC	Armoured Personnel Carrier
BL	Blue Line
CAO	Chief Administrative Officer
CIMIC	Civil-Military Cooperation
CSA	Comprehensive Settlement Agreement
DDPCA	Deputy Director of Political and Civil Affairs
DDR	Demobilisation, Disarmament, and Reintegration
DFC	Deputy Force Commander
DPCA	Director of Political and Civil Affairs
DO	Designate Official
DPO	Department of Peacekeeping Operations
DRC	Democratic Republic of Congo
DUF	Directive for Use of Force
EOD	Explosives Ordnance Disposal
FC	Force Commander
HoM	Head of the Mission
IDF	Israeli Defence Forces
IDP	Internally Displaced Personnel
INTERFRET	International Force in East Timor
LAF–N	Lebanese Armed Forces Navy
LAF	Lebanese Armed Forces

LMAC	Lebanon Mine Action Centre
MACC SL	Mine Action Coordination Centre, South Lebanon
MINUSMA	UN Multidimensional Integrated Stabilization Mission in Mali
MINUSCA	United Nations Multidimensional Integrated Stabilization Mission in the Central African Republic
MoE	Measure of Effectiveness
MoU	Memorandum of Understanding
MONUSCO	United Nations Stabilisation Mission in Congo
MPLA	Movimento Popular de Liberatcao de Angola
MTF	Maritime Task Force
NATO	North Atlantic Treaty Organisation
OIOS	Office of Internal Oversight Services
ONUSAL	United Nations Observer Group in El Salvador
PCC	Police Contributing Country
POC	Protection of Civilians
PKO	Peacekeeping Operation (s)
PFLP	Popular Front for the Liberation of Palestine
PLO	Palestine Liberation Organisation
RUF	Revolutionary United Front
QRF	Quick Reaction Force
QUIP	Quick Impact Project
SCR	Security Council Resolution
SG	Secretary General
SLA	South Lebanese Army
SOFA	Status of Forces Agreement
SOMA	Status of Mission Agreement
SPLA	Sudan People's Liberation Army
SRSG	Special Representative of the Secretary General
TCC	Troop Contributing Countries
UAV	Unarmed Aerial Vehicle
UN	The United Nations
UNAMA	United Nations Assistance Mission in Afghanistan
UNAMET	United Nations Assistance Mission in East Timor
UNAMI	United Nations Assistance Mission in Iraq

UNAMID	United Nations Hybrid Operation in Darfur
UNAMIK	United Nations Interim Administration in Kosovo
UNAMIR	United Nations Assistance Mission for Rwanda
UNAMSIL	United Nations Mission in Sierra Leone
UNAVEM II	United Nations Verification Mission in Angola II
UNCRO	UN Confidence Restoration Operation in Croatia
UNDOF	UN Disengagement Observer Force
UNEF	United Nations Emergency Force
UNFICYP	United Nations Peacekeeping Force in Cyprus
UNHCR	United Nations High Commissioner for Refugees
UNIFIL	UN Interim Force in Lebanon
UNITA	Uniao Nacional para Independencia Total de Angola
UNITAF	United Task Force Somalia
UNMACC	United Nations Mine Action Coordination Centre
UNMEE	UN Mission in Ethiopia and Eretria
UNMISS	United Nations Mission in South Sudan
UNMOGIP	UN Military Observer Group in India and Pakistan
UNOMOZ	United Nations Operations in Mozambique
UNOSOM	United Nations Operation in Somalia
UNPROFOR	United Nations Protection Force in former Yugoslavia
UNSMS	UN Security Management System
UNSCOL	United Nations Special Coordinator for Lebanon
UNTAC	United Nations Transitional Authority in Cambodia
UNTAES	United Nations Transitional Authority in Eastern Slovenia
UNTAET	United Nations Transitional Authority in East Timor/Timor-Leste
UNTAG	United Nations Transition Assistance Group

INTRODUCTION

UN Peacekeeping and its Relevance

From its inception in 1948, until December 2020, 71 Peacekeeping operations (PKO) have been deployed by the UN.[1] As per many analysts, the UN has been effective in ending conflicts and ensuring reconciliation in Cambodia, El Salvador, Guatemala, Mozambique, Namibia, and Tajikistan. In Sierra Leone, Burundi, Ivory Coast, Timor-Leste, Liberia, Haiti, and Kosovo, the UN was able to make some difference and provide a security guarantee supporting a political transition. However, in places like Rwanda, Somalia, and the former Yugoslavia, the UN was found to be failing in its performance.

Some of the missions were closed and some troop-contributing countries (TCCs) pulled out their contingents due to the high-security threat to the peacekeepers. Analyses to determine the effectiveness of past missions in Bosnia, Somalia, Rwanda, Congo, and, even South Sudan give the impression that the instrument of UN PKO is a big failure and is not the answer to resolving conflicts. In addition, in general, avid researchers like Chiyuki, Coning, and Thakur have noted that all peace operations have side effects in terms of unintended consequences. When the unintended consequences are negative and are of such magnitude that they go beyond the scope of the mission, such as sexual abuse by peacekeepers in DRC, the unintended and negative consequences impact negatively on the success of the peace operations.[2] In a similar vein, Soeters also noted that unintended consequences are generally related to extreme poverty and disparities in the economic standard in society. Therefore, he believed that to expect only positive results from peace operations would be a romantic illusion.[3]

Connaughton mentioned that in the case of Somalia, the United Nations Operations in Somalia II (UNOSOM II) ended immediately after a US helicopter was shot down. In Rwanda, Belgium pulled out its military contingent after Hutu militias killed ten soldiers in April 1994.[4] In Sierra Leone, the opposing factions took ten UN military observers hostage. In Bosnia and Herzegovina, to deter North Atlantic Treaty Organization (NATO) air strikes, Bosnian Serb forces took Dutch peacekeepers hostage in July 1995, after which the massacre in Srebrenica evolved.[5]

All such developments triggered the contributing nations to express reservations and the UN was left with no option but to terminate many such PKO. Explaining UN decision-making vis-à-vis peacekeeping, Lipson described the UN as organised anarchy and a system of loosely coupled elements with preferences of the member-states that are greatly influenced by their political priorities. Even within the United Nations Security Council (UNSC), there is a lack of coherence in defining problems. Lipson also cited a lack of clarity in the organisational mechanism for making policy decisions. He identifies a lack of continuity among non-permanent members of the UNSC and other important UN bodies such as the Special Committee on PKO, responsible for supporting the PKO, having a negative impact on its functioning. This results in inconsistencies in the decision-making for participation – and the ending thereof – of peacekeeping.[6] Therefore, the causes for closing missions were both because of diplomatic incongruity and the conditions on the ground.

After learning lessons from past bitter experiences, the international community tried to introduce reforms in the field of peacekeeping. One of the most significant contributions was the recommendations by the Panel on UN Peace Operations under the chairmanship of Lakhdar Brahimi.[7] In this context, a few of the current peace operations such as the UN Stabilisation Mission in Congo (MONUSCO) and the UN Mission in the Republic of South Sudan (UNMISS) are positive reflections of the international community's better understanding of the dynamics of the new type of complex conflicts and the need for a multi-functional approach.

Besides conceptual evolution, the criteria for success in PKO have also attracted some attention from many authors. Measuring the performance of all stakeholders of PKO helps to monitor the progress of implementation of the plans, identify challenges and drawbacks, and take corrective action to fulfil its goals. To enhance the effectiveness of peace operations, the UN, on its part though, has tried to introduce several reforms in the past 30 years. Measuring the performance, however, has never been easy because there is no standard method in place. A review of the vast literature and numerous publications on the peacekeeping success criteria shows that defining such an evaluation framework requires grounding it with practical realities from PKO themselves in terms of understanding why a peace operation either succeeds or fail.

There is no single way to determine the effectiveness of PKO. Opinions vary and the literature is scant. Available scholarly work on the evaluation criteria is based on studies of different UN PKO deployed mostly in intra-state conflict zones. These criteria are mission-specific and hence cannot be used as a template to evaluate traditional PKO.

General set-up of the Book

This book is about assessing the effectiveness of a traditional UN Peace Operation based on the updated and revised version of the author's research on *'United Nations Interim Force in Lebanon: Assessment and Way Forward'* from Tilburg University, the Netherlands. The author was awarded a PhD by the University on 1 July 2021.

The book first goes on to develop a conceptual framework for the evaluation of UN peace operations and apply that to assess the performance of a traditional UN Peace Operation with UNIFIL as a case study following a combination of quantitative and qualitative inductive research approaches. Case study research that combines qualitative and quantitative methods based on primary and secondary data has its advantages. Because, building a theory from a case study is likely to have novelty, testability, and empirical validity. Besides, quantitative data supports qualitative data, and add the convergence of findings to the empirical groundings.[8] Walter, Howard, and Fortna mentioned that the findings of qualitative study tend to focus on the failures of peacekeeping and hence appear somewhat pessimistic. On the other hand, analysis based on quantitative data, which covers a broad range of cases, is not pessimistic at all. However, quantitative studies have flaws of their own. The authors hence contend that both approaches are necessary (this will be covered in detail later in Chapter 3).[9]

The study used the concept of a pillar question given that it is highly practical.[10] The empirical observations made from the answers to the pillar questions, obtained after interviewing selected participants combined with historical content were synthesized with publicly available data/statistics/records. Various interviewees were (or had been) personally involved in the dynamics of the mission and because of the personal experience of the researcher/author who held a senior-level appointment in the mission for two years. Hence, working towards expressing the interviewees' experiences that are as complete as possible was important.[11] It required a lot of time and effort to coordinate the interviews. It was also difficult to find adequate an number of practitioners and subject matter experts (including members of IDF) for the interview because of their hesitance to air their opinions due to either their preoccupations or the sensitivity of the subject.

The collection of data from the interviewees commenced in 2015. Ethical considerations such as honesty, carefulness, transparency, independence, and responsibility guided the set-up and execution of this study. The primary data collection at three levels was done as follows:

- The first category of respondents refers to members of an Indian military contingent who had recently returned from UNIFIL. Two hundred and thirty-seven contingent members (mostly soldiers and NCOs) filled out a questionnaire. These data, however, did not prove to be useful because of similarity in the responses (see Appendix E for the summary of data and analysis of responses). This may be due to their employment at the tactical level, making them unaware of the larger picture of the conflict, and because they experienced a strict military hierarchical system and culture not allowing them to diverge from the average opinion.
- The second segment includes former military peacekeepers of officer rank, who served in UNIFIL at some point in time after the war of 2006. The same questionnaire that was distributed among Indian peacekeepers was sent to several contacts using a Google spreadsheet, hence constituting this second segment. There were about 110 officers of the ranks of Captain to Colonel, posted in UNIFIL HQs in different capacities at the time of the researcher's tenure in Lebanon (this strength fluctuates from time to time but generally remains at this level). Of these, 60 officers of the ranks of Major to Colonel, who were holding important assignments such as operational planning and who were more aware of the dynamics of the conflict, were picked up randomly and approached for their views. Forty-one of the people that were addressed, filled out the questionnaire (a response rate of 68 per cent). Since all the respondents were serving officers, to maintain confidentiality, they were asked not to disclose their names and nationality.

- The third segment comprises a sample of subject matter experts and a few serving and former peacekeepers who agreed to be interviewed in a semi-structured manner. The interviews included semi-structured face-to-face and online interaction with open-ended questions.[12] Identifying the subject matter experts for the interview was a challenge because the researcher had already returned to India four years earlier and re-establishing contact with the appropriate experts was problematic. Besides, the Syrian civil war was at its peak. With difficulty, it was possible to contact 38 experts. One senior civilian employee and one Lebanese civilian employee in UNIFIL, and one Lebanese Armed Forces (LAF) officer refused to be interviewed. At least two former military peacekeepers agreed but never responded after the questions were sent to them. Several others did not even acknowledge the initial contact that was made through an earlier local acquaintance. Finally, 25 key stakeholders from past and existing missions (2008 to 2017), as well as experts from all sides of the spectrum, agreed and were interviewed. They included former high-ranking and middle-level military officers holding important assignments at UN HQs and in UNIFIL, senior UNIFIL civilian employees, former high-ranking officers from LAF, former Israeli security experts and academics who are subject matter experts. The topic list for these interviews was formulated based on the key goals set by UNIFIL and followed the general content of the questionnaires. The interviews were mostly conducted through Skype connections. Three of the interviewees, however, insisted on answering the questions in writing, as they were not comfortable in a face-to-face interview. Records of the interviews were stored either in the form of audio files or written format. In both cases, transcripts were converted into a more readable format as far as possible without distorting the meaning of what the interviewees wanted to state. In a few cases, transcripts were left untouched. Thereafter, the transcripts were shared with the interviewees for 'Member Check' (their approval). The analysis of the data consisted of a qualitative content analysis of the transcripts of the interviews, paying attention to the main tendencies as well as outlying views.

For the application of the evaluation framework, the study has been confined to the case study and geographical entity of South Lebanon. Moreover, except for the secondary data, which are available in terms of reports of the Secretary-General of the UN, reports of the UNIFIL, and published material on UNIFIL including media reports, only limited inputs are available from the UN HQ at the time of the establishment of the mission in the 1970s and the events that followed directly thereafter.

Layout of the Chapters

The main objective of the book is to assess the effectiveness of a traditional peace operation with UNIFIL as a case study. I begin the book with a description of the concept and a few important operational definitions of UN Peace Operations, which I will be referring to in the main body of the book. The layout of the book will be in six chapters as under:

1. Chapter 1 will briefly dwell on the concept of UN Peacekeeping, and a few important operational definitions.
2. Chapter 2 reviews the literature on the causes of success and failure of UN Peace Operations and how they can vary from strategic to operational and tactical reasons and will depend on mission-specific conditions.
3. Chapter 3 is devoted to developing the evaluation framework and identifying criteria to evaluate the performance or effectiveness of peacekeeping.
4. Chapter 4 is dedicated to how the conceptual framework for assessment can be applied to UNIFIL, which is unique in terms of its size, composition, capability, robust Rules of Engagement, and having to navigate in a sensitive political and security environment in the Middle East. This chapter will also look at how *one,* UNIFIL has been able to create conditions to maintain the present status quo and thus enabling the people to live their daily life with minimum disruption for close to two decades; and *two,* how UNIFIL could earn credibility by creating a predictable security environment that is less dangerous than what was prevailing before 2006.
5. Chapter 5 seeks to synthesise information about the operational activities of UNIFIL since 2006 when the new UNIFIL started after Israel had withdrawn its troops from South Lebanon. This chapter covers an assessment of UNIFIL's performance from 2006 (post the Israel-Lebanon war) until July 2020. Following up on the conceptual framework of Chapter 3, this chapter aims to present the assessment after collating the information based on operational data and records that are available in open sources, observations from publicly

available reports of the UN and UNIFIL, and opinions of the subject matter experts found in peacekeeping-related books and research studies. At the same time, reports and statistics – no matter how specific – do not reveal the true picture unless they are corroborated by the views of the stakeholders. This is done by taking into consideration the responses of three different segments of stakeholders: members of the Indian military contingent who returned from Lebanon, former military peacekeepers of officer rank who served in UNIFIL at some point after the war of 2006 and – most importantly – the subject matter experts.

6. Chapter 6 will cover the final assessment and make recommendations for enhancing the effectiveness of UN Peace Operations.

ENDNOTES

1. UN Department of Peace Operations, Peacekeeping Operations Fact Sheet (December 31, 2020), https://peacekeeping.un.org/sites/default/files/peacekeeing_factsheet_12_ 2020_english_1.pdf
2. Aoi Chiyuki, Cedric de Coning and Ramesh Thakur, "Unintended consequences, complex peace operations and peace building systems: Unintended consequences, complex peace operations and peace building systems". In *Unintended Consequences of* PKO, ed. Aoi Chiyuki, Cedric de Coning and Ramesh Thakur (Tokyo/New York/ Paris: United Nations University, 2007), 3-19.
3. Joseph Soeters, *Sociology and Military Studies: Classical and Current Foundations* (London and New York: Routledge, 2018), 70.
4. Richard Connaughton, "Rwanda-Tropical Nazism," *Military Intervention and Peacekeeping: The Reality* (Hampshire, England: Ashgate, 2001), 139-90.
5. Séverine Autesserre, "The Crisis of Peacekeeping: Why the UN Can't End Wars," *Foreign Affairs,* January/February 2019:101-116, https://www.foreignaffairs.com/ articles/2018-12-11/crisis-peacekeeping
6. Michael Lipson, "A 'Garbage Model' of UN Peacekeeping," *Global Governance*.13, no. 1 (January-March 2007): 79-97.
7. UN General Assembly, *Report of the Panel on United Nations Peace Operations,* A/55/ 305-S/2000/809 (August 21, 2000).
8. Kathleen M. Eisenhardt, "Building from Case Study Research," *The Academy of Management Review* 14, no. 4 (October 1989): 546-48. Also, see Gerald L. Fetner, *Immersed in Great Affairs: Allan Nevins and the Heroic Age of American History* (Albany: State University of New York Press, 2004): 4 and Carter V. Good, *Introduction to Educational Research* (New York: Appleton-Century-Crofts, 1959).
9. Barbara F. Walter, Lise Morje Howard, and Virginia Page Fortna, "The Extraordinary Relationship between Peacekeeping and Peace," *British Journal of Political Science* (2020): 8-10, doi: 10.1017/S000712342000023X; Jacob Kathman, "Personal composition and member state contributions to United Nations peacekeeping operations," in G. Clayton, ed., "The known knowns and known unknowns of peacekeeping data,"

International Peacekeeping 24, no.1 (2017): 3-4, DOI: 10.1080/13533312.2016.1226768

10. Patricia M. Shields and Nandini Rangarajan, *A Playbook for Research Methods: Integrating Conceptual Frameworks and Project Management* (New Forum Press, 2013), 109-57.
11. For data collection, see Ference Matron and Shirley Booth, *Learning and Awareness* (New Jersey: Lawrence Erlbaum Associates, 1997). Also, see K. N. Krishnaswamy, A. I. Sivakumar and M. Mathirajan, *Management Research Methodology: Integration of principles, methods and techniques* (1st edn.) (New Delhi: Dorling Kindersley Pvt. Ltd., 2013); John W. Best, James V. Kahn and Arbind K. Jha, *Research in Education* (10th edn.) (New Jersey: Pearson Education Inc, 2011) and Marianne Daher, David Carré, Andrea Jaramillo, Himmble Olivares, and Alemka Tomicic, "Experience and Meaning in Qualitative Research: A Conceptual Review and a Methodological Device Proposal," *Forum: Qualitative Social Research* 18, no. 3 (September 2017), https://doi.org/10.17169/fqs-18.3.2696
12. James Griffith, "Survey Research in Military Settings," in *Routledge Handbook of Research Methods in Military Studies,* ed. Joseph Soeters, Patricia M. Shields and Sebastian Rietjens (New York: Routledge, 2014), 179-93.

CHAPTER 1

EMERGING CONCEPT OF UN PEACEKEEPING

Concept of UN Peacekeeping

The concept of UN PKO has evolved over the last 70 years with several successes and failures in various missions. Along with the evolution of the PKO concept, aspects of criteria of success have been studied and conceptualised by many authors. This introductory chapter deals with the concept, and evolution of the UN PKO and, some operational definitions that would be referred to in the book subsequently.

The history of UN PKO goes back to the time of the Cold War when superpower rivalries frequently paralysed the function of the UNSC. The first two PKO deployed by the UN were the UN Truce Supervision Organization (UNTSO) in Jerusalem and the UNMOGIP. Both missions continue to this day and are of the small-sized traditional observation and monitoring type. UN military observers are unarmed to assure the warring parties of their noble intent. The earliest armed PKO was the First UN Emergency Force (UNEF I) deployed in Gaza in 1956, to keep peace in the face of the Suez Crisis.[1]

The UN Charter was signed on 26 June 1945 in San Francisco after the UN Conference on International Organisation and came into force on 24 October 1945. The UN Charter is the basic document that guides most UN activities. Articles and chapters enshrined in the Charter provide legitimacy to the UN PKO.[2] As given in the Charter, the UN was established to "save succeeding generations from the scourge of war" and one of its main purposes is to maintain international peace and security. UN peacekeeping is one of the tools used by the UN to fulfil this objective. Even though the word 'peacekeeping' is specifically not mentioned in the Charter, this tool has evolved over a period. The UN Charter gives the UNSC the primary responsibility for the maintenance of international peace and security.

The UNSC is the main organ responsible to maintain international peace and security having the authority to establish any PKO. However, whenever there is an extreme threat to peace and security and the UNSC is unable to decide because of a lack of unanimity, the UN General Assembly, vide resolution 377 (V) of 3 November 1950, also known as the "Uniting for Peace" resolution, can authorize a PKO. The UNEF I was adopted under the procedure established by the "Uniting for Peace" resolution.[3]

Conflict resolution is an overall objective of all peacekeeping initiatives by the UN and it implies the settlement of disputes that underline a conflict. It includes conflict prevention, peace-making, peace-building, and finally conflict termination. According to former UN Secretary-General, Boutros Boutros-Ghali, "Peacekeeping is the deployment of a UN presence in the field, hitherto with the consent of all the parties concerned, normally involving the UN military and/or police personnel and frequently civilians as well".[4] Peacekeeping, therefore, while making an overall contribution to conflict resolution, technically falls under 'conflict management.'

UN PKO have evolved over the past six decades with a visible shift in their original nature. The nature of conflicts changed from inter-state to intra-state, increase in the loss of lives of innocent civilians, destruction of infrastructure and basic services, and crumbling of government institutions.[5] The complex nature of conflicts has posed more challenges to the international community. The changing complexity and the varying nature of UN PKO roles show the differences over various generations.

Although there is a thin line delineating one generation of PKO from the next, Kenkel divided it into five different generations, in his *Five generations of peace operations: from the "thin BL" to "painting a country blue."*[6] They are as follows:

(a) **First Generation: Traditional Peacekeeping**. These are mandated under Chapter VI of the Charter with lightly armed peacekeepers and strict adherence to the basic principles of peacekeeping. UNMOGIP, UNFICYP, UNEF and UNIFIL fall in this category.

(b) **Second Generation: Civilian Tasks**. These missions are mounted in a complex environment where the rebuilding of a broken society gets more or equal importance. These missions are characterized by the addition of civilian tasks related to political transformation from the conflict without an increase in the permission to use force. UNTAG, UNOMOZ and ONUSAL fall in this generation of PKO.

(c) **Third Generation: Peace Enforcement**. These missions are under Chapter VII of the Charter and essentially enforce the mission's mandate even if it amounts to the use of force. UNAMSIL and MONUSCO fall in this category.

(d) **Fourth Generation: Peace-building**. These are essentially political missions and robust peace-building operations with more intrusive civilian tasks.[7] UNAMI, UNSCOL and UNAMA are three such missions out of several. The extreme form of peace-building operations is when the civilian tasks include exercising interim transitional governance of a sovereign state. UNTAET and UNMIK fall in this category.

(e) **Fifth Generation: Hybrid Mission**. These are hybrid missions with uniformed peacekeepers drawn from both the UN and regional organizations under a separate mandate and chain of command. An example is UNAMID.

Scholars have used logic to categorise PKO in different ways as peacekeeping operations have evolved over a period. For the sake of clarity and simplicity, UN PKO can be broadly classified as peacekeeping missions (under Chapter VI and enforcement missions under Chapter VII), and Political Missions. This study will remain limited to the first-mentioned PKO, of which 12 are currently ongoing.[8] PKO, in general, includes peacemaking, peacekeeping and peace-building as three complementary strategies for reducing violence and restoring normalcy in a conflict zone.[9] While peacekeeping is generally referred to as the involvement of uniformed men (both military and police), it is the non-uniformed civilians who play a critical role in the two other activities. Both military and civilian peacekeepers bring with them an array of tools for complementary activities in reducing violence and creating a safe environment for the political process to move ahead.[10] In the whole spectrum of this peace process, the military plays a critical role in securing the environment and giving peacemakers and negotiators the space to operate.

PKO are guided by three basic principles of peacekeeping—consent, impartiality and non-use of force.[11] More often than not, these principles have been interpreted differently by different TCCs, more specifically in the context of the use of force for self-defence. There are varying interpretations of the term 'self-defence'. According to one of the former Secretaries-General of the UN, Mr Kurt Waldheim, self-defence includes "resistance to attempts by forceful means to prevent it from discharging its duties under the mandate of the Security Council".[12] This is one of the reasons why the assessment of PKO has not been easy. The ambiguities in the interpretation of the principles that impact the performance of peace operations will be discussed in more detail in Chapter 2.

Operational Definitions

Some of the common and important peacekeeping-related definitions are:[13]

(a) **Peacekeeping**. Peacekeeping is an instrument designed to preserve the peace, however fragile, where fighting has halted, and to assist in implementing agreements achieved by the peacemakers. It was the brainchild of Lester Pearson, Canada's Minister of External Affairs (later Prime Minister), and the UN Secretary-General, Dag Hammarskjold. It was a concept conceived as a diplomatic key to open the path to further negotiations for a peaceful resolution of conflicts. It, therefore, is part of the whole process of peace and tested for the first time in UNEF I.[14]

(b) **Peace Operations**. The term 'UN peace operations' embraces a broad suite of tools managed by the UN Secretariat ranging from special envoys and mediators, political missions (including peace-building missions), preventive diplomacy initiatives, peacekeeping missions including observation missions (both ceasefire and electoral missions) to small, technical specialist missions, multi-disciplinary operations, both large and small, drawing on civilian, military and police personnel to support the peace process implementation, as well as advance missions for planning.[15] Hereafter, in this study, the terms 'peacekeeping operation', 'peace operation', and 'peacekeeping mission' are used interchangeably.

(c) **Peace enforcement**. Peace enforcement involves the application, with the authorisation of the Security Council, of a range of coercive measures, including the use of military force. Such actions are authorized to restore international peace and security in situations where the Security Council has determined the existence of a threat to the peace, a breach of the peace, or an act of aggression. The Security Council may utilize, where appropriate, regional organisations and agencies for enforcement action under authority. This is also often referred to as military intervention, which is the most controversial and often debated subject amongst the international community.[16]

(d) **Peace-building**. Peace-building involves a range of measures targeted to reduce the risk of a situation lapsing or relapsing into conflict by strengthening national capacities at all levels for conflict management and laying the foundation for sustainable peace and development.

(e) **Peacemaking**. Peacemaking generally includes measures to address conflicts in progress and usually involves diplomatic actions to bring hostile parties to a negotiated agreement. Peacemakers may also be envoys, governments, groups of states, regional organizations, the United Nations, unofficial and non-governmental groups, or a prominent personality working independently.

(f) **Robust peacekeeping**. Robust peacekeeping involves the use of force at the tactical level with the consent of the host authorities and/or the main parties to the conflict.

(g) **Rules of Engagement (RoE)**. The use of force of any kind by a member of a peacekeeping contingent is defined by the RoE. The RoE is tailored to the specific mandate of the mission and the situation on the ground.[17]

In addition, some of the other common terms that are associated with peacekeeping are:

(a) **Inter-State Conflict**. Inter-state violence is a conflict between two or more states (both members of the international system), who use their respective national forces in the conflict.

(b) **Intra-State Conflict**. When there is conflict within a state like civil war, it is known as an intra-state conflict. Arab Spring uprisings in Libya, Syria, and Yemen, or different groups fighting a turf war in places like South Sudan and DRC are some examples of intra-state conflict.

(c) **Multidimensional Peacekeeping.** Until the end of the Cold War, the role of peacekeeping was primarily limited to observing, mediating, and preventing hostilities. Post the Cold War, as inter-state conflicts decreased and there was an increase in intra-state conflicts, there was a shift in the concept of peacekeeping with more focus on the implementation of peace agreements and other capacity-building measures for a durable peace. As a result, peace operations are increasingly mandated with multidimensional tasks like significant electoral, civil administrative, policing, human rights, repatriation, rehabilitation, and reconstruction functions. UNTAC, MONUSCO and UNMISS fall in this category.[18]

ENDNOTES

1. UN Department of Peace Operations, accessed July 30, 2020, http://www.un.org/en/peacekeeping/operations/early.shtml
2. UN Department of Public Information, *Charter of the United Nations* (New York: UN Department of Public Information, 1945).
3. UN General Assembly, Resolution A/RES/1000 (ES-I) (November 5, 1956).
4. Butros-Butros Ghali, *An Agenda for Peace*, A/47/277-S/24111 (New York: The United Nations, 1992).
5. Alex J. Bellamy and Paul D. Williams, *Understanding Peacekeeping* (Cambridge: Polity, 2010), 397-402.
6. Kai Michael Kenkel, "Five generations of peace operations: from the 'thin BL' to 'painting a country blue'," *Revista Brasileira de Politica International* 56, no. 1 (2013), Institute of Brasileira de Relacoes Internacionais: 122-143, http://dx.doi.org/10.1590/S0034-73292013000100007
7. UN Political Missions, *Report of the Secretary-General*, accessed June 15, 2018, https://peaceoperationsreview.org/wp-content/uploads/2015/07/united_nations_report_secretary_general.pdf
8. UN Department of Peace Operations, Peacekeeping Operations Fact Sheet (November 30, 2021), https://peacekeeping.un.org/sites/default/files/peacekeeping_missions_factsheet_246_nov2021_en.pdf
9. Butros-Butros Ghali, *An Agenda for Peace*, A/47/277-S/24111 (New York: The United Nations, 1992).
10. Tim Wallis, "Nonviolent Peaceforce," in *Civilian Peacekeeping*, (*Oxford Encyclopaedia of Peace*, 2020).
11. *United Nations Peacekeeping Operations: Principles and Guidelines* (New York: UN Department of Public Information, 2008).
12. UN Security Council, *Report of the Secretary-General on the Implementation of Security Council Resolution 340 (1973)*, S/11052/Rev. 1 (October 27, 1973). Also, see Katherine E. Cox, "Beyond Self-Defence: United Nations PKO and the Use of Force," *Denver Journal of International Law and Policy* 27 (1999), 271; A. K. Bardalai, *Changing Security Scenario: Implications for UN Peacekeeping* (New Delhi: Knowledge World for United Service Institution of India, 2006) and Anddrej Sitkowski, *UN Peacekeeping: Myth and Reality* (Westport: Praeger Security International, 2006), 111-124.
13. *United Nations Peacekeeping Operations: Principles and Guidelines* (New York: UN Department of Public Information, 2008).
14. Indar Jit Rikhye, *The Theory & Practice of Peacekeeping* (New York: C. Hurst & Company, 1984), 224-27.

15. UN General Assembly Security Council, *Report of The Independent High-Level Panel on Peace Operations*, A/70/95–S/2015/446 (June 17, 2015).
16. Martha Finnemore, *The Purpose of Intervention: Changing Beliefs about the use of Force* (New Delhi: Manas Publications, 2004).
17. UN Department of Peacekeeping Operations, *UN Handbook on United Nations multidimensional PKO* (New York: Peacekeeping Best Practice Unit, 2003).
18. For more, please see, Cecilla Cavero Sanchez, "Multidimensional Peacekeeping: A New Tool for Democracy," *RCIS*, November 28, 2019, https://www.ocf.berkeley.edu/~rics/multidimensional-peacekeeping-a-new-tool-for-democracy/; Adm Day, "The Future of Multidimensional Peacekeeping," *IPI Global Observatory*, September 15, 2020, https://theglobalobservatory.org/2020/09/future-multidimensional-peacekeeping/discourses

CHAPTER 2

UNITED NATIONS PEACEKEEPING OPERATIONS: CAUSES FOR FAILURE AND CONTINUING RELEVANCE[1]

Introduction

Despite the long history of UN peacekeeping, barring a few, the UN cannot boast of many successes. As per the UN Panel's observations, most of these operations have been characterised by late deployment, weak mandates, inadequate resources, and ill-equipped and untrained peacekeeping troops. Several UN reports and various experts have also talked about the lack of commitment of troop-contributing countries (TCCs).[2] Given such a track record, there is now a question mark on the continued relevance of UN PKO, or, to put it differently, on its ability to implement its mandates. The real story however is that (as mentioned in Chapter 1), despite many challenges, UN peacekeeping has been remarkably effective in bringing peace.[3] The dominant narrative on the failure in UN peacekeeping is probably because there is no fixed standard to evaluate whether a PKO has been successful or not. As stated by Bratt, except for a very few, most scholars have not been able to identify and specify the criteria for the evaluation of a PKO.[4] Hence, such evaluations are unlikely to be perfect. Even though the knowledge gained from books is necessary, unless such knowledge is applied along with practical experience, the learning process will not be complete. One can gain knowledge by reading but one cannot get to know the core of any subject without practical experience.

To determine whether the PKO have succeeded or not, the identification of a framework for evaluation of PKO is a prerequisite. However, to develop either the framework or identification of standard criteria, a good comprehension of the causes for the success and failure of PKO is a priority. Most discussions related to the performance of PKO, including the Brahimi Report, attribute the failure of PKO to a vague mandate, inadequate troops, and lack of equipment and training.[5] Fortna mentioned that critics of peacekeeping are only fond of highlighting the dramatic failures of peacekeeping but are also biased in their case selection.[6] Walter, Howard, and Fortna noted similarly and stated that there is more literature on the failure of peacekeeping because critics are unable to highlight the good works even though UN peacekeeping "is remarkably effective in bringing peace."[7] While a PKO may fail to implement the mandate because of its weaknesses, there are numerous conceptual, organisational, and conflict-specific variables, on which peacekeeping missions and peacekeepers have little control but directly impact the outcome of the PKO. Therefore, it will be unfair to blame the PKO simply for not being able to implement the mandate without understanding the reasons for the failure. There is also a huge gap between the conceptual thinking on UN PKO and how it is construed for its implementation.

Thus, to assess the relevance of PKO, there is a need to study the causes for success and failure as well as the development of a framework for evaluation, followed by an assessment of the PKO. The contribution of this chapter is on a few important but less-talked-about factors that have an overriding influence on the outcome of the PKO. The chapter also aims to provide a perspective on the relevance of PKO in the context of challenges in conceptualising, planning, deployment, and execution.

UN PKO can be deployed only after the approval of the UNSC. The budget for the operation is approved by the UN General Assembly (UNGA) after the Council has adopted a resolution for its deployment. Before and after its deployment, the three interrelated principles of peacekeeping—consent, impartiality, and use of force only in self-defence—become the guiding factors for all PKO. Interpretation of these principles is fraught with ambiguity, which impacts the performance of the peace operations (this will be discussed in the following section). There is, however, no direct reference to the principles in the UN Charter. These principles were evolved and adopted after UN experiences in Gaza. If a peace agreement indicating consent for the deployment of a PKO is concluded by the parties to the conflict even before the UNSC approves the deployment, the PKO stands a better chance of survival.

The role of the UNSC does not end with approving the deployment of a PKO. It is the highest organ of the UN that not only approves but also has the responsibility to ensure that the peacekeeping mission continues to receive the required support to implement its mandate. Similarly, if there is inadequate budgetary support, the peacekeeping mission will be either understaffed and below strength or have to be closed prematurely.

In summary, I argue herein that a mission's performance is affected by the following: (1) ambiguity in the understanding of peacekeeping principles and the mandate; (2) the presence of a comprehensive and inclusive peace agreement; (3) inclusivity and local actors; (4) the degree to which support from the UNSC is continued; and (5) the size of budgetary support. Before taking up these aspects, I will first delve somewhat deeper and examine the question of when peacekeeping fails and when it does not.

When does Peacekeeping fail and when does it not?

Owing to a series of failures in the 1990s, the UN ordered a comprehensive review of UN PKO. The Brahimi Report concluded that 'the UN has repeatedly failed to meet the challenges.'[8] The same is true even today. As observed by Jacobson, 'The primary successes of the UN have been in the areas of elections and communications (after peace agreement), diplomacy and hindsight analysis of failures.'[9] Autesserre, on the other hand, referring to UN peacekeeping in DRC, commented that the international community's inability to address the root cause of the conflict was one of the main reasons for the failure of peacekeeping operations.[10] Barring a few, most researchers have touched upon only individual factors (such as peace agreement, mandate, use of force, etc.) impacting the outcome of the PKO. However, the most comprehensive work in this field has been done by Doyle and Sambanis, Diehl, Jett, Howard and Pepra. Bratt, Diehl, and Druckman reported on the success and failure and identified the success criteria for the evaluation of PKO.[11] Diehl, Jett, Howard, and Pepra have been able to analytically identify several factors/causes after a detailed analysis of a few selected PKO. Strategic factors are derived from conceptual thinking on the management of PKO. For example, factors relating to peace agreements and the UNSC can be termed as strategic. Similarly, different standards of operational capability and varying interpretations of principles/rules of peacekeeping impact the PKO at the operational and tactical levels. It is, however, difficult to draw a clear dividing line separating these two different clusters. For instance, discussion on the use of force, which is one of the basic principles of peacekeeping, can transcend from the strategic to the tactical level.

Based on research by various scholars who have been named earlier, some of the important strategic and operational/tactical factors impacting the success and failure of UN PKO are as follows:

Strategic Factors

1. The principle of neutrality and its replacement by the principle of impartiality including possible confusion over its interpretation in the field.
2. The presence or absence of a comprehensive peace agreement.
3. The degree of consensus in the international community, most importantly among the Permanent Members of the UNSC, in defining the problem and comprehending the real motive of the warring parties agreeing for UN mediation as well as sincerity and commitment among the relevant stakeholders.
4. The quality and comprehensibility of the compromised mandate.
5. The size of resources and the quality of peacekeepers.
6. The clarity of the method for implementation of the mandate.
7. The degree of consent from the host government that is in real control, stable in time and based on cooperation from the warring groups/parties.
8. The influence of external powers and internal/sub-national actors in the continuation of the conflict.
9. The degree of understanding of the root cause of the conflict.
10. The ability to learn from the best practices.
11. The presence of peacekeepers from developed countries.

Operational/tactical Factors

1. The timely deployment of the peacekeeping force—the time lag between the ceasefire agreement and the arrival of the peacekeepers.
2. The capabilities of the PKO—the adequacy of the peacekeepers, their equipment and the mission's infrastructure.
3. Adequacy of budgetary support.
4. The match between the mandated task and resources.
5. The influence of external and internal/sub national actors.
6. The effectiveness of mission leaders (HoM and FC)—their vision and capability to resolve conflicts.

7. The use of force, or the lack of it because of fear of retaliation.
8. The degree to which the interpretation of the principles of peacekeeping varies.
9. The degree of sensitivity to local culture and tradition.
10. The challenges of operational interoperability and integration of multinational peacekeeping contingents due to a cultural divide, different training standards and operational philosophy and undue emphasis on national identity.

The list of factors/causes for the success or failure is not exhaustive since they will vary from conflict to conflict, each requiring its specific diagnosis and treatment.[12] The outcome of the PKO can be affected by either one or more, or a combination of the above-listed strategic and operational/tactical factors. For instance, the UN spent a whopping amount of $ 1.68 billion on UNOSOM I and II from 1992 to 1995. Yet, its effort in Somalia ended in disaster, despite the US decision to intervene militarily.[13] Initially, the USA had resisted a UN peacekeeping role in Somalia.[14] Also, depending on the dynamics of the conflict, either the strategic or operational/tactical factors can have an overriding influence on the performance of a PKO. For example, the PKO in the former republic of Yugoslavia was doomed from the very beginning. Despite having all the resources in hand, there was no peace agreement between the parties to the conflict or any consensus among the powerful nations in defining the actual problem or a workable strategy to restore peace. As a result, the international community could not decide on a common plan to protect the safe areas. The mission did not use force, not even in self-defence. Similarly, the failure of the PKO in Rwanda can be attributed to a combination of strategic and operational/tactical reasons. Even though a peace agreement was signed before the deployment of the PKO, decision-makers were unaware of the presence of the strong undercurrent amongst the Hutu community, which was against any political reconciliation. On the operational level, the mission was below strength and some of the contingents lacked the will to intervene to protect civilians from the wrath of Hutu militias when the genocide began in April 1994.

The Ambiguity in Principles of Peacekeeping

When peace operations are deployed, they are expected to follow the UN norms. Following the norms provides credibility and legitimacy to peacekeeping. What are UN norms? Laurence described norms as "Collective expectations for the proper behaviours of actors with a given identity".[15] The list of the norms is not finite; it can include anything that is expected from a peacekeeper such as adherence to the principles of peacekeeping, maintaining good conduct and discipline, sensitivity to gender, environmental friendliness, respect for human rights, etc.[16] Barring the principles of peacekeeping, most of the norms are clear-cut. In the case of peacekeeping norms, there is however a huge gap between the theories of the principles of peacekeeping and their practice. In this section, I will take a close look at the ambiguity in the interpretation of the principles and how it impacts the peace operation. *Consent*, *impartiality*, and *use of minimum force* are the three principles of peacekeeping, which at times are referred to as the *holy trinity*.[17] As a principle, UN PKO are deployed with the consent of the main parties to the conflict. This signifies a commitment by them to the political process and their acceptance of the UN PKO, with the necessary freedom of action, both political and physical, to carry out its mandated tasks. Regarding impartiality, UN PKO are expected to remain impartial in their dealings and not take sides. Failure to adhere to this principle may undermine their credibility, followed by the withdrawal of consent. Use of minimum force means that it will be used only as a last resort and that too in self-defence unless it is an enforcement action.

Adherence to these three principles is crucial because it provides legitimacy to the PKO. Whalan explained that when peacekeepers' actions are in coherence with UN norms and adhere to the principles, peacekeeping is legitimised. She further noted, "Peacekeepers are legitimised when the local actors perceive them to be legitimate."[18] However, these principles have their limitations in terms of their interpretation by the TCCs, thus creating confusion in the field and, many times, resulting in inaction on the part of the peacekeepers. The often-talked-about inability of peacekeepers to implement the mandate, more specifically when it comes to saving human lives, seems more because of a lack of clarity in understanding the principles of peacekeeping and less due to a lack of will and inadequate capability.

Consent at the strategic level for the deployment of the PKO does not necessarily mean that there will be consent at the tactical level too. Availability of consent at both the strategic operational and tactical levels is rare. Often, consent given is out of compulsion, either due to a threat or some other incentive. And when any of these is diluted, consent is withdrawn. Withdrawal of consent at the tactical level does not necessarily mean the withdrawal of consent at the strategic level (because there are smaller groups in intra-state conflicts and because orders originating at the apex level need not necessarily be strictly complied with at the lowest level). However, the withdrawal of consent at the strategic level is bound to affect the PKO at the operational and tactical levels. Curran noted that the absence of the main parties to the conflict risk drawing the peacekeeping mission into the conflict and enforcement action. He mentioned that at the same time, "a blind reliance on the consent of all parties (large and small) may lead a peacekeeping force to lose not only effectiveness but also legitimacy."[19] In Cambodia, the Khmer Rouge had earlier consented to the peace process but later withdrew. It was a case of withdrawal of consent at the tactical level. However, due to the maturity and ability of the senior mission leaders to understand the larger picture of the peace process, the PKO was able to fulfil the better part of the mandate. Although, according to Sanderson, the FC of the United Nations Transitional Authority in Cambodia (UNTAC), the results could have been better if only the mission had been better planned.[20] Somalia can be cited as an opposite example of how the mission leader managed to persuade the rebel leader to give his consent—a consent that was initially denied, then given and later again withdrawn, with catastrophic results for the mission.

While explaining peace operations in a complex environment of intra-state conflict where there is no effective government, Alao, Mackinlay, and Olonisakin observed, "In the absence of an effective government from which to obtain the consent, a strong regional consensus was needed. It might exercise an overwhelming pressure, confronting the lawless and imposing unbearable financial deprivation or arrestable rewards".[21] In an environment, where there are a large number of armed groups, external powers intervene to change the course of the conflict to their advantage. The consent does not remain the prerogative of the host government. As a result, it becomes extremely difficult or near impossible to obtain the consent of a similar degree from all the parties to the conflict. Consent then gradually becomes irrelevant and is replaced by consensus. This was the case in Somalia where there was an institutional collapse by the time the PKO was to be deployed in Somalia.[22] Doyle and Sambanis reported that because of the lack of legitimate central authority in Somalia, most local warlords favoured war to maximise their control over their territory.[23] Given the events leading to the civil war in the wake of the overthrowing of Mohamed Siad Barre, who had ruled the country for more than two decades, no leader could give consent. Among the two primary disputants who were fighting for power, Ali Mahdi consented, but, Aideed had to be persuaded by Mohamed Sahnoun, the Special Representative of the Secretary-General

(SRSG), to accept the deployment of 500 peacekeepers for the protection of humanitarian convoys.

However, Aideed withdrew his consent when Secretary-General Butros Butros-Ghali suggested to the Security Council to deploy 3,000 peacekeepers without consulting either Sahnoun or Aideed. This enraged Aideed, who considered this a breach of faith. What followed immediately was an escalation of violence. The first catastrophic event was in June 1993 in which 24 Pakistani troops were killed and 56 injured while trying to inspect a weapon storage site belonging to Aideed. The attack on the Somalis during a peace meeting by the American-led peacekeeping mission on 12 July 1993 ended the remaining hope of salvaging the peace. As reported by Peterson from the front lines in Africa for London's *Daily Telegraph*, the Somalis really wanted peace and a peace agreement could have been achieved it. But the attack by more than half a dozen Cobra helicopters, first by TOW missiles and then by 20 mm cannon guns killed hundreds of civilians. A few of them were killed while trying to run away. It was a Bloody Monday and to the Somalis, an act of war.[24] Later, on 3 and 4 October 1993, during the United States (US) Army Rangers' raid on Aideed's compound, 18 Rangers were taken hostage and killed, and one was dragged through the streets of Mogadishu. The withdrawal of consent by Aideed was the turning point for the PKO in Somalia.[25] The initial consent for the deployment of a PKO in Somalia was possibly influenced by the personal motives of the main parties to the conflict. On the one hand, the main rivals—Ali Mahdi and Mohammed Aideed—considered the presence of the mission and the task of protecting the personnel, installations, and equipment of the UN and its agencies as a clear threat and obstruction to their power struggle.[26] On the other hand, these two leaders desperately needed the UN to obtain economic aid even though remaining sceptical of the international organisation's likely hidden agenda.[27] What followed thereafter in Somalia, and its consequent effect on the subsequent missions elsewhere (for example, in Rwanda), is a sad commentary on the UN's peacekeeping history.[28]

Impartiality, the second principle, is either not understood or is confused, or deliberately misinterpreted. It was Dag Hammarskjold's study on peacekeeping, which was presented to the UNGA after the deployment of the UNEF in 1956 that led to the identification of certain basic principles that would later provide an acceptable framework for the subsequent PKO.[29] Though derived from the report of Hammarskjold, this principle was not mentioned as *impartiality* but inferred from what Hammarskjold explained.

To limit the scope of a possible difference of opinion, the UN followed it by deciding not to include peacekeepers from any of the Permanent Members of the Security Council, and from any country that, because of its geographical position or for other reasons, might be considered as possibly having a special interest in the situation that had called for the operation. Hammarskjold reported: 'In the case of UNEF, the policy has been to exclude military personnel belonging to any of the Permanent Members of the Security Council or any country which, for geographical or other reasons, might have a special interest in the conflict.'[30] He believed the PKO did not involve the use of force as envisaged under Chapter VII of the UN Charter, which was drafted during the Cold War era when conflicts were generally inter-state and not intra-state. Even though it is referred to as impartiality in the Capstone Doctrine, the Brahimi Report referred to it as *neutrality/ impartiality* leaving it open for scholars and academicians to split hairs in various academic discourses. According to Yamashita, "Impartiality and neutrality both meant equidistance, and there was no conceptual distinction between the two". In his article explaining how impartiality had been put into practice, he went on to state, "Impartiality is here defined as loyalty to the mission mandate and to the Charter principles. Impartiality in this understanding constitutes a different code of action from neutrality because it potentially enables peacekeepers to use force against those who act against their mandates and the 'Charter principles' on which they are based."[31] This corroborates what is mentioned in the Capstone Doctrine:[32]

> The need for even-handedness toward the parties should not become an excuse for inaction in the face of behaviour that clearly works against the peace process. Just as a good referee is impartial, but will penalize infractions, so a peacekeeping operation should not condone actions by the parties that violate the undertakings of the peace process or the international norms and principles that a United Nations peacekeeping operation upholds. Notwithstanding the need to establish and maintain good relations with the parties, a peacekeeping operation must scrupulously avoid activities that might compromise its image of impartiality.

However, given complex internal conflicts where extreme violence has become the norm, reining in warmongers (multiple parties to the conflict) requires well-trained and well-equipped military peacekeepers, who have always been at a premium, except for the Permanent Members of the UNSC and a few other developed nations. Therefore, the very rationale of neutral troops does not make much sense. As observed by Frazer, "The decision to deploy peacekeepers in and of itself is not neutral and is reflective of the political and strategic interests of the UN Security Council in general, and the P5 in particular".[33] Over time, as UN PKO became a more practical alternative for conflict resolution, impartiality, rather than neutrality, has assumed greater importance. Even the UN official document mentions impartiality as a principle.[34] The shift in conceptual thinking from neutrality to impartiality took place around 1998, after the debacles in Srebrenica and Rwanda. Even then, neutrality and impartiality were often confused; they have different meanings and significance: neutrality usually means not taking sides with warring parties, and impartiality refers to non-discrimination, i.e., peacekeepers must be neutral but implement the mandate without favour and prejudice to any party.[35] Describing this as 'the neutrality–impartiality dilemma', Malito has questioned the very concept of the possibility of peace in a neutral space.[36] While the principle of neutrality has been replaced by impartiality, given the multiple groups fighting in the same conflict and with high chances of either lack or withdrawal of consent by one or more groups, the peace operation cannot remain impartial even in principle.[37]

However, to some, impartiality is synonymous with neutrality, and not taking action against perpetrators of violence because of a lack of understanding of the mandate is considered impartial. Impartiality is not limited to deeds alone but also to the way stakeholders look at the peacekeepers' impartial status. There is no better example to understand this relationship than what happened when Hutu militias came down on the Tutsis in Rwanda on 6 April 1994 and killed Prime Minister Agathe Uwilingiyimana who was a Hutu, in addition to killing 10 Belgian peacekeepers.[38] Even though General Dallaire, the FC of the UNAMIR, tried his best to protect the civilians with whatever little means the mission had, one of the military contingents stood by silently as mute spectators to what was happening, possibly waiting for orders from their national capital. France, Italy, Belgium, and the USA instructed their contingents to evacuate only their nationals.[39] These nations probably wanted to remain neutral by not taking action against the perpetrators of violence. According to General Dallaire, it was 'cynical manoeuvring by France, Belgium, and the USA.'[40] Commenting on the implications of the impartiality of UN peace operations, Rhoads quoted Mona Khalil (former senior UN legal officer) saying that impartiality, "requires UNPKO to act independently when the host government is unable or unwilling to even take action against the host government forces where and when they pose a threat to civilians."[41]

Rhoads's observation was in the context of a lack of response on the part of UMISS during the violence between Kiir and Machar in July 2016, when the government forces were the perpetrators of the violence. A total of 73 civilians were killed including 20 at the PoC sites. She also provided an opposite example, i.e., the impartial stand taken by the UN in the same mission following the civil war in 2013. In May 2014, the UN, by its resolution 2155, took away the state-building and peacebuilding functioning of UNMISS. This was a strong signal from the UN that a government that abuses its people will not be supported.[42] In the former case, the lack of response on the part of the peacekeepers was attributed to the overstretched peacekeepers in trying to protect PoC sites while ignoring the threat to them. There were also other side issues such as an increase in crimes, rapes, and violence inside the PoC sites. While the actual reason why the peacekeepers did not react is difficult to state, UNMISS failed to take an impartial stand to protect the civilians.[43]

From the time the Belgian contingent of 450 para commandos landed in November 1993, Belgium's impartial status, being the former colonial master of Rwanda, has been doubted by the Government of Rwanda. Their attitude further vitiated the atmosphere. Most of the soldiers had joined UNAMIR after their tour of duty in Somalia, which was a Chapter VII mission. Describing the aggressive attitude of the Belgian soldiers, General Dallaire quoted his staff officers: "My staff soon caught some of them bragging at the local bars that their troops had killed over two hundred Somalis and that they knew how to kick the "nigger" arse in Africa."[44] On the other hand, France had a good relationship with the Hutu government. Therefore, when the Tutsi regained power and slowly recovered ground, they did not see France's role in Operation Turquoise as impartial. General Dallaire noted that the inertia and interference from the TCCs cost many innocent lives in Rwanda.[45] Whether on account of the term's deliberate/ unintentional misinterpretation of the history of the peacekeepers/ contingent, or political manoeuvring by powerful nations, once lost, the impartial status of the peacekeeper is difficult to get back. Therefore, the need to deal with the humanitarian crisis has necessitated revisiting 'neutrality' and replacing it with 'impartiality'.

After the genocide in Rwanda, Kofi Annan stated that "Impartiality does not—and must not—mean neutrality in the face of evil; impartiality means strict and unbiased adherence to the principles of the Charter, nothing more, and nothing less".[46] Similarly, the Report of the Panel on United

Nations Peace Operations in 2000 also stated that 'Impartiality for the United Nations must mean adherence to the principles of the Charter and to the objectives of a mandate that is rooted in those Charter principles'.[47] The same was endorsed by the General Assembly's Special Committee on Peacekeeping Operations.[48] The necessity of adhering to the principle of impartiality must, however, not be restricted to the implementation of the mandate alone. It must begin with the formulation of the mandate by the UNSC. However, whenever the UNSC mandate has a clear political objective, it is no longer possible for the UN to remain impartial. The principle of impartiality is also intrinsically connected to the third principle—the *use of force*—which is the most controversial of the three.

Even though Hammarskjold believed that peace operations, in general, did not involve the use of force as envisaged under Chapter VII of the UN Charter, a peace operation under Chapter VI can also use force in self-defence. There is however a misunderstanding that force can be used only under Chapter VII of the UN Charter. As analysed by Labuda, this needs some explanation and going back to what Hammarskjold explained in his report to the General Assembly *Summary study of the experience derived from the establishment and operation of the Force.*[49]

Hammarskjold stated, "A problem arises in this context because of the fact that a wide interpretation of the right of self-defence might well blur the distinction between operations of the character discussed in this report and combat operations, which would require a decision under Chapter VII of the Charter and an explicit, more far-reaching, delegation of authority to the Secretary-General than would be required for any of the operations discussed here".[50] This amplified to *firstly*, use of force is permissible even under Chapter VI. *Secondly*, there is a distinction between the use of force in self-defence under Chapter VI and enforcement action under Chapter VII. *Thirdly*, the line between the use of force in self-defence and combat action even under Chapter VI as seen later in Congo (1960–1964) is blurred.[51] The line became more blurred as subsequent peacekeeping missions got multidimensional and expansive mandates, some under Chapter VII, and some with authority for wider use of force even under Chapter VI (it will be explained in more detail later).

As the peace operations evolved, along with the expanded mandates, came phrases like 'in defence of the mandate', 'robust peacekeeping', 'aggressive peacekeeping', 'use all necessary means', etc. When seen in the context of the spirit of the principles as illustrated by Hammarskjold, these phrases have added further confusion to the understanding of their meaning. *One*, the principle of use of force is mentioned as 'Non-use of force except in self-defence and defence of the mandate ' in the Capstone Doctrine. There is however no explanation as to how much force is enough and what is the meaning by the defence of the mandate or is proactive use of force to implement the mandate covered by this principle. *Two*, Phrases like 'robust peacekeeping', 'aggressive peacekeeping', and 'use all necessary means' are generally understood because of their association with the Chapter VII mandate. At the same time, even under a Chapter VI mandate, "Robust peacekeeping involves the use of force at the tactical level with the authorization of the Security Council and consent of the host nation and/ or the main parties to the conflict".[52] However, there are examples of past missions like the United Nations Mission in Liberia (UNMIL) and the United Nations Stabilisation Mission in Haiti (MINUSTAH), which though mandated under Chapter VII, were not authorised to use force.[53] On the other hand, the mandate of the United Nations Interim Force in Lebanon (UNIFIL) uses phrases like "authorises UNIFIL to take all necessary actions..." under a Chapter VI mandate.[54]

Even this phrase, 'all necessary means', raises the question of the limit of using force. Bourgeois argued that 'necessary' cannot be a 'blank cheque.' Defining 'necessary' in the context of its legality, she concluded that UN peace operations or UN-mandated peace operations simply cannot resort to any amount of force to protect civilians. The Security Council's using this phrase to authorise peace operations to protect civilians leaves room for discussion and ambiguity.[55] It, in turn, allows being interpreted differently by different TCCs and peacekeepers to suit themselves. Bourgeois however identified an upper limit to what UN (mandated) peace operations may lawfully do to protect civilians. "First, any use of force needs to strictly comply with the norms of *ius cogens*. Second, the overall levels of force used when carrying out a UNSC mandate need to be necessary and proportionate to obtain the general objective(s) set out in the mandate. Third, specific instances of the use of force need to comply with HRL, IHL (if applicable), and relevant domestic laws of the host State and the TCC(s)".[56] To my understanding, 'necessary' means only what is 'essential' or the 'minimum' use of force that is necessary. But the question is how to determine what 'minimum' is.

The normative ambiguity and its legal implications in the context of Human Rights Law (HRL) and International Humanitarian Law (IHL) have hence further compounded the application of the principle of use of force. Mission HQs, however, for their part, try to remove the ambiguity by way of issuing guidelines to make the use of force simpler. These come in the form of RoE, which is approved at the level of UN Headquarters (HQs). The RoE, though exhaustive, are only general guidelines to commanders for their intelligent interpretation on a case-by-case basis. There have been many instances in the past when peacekeepers did not use force even in self-defence.[57] The hesitation to use force can be caused either because of an obsession with the fear of loss of legitimacy if viewed as partial by the party on which force is applied or by the fear of sustaining casualties as a result of retaliation from rogue elements. Howard and Dayal argued along similar lines. They noted that using force not only compromised the principle of impartiality but also made the peacekeepers vulnerable to attacks by armed groups against whom force was used. Besides, when peacekeepers fail to implement important mandated tasks such as the protection of innocent civilians, it can be perceived by the local population as a consequence of either inadequate troops or a weak mandate. Therefore, a stronger mandate to use force generates hope in the peacekeepers' ability to achieve something which they could not do earlier. Howard observed that such high expectation is another negative effect of using force by peacekeepers.[58] What is implied is simply to live up to the expectations of the mandate, there is a chance that peacekeepers use excessive force even in self-defence.

The likelihood that the use of force leads to fatal retaliation is probably the primary factor dwelt upon by the commander regarding whether to use force or not. Such was the case in Bosnia when, between 7 and 11 July 1995, Bosnian Serbs attacked Srebrenica, killed innocent civilians and took 50 Dutch peacekeepers hostage. Repeated requests for North Atlantic Treaty Organization (NATO) airstrikes by the Dutch battalion against the attacking Bosnian Serbs went unheeded until 11 July 1995. Barnett and Finnemore related this incident to Akashi, the HoM's, and French General Bernard Janvier's obsession with the UN's commitment to the rule of neutrality, that is, not to use force, which eventually resulted in the UN's failure to protect the safe havens.[59] According to a Human Rights Watch report, had airstrikes been done in time, the fate of Srebrenica would have been different.[60] Quoting from the inquiry by the UN official, David Harland, Porter stated that the request for an airstrike by the Dutch contingent commander, Colonel Ton Karremans, was deliberately delayed by Janvier.

According to Porter, 'He was, of course, playing for time, doing anything rather than taking direct action, which he believed would inflame the Serbs.'[61] In other words, both Yasushi Akashi and General Janvier, fearing retaliation from the Serbs, chose to stringently adhere to the principle of peacekeeping, namely, minimum use of force only in self-defence, rather than using it to save thousands of innocent lives.

Novosseloff also attributed such inaction on the part of the senior leaders to their fear of losing the status of impartiality and fear of retaliation, which prevented them from using force even if it was a just and fit case.[62] Whether it was a case of abdicating moral responsibility to save human lives or was the notion of getting legitimacy by not using force that could have influenced the decisions of Akashi and Janvier is not known. In this regard, against the backdrop of what Tripodi observed when he stated that "when peacekeepers are placed in a position to prevent moral catastrophes, they cannot step aside and "allow" the killing of those who believed the soldiers were there to protect them" it can reasonably be concluded that both Akashi and Janvier did not fulfil their moral obligation.[63] Goulart calls it a lack of 'combat motivation', which inspires the peacekeepers to fight armed opponents in the conflict zone. Noting that there can be several different combat motivating factors, Goulart observed that the legitimacy of the cause is the predominant factor. Citing examples from contemporary peace operations like MONUSCO and UNMISS, he explained that the sense of legitimacy of the cause for defending the sovereignty of their own country is different from that of peacekeepers taking the risk to save the lives of some foreign nationals in the conflict zone. He reported that, among others, the lack of combat motivation was one of the main reasons for the failure of peace operations.[64]

While describing the relationship between power, legitimacy, and effectiveness, and its impact on the local population, Whalan highlighted the challenging and unpredictable environment in which peacekeepers are required to work. She observed that peacekeepers use the power of coercion, inducement, and legitimacy to shape local behaviour. She, however, cautioned that coercion by using force may tend to breed resentment which adversely affects the quality of behaviour that is expected to be shaped.[65]

As mentioned in the previous section, impartiality is closely linked to the use of force. Laurence reported that impartiality is a core legitimating norm for UN peace operations, which is contested because there is a genuine shift in the explanation of impartiality. He explained such a shift by citing examples from DRC. He observed that even though it adopted a forceful stance after Joseph Kabila came to power in 2006, MONUSCO did nothing when the rebel group M-23 (Mouvement du 23 mars) overran Goma in 2012. Later, however, the Force Intervention Brigade (FIB), comprising troops from South Africa, Tanzania and Malawi, joined hands with the government forces and used lethal force against M-23.[66] While UN officials contest the critics of FIB that it was impartial because it took the side of the mandate, Laurence however noted that impartiality persists but the ways of being impartial have proliferated. Therefore, according to him, "insisting that a force like the FIB is impartial can be a deliberate strategy for glossing over normative and political disagreements".[67]

Instances of the United Nations Protection Force (UNPROFOR) and UNAMIR clearly illustrate the failure on the part of senior leaders as well as that of the peacekeepers to save innocent lives.[68] Legitimacy, nevertheless, is a subjective perception that varies depending on how the outcome of the operation affects different stakeholders, including the local population. The opinions of host-nationals, since they suffer the most and are also the primary beneficiaries of positive peace, should be central to the way the effectiveness of a PKO is measured. Hence, the peace process must consider the views of the local population.

For peace operations to succeed, the legitimacy of the operation, both at the strategic and local levels, is necessary. When a peace operation can implement a large part of the mandate, it gains credibility. Newby put it as the ability to deter conflict and provide human security. Therefore, it has to be earned and constantly supported by evidence. Once a mission has established credibility, it earns confidence. On the other hand, local legitimacy enables the mission to win cooperation from the local population. Hence, local legitimacy is linked to trust but can be eroded over time by unreliable behaviour on the part of those who are trusted.[69] Simply because a PKO is a multinational force that is either led or authorised by the UN, it does not mean that it will be viewed as legitimate by the local population.[70] Explaining this as local legitimacy, Whalan noted that "Local legitimacy refers to evaluations by local actors about a peace operation's rightness, fairness, and appropriateness—that is, whether its practices rightfully cohere with the relevant framework of rules and values, are fair, and produce appropriate outcomes."[71] In Bosnia, in evaluating the poor Bosnian Muslim population, the UN operation failed to protect their lives. Howard stated that 'the UN gains enormous moral and ethical legitimacy in the field by not using force'.[72] However, not using force in Bosnia, while technically legitimate, was both morally and ethically wrong and ethically illegitimate.

Implementation of Mandate

Different interpretations of the peacekeeping principles directly impact mandate implementation, which is the second aspect we discuss here. Very often, a vague mandate has been quoted as the root cause of the problem. The failures of PKO in the former Yugoslavia and Somalia and Rwanda are often attributed to the mandate, which was flawed and unachievable. Even though a perfect mandate would have helped to improve the chances of success of the operations, it is difficult to formulate a flawless mandate because of political compulsions. Such was the case even during the UN operations in Katanga. On 12 July 1960, the President and Prime Minister of the Republic of Congo accused Belgium of inciting and helping a secessionist movement in Katanga for colonial benefit. Describing Belgium's action as a threat to international peace and security, they requested the UN for military assistance to protect the national territory of Congo against this external aggression.[73] Recognising the urgency of the situation, Dag Hammarskjold, the then Secretary-General, exercising his power under Article 99 of UN Charter XV, called for an immediate meeting of the Security Council. The reasons for the Secretary-General taking the initiative to call for a meeting of the Security Council are interesting. In normal circumstances, the President of the Security Council calls a meeting if a dispute or situation is brought to the its attention under Article 35 or under Article 11 (3) of the Charter. In the instant case, by exercising his power of Article 99, the Secretary-General took the lead to hasten the process. Besides, on 17 July, the Congolese President and the Prime Minister informed the representative of the Secretary-General in Congo that if the UN were unable to ensure the withdrawal of the Belgian troops within 48 hours, they would be forced to request the intervention of the USSR.[74] As observed by Aksu, to the West, reports of Belgium's involvement were a matter of concern and so were the political and economic implications of the situation. To the Eastern bloc, more specifically the USSR, it was a good opportunity to be used to highlight the imperialistic idea of the West if no action was taken. Overall, everybody wanted to do 'something'. All that remained was how the Secretary-General could work around all the members and build a consensus. Hammarskjold dominated most of the discussions that followed and indirectly forced the hands of the Security Council to act.[75] The initiative of the Secretary-General in terms of taking up the issue under Article 99 of Chapter XV was a clever move enabling the UNSC to authorise him to provide the necessary assistance.[76] This was a case of political compromise even though it was for the benefit of Congo.

On 14 July 1960, the Security Council adopted Resolution 143 calling for the withdrawal of Belgian troops and authorising the Secretary-General "to take all necessary steps" to provide the Congolese government with "such military assistance as may be necessary" until national security forces are able "to meet fully their tasks". A total of five resolutions were adopted by the Security Council associated with the withdrawal of the Belgian military and mercenaries and the goal of internal stability.[77] Fearing intervention by the USSR and the dawn of the Cold War prompted the Council to take more vigorous action by adopting Resolution 145 which used strong words like *"Calls upon the Government of Belgium to implement speedily Security Council Resolution 143 (1960) on the withdrawal of its troops and authorizes the Secretary-General to take all necessary action to this effect"*.

However, unlike the situation before 2000, the mandates of most contemporary peacekeeping missions have become more clear and stronger, with detailed and multifarious tasking for the peacekeepers. Peter reported, "The UN not only is using force to protect the peace agreement, civilians, or itself—all established reasons for the use of force—but also to protect and assist the host state and its government".[78] Peter's statement should be seen in the context of what Tardy had mentioned earlier while critiquing the concept of Robust Peacekeeping.[79] He observed that after the tragedies of Rwanda and Srebrenica, where the peacekeepers failed to protect human lives, the calls for stronger political backup and operational teeth for peacekeepers were widely accepted across the world. Accordingly, the doctrine on the use of force started to re-evolve. Peace operation mandates became stronger, the peacekeeping force became better equipped with the protection of civilians (PoC) as the core objective of all peace operations (this will be discussed in the following section). The idea of robustness was enshrined in this new thinking. Robustness is to give operational capability while acting against spoilers. The term 'Robust Peacekeeping' has now been mentioned in the 'Principles and Guidelines' issued by UN HQs. Tardy argues that the UN definition of 'robust peacekeeping' demands the use of force at the tactical level with the consent of the host state.[80] He however questioned the acceptability by the host state of the use of force by peacekeepers at the tactical level when either the state or one of the parties is the perpetrator of the violence in the conflict. Moreover, under such given circumstances, whenever force is used even against the spoilers, the principle of impartiality will be lost or seen to be lost by one or more affected parties to the conflict.

Protection of Civilians

Despite the ambiguity in understating the use of force, the mandates of contemporary peace operations have become stronger with the primary objective to save innocent human lives. But *how* to implement this has not been defined. Whether it is to provide some space either to the field commanders to use their discretion or to the main disputants in exchange for their consent is not known. No matter what the exact intention might be, it does impact mandate implementation. For instance, in the context of the mandate of protecting civilians inside a camp, is it to be done simply by providing perimeter defence and waiting for the perpetrators of the violence to come close to the camp? Or moving out of the camp to deter them at a distance by patrolling or, whether laying ambushes would be better options? What happened in the civilian camp in Malakain South Sudan in February 2016 is an example that shows how difficult and precarious such situations can be.[81]

Further, how does one provide protection when one of the parties responsible for the violence is state-sponsored? Such was the story on 11 July 2016 when about 80-100 government soldiers from the Sudan People's Liberation Army (SPLA) stormed the Terrain Hotel compound. They singled out the Americans, abused and beat them, and thereafter shot dead the South Sudanese reporter, John Gatluk, who worked for *Internews* (a US-funded media development organisation) right in front of the foreign aid workers, gang-raped several foreign women, and carried out mock executions. Desperate pleas to the UN peacekeeping mission, located less than a mile away, went unheeded.[82] It is still not clear if the peacekeeping contingent/s, located not far away, was/were either incapable of or unwilling to respond to the calls for help to avoid putting the interest of its/their TCCs in South Sudan at risk. UNIFIL aptly amplifies the other reason—providing space to the disputants—for lack of clarity in the mandate. For example, without the Hezbollah's unwritten consent, the current mandate could not have been adopted and, hence, any action against it would not be acceptable to them.[83] Consequently, any retaliation consequent to the use of force by UNIFIL will not be acceptable to the TCCs.

Accordingly, UNSCR 1701 is silent on both the Hezbollah's role in Lebanon and the role of both UNIFIL and the LAF in disarming the outfit.

Despite being a core objective of the UN, the mandate to protect civilians has become increasingly challenging. Mamiya, the author of the International Peace Institute (IPI) report, 'Protection of Civilians and Political Strategy', pointed out the tension between politics and the urgent need for the protection of civilians. According to him, such a strain can prevent creating consensus in the UNSC for taking important decisions like the protection of civilians. The UN policy of 2019 has outlined the PoC operational concept in three-tier action.[84] This concept is largely endorsed. However, Bode and Karlsrud have observed that those who implement the concept, have a different understanding of the norm. Hence, it is challenging to practise this concept.[85] Protection of civilians is much more than this policy. Citing the joint operations by the Congolese Army (FARDC) and the Ugandan Military (UPDF) against the Allied Democratic (ADF) in Beni territory of DRC on 3 November 2021, Spound observed that the peacekeeping missions are wrapped in the legal implications of the use of force as well as the likelihood of an increased threat to civilians as revenge. This gets complicated in the fear of casualties to the peacekeepers because of retaliation by the rebels against their using force to protect civilians. The resultant inaction by the peacekeepers is seen by the civilian population as unwillingness on the part of peacekeeping missions to protect civilians. Dayal calls it the crisis of consent by the local population.[86]

There is however a tendency in some quarters to confuse PoC as a core obligation with responsibility. The centrality of PoC is well understood because saving human lives is the moral responsibility of human beings. However, the primary responsibility to protect civilians is that of the host state. Shifting the responsibility to the peacekeepers will encourage them to shun their obligation and become a drain on the peacekeeping resources. It was observed similarly by Day and Hunt, "First, the gravitational pull of PoC can distract attention and scarce resources from other, often interdependent, priorities. Second, how PoC has been pursued can distort intended impacts and in some circumstances even do harm. Third, these distractions and distortions can combine to produce dilemmas for mission leaders, Secretariat officials, and the Security Council."[87] The UN's Report of the Special Committee on Peacekeeping Operations reaffirmed the importance of PoC as the core objective of the peacekeeping operations. Yet, this report only encourages and reminds the member-states and TCCs of their obligations to protect civilians under the relevant international law.[88] Coning, while explaining stabilisation operations, stated, "There will always be a gap between doctrine and practice, but it is the responsibility of the policy makers to keep that gap as small as possible. The wider the gap the more likely there will be negative consequences".[89]

Interestingly, after examining the work of the UN mission in Sierra Leone from 1997 to 2001 to study how peacekeepers can reduce violence, Salvatore concluded that since the increase or decrease in violence is also conditional on the local balance of power and the territorial control held by the warring parties, increasing the number of peacekeepers even though it helps, does not automatically reduce violence against civilians.[90] Therefore, it is still possible for peacekeeping contingents to honour the commitment they made to fulfil their duty, i.e., to save innocent human lives.[91] While UNPROFOR and UNAMIR generally are quoted for their failure to save innocent lives, there were also examples in the same missions—dating back to the 1990s, much before the protection of civilians became the core issue for the UN—when peacekeepers held their ground, including making the supreme sacrifice to protect civilian lives disregarding orders from their political superiors. In Bosnia, in December 1993, a NORDBAT platoon (from the Scandinavian contingent), despite being heavily outnumbered by a Croatian battalion-size force, refused to hand over two Muslim nurses to the Croats for more than 12 hours. Ingesson has defined such firmness to achieve the mission objective by disregarding the highest political authority and without worrying about one's future career as a culture of 'mission command', which takes decades to grow and develop.[92] Similarly, during the genocide in Rwanda, the actions of Captain Mbaye Diagne, a Senegalese unarmed military observer, were a rare example of commitment and dedication to protecting civilian lives when others were running away from the battlefield. Finally, on 31 May 1994, he was killed by a shrapnel attack by Hutu militias.[93] Therefore, rather than the very idea of a vague mandate, it is the lack of determination on the part of senior leaders as well as the peacekeepers themselves that seems to be the primary reason for the failure of PKO. A clear mandate does help to provide a well-defined direction to the peacekeepers. Unless there is a will to honour the commitment, no amount of clarity can help to protect innocent lives. Another related challenge arises when PoC is linked to the concept of Responsibility to Protect (R2P) because even though they are distinct, they are closely related.[94]

Peace Agreement

A peace agreement is essentially a contract between disputants to end the conflict. In the context of UN PKO, a ceasefire agreement is a type of peace agreement, which, however, varies from conflict to conflict. In general, a peace agreement indicates the willingness of the parties to the conflict to restore peace by means other than violence, hence making it a moral obligation for the disputants to honour their commitments made in the peace agreement. To this end, a UN PKO is one of the institutions or organisational tools to monitor the implementation of the peace agreement.[95]

Even though the signing of a peace agreement does not guarantee peace, a PKO has better chances of success after fruitful negotiations resulting in an agreement that displays a sincere change in the positions of the disputants. After analysing 32 peace operations since 1948, Pushkina, Siewert, and Wolff concluded that besides lack of consent and cooperation, the absence of a peace agreement is sufficient for failure of a peace operation.[96] Hence, such negotiations must include the major disputants as well as the external powers that have the power to influence the peace process. For instance, in Cambodia, when China and Vietnam withdrew their support to the adversary parties they were backing, the peace process fell into place.[97]

Angola was a case of pronounced external involvement in supporting the warring groups even after the signing of the Bicesse Accord in 1991.[98] The United Nations Angola Verification Mission (UNAVEM) II was deployed in May 1991 but the main disputants—Movimento Popular de Liberatcao de Angola (MPLA) and United Nacional para Independencia Total de Angola (UNITA)—continued to be supported by outside powers. Violence recurred when Savimbi, leader of UNITA, lost the election. The resumption of violence, which cost around 300,000 lives, was primarily due to several reasons. First, the Bicesse Accord did not include any provision for a third-party guarantee to ensure that the disputants would adhere to the accord. Second, the international community could not determine what exactly was in Savimbi's mind. Third, the election was held even when the security situation was not conducive. Fourth, since the USA had always supported UNITA and was only looking at it coming to power, the PKO was grossly below strength.

The Lusaka Protocol is the second agreement that was signed in November 1994 but at a time when Savimbi was losing territory and under pressure to buy time. Just before signing the agreement, the USA did a volte-face by supporting sanctions on its protégé, UNITA. Moreover, since the agreement considered UNITA illegitimate, UNITA had to disarm itself, but this was not so for the government forces. Further, as there was no mention of the prevention of importing arms by any party in the protocol, the earlier sanction that was imposed on UNITA before the signing of the agreement remained, thus making it biased towards the sitting government of the MPLA. Finally, when the MPLA launched an attack on UNITA soon after agreement was reached, Savimbi withdrew his consent and again picked up arms, which that had been carefully cached deep inside the jungle.[99] In Angola, the Bicesse and Lusaka agreements were inconclusive; they favoured only one party and powerful nations like the USA were not interested in the peace process. According to Howard, "While the Lusaka Peace Accord was detailed, and both sides consented to it and UN's oversight, these otherwise favourable situational conditions were tinged with ambiguity as to the depth of consent".[100]

The UNAMIR mission was deployed in Rwanda after the conclusion of the Arusha Accord in August 1993.[101] The Arusha Accord was fraught with challenges from the very beginning. According to Willard, political impasse, a lack of strategy for reintegration of demobilised soldiers, turf battles between different agencies on funding to support the demobilisation programme and, above all, a lack of sincerity on the part of the UNSC were some of the causes of failure to implement the accord.[102] Howard also observed that even though the warring parties—the Hutus and the Tutsis—had signed the Arusha Accord before the deployment of the mission, the Hutu majority that had been dominated by the Tutsi minority in the past, remained hostile against the latter. She reported, "During the peace process, a new political force (sometimes referred to as 'Hutu Power') had been gaining strength".[103] According to her, this new power centre, which was against any political reconciliation, was unknown to the UN and the Rwandan government. Therefore, consent by the Hutus was at best symbolic and it needed an incident like the death of Hutu General Habyarimana on 6 April 1994 to trigger violence. The international community was either oblivious or refused to see the gaps in the agreement and had pinned too much hope on the success of the agreement, which was flawed from the very beginning. As a result, the requirement of a peacekeeping force of reasonable size was neither supported nor approved by the decision-makers at UN HQs.[104]

On the other hand, the situation prevailing in Bosnia and Herzegovina was different from these other three conflicts.[105] There was neither a peace agreement nor a stalemate on the battlefield and the mission did not enjoy the full consent of all the parties (especially not from the Bosnian Serbs).[106] According to Doyle and Sambanis, it was a lack of unanimity in the UN Security Council about the actual problem. Citing examples of the UN Protected Areas, which were vulnerable and not protected well, the Europeans were more worried about the Muslims using the safe areas to launch attacks on the Serbs. On the other hand, the USA would not risk its forces on the ground. As a result, the international community was not effective and failed to exert pressure on the Serbs.[107] Therefore, the mission began on the wrong footing. Even General Satish Nambiar—the first HoM and FC of UNPROFOR—attributed the failure of UNPROFOR in Bosnia largely to lack of a peace agreement, inadequacies in the mandate, interference by influential nations, including the USA, and inadequacy of troops. According to him, an agreement like the Dayton Peace Agreement of 14 December 1995 should have been concluded before the decision to establish a PKO was taken.[108]

The case of the Democratic Republic of Congo (DRC) is more complicated because of the distinct involvement of Angola, Rwanda, and Uganda in the internal affairs of DRC from the very beginning of the First Congo War in 1996. The alignment and the number of foreign actors, as well as internal armed groups, continued to change as the war progressed. The five different agreements—the Lusaka Ceasefire Agreement (1999), the Sun City Agreement (April 2002), the Pretoria Agreement (July 2002), the Luanda Agreement (July 2002) and, finally, the Global and Inclusive Agreement of December 2002—never helped to end the conflict because they did not sufficiently address the grievances of all the armed groups. The latest comprehensive agreement of 31 December 2017 that stipulated the end of the two terms of the current President Kabila (according to the DRC Constitution), who agreed not to contest in the next election, appears to be quite an achievement. Kabila proposed his former Interior Minister, Emmanuel Ramazani Shadary, who has the dubious distinction of being one of the individuals internationally sanctioned in 2017, to succeed him. In this way, Kabila wanted to continue to rule DRC by proxy even after he relinquished power, possibly his reward for the significant concessions he made.[109] Even though it was Felix Tshisekedi, the opposition leader, who won the election (allegedly disputed) and there were expectations for improvement, nothing has changed after two-and-a-half years of the government in power. According to Kambale and Dizolele, the corrupt and dysfunctional government has not been able to control the armed militias.

One of these groups killed the Italian Ambassador to DRC along with his driver and bodyguard in February 2021.[110] The current situation is pretty much the same as what Autesserre had described earlier in 2008 and 2010. She had reported that "Until the local grievances that are feeding the violence throughout eastern Congo are addressed, security in the entire country and the Great Lake Region overall will remain uncertain."[111] Therefore, the conflict in DRC is not likely to be over as long as the peace agreements do not address the grievances of all the actors. In fact, the lack of honesty in these agreements has only helped to re-ignite the conflict that has been fuelled by various multinational corporations (MNC) that want access to the rich natural resources of the country.[112]

Similarly, the Comprehensive Peace Agreement (CPA) that marked the end of two decades of civil conflict in Sudan fell short of an inclusive agreement. This agreement is a collection of documents negotiated over two years and signed in Kenya on 9 January 2005.[113] A detailed description of the shortcomings of the peace agreement has been given by Guehenno, who was the Under-Secretary-General of the UN and closely involved in the progress of the signing of the agreement in his memoirs of peacekeeping. Guehenno observed, "The agreement signed on 9 January 2005 was actually a very fragile foundation for peace".[114] Amongst others, the CPA required holding a referendum at the end of six years, that was in January 2011, to allow the people of southern Sudan to decide whether they wanted to remain with Sudan or be part of an independent sovereign state in the south. They chose independence, but only to be engulfed by their internal problems. If the provision for an independent South Sudan was already part of the CPA, the drafters should also have catered for a smooth transition and made provisions for necessary assistance for subsequent governance of a new state. According to Ottaway and Hamzawy, 'the signing of the agreement was due to skilful international mediation and diplomacy, rather than a sincere change in the position of the two states.'[115] In yet another attempt to give a chance to peace, the President of South Sudan, Salva Kiir, and his former Vice President, Riek Machar, signed a peace deal in Khartoum on 27 June 2018.[116] The talks were mediated by President Omar al-Bashir of Sudan and President Yoweri Museveni of Uganda. This agreement was a welcome change to the ongoing conflict. However, as *The New York Times* reported, the country has already suffered a lot with approximately 2.5 million citizens fleeing the country and hundreds of thousands internally displaced. A peace deal like this, which looks elite, is not going to succeed if the same issues are perpetuated again and those who have suffered the most are not taken on board unless it includes reforms designed to fight corruption and build more accountable public finances. The landmark 2005 agreement that paved the way for its secession from Sudan gave Juba 50 per cent of the south's oil revenue, allowing billions to be pumped into the new semi-independent government as it prepares for complete independence.[117] Another reason why this agreement could fall apart is that it is not inclusive. The United Nations' "sustaining peace" agenda recognises that peace is a process that builds a common vision of society that ensures that all population's needs are considered. This inclusivity is both an objective and a principle.

Inclusivity is defined as the extent to which the views and needs of parties to the conflict and other stakeholders are represented, heard, and integrated into peace processes. This is important throughout the whole peace process—from mediation to institution building.[118] As South Sudan completes its tenth anniversary of independence, the people who fought for it feel betrayed since South Sudan is not democratic as planned. The security sector reforms lacked strategy and almost 400,000 people lost their lives during the internal strife. Even the comprehensive peace agreement that focused only on the President and the Vice President, who failed to live up to their promises, suffered from the following problems:[119]

- The DDR strategy was more focused on ethnic packing and integrating rival armed groups who were more loyal to their ethnic leaders into one tent.
- Stakeholders were unable to agree on the objective of security reforms.
- It lacked a demobilisation program aimed at reducing the size of SPLA and allowing the combatants to join civilian life. Only 13 per cent of the former fighters entered the program; the rest were technically ineligible leaving them with no option other than to lose faith in the security reforms.

Therefore, unless there is a comprehensive peace agreement before the UNSC approves a PKO, its continuance will be purely out of political necessity and because there is no exit strategy. For instance, UNIFIL was established without a peace agreement and in a hurry. The Security Council failed to fully support it. The Soviet Union abstained from voting on all the resolutions from 1978 to 1986 on the ground that firstly, UNIFIL's function of assisting the return of an effective government of Lebanon was not practical, and secondly, there was no exit strategy for UNIFIL. The Soviet Union, however, did a U-turn in 1986 when the USA's role in the Middle

East began to decline.[120] Goulding described the background to establishing UNIFIL as:

> It is an operation about whose viability the then Secretary-General and his senior advisers had doubts. It was nevertheless pushed through the Security Council by the United States for pressing, if passing, political reasons. President Carter was launching the negotiations, which were to lead to the Camp David Accord and did not want the process derailed by the Israeli invasion of Lebanon that had just taken place.[121]

Inclusivity of Local Actors

It is, however, a challenge to conclude a comprehensive peace agreement when there are several parties to the conflict and armed groups are fighting for their share of the profits. Ginty and Richmond noted that the current method of peacebuilding is not inclusive and leaves local actors out of the process. They contend that there are a large number of local-based agencies that are present within a conflict or post-conflict zone and working for the peace process. These agencies, along with the local population, are better equipped in peacebuilding tasks and better suited to suggest workable practices to examine peace. However, the current concept of building peace, in their eyes, is a kind of Western colonial narrative projecting dominance of the global North rather than of autonomy, democracy, rights, and cooperation.[122] In the same manner, Newby pointed out the importance of gaining credibility to win the cooperation and confidence of the local population.[123]

Autesserre also commented that the international community's inability to address the root causes of conflicts including the role of local agents is one of the main reasons for the failure of peacekeeping operations.[124] She reported that the local agendas of the family, clan and community partly drive continuation of the conflict. Recurrence of the power struggle within the local political parties in South Africa after the end of apartheid and the dispute in Burundi for access to land and inter-clan tension in Somalia are a few examples of local agendas driving conflicts.[125] DRC is another example where, despite so many peace agreements, the current situation is still in a mess. According to her, what began as a grass-root conflict over access to land and power politics between the so-called indigenous Congolese in Kivus (eastern Congo) and the Congolese of Rwanda descent who had migrated to Congo, first escalated into a national political issue and then into a regional conflict. Even after the end of the war in 2003, the micro-level antagonism continued to fuel the insurgencies. Nevertheless, the strategy to build peace has been based on the dominant narrative that the current situation is a fallout of the large-scale violence of the two Congo wars. As a result, the international community looked at the local tension and antagonisms as nothing but criminal activities, which festered because of the absence of national authority. Since the focus was only on the macro-level issues with the root cause of the conflict unsolved, numerous armed groups supported by both government and external powers continue to fight to control the mineral-rich territory of DRC. Autesserre noted, "The illegal exploitation of Congolese mineral resources thus holds a central place as one of the primary motivations for violence waged by regional and national actors".[126]

The role-play of the local actors was visible even in Somalia and Rwanda. Doyle and Sambanis reported that the failure of the UN in Somalia was both at the macro and micro levels. The UN's understanding of Somali political culture was poor and it failed to use the correct conflict resolution tool that could sustain a locally based peace. At the micro-level, when the UN invited the warlords to participate in a conference and sought their cooperation for the distribution of humanitarian assistance, it legitimised their claims over their respective territories. On the other hand, it prevented those groups that were excluded from such conferences from promoting peace initiatives and, most importantly, the UN was unable to identify a legitimate authority in the state where there was no central legitimate authority.[127] The case of Rwanda was slightly different in the sense that a peace agreement (Arusha Peace Agreement) was in place even though it was complicated because of the unstable coalition group. That aside, Rwandan President Habyarimana signed the agreement under duress. Most remember Rwanda for the UN's failure to prevent the genocide of the Tutsis by the Hutus in 1994. What the UN, however, failed to relate is the action of the Hutus to the historical legacy of 1959, when they rose against the Tutsi minority followed by the first full-scale war in 1963-1964, killing around 3,000 Tutsi exiles and 10,000 innocent Tutsi civilians as retaliation by the Rwandan government. Soon after the war, then-President Gregoire Kayibanda began fostering the ideology of *being Hutu*.[128] The same ideology later became the core of the Hutu power centre that emerged during the presidency of Habyarimana and the spirit behind the massacre of the Tutsi minority in April 1994.

Leadership

While explaining the ambiguity of the UN norms in the context of Srebrenica, I had earlier mentioned the crucial role of the mission leaders in implementing the mandate. UN peace operations are military operations but with the UN mandate to operate outside the contingents' home state. Defining command of a military force, King mentioned that "Command consists of three intimately connected functions: mission objective, mission management and mission motivation."[129] He further stated that these three elements are inseparable and that the leader, who can define these competently, is also able to motivate his troops. Like all military operations, the peacekeeping force is led by a uniformed man. But barring two missions, the HoM is a civilian UN employee who is generally the Special Representative of the Secretary-General. These senior mission leaders do not have an enviable task for primarily two reasons. *One*, the decision-making process in the complex politico-military environment is complex and challenging. *Two*, even though the HoM draws his authority from the Secretary-General, based on the UN charter, the command and control are generally not like a military command channel.

Even the FC faces similar challenges of mission management and mission motivation primarily because of participation in peacekeeping by choice and the general dislike in the UN towards the words '*command and control*.' Therefore, command and control are more a product of coordination, cooperation and management. In a diverse force, good comprehension of the challenges and how to make the best of the contingents is the art of leadership. For instance, UNIFIL is one unique mission, where the diversity is between the contingents from the Western and non-Western nations. Some of them are equipped with advanced weapon systems which are rare in UN peacekeeping. Useful employment of these capable peacekeepers from the West and skilled peacekeepers from non-Western nations depends on the prevailing circumstances as well the ingenuity of mission leaders. This apart, even the other leadership trait such as the ability to take risks, contributes to the effectiveness of peace operations.

In UN integrated missions, SRSG is the top political representative of the Secretary-General who is expected to play a coordinating role inside as well as outside the UN. Karlsrud noted that mission leaders have to navigate in unchartered waters and operate between conflicting parameters of adherence to norms and principles of peacekeeping and deliver in the field. He went on to state that "The rules and norms of an organization are more than bounded rationality, distinct from the environment—they shape the rationality of the organization's actors and guide individual action".[130] When it comes to taking a crucial decision, the leader interprets the mandate according to his interpretation of the UN Charter and in terms of personal gain or loss of prestige. While some leaders calculate the loss should the decision become counterproductive, some SRSGs may walk the extra mile when it comes to saving lives. For instance, as mentioned earlier, in Bosnia, the leaders, despite having the resources at hand, refused to call for an airstrike by NATO when the Bosnian Serbs killed thousands of unarmed civilians and took Dutch peacekeepers hostage.[131] In contrast, in Rwanda, Gen. Dallaire, the FC, and his staff risked their lives to save as many innocent Rwanda civilians as they could from the genocide by the Hutus in April 1994.[132] Similarly, in 2005, the UN Stabilization Mission in Haiti (MINUSTAH) fired more than 20,000 rounds of ammunition, grenades and mortar fire and killed the gang leader, Emmanuel "Dread" Wilme, and many of his followers.[133] Likewise, in April 2011, in Cote d'Ivoire, when the country's internal situation of the country was going out of hand because of violence perpetrated by the Defence and Security Forces of Cote d'Ivoire (FDSCI), the UN, along with French Licorne forces, attacked with heavy weapons, entered the presidential palace and captured President Gbagbo.[134] Even if Rwanda was considered a failure, the FC was effective in saving hundreds of lives. Similarly, the leaders in Haiti and Cote d'Ivoire took risks to implement the mandate. Essentially, it is individual leadership characteristics that can be the turning point in the trajectory of peace operations.

UNSC, Budgetary Support and other Policy-related Factors

The UNSC has the sole authority to approve the deployment of a new PKO. Even after a PKO is deployed, its mandate has to be renewed every six months. In addition to the difficulties of formulating a mandate, during the entire period—from the time of its deployment until a mission closes—the UNSC faces many challenges. To begin with, the decision to mount a PKO may be taken without assuming there are good chances of success. There may be times when the UNSC may decide to act under the influence of international media and domestic pressure even if the chances of success are poor.

Howard and Stark pointed to a lack of consensus in defining the actual problem as another major weakness of the UNSC that affects the mandate, structure, the budget to support the operation and the exit strategy of the PKO. For example, in the case of the former Republic of Yugoslavia, the USA perceived the conflict as an instance of ethnic hatred and, hence, intervention would be futile. France considered it as a tension between the elites and the public; and for China, it was an internal problem. Only a few European nations such as Germany and the Non-Aligned Group, considered the problem of external aggression by the Serbs and recommended military intervention. On the whole, the UNSC was completely confused. The military, on the other hand, had a different perspective on how to protect safe areas.[135] The net result was the establishment of a PKO that lacked a strategy and the required strength and clarity in the mandate. It was a PKO that was doomed to fail from the very beginning.

Sitkowski commented that to expect the UNSC to manage the security function of the world is an illusion dreamt in 1945 at the time of adoption of the UN Charter at San Francisco. It is primarily because the big powers did not consider the UNSC anything else other than an extension of their national diplomacy. He further noted that except for the intervention in Korea in the 1950s and the Gulf in 1991, the UNSC has never performed its functions in accordance with the Charter.[136] Bara and Hultman observed that "behind any UN deployment is the consensus of the P5 members that the conflict poses a threat to global or regional peace and security".[137] However, the decision of the P5 members depends on how such conflicts threaten their countries. The deployment of a PKO based on a Security Council resolution is only the first step to bringing order to a conflict zone. Such a decision must be followed by a sincere commitmet to continuous political support, provision of adequate resources (soldiers and equipment), financial support and support for any mid-course correction of the mandat, if required.

Critics also like to argue that it is the Security Council that is to be largely blamed for failing in its responsibility to either prevent a conflict or even allowing it to progress in some cases. The inability to prevent Russian from invading Ukraine in February 2022 and ending the conflict is the latest example of the Security Council's failure (even if it is because of the organisational constraints of the Security Council with a P5 member involved in the conflict). Earlier, explaining the conflicts between Israel and Lebanon, Nasu mentioned that the Security Council took four days to react after Israel's first invasion of Lebanon in March 1978. In the second military incursion in June 1982, the Security Council shifted the responsibility to a multinational force because of the US veto. In the case of the 2006 war, which began on 12

July 2006, the Security Council waited until 11 August 2006 to adopt Resolution 1701. According to him, it seemed like there was tacit approval from the Security Council for the 2006 war to continue under the pretext of self-defence by Israel. Nasu believed that the Security Council's decisions have been selective and hostage to the interests of the P5 members.[138] Jones and Hart had similar views. They observed that in the Middle East, the USA was never in favour of any UN peacekeeping because Israel would not accept any UN peacekeeping. They stated that "The United States repeatedly raised the prospect of closing down UNIFIL, which Lebanon resisted, citing first and foremost the economic impetus to the south provided by UNIFIL's presence".[139] Later, explaining the role of the Security Council on sustainable peace, Sambanis mentioned that the lack of sincere commitment on the part of the Security Council is a big impediment to sustainable peace. Sambanis's remark, however, was more related to the post-operation peacebuilding activities. Even then, her comment that "the Security Council recognizes the severity of the conflict but is unwilling or unable to give troops an adequate mandate to resolve the conflict (that is, a mismatch between the problem and the treatment)," can be related to several current peace operations.[140]

Decisions of the Security Council must be accompanied by a consensus amongst all the Permanent Members on the correct definition of the problem, along with a comprehensive strategy to move the peace process forward. Williams observed that the Permanent Members, who influence the decisions of the UNSC, generally do not participate in PKO with troops. Consequently, the non-powerful nations who participate with troops in such complex operations are unable to resolve the instability in the theatres of operation because they lack leverage over the conflicting parties and the host nations to alter the security situation.[141]

The appointment of senior leaders is another area where the UNSC has a poor track record. For instance, the appointment of the Secretary-General, who has an enormous responsibility to bring to the attention of the UNSC any matter that threatens international peace and security, is political. By and large, this appointment is decided by the support of the Permanent Members of the Council. Rikhye commented that the Secretary-General has an important role to play because he or she is the one who is ultimately responsible for the effective management of the PKO. Brahimi states: 'Effective dynamic leadership can make the difference between a cohesive mission with high morale and effectiveness and one that struggles to maintain any of these attributes'.[142] However, the process of appointment of the Secretary-General, and the appointment of the HoM, is influenced by the members of the UNSC. Chesterman and Franck observed that the Permanent Members of the Council are always interfering in the Secretary-General's appointment and functioning, thereby potentially reducing him or her to be a figurehead.[143] The debacles in Somalia, Rwanda, and Bosnia and Herzegovina amplify how ineffective leaders can negatively contribute to the failures of PKO.

Additionally, PKO are expensive and therefore must have adequate budgetary support. For 2019-20, the budget for UN PKO was approved at $ 6.5 billion for 12 operations and the UN logistical support operation in Somalia.[144] In comparison, this is 1.9 per cent less than the budget for the year 2018-19.[145] Even the approved budget for 2018-19 was nearly $ 580 million, less than the amount requested by the Secretary-General.[146] The budget continues to decrease. The approved budget for the fiscal year 2021-22, which is $ 6.38 billion, shows an average decrease of 2.1 per cent from the budget for 2020-21. The budget for the fiscal year 2022-23 is $ 6,45 billion which grew by 1.16 per cent, is because of the rising operational cost and increased pay of civilian personnel. Hence, it should not be considered as precedence for subsequent years.[147] The aspect of budgetary support remains in the domain of the UNGA. The budget for PKO is sourced from the member-states' annual contributions, with their share calculated according to a formula considering their economic health. The Permanent Members of the UNSC have to pay a larger share because of their special responsibility for the maintenance of international peace and security. Currently, based on the effective rates of assessment for 1 January 2019 to 31 December 2021, the USA tops the list of contributors with 28.40 per cent of the budget, followed by China (10.23 per cent), France (6.28 per cent), the United Kingdom (UK) (5.77 per cent) and the Russian Federation (3.99 per cent).[148]

The report of the Secretary-General on the need to establish a new PKO is accompanied by a document, called the 'Outline Financial Implication'. Once the UNSC approves a PKO, the advance mission HQ (which should be established soon) prepares a detailed budget and submits it to the UN HQs. The Secretary-General thereafter forwards the budget proposal to the Advisory Committee on Administrative and Budgetary Questions (ACABQ) of the UNGA for review, and its further recommendations to the Assembly's Fifth Committee for final approval. Disagreement among the members of the UNSC and tension between the Security Council and the Fifth Committee may result in a truncated PKO *ab initio* or midway, or premature closure of the mission. For example, in Rwanda, even months after the UNSC approved the deployment of UNAMIR II in May 1994, the member-states that voted in favour of the deployment found one excuse after another not to send their troops.[149] The US government at that time, for instance, argued that the African problems can be best solved by the Africans.[150] A considerable mismatch between the task and the resources resulted. Against a requirement of 35,000 troops, UNSCR 836 approved only 7,500. Looking back in hindsight, Rwanda was a victim of the consequences of the suffering in Somalia. Howard noted that there were differences of opinion between the Secretariat and the field. She observed that the UNSC neither wanted to abandon nor approve a large peacekeeping force to control the genocide that commenced on 6 April 1994, so much so that it defined the problem not as a systematic, well-planned genocide but as a chaotic civil war and ethnic massacre.[151] Such definitions justified their inaction in the face of the genocide. Eventually, when UNAMIR II was authorised after 31 May 1994, '...while the council did not endorse a mandate with adequate support, it did pass many resolutions on that matter'.[152] When compared to Somalia, the Security Council's decisions on Rwanda were neither consensual nor consistent, because while UNAMIR I was mandated under Chapter VI, the French-led 'Operation Turquoise' that took place at the same time was endorsed under Chapter VII. In contrast, interestingly, the decisions of the Security Council for Somalia were consensual and without any abstentions. Even the mission budget overshadowed all the other missions of that time.[153] Yet, failure in Somalia cast a dark shadow on the minds of the members of the Security Council when it came to dealing with the genocide in Rwanda.

Since the Fifth Committee is the final authority for the approval of the budget and the committee members come from the same countries that are members of the UNSC (and a few others), the clout of the Council in the budgetary process is inevitable. Therefore, the number and intensity of peacekeeping-related debates taking place in the UNSC reflect the Permanent Members' seriousness and commitment (or lack of it!) to face new and complex challenges that may threaten international peace and security. However, a greater number of discussions or debates do not guarantee a sincere commitment by the members of the UNSC. At the same time, such discussions do help in bringing clarity in formulating the mandate and garnering support for the required budget. According to Howard, a degree of interest shown by the UNSC in the form of debates, whether or not the resolutions are unanimous and whether or not their interests changed during the peace negotiations or implementation, contributes to the fate and success of a mission.[154] A valid discussion has been raised by Fortna in her incisive research paper on international intervention after civil wars. The inference that peacekeeping after civil wars does indeed make an important contribution to the stability of peace is important.[155]

Conclusion

In the absence of a conceptual framework, it is difficult to unequivocally evaluate the performance of PKO. Consequently, commenting on the relevance of PKO is problematic. For instance, after assessing 17 peacekeeping missions between 1945 and 1998, Pushkina classified them as 'successful', 'partially successful', and 'failed'.[156] Different scholars have identified different causes for the success or failure of PKO. All of them are relevant and have impacted the outcome of the PKO one way or the other. The situation surrounding the conflict and circumstances leading to the peace agreement, the availability of the consent of the disputants, support of the international community, the decision-making process, and the relevance of the principles of peacekeeping are the most common causes impacting the outcome of the peace process. Furthermore, factors like the support of the UNSC, including the intensity of the debate, and funding for the operation also affect the peace process. However, unless there is coherence between the mandate, strategies, plans, programme initiatives, structures, processes, and networks, a PKO cannot be a success.

As indicated in this chapter, despite so many studies undertaken to find ways to meet these challenges, nothing much has changed from Rwanda in 1994 to South Sudan in 2016.[157] This is because there is a large gap between what is professed conceptually and how it is interpreted during implementation. The way the basic principles of peacekeeping are interpreted is the biggest challenge impacting all PKO and, most importantly, affecting those nations that contribute with their peacekeepers in large numbers. To reiterate, the often-spoken inability of the peacekeepers to implement the mandate, more specifically when it comes to saving human lives, seems chiefly because of the lack of clarity in understanding the principles of peacekeeping and the mandate, and less due to their deficient capabilities.[158]

However, what has also emerged after further study is that one cannot always lay all the blame on the lack of clarity in the mandate or insufficient understanding of the principles of peacekeeping. Despite clear tasking, there were instances when commanders on the spot succumbed to the pressure of their political bosses, who were afraid of the domestic fallout if their military contingents used force to protect innocent civilians, which was their mandate. Astonishing mishaps in UNPROFOR and UNAMIR clearly illustrate this paradox. On the other hand, there were instances in the same two missions when peacekeepers held their ground and even died protecting civilians, disregarding orders from their political superiors.

The subject of success and failures will remain an enigma because first, defining success itself is a problem. Second, while there are common causes for success and failure, they vary from conflict to conflict. According to Rikhye:

> "Each conflict is different; each requires its diagnosis and treatment. UN peacekeeping forces can only prove effective if their mandate and resources are tailored to the needs of their missions for which they depend on the decision by the Security Council and mandates that it provides."[159]

Since there are no standard criteria for evaluation, most of the past assessments of PKO have been made by scholars who develop their success criteria based on their perceptions and convictions. Hence, their conclusions may be debatable. Despite this, there is some commonality in their deductions. The PKO that have failed to protect innocent lives have generally been branded failures. In such cases, the peacekeepers' inability to deliver in the field was due to the direct consequences of the deficit in conceptual thinking, the decision-making paralysis and confusion at the highest level, and a lack of will on the part of the peacekeepers to implement the mandate.

Ambiguity in the understanding of peacekeeping principles is always exploited and interpreted to suit the national interests of a few TCCs. Yet even though peace agreements do not guarantee peace, they do improve the chances of success. At the same time, it is better to deploy a PKO without a peace agreement rather than concluding an agreement that is not inclusive and has loopholes. Peacekeepers find themselves unprepared to face challenges of recurrence of violence when they pin false hopes on inconclusive and bad agreements. Such agreements, built on mistrust, also become an excuse for the disputants to derail the peace process. As to deficient resources, Angola and Rwanda are two clear examples of minimal means to meet the enormous challenges that the PKO faced. As for the mandate, even though they have become clearer and stronger, TCCs and the disputants will continue to take advantage of their inherent weaknesses.

Given the challenges and the slow progress in peacekeeping reform, the relevance of the PKO will have to be examined in the context of the availability of alternative mechanisms to restore normalcy in the conflict zone.[160] The number of conflicts triggered by greed for money and power has necessitated an instrument to bring back normalcy. Global policing, like the US intervention in Iraq, Libya and Afghanistan and, more recently, by some major powers in Syria, is coming under severe international criticism. This urges powerful nations to be more careful in exercising such an option. What, however, will not change is that it is national interests that have an overriding influence on a country's decision for participation with troops in either UN PKO or UN-authorised PKO. Consequently, though powerful and capable nations will be more cautious and weigh the cost of participation in complex missions carefully, at the same time they will not shy away from participating with uniformed peacekeepers in non-UN operations far away from their homeland, provided such participation is deemed to be in the interests of their national security.

Due to the uncertain commitment of capable nations vis-à-vis their participation in PKO, the usefulness of UN PKO will remain a challenge unless it is regionally based (such as the Economic Community of West African States Monitoring Group participating in peacekeeping operations in the African region) and there is an adequate incentive for increasing participation by non-Western nations. Besides, since there is a growing reluctance on the part of the main donors like the USA to fund UN PKO, their size will gradually become smaller and will not be able to meet the complex challenges of the vicious conflicts of the future. Therefore, there is a dire need for a conceptual shift in restructuring the peacekeeping force relying more on technology and rapid response capability than on heavy footprints. Finally, in the absence of any other, better, substitute, it is reasonable to believe that UN PKO is going to stay as one of the main alternatives for restoring peace in conflict zones. Going by the words of former UN Secretary-General Dag Hammarskjold—'The UN was not created to take mankind into paradise, but rather to save humanity from hell'—the UN is not a failure'.[161] After studying the causes for the failure of the peacekeeping operation, and their continued relevance, Chapter 3 will look into developing a conceptual framework for the assessment of a traditional UN peacekeeping operation.

ENDNOTES

1. This chapter is a revised and updated version of A.K. Bardalai, "United Nations Peacekeeping Operations: Causes for Failure and Continuing Relevance," *Journal of Defence Studies* 12, no. 4 (October-December 2018): 5-34.
2. UN General Assembly Security Council, *Agenda for Peace*, A/47/277 – S/24111 (June 17, 1992); UN General Assembly, *Report of the Panel on United Nations Peace Operations*, A/55/305-S/2000/809 (August 21, 2000); UN General Assembly Security Council, *High-Level Independent Panel Report*, A/70/95–S/2015/446 (June 17, 2015).
3. Barbara F. Walter, Lise Morje Howard and Virginia Page Fortna, "The Extraordinary Relationship between Peacekeeping and Peace," *British Journal of Political Science* (2020): 1, doi:10.1017/S000712342000023X; Barbara F. Walter, Lise Morje Howard and Virginia Page Fortna, "The Astonishing Success of Peacekeeping: The UN Program Deserves More Support—and Less Scorn—From America," *Foreign Affairs*, November 29, 2021, https://www.foreignaffairs.com/articles/world/2021-11-29/astonishing-success-peacekeeping; Also see Virginia Page Fortna, "Does Peacekeeping Keep Peace? International Intervention and the Duration of Peace After Civil War," *International Studies Quarterly* 48, no. 2 (2004): 285, https://doi.org/10.1111/j.0020-8833.2004.00301
4. Duane Bratt, "Assessing the Success of UN Peacekeeping Operations," *International Peacekeeping* 3, no. 4 (Winter 1996): 64.
5. UN General Assembly Security Council, *Comprehensive Review of The Whole Question of Peacekeeping Operations in all their Aspects*, A/55/305–S/2000/809 (August 21, 2000).
6. Virginia Page Fortna, "Does Peacekeeping Keep Peace? International Intervention and the Duration of Peace After Civil War," *International Studies Quarterly* 48, no. 2 (2004): 269, https://doi.org/10.1111/j.0020-8833.2004.00301
7. Barbara F. Walter, Lise Morje Howard and Virginia Page Fortna, "The Extraordinary Relationship between Peacekeeping and Peace," *British Journal of Political Science* (2020): 1-2, 14, doi:10.1017/S000712342000023X
8. UN General Assembly, *Report of the Panel on United Nations Peace Operations*, A/55/305-S/2000/809 (August 21, 2000).
9. Tomas W. Jacobson, "UN Peacekeeping: Few Successes, Many Failures, Inherent Flaws", *International Diplomacy & Public Policy Centre*, LLC, Colorado (March-April 2017): 1,www.IDPPCENTER.com
10. Severine Autesserre, "The Trouble with Congo: How Local Disputes Fuel Regional Conflicts," *Foreign Affairs*, 87, no. 3 (May-June 2008): 95, https://www.jstor.org/stable/20032653
11. Duane Bratt, "Assessing the Success of UN Peacekeeping Operations," *International Peacekeeping* 3, no. 4 (Winter 1996): 64–81; Paul F. Diehl and D. Druckman, *Evaluating Peace Operations* (New Delhi: Viva Books in arrangement with Lynne Rienner, 2011).
12. Indar Jit Rikhye, "The United Nations Operation in the Congo: Peacekeeping, Peacemaking and Peacebuilding," in *Beyond Traditional Peacekeeping*, ed. Donald C. F. Daniel and Bradd C. Hayes (London: Macmillan, 1995), 207–27.
13. Aisha Ahmad, "Agenda for Peace or Budget for War? Evaluating the Economic Impact of International Intervention in Somalia," *International Journal* 67, no. 2 (Spring 2012): 313-331,http://www.jstor.org/stable/23266009
14. Jonathan Mermin, "Television News and American Intervention in Somalia: The Myth of a Media-Driven Foreign Policy," *Political Science Quarterly* 112, no. 3 (1997): 389, accessed October 10, 2020. doi: 10.2307/2657563

15. Marion Laurence, 'An 'Impartial' Force? Normative Ambiguity and Practice Change in UN Peace Operations,' *International Peacekeeping* 26, no. 3 (January 2019), 258: 256-280, DOI: 10.1080/13533312.2018.1517027
16. John Karlsrud and Kseniya Oksamytna, "Norms and Practices in UN Peacekeeping: Evolution and Contestation," *International Peacekeeping* 26, no. 3 (2019), 253-254, DOI: 10.1080/13533312.2019.1600637
17. E.P. Rhoads and M. Laurence, "Peace Operations, Principles, and Doctrine," in *The Palgrave Encyclopaedia of Peace and Conflict Studies,* ed. O. Richmond and G. Visoka (October 15, 2019): 1-7, DOI: https://doi.org/10.1007/978-3-030-11795-5_20-1
18. Jeni Whalan, "The Local Legitimacy of Peacekeepers," *Journal of Intervention and Statebuilding,* 11, no. 3 (2017): 309, https://doi.org/10.1080/17502977.2017.1353756. Also see Vanessa Frances Newby, *Peacekeeping in South Lebanon: Credibility and Local Cooperation* (New York: Syracuse, 2018), 25-81.
19. David Curran, "Muddling on through? Cosmopolitan Peacekeeping and Protection of Civilians," *International Peacekeeping* 24, no.1 (2017), 72.
20. John Sanderson, "The Cambodian Experience: A Success Story Still?" in *United Nations Peacekeeping Operations: Ad hoc Missions, Permanent Engagement,* ed. Ramesh Thakur and Albrecht Schnabel (Tokyo/New York/Paris: The United Nations University, 2001), 155–66.
21. Abiodun Alao, John Mackinlay, and Funmi Olonisakin, "Regional Peacekeeping after the Cold War," *Peacekeepers, Politicians and Warlords: The Liberian Peace Process* (Tokyo: United Nations University, 1999), 7.
22. Aisha Ahmad, "Agenda for Peace or Budget for War? Evaluating the Economic Impact of International Intervention in Somalia," *International Journal* 67, no. 2 (Spring 2012): 313–31, http://www.jstor.org/stable/23266009
23. Michael W. Doyle and Nicholas Sambanis, *Making War and Building Peace: United Nations Peace Operations* (Princeton: Princeton University Press, 2006), 154.
24. Scott Peterson, "Bloody Monday," *Me Against my Brother: At War in Somalia, Sudan and Rwanda* (New York/London: Routledge, 2000), 117–136.
25. Lise Morje Howard, *UN Peacekeeping in Civil Wars* (Cambridge: Cambridge University Press, 2008), 25–27.
26. UN Security Council, Resolution S/RES/897 (February 4, 1994).
27. Joshua S. Goldstein, *Winning the War on War: The Decline of Armed Conflict Worldwide* (London: Penguin Books Ltd., 2012), 78.
28. Lise Morje Howard, *UN Peacekeeping in Civil Wars* (Cambridge: Cambridge University Press, 2008), 25–27.
29. Norrie MacQueen, *Peacekeeping and International System* (New York: Routledge, 2006), 74–78; United Nations, "*Summary Study of the Experience Derived from the Establishment and Operation of the Force: Report of the Secretary-General, A/3943,*"(October 9, 1958).
30. Ibid., 11.
31. Hikaru Yamashita, "Impartial Use of Force in United Nations Peacekeeping," *International Peacekeeping* 15, no.5 (November 2008):.615–630, DOI: 10.1080/13533310802396152
32. United Nations Peacekeeping Operations: Principles and Guidelines (New York: UN Department of Peacekeeping Operations, 2008), p. 33.
33. Trudy Fraser, "Peacekeeping and Rule of Law: Challenges posed by Intervention Brigades and other Coercive designation in support of the Protection of Civilians," in *Perspective on Peacekeeping and Atrocity Prevention: Expanding Stakeholders and Regional*

Arrangement, ed. David Curran, Trudy Fraser, Larry Winter Roeder Jr., and Robert Zuber (New York/Dordrecht/London: Springer, 2015), 69.

34. *United Nations Peacekeeping Operations: Principles and Guidelines* (New York: UN Department of Peacekeeping Operations, 2008), 31.
35. Ibid., 33.
36. Debora Valentina Malito, "Neutral in Favour of Whom? The UN Intervention in Somalia and Somaliland Peace Process," *International Peacekeeping* 24, no. 2 (April 2017): 280–303.
37. Mateja Peter, "Between Doctrine and Practice: The UN Peacekeeping Dilemma." *Global Governance* 21 (2015): 351–70.
38. In Rwanda, after the Hutu President died in an air crash, Hutu militias started the genocide on 6 April 1994, which killed around 800,000 innocent lives of the Tutsi minority community.
39. While Belgium was part of UNAMIR, France entered Rwanda with an intervention force to undertake a UN-mandated humanitarian operation, 'Turquoise', in June 1994. The USA, however, was never part of it.
40. Romeo Dallaire, *Shake Hands with the Devil* (Cambridge: Da Capo Press, 2003), 414.
41. Emily Paddon Rhoads "Putting Human Rights up Front: Implications for Impartiality and the Politics of UN Peacekeeping," *International Peacekeeping* 26, no. 3 (January 2019): 281-301, DOI: 10.1080/13533312.2018.1561184
42. Emily Paddon Rhoads "Putting Human Rights up Front: Implications for Impartiality and the Politics of UN Peacekeeping," *International Peacekeeping* 26, no. 3 (January 2019): 281-301, DOI: 10.1080/13533312.2018.1561184: S/RES/2155 (2014), May 27, 2014.
43. "UNDER FIRE: The July 2016 Violence In Juba and UN Response," *Centre for Civilians in Conflict*, 2016, www.civiliansinconflict.org
44. Romeo Dallaire, *Shake Hands with the Devil* (Cambridge: Da Capo Press, 2003), 113.
45. Ibid.
46. Kofi Annan, "Podium: Impartiality Does Not Mean Neutrality," *Independent*, January 22, 1999, https://www.independent.co.uk/arts-entertainment/podium-impartiality-does-not-mean-neutrality-1075401.html
47. UN General Assembly, *Report of the Panel on United Nations Peace Operations*, A/55/305-S/2000/809 (August 21, 2000).
48. UN General Assembly, *Report of the Special Committee on Peacekeeping Operations and its Working Group, Official Records Fifty-ninth Session Supplement*, No. 19, A/59/19/Rev.1 (January 31–February 25 and April 4 -8, 2005).
49. Patryk I. Labuda, "UN Peacekeeping as intervention by invitation: host-state consent and the use of force in Security Council-mandated stabilisation operations," *Journal on the Use of Force and International Law* 7, no. 2 (2020): 329, 317–56, DOI:10.1080/20531702.2020.1805886
50. UN General Assembly, "Summary study of the experience derived from the establishment and operation of the Force", Report of the Secretary-General to the General Assembly, A/3943, October 9, 1958 (para 179, page 31).
51. Jane Boulden, "United Nations Operation in the Congo (ONUC)." in *The Oxford Handbook of United Nations Peacekeeping Operations*, ed. Joachim A. Koops, Norrie Macqueen, Thierry Tardy and Paul D. Williams (Oxford: Oxford University Press, 2015), 160–70.
52. "The Basic Principles of United Nations Peacekeeping," *United Nations Peacekeeping*

Operations: Principles and Guidelines (UN Department of Peacekeeping Operations: New York, 2008), 34.

53. UN Security Council Resolutions S/RES/1509 September 19, 2003, and S/RES/1542 April 30, 2004.
54. UN Security Council Resolution S/RES/1701 August 11, 2006.
55. Hanna Bourgeois, "All Necessary Means' to Protect Civilians: The Interpretation and Implementation of UN Security Council Mandates Authorising the Protection of Civilians," *Journal of International Peacekeeping* 24, no. 1-2 (2020): 53–114, DOI: https://doi.org/10.1163/18754112-20200006
56. Hanna Bourgeois, "All Necessary Means' to Protect Civilians: The Interpretation and Implementation of UN Security Council Mandates Authorising the Protection of Civilians," *Journal of International Peacekeeping* 24, no. 1-2 (2020): 113, 53–114, DOI: https://doi.org/10.1163/18754112-20200006
57. OIOS, Inspection and Evaluation Division, *Evaluation of the Effectiveness of United Nations Peacekeeping Operations in Deterring and Confronting Armed Elements in the Democratic Republic of Congo, Mali, and the Central African Republic*, IED-17-013, 2 October 2017, para. 104, and *Triennial Review of Implementation of Recommendations Contained in the OIOS Evaluation Report on the Implementation and Results of Protection of Civilians Mandates in United Nations Peacekeeping Operations*, IED-17-010, 4 October 2017.
58. Lise Morje Howard and Anjali Kaushlesh Dayal, "The Use of Force in UN Peacekeeping," *International Organisation* 72, no. 1(Winter 2018), 72, https://doi.org/10.1017/S0020818317000431
59. Michael N. Barnett and Martha Finnemore, "The Politics, Power and Pathologies of International Organizations," *International Organizations* 53, no. 4 (Autumn 1994): 725.
60. Human Rights Watch, *The Fall of Srebrenica and the Failure of UN Peacekeeping: Bosnia and Herzegovina*, 7, no. 13 (October 1995) and Dennis C. Jett, *Why Peacekeeping Fails* (New York: Palgrave, 2001), 15–18.
61. Henry Porter, "Days of Shame," *The Guardian*, November 17, 1995. https://www.theguardian.com/theguardian/1999/nov/17/features11
62. Alexandra Novosseloff, "Can We make UN Peacekeeping Great Again," *Global Peace Operations Review*, 9 May 2017, http://peaceoperationsreview.org/thematic-essays/can-we-make-un-peacekeeping-great-again
63. Paolo Tripodi, "Soldiers' Moral Responsibility in Peace Support Operations," *International Journal on World Peace*, XXV, no. 1 (March 2008), 11; Paolo Tripodi, "When Peacekeepers Fail Thousands are Going to Die. The ETO in Rwanda: A Story of Deception," *Small Wars and Insurgencies* 17, no. 2 (June 2006): 234; "Peacekeepers, Moral Autonomy and the Use of Force Peacekeepers," *Journal of Military Ethics* 5, no. 3 (2006): 214–32.
64. Fernando Rodrigues Goulart, "Blue Helmets, Armed Groups, and Peace at Stake: Does Combat Motivation Matter for Robust Peacekeeping to Succeed?" *International Peacekeeping* (2020), DOI: 10.1080/13533312.2020.1827950
65. Jeni Whalan, "Power, Legitimacy, and their relationship," *How Peace Operations Work: Power, Legitimacy and Effectiveness* (Oxford: Oxford University, 2013), 55.
66. Marion Laurence, "An Impartial Force? Normative Ambiguity and Practice Change in UN Peace Operations," *International Peacekeeping* 26, no. 3 (January 2019): 256–280, DOI: 10.1080/13533312.2018.1517027

67. Marion Laurence, "An Impartial' Force? Normative Ambiguity and Practice Change in UN Peace Operations," *International Peacekeeping*, 26, no.3 (January 2019), 257: 256–280, DOI:10.1080/13533312.2018.1517027
68. D. Blocq, "Western soldiers and the protection of local civilians in UN peacekeeping operations: Is a nationalist orientation in the armed forces hindering our preparedness to fight?" *Armed Forces & Society*, 36(2) (2010): 290–309.
69. Vanessa Frances Newby, "The Role of Credibility in Peacekeeping," *Peacekeeping in South Lebanon: Credibility and Local Cooperation* (New York: Syracuse, 2018), 25–57.
70. Sophia Sabrow, "Local Perceptions of the Legitimacy of Peace Operations by the UN, Regional Organizations and Individual States: A Case Study of the Mali Conflict," *International Peacekeeping* 24, no. 1 (2017): 176.
71. Jeni Whalan, "Power, Legitimacy, and their relationship," *How Peace Operations Work: Power, Legitimacy and Effectiveness* (Oxford: Oxford University, 2013), 62–63
72. Lise Morje Howard, *UN Peacekeeping in Civil Wars* (Cambridge: Cambridge University Press, 2008), 339.
73. "Cable dated 12 July 1960 from The President of The Republic of The Congo and Supreme Commander of The National Army and The Prime Minister and Minister of National Defence addressed to The Secretary-General of The United Nations," the UN Security Council, S/4382, July 13, 1960.
74. "Questions Relating to the Situation in the Republic of Congo (Leopoldville)," https://www.un.org/depts/dhl/dag/docs/congo60.pdf
75. Eºref Aksu, " The UN in the Congo conflict: ONUC", in *The United Nations, intra-state peacekeeping and normative change* (Manchester, England: Manchester University Press, 2018), 100–29, https://doi.org/10.7765/9781526137906.00009
76. Arthur Lee Burns and Nina Heathcote, *Peacekeeping by UN Forces* (London: Pall Mall Press, 1963), 23–35.
77. The UN Security Council Resolutions S/RES/143, July 14,1960; S/RES/145, July 22,1960; S/RES/146, August 9,1960; S/RES/161, February 21, 1961; S/RES/169, November 24, 1961.
78. Mateja Peter, "Between Doctrine and Practice: The UN Peacekeeping Dilemma." *Global Governance* 21 (2015), 360.
79. Thierry Tardy, "A Critique of Robust Peacekeeping in Contemporary Peace Operations," *International Peacekeeping* 18, no. 2 (2011): 152-167, DOI: 10.1080/13533312.2011.546089
80. *United Nations Peacekeeping Operations: Principles and guidelines* (New York: UN Department of Public Information, 2008).
81. The civilian camp, co-located with the UN base, housed more than 37,000 people, mainly from the Dinkar and Nuer communities. When fighting broke out between them, many civilians rushed towards to the UN base for shelter. Despite fearing a situation that could go out of control, the peacekeeping contingent failed to react.
82. Lauren Spink and Matt Wells, "Under Fire: The July 2016 Violence in Juba and UN Response," *Centre for Civilians in Conflic*t, October 5, 2016, https://civiliansinconflict.org/publications/research/fire-july-2016-violence-juba-un-response
83. UN Security Council, Resolution S/RES/1701 (August 11, 2006).
84. UN, The Protection of Civilians in United Nations Peacekeeping, *The UN Department of Peace Operations*, Ref. 2019.17. November 1, 2019.
85. Ingvild Bode and John Karlsurd, Implementation in Practice: The Use of Force to Protect civilians in United Nations peacekeeping," *European Journal of International Relations* 25, no. 2 (2019): 458–485, doi: 10.1177/1354066118796540

86. Daniel Levine-Spound, "Ugandan and Congolese Troops Are Conducting Joint Operations: What Could that Mean for MONUSCO?" *IPI Global Observatory*, December 20, 2021, https://theglobalobservatory.org/2021/12/ugandan-congolese-troops-joint-operations-monusco/. Also see Anjali Dayal, "A Crisis of Consent in UN Peace Operations," *IPI Global Observatory*, August 2, 2022, https://theglobalobservatory.org/2022/08/a-crisis-of-consent-in-un-peace-operations/
87. Adam Day and Charles T. Hunt, "Distractions, Distortions, and Dilemmas: The Externalities of Protecting Civilians in United Nations Peacekeeping," *Civil Wars* (2021), DOI: 10.1080/13698249.2022.1995680
88. UN General Assembly, *Report of the Special Committee on Peacekeeping Operations, Official Records Seventy-Fifth Session Supplement No 19* A/75/19, 15 February–12 March 2021.
89. Cedric de Coning, "Is stabilization the new normal? Implications of stabilization mandates for the use of force in UN peace operations," in *The Use of Force in UN Peacekeeping* (1st edn.) ed. Peter Nadin (London: Routledge, 2018), 85–99.
90. Jessica Di Salvatore, "Obstacle to Peace? Ethnic Geography and Effectiveness of peacekeeping," *British Journal of Political Science 50*, no. 3 (2020): 1089–1109, DOI: 10.1017/S0007123418000200
91. Ralph Mamiya, "Protection of Civilians and Political Strategies," *International Peace Institute Issue Brief*, May 2018, https://www.ipinst.org/2018/05/protection-of-civilians-and-political-strategies.
92. Tony Ingesson, *The Politics of Combat: The Political and Strategic Impact of Tactical-level Subcultures, 1939–1995* (Lund: The Faculty of Social Science and Department of Political Science, 2016): 231–282, http://lup.lub.lu.se/record/8871111; Tony Ingesson, "Trigger-happy, Autonomous, and Disobedient: Nordbat 2 and Mission Command in Bosnia," *The Strategy Bridge*, September 21, 2017, https://thestrategybridge.org/the-bridge/2017/9/20/trigger-happy-autonomous-and-disobedient-nordbat-2-and-mission-command-in-bosnia
93. Paolo Tripodi, "Soldiers' Moral Responsibility in Peace Support Operations," *International Journal on World Peace*, XXV, no. 1 (March 2008), 19.
94. Paul D. Williams, "The R2P, Protection of Civilians, and UN Peacekeeping Operations," in *The Oxford Handbook of the Responsibility to Protect*, ed. Alex J. Bellamy and Tim Dunne (Oxford University Press, 2016), 524–544.
95. Nita Yawanarajah and Julian Ouellet, "Peace Agreements," in *Beyond Intractability*, ed. Guy Burgess and Heidi Burgess (University of Colorado, September 2003), https://www.beyondintractability.org/essay/structuring_peace_agree
96. Darya Pushkina, Markus B. Siewert, and Stefan Wolff, "Mission (im)possible? UN military peacekeeping operations in civil wars," *European Journal of International Relations*, 28, no. 1 (2022): 158-86, https://doi.org/10.1177%2F13540661211046602
97. Dennis C. Jett, *Why Peacekeeping Fails* (New York: Palgrave, 2001).
98. The Bicesse Accord is a comprehensive agreement that includes four documents: a ceasefire agreement; fundamental principles for the establishment of peace in Angola; concepts for resolving issues still pending between the government and the National Union for the Total Independence of Angola (UNITA); and the Protocol of Estoril that includes elections, military monitoring, internal security, political rights of UNITA, administrative structures and formation of the Angolan Armed Forces.
99. Christine Messiant, "Why did Bicesse and Lusaka Fail: A Critical Analysis," *Accord*, no. 15 (2004), http://www.c-r.org/accord-article/why-did-bicesse-and-lusaka-fail-critical-analysis

100. Lise Morje Howard, *UN Peacekeeping in Civil Wars* (Cambridge: Cambridge University Press, 2008), 38.
101. TheArusha Accord was signed in Arusha, Tanzania, between the Rwandan government and the Tutsi Rwandan Patriotic Front (RPF). The signing of theAccord followed a ceasefire agreement that was concluded in July 1992.
102. Emily Willard, *Rwanda: The Failure of Arusha Peace Accords,* National Security Archive Electronic Briefing Book No. 469,May 21, 1994, https://nsarchive2.gwu.edu/NSAEBB/NSAEBB469/
103. Lise Morje Howard, *UN Peacekeeping in Civil Wars* (Cambridge: Cambridge University Press, 2008), 30.
104. Ibid., 34.
105. The UNPROFOR was initially established for Croatia on 21 February 1992 for demilitarisation and protection of United Nations Protected Areas (UNPA), and also to assist UN humanitarian agencies. It is only later, on 31 March 1995, that its operations were extended to Bosnia and Herzegovina. When UNPROFOR was reconstructed into three different missions for Croatia, Macedonia, Bosnia and Herzegovina, it was rechristened with different names for Croatia (United Nations Confidence Restoration Operation in Croatia [UNCRO]); for Macedonia (United Nations Preventive Deployment Force [UNPREDEP]) but retained its original nomenclature for Bosnia and Herzegovina.
106. Lise Morje Howard, *UN Peacekeeping in Civil Wars* (Cambridge: Cambridge University Press, 2008), 44.
107. Michael W. Doyle and Nicholas Sambanis, *Making War and Building Peace: United Nations Peace Operations* (Princeton: Princeton University Press, 2006), 167.
108. Interview with Lieutenant General Satish Nambiar, who was the HoM and FC of UNPROFOR from March 1992 to March 1993.
109. Michelle D. Gavin. "Kabila Will Not Stand in Elections, but Will Congo Really Change?" *Council on Foreign Relations,* August 15, 2018, https://www.cfr.org/blog/kabila-will-not-stand-elections-will-congo-really-change
110. Pascal Kalume Kambale and Mvemba Phezo Dizolele, "Power Shift in Congo: The President and the Pursuit of Reform," *Foreign Affairs,* February 25, 2021, https://www.foreignaffairs.com/articles/democratic-republic-congo/2021-02-25/power-shift-congo
111. Severine Autesserre, "The Trouble with Congo: How Local Disputes Fuel Regional Conflicts," *Foreign Affairs* 87, no. 3 (May-June 2008): 95, https://www.jstor.org/stable/20032653; Severine Autesserre, *The Trouble with Congo: Local Violence and the Failure of International Peacekeeping* (New York: Cambridge University Press, 2010). Also see Michael W. Doyle and Nicholas Sambanis, *Making War and Building Peace: United Nations Peace Operations* (Princeton: Princeton University Press, 2006); Oliver P. Richmond, "UN Peace Operations and Dilemmas of Peacebuilding Consensus," *International Peacekeeping* 11, no. 1 (March 2004): 83–101, DOI: 10.1080/1353331042000228403
112. John Ahere, "The Peace Process in the DRC: A Transformation Quagmire, *Accord,* December 6, 2012, http://www.accord.org.za/publication/peace-process-drc/
113. The CPA was signed in Kenya by the National Congress Party (NCP) and the Sudan People's Liberation Movement/Army on 9 January 2005. The negotiations were facilitated by the Intergovernmental Authority of Development (IGAD) as well as the United Kingdom (UK), Norway, the USA, and Italy.

114. Jean-Marie Guehenno, "Sudan: Dangers of Fragmented Strategy for a Fragmented Country," *The Fog of Peace* (Washington: Brookings Institution, 2015), 172.
115. Marina Ottaway and Amr Hamzawy, "The Comprehensive Peace Agreement," Carnegie Endowment for International Peace, January 4, 2011, https://carnegieendowment.org/2011/01/04/comprehensive-peace-agreement-pub-42223
116. "Khartoum Declaration of Agreement Between Parties of the Conflict in South Sudan," https://igad.int/programs/115-south-sudan-office/1874-khartoum-declaration-of-agreement-between-parties-of-the-conflict-in-south-sudan
117. "A Peace Deal for South Sudan is Signed. Will it Last?" *The New York Times*, June 27, 2018, https://www.nytimes.com/2018/06/27/world/africa/south-sudan-peace-deal.html
118. Liezelle Kumalo, "South Sudan can learn from Liberia's road to peace," *ISS*, September 3, 2018, https://issafrica.org/iss-today/south-sudan-can-learn-from-liberias-road-to-peace?utm_source=BenchmarkEmail&utm_campaign=ISS_Today&utm_medium=email
119. Luka Biong Deng Koul, "Lessons from a Decade of South Sudanese Statehood," *Peacebuilding, Regions and Power,* Prio Blogs, July 11, 2021, https://blogs.prio.org/2021/07/lessons-from-a-decade-of-south-sudanese-statehood/
120. Ray Murphy, *UN Peacekeeping in Lebanon, Somalia and Kosovo: Operational and legal issues in practice* (New York: 2009), 44.
121. Marrack Goulding, "The Evolution of United Nations Peacekeeping," *International Affairs* 69, no. 3 (1993), 453.
122. Roger Mac Ginty and Oliver P. Richmond, "The Local Turn in Peace Building: a critical agenda for peace," *The Third World Quarterly* 34, no. 5 (2013): 772, https://doi.org/10.1080/01436597.2013.800750
123. Vanessa Frances Newby, "The Role of Credibility in Peacekeeping," *Peacekeeping in South Lebanon: Credibility and Local Cooperation* (New York: Syracuse, 2018), 53.
124. Severine Autesserre, "The Trouble with Congo: How Local Disputes Fuel Regional Conflicts," *Foreign Affairs* 87, no. 3 (May-June 2008): 107, https://www.jstor.org/stable/20032653
125. Severine Autesserre, *The Trouble with Congo: Local Violence and the Failure of International Peacekeeping* (New York: Cambridge University Press, 2010), 6.
126. Severine Autesserre, "A Top-Down Problem," *The Trouble with Congo: Local Violence and the Failure of International Peacekeeping* (New York: Cambridge University Press, 2010), 62.
127. Michael W. Doyle and Nicholas Sambanis, *Making War and Building Peace: United Nations Peace Operations* (Princeton: Princeton University Press, 2006), 160.
128. Ibid., 285.
129. Antony King, "Defining Command," *Command: The Twenty-First Century General* (Cambridge: Cambridge University Press, 2019), 69.
130. John Karlsrud, "Special Representatives of the Secretary-General as Norm Arbitrators? Understanding Bottom-up Authority in UN Peacekeeping," *Global Governance*, no. 19 (2013), 525–544
131. Michael N. Barnett and Martha Finnemore, "The Politics, Power and Pathologies of International Organizations," *International Organizations* 53, no. 4 (Autumn 1994): 725.
132. Romeo Dallaire, *Shake Hands with the Devils,* (Cambridge: Da Capo Press, 2005).
133. Colum Lynch, "UN Peacekeeping More Assertive, Creating Risk for Civilians," *Washington Post*, 15 August 2005.

134. John Karlsrud, "Special Representatives of the Secretary-General as Norm Arbitrators? Understanding Bottom-up Authority in UN Peacekeeping," *Global Governance*, no. 19 (2013), 525–544.
135. Lise Morje Howard and Alexandra Stark, "How Civil Wars End: The International System, Norms, and the Role of External Actors," *International Security* 42, no. 3 (Winter 2017/18): 155–61.
136. Andrzej Sitkowski, *UN Peacekeeping: Myth and Reality* (London: Praeger Security International, 2006), 22.
137. Corinne Bara and Lisa Hultman, "Just Different Hats? Comparing UN and Non-UN Peacekeeping," *International Peacekeeping* 27, no. 3 (2020), 363. DOI:10.1080/13533312.2020.1737023
138. Hitoshi Nasu, "The Responsibility to React? Lessons from the Security Council's Response to the Southern Lebanon Crisis of 2006," *International Peacekeeping* 14, no. 3 (2007):342–45.
139. Bruce Jones and Andrew Hart, "Keeping Middle East Peace?" *International Peacekeeping* 15, no. 1 (2008), 112.
140. Nicholas Sambanis, "Short- and Long-Term Effects of United Nations Peace Operations," *The World Bank Economic Review* 22, no. 1 (2008): 17.
141. Paul D. Williams, *Enhancing US Support for Peace Operations in Africa*, Council Special Report, no. 73 (May 25, 2015), 3; M. Lipson, "A Garbage Can Model of UN peacekeeping," *Global Governance* 13 (1): 80.
142. UN General Assembly, *Report of the Panel on United Nations Peace Operations*, A/55/305-S/2000/809 (August 21, 2000).
143. Simon Chesterman and Thomas M. Franck, "Leadership in Peace Operations: A Secretary General or a General," in *The Management of Peacekeeping*, ed.Julian Junk, Francesco Mancini, Wolfgang Seibel and Till Blume (London: Lynne Rienner Publishers, 2017), 292–298.
144. UN General Assembly, *Approved resources for peacekeeping operations for the period from 1 July 2019 to 30 June 2020*, A/C.5/73/21 (July 3, 2019).
145. UN General Assembly, Approved resources for peacekeeping operations for the period from 1 July 2018 to 30 June 2019, A/C.5/72/25 (July 5, 2018).
146. Jack Sherman, "With Peacekeeping Budget Approved, More Contentious Negotiations Lie Ahead," *IPI Global Observatory*, July 13, 2018, https://theglobalobservatory.org/2018/07/peacekeeping-budget-approved-contentious-negotiations ahead/
147. United Nations News "How we are funded," https://peacekeeping.un.org/en/how-we-are-funded, accessed June 7, 2022 and Daniel Forti, "The 2022 UN Peacekeeping Budget: Signs of Progress or a Fleeting Moment of Consensus?" *IPI Global Observatory* July 20, 2022, https://theglobalobservatory.org/2022/07/2022-un-peacekeeping-budget/
148. UN Department of Peace Operations, "How We are Funded," accessed November 28, 2020, https://peacekeeping.un.org/en/how-we-are-funded; UN General Assembly, *Implementation of General Assembly resolutions* 55/235 and 55/236, A/73/350/Add.1 (December 24, 2018).
149. For an analysis of this, see Michael Lipson, "Peackeeping: organized hypocrisy?" *European Journal of International Relations*, 13 (1): 5–34.
150. Romeo Dallaire, *Shake Hands with the Devil* (Cambridge: Da Capo Press, 2003), 414.
151. Lise Morje Howard, *UN Peacekeeping in Civil Wars* (Cambridge: Cambridge University Press, 2008), 32–33.

152. Ibid., 34.
153. Ibid., 24.
154. Ibid., 34.
155. Virginia Page Fortna, "Does Peacekeeping Keep Peace? International Intervention and the Duration of Peace After Civil War," *International Studies Quarterly* 48, no. 2 (2004): 285, https://doi.org/10.1111/j.0020-8833.2004.00301
156. Darya Pushkina, "A Recipe for Success? Ingredients of a Successful Peacekeeping Mission," *International Peacekeeping* 13, no. 2 (June 2006): 135.
157. A.K. Bardalai, "UNPKO and Military Contributions: Challenges and Opportunities for Asia Pacific Governments," *Journal of the United Service Institution of India*, GXLVII, no. 607 (January–March 2017): 26–34.
158. Ibid.
159. Indar Jit Rikhye, "The United Nations Operation in the Congo: Peacekeeping, Peacemaking and Peacebuilding," in *Beyond Traditional Peacekeeping*, ed. Donald C.F. Daniel and Bradd C. Hayes (London: Macmillan, 1995), 226.
160. M. Lipson, "Peacekeeping reform: managing change in an Organized Anarchy," *Journal of Intervention and Statebuilding* 6, no. 3 (2012): 279–98.
161. Nick Bryant, "UN: Seventy years of Changing World," *BBC News*, September 20, 2015, http://www.bbc.com/news/world-us-canada-34310354

CHAPTER 3

A CONCEPTUAL FRAMEWORK FOR ASSESSING TRADITIONAL PEACE OPERATIONS[1]

Introduction

Despite its more than seven decades of history, most of the UN peace operations have come under serious criticism because of their late deployment, weak mandate, inadequate resources, and, above all, ill-equipped and not optimally prepared peacekeeping troops. Given such a track record, there is now a question mark on the continued relevance of the UN peace operations; indeed, their very ability to implement the mandate has been repeatedly questioned.

The UN understands that ultimately it is about performance. In this regard, during a thematic debate on peacekeeping operations on 12 September 2018, the Under-Secretary-General (USG), Jean-Pierre Lacroix, confirmed to the United Nations Security Council (UNSC) that a clear framework of performance standards and assessment based on the performance by separate military units has already been established. He further confirmed that all missions would be expected to use this framework by 2020.[2] A resolution to that effect was adopted by the UNSC on 21 September 2018.[3] The USG, however, did not mention anything about the performance evaluation of the *whole* mission; but it may be safe to assume that the framework will be further developed for its application to the whole mission.

To determine whether peace operations have succeeded or not, a conceptual framework for the evaluation of peace operations is a prerequisite. However, as mentioned in Chapter 2, to develop such a conceptual framework, a good comprehension of the causes for the success and failure of peace operations is imperative.[4]

It is pertinent to note that no established theoretical framework on PKO has been found in the extant literature, for which reason research has to focus on a conceptual framework. Fetherston developed a theory towards peacekeeping in 1994. Peacekeeping is then placed within a contingency framework and the contingency theory has been analysed in the book. Another theory relates to conflict theory in the field of international relations. It relies heavily on academic literature on peaceful third-party intervention. Concepts such as conflict management, conflict resolution, facilitation, and mediation are used as key constructs of a successful PKO. No structured model emerges and hence the success criterion needs to look elsewhere to conceptualise the practice.[5] The aim here is to develop a framework and identify common success criteria to evaluate the performance or effectiveness of a peace operation. The UN's effort to establish such a framework would, by now, be in an advanced stage. Hence, this is an appropriate time for troop-contributing countries (TCCs) to use the suggested framework to pitch in with their contributions. In this connection, it will be argued that a concept based on Diehl and Druckman's idea of goal setting, and that of pillar questions by Shields and Rangarajan, can act as guides for the assessment of peace operations.[6] Accordingly, key or pillar questions can be framed to determine the extent to which a mission's goals have been achieved. This chapter provides the goals, key questions, and success criteria that can be used as a template for the assessment of traditional peace operations.

Evaluation Practices and the Development of an Evaluation Framework

Before developing the framework, it will help to have a brief look at the current evaluation methods followed by the UN and its weaknesses.

UN Performance Evaluation

At the UN Headquarters (HQs), the Inspection and Evaluation Division (IED) of the Office of Internal Oversight Services (OIOS) is mandated to evaluate the performance of all peace operations.[7] However, apart from generic guidelines, the *Inspection and Evaluation Manual* is silent on the detailed modalities for evaluation.[8] According to K.B.S. Sirohi, an Indian Army officer who was the former section chief of IED and who recently retired from UN services, much is left to the interpretation of the evaluation team, although the process of evaluation generally follows the guidelines given in the manual.[9] Coning and Brusset have stated that the main weakness of the current performance system is that it lacks a common frame of reference. Different tools serve different purposes without clearly distinguishing between their accountability, feedback on implementation, and organisational learning roles.[10]

To that end, the Effectiveness of Peace Operations Network (EPON), which is coordinated by the Norwegian Institute of International Affairs (NUPI), has done pioneering work to assess the effectiveness of UN peace operations. Its assessment report of the UNMISS concludes that 'UNMISS's role here in pushing for inclusivity and in supporting more local level agreements in support of the agreement, does appear to have positively influenced the process. It goes on to state, 'When considering how to measure the impact of the UN on the political landscape of South Sudan, a significant degree of humility about its ability to transform the system of power and authority is warranted'.[11] Though the report complements UNMISS for its effort, at the same time it hints that it is required to do much more than what it is doing.

Similarly, in the case of MONUSCO, the report, noticing the presence of numerous political and security dilemmas, acknowledges that the mission has been able to re-invent and adapt to the changing conflict dynamics.[12] These reports have tried to assess the effectiveness across a few critical dimensions. The different dimensions for different missions have been derived from the concept of the operations and from what has been identified as critical to the effectiveness of the mission. Likewise, the dimensions selected for the assessment of the United Nations Multidimensional Integrated Stabilization Mission in Mali (MINUSMA) are different from UNMISS and MONUSCO.[13] All three reports have generally left the conclusion of the overall performance of the missions to the interpretation of the readers. In the case of MINUSMA, the report has concluded that since 2016, its effectiveness has decreased.

Nonetheless, these reports have probably provided the input for the formulation of the UN tool for performance evaluation of the whole mission, according to Ahmed, who has served in the United Nations Interim Security Force for Abyei (UNISFA) as a political affairs officer:

> This proves the UN's responsiveness to the long-standing critique that it does not have a sufficiently robust system of performance

evaluation. It has apparently taken the benefit of several studies dwelling on an assessment framework and has a working one in place. It is now forming part of the reports of the Security Council for some pilot missions. This is a positive step that needs to be taken further and the framework needs to be kept updated.[14]

That the report of the Secretary-General on UNMISS also devotes a paragraph to the performance evaluation of the military component is an indication of the UN's sincerity in this field.[15] Since all reports of the Secretary-General are drafted by the respective missions, the performance evaluation of the military component of UNMISS is the reflection of the Head of the Mission of UNMISS and not the Secretaries-General. One could question, however, if the audit or assessment of any organization made by its head can ever be reliable. Keeping this aside, it is also an indication of the first step of acknowledging the need for performance evaluation at each level. Otherwise, best practices learnt over decades will be consigned to the archives of the UN. Given that criticism of the absence of a performance assessment framework, as well as the impression that the UN continues not to have one, may not be correct.

Performance evaluation of peace operations has always been difficult because the system lacks a common reference point. Setting the parameters for the conceptual framework for performance evaluation, or the benchmarks, and identification of correct indicators are the most crucial elements of the process of establishing a framework for performance evaluation.

The UN Department of Peacekeeping Operations (later renamed Department of Peace Operations), in particular, the Department of Field Support (DPO–DFS) has launched a planning toolkit that provides guidelines, checklists and templates that can be used for different plans, including the strategic framework a the mission's result-based budget (RBB).[16] While the toolkit focuses only on the planning aspects of the program, the list of do's and don'ts and the overview of examples are good inputs for setting benchmarks for budget planning. The do's and don'ts can be applied even to set goals (derived from the mandate) by peacekeeping missions. The toolkit also contains examples of good and bad indicators to measure progress towards expected accomplishments. Even though the toolkit provides good guidelines and techniques to measure progress for RBB and other programs, it is not enough to use it as a framework for performance evaluation of the whole peace mission. The RBB toolkit, which is meant for budget planning, is a useful input for creating a mathematical model to audit the spending of the allocated budget by peacekeeping missions in respective financial years. A pure mathematical evaluation will be quantitative and will fall short of a comprehensive assessment of the peace operation. Success, however, is often confused with effectiveness. In the context of a peacekeeping operation, success can be defined as achieving what was intended. Hence, it will be measurable. Effectiveness can be defined as a mission's ability to go through the process to produce results. Behavioural scientist Luthans noted that trying to make the distinction however seems like 'splitting hairs.'[17] Therefore, these two words will be used interchangeably in the subsequent sections.

Evaluation Design: Qualitative or Quantitative

As indicated in Chapter 2, after a thorough review of previous empirical research on the role of peacekeeping in reducing violence around the world, Walter, Howard, and Fortna concluded that peacekeeping had been remarkably effective in bringing peace. Their conclusion was based on a review of the earlier research that used different datasets and statistical models, covering different periods and measuring effectiveness in different ways. They reported with overwhelming evidence that all the quantitative research that they reviewed was consistent with their findings that peacekeeping operations had a statistically significant effect in bringing peace by a) reducing and preventing violence from recurring; b) containing its spread within and across borders; c) reducing civilian and military deaths, and d) making post-conflict settlement easy. An important conclusion of their study was that the positive effect of UN peacekeeping on bringing peace was a result based on quantitative studies and not on qualitative ones. According to them, quantitative data until now has been able to identify a significant and positive relationship between the presence of UN peacekeepers and their positive output in the field. They reported that, unlike qualitative studies, quantitative studies are more positive because quantitative scholars tend to examine the full range of cases to determine larger patterns over time across cases. That aside, as mentioned earlier, the authors also contended that the quantitative method has its limitations for several reasons. Firstly, most quantitative studies rely heavily on macro-level data in terms of space and time, and hence, the recommendations fall short of detailed policy recommendations for practitioners. On the other hand, qualitative data cover a range of other subjects like mandates, the success of peacebuilding measures, progress in nation-building and perceptions of the local population on the efficiency of peace operations. These subjects are difficult to quantify. To give an example, quantitative data can be used to find the financial and material contributions made by peacekeeping contingents in developmental projects in the field. However, the same data cannot be used to gauge the local population's perception of the usefulness of such contributions. Secondly, the findings of quantitative data analysis can be less than perfect because of sometimes unreliable data, untenable assumptions, and varying parameters for measuring performance. An analysis of qualitative data collected at the local level that includes the local population, practitioners, and subject matter experts can help bridge such a gap.

Walter, Howard, and Fortna believed that to get better clarity on how a peace operation has been able to contribute effectively, both quantitative and qualitative studies are necessary. Another important conclusion was the lack of knowledge about the full range of the usefulness of peacekeeping. To this end, they recommended more thorough evaluation research in institutions that can be created especially for research on peacekeeping policy.[18] After qualitatively and quantitatively investigating how the often neglected subject of the distance between the peacekeepers and local populations can affect the effectiveness of peacekeeping, Bove, Ruffa and Ruggeri also concluded that "Combining qualitative and quantitative investigations is important to better understand the role of similarity/dissimilarity between the Blue Helmets and local population."[19] However, there are some other factors and parameters that should form part of the framework to assess the effectiveness of peacekeeping operations; they are discussed in the following sections.

Mission Effectiveness, its Dynamics, and its Antecedents

There is no fixed definition of mission effectiveness.[20] In the context of UN peace operations, apart from the periodic UN Secretary-General's report to the Third Committee of the UN General Assembly and the UNSC, there are no objective criteria to measure the effectiveness of any peace operation.[21] This is not so strange. Different organizations use different measures to assess their achievements and effectiveness. For example, the corporate world, using multidimensional research instruments designed to capture consumer expectations and perceptions, looks at the wealth of shareholders and capital formation.[22] Yet, while measuring performance, another indicator that needs to be considered along with effectiveness is efficiency.[23] For example, an organization may employ hundreds of individuals who are efficient employees, but it may not be able to deliver because of certain constraints that are beyond the control of the organization. Similarly, if management can get the best out of its inefficient employees, the organization may still be able to deliver. Therefore, while efficiency is derived from the comparison between output and input, effectiveness is the overall contribution towards achieving goals. Mitchell explains that most non-profit leaders define organizational effectiveness as the extent to which an organization achieves specified levels of progress, cost efficiency, and goals.[24]

In the case of UN peace operations, cost and resources are the inputs and the end state is the output. However, like other organizational set-ups, the comparison between input and output in the case of peace operations is complicated. This is because, first, the inputs that contribute towards a peace operation, like the structure of the mission, leadership, the work culture of different peacekeeping contingents, communication, and quick reaction capability, are difficult to be quantified. Second, in a commercial organization, there usually is a commonality in the workers' backgrounds, professional skills, culture, and tradition. However, a peace operation comprises diverse contributors in terms of military, police, and civilian peacekeepers coming from all over the world, with different work ethos, cultures and traditions, religions, standards of training and operational ethos, and that too for a short duration. Therefore, the interpretation of the relationship between effectiveness and efficiency, and its application to peace operations, will be different from that of commercial organizations.

For instance, despite a mission comprising capable and well-equipped peacekeepers, it may still not be effective on the ground. To elaborate further, a capable quick reaction force (QRF) may not be able to take control of a sensitive situation in time because of the adverse effect of the underdeveloped terrain on its mobility. On the other hand, despite a good communications network, an inefficient QRF may not be effective to control a similar situation. Hence, in the case of the former, labelling the peace operation as ineffective will be unfair. The commonality between the effectiveness of a commercial organization and a UN peace operation is that both can be judged from their achievement of set targets or goals. At the same time, the multiple variables make it difficult to measure the effectiveness of a peace operation in achieving its goals.

Howard observed that even though peacekeepers are not consistent in achieving their intended goals, by most assessments, peacekeeping is effective. According to her, the effectiveness of peacekeepers comes from their power to convince others—warring parties, the government, and civilians to behave in a manner that they would not be willing to do otherwise. She calls it the *power of peacekeeping*. She reported that such power comes in the form of *coercion*, which is about limiting choices, *inducement* by offering material help and *persuasion*, which falls in the realm of ideas.[25]

Sandler compared effectiveness with the benefit of the free flow of transnational public goods and described the effectiveness of peacekeeping as its ability to achieve stability.[26] Raab and Soeters observed, "The mission's effectiveness is measured on the basis of a political and military assessment of the general situation (e.g., hostilities have ceased, public order and safety have been restored) as well as using figures of produced output (the number of explosive devices and bombs defused, the number of medical contacts with the local population, and the amount of money spent on projects)."[27] Salvatore and Ruggeri, after reviewing several studies on the effectiveness of peacekeeping, commented that despite the wide range of functions performed by UN peacekeepers, curbing violence remains the priority agenda for them. Noting that most of the peacekeeping literature is focused on negative peace, i.e., the absence of violence, they reported that "widely used indicators of effectiveness seem to be dominantly security-focused".[28] There is more, however. Aoi, Coning, and Thakur noted that there could be unintended consequences of peace operations. In this context, they observed that even reports of sexual abuse by peacekeepers might become the determining factor in the success of peace operations. At the same time, when such negative consequences can be anticipated, it helps in the overall improvement of the peace operation.[29] Coning, while explaining the complexity theory in political science and the utility of adaptive peace operations, put forward the idea of the Comprehensive Performance Assessment System (CAPS). CAPS is an iterative adaptive cycle that starts with the planning process and ends with adjustments made to future plans and operations. Such adjustment, which is required to improve the performance of the mission, is made based on an analysis of the feedback obtained from the environment.[30]

It was Johan Galtung who first talked about *negative peace*. He explained that peace has two sides: the *absence of personal violence* and the *absence of structural violence*. He referred to these as *negative peace* and *positive peace*, respectively.[31] Similarly, in Bove, Ruffa, and Ruggeri's concept, the central variable of peacekeeping effectiveness is "'negative peace': a decline in civilian victimization and battle-related deaths."[32] Howard's views are similar. She considered negative peace as one of the indicators to assess the effectiveness of the peace operation. According to her, ceasefire and the absence of violence is negative peace.[33] Richmond, however, cautioned that the benefit of negative peace should be available even to local actors and not limited to regional and international actors. He argued that it is important to visualise how peace should look from inside the conflict zone and not like the Western models that search for a solution from outside.[34]

In another publication, Ruffa differentiated between the effectiveness of the military in military operations and peace operations. She noted that "Military effectiveness traditionally refers to assessing behaviour without looking at the actual impact on, namely, victory and defeat; in the peace and conflict literature; effectiveness refers to the impact on the ground".[35] Accordingly, in examining the effect of military culture in multinational operations, Ruffa used the concept of Unit Peace Operation Effectiveness (UPOE) to explore the varying behavioural impacts of military contingents on the ground. This concept is derived from distinct military cultures of different military units, which shape their behaviour when employed in multinational operations. For her study, she selected two military contingents, one each from France and Italy in UNIFIL from 2007 to 2013, and used five indicators of effectiveness: responsiveness, integration, military and non-military skills, quality, and interoperability. These indicators are mission-specific and will impact differently on different peace operations.[36] She concluded that when employed in multinational operations, the behavioural impact of both the French and Italian contingents on the ground was different. The French peacekeepers, who were assertive by nature, considered participating in UNIFIL as in any other military operation outside their country. To them, the Hezbollah or Islamist terrorists, or for that matter anyone who can prevent them from implementing the mandate, posed a threat. This also includes IDF or even local citizens. Force protection being a high priority, French peacekeepers used heavy armoured vehicles including Leclerc tanks even for routine operational patrolling. As a result, the French peacekeepers are generally seen as more arrogant by the local population of South Lebanon. On the other hand, the Italians considered UNIFIL as a traditional peacekeeping operation and hence did not see any enemy in South Lebanon. They believed that their presence in UNIFIL is only for political reasons and laid a lower priority on force protection but a higher one on CIMIC activity. Except for the heavy tanks with the French contingent, both contingents generally had similar equipment profiles, the same standard of training and around the same strength. While the French contingent appears to be militarily skilled and professional, the Italians were more acceptable to the local population because of their relatively softer behaviour on the ground.[37] Likewise, using the same parameters, the military contingents from other nations would also have behaved differently with varying impacts on the ground. Similarly, Soeters and Meulen cited the example of how the cultural sensitivity of Turkish soldiers made it easier for them to interact with the local population.[38] In this regard, Soeters and Manigart earlier noted that it is important for military personnel to be trained in cultural awareness and develop cultural intelligence.[39]

Rietjens and Ruffa reported that coherence also affects the effectiveness of peacekeeping operations. They observed that as UN peacekeeping operations, comprising peacekeepers with varying standards of training, equipment and cultural diversity, are being regularly tasked with more diverse mandates, the success of these missions lies in integrating the resources to a common understanding and execution of mission goals. This is what the UN calls integration and cooperation or coherence as Rietjens and Ruffa speak about this. They picked up MINUSMA as a case study to assess the coherence of the mission. They used three key areas to assess cohesion: *mutual dependency and compatibility between strategies and organisational partners; the extent of alignment between individuals and organisational culture* and the *extent of alignment between the resource and the modus operandi*. The study revealed that MINUSMA fared poorly in all three areas. They concluded, "If we consider the effectiveness of peacekeeping operations as the level of goal realisation (i.e., fulfilling the UN mandate), our analysis suggests a positive and rather strong relation between the coherence and effectiveness".[40] Since military culture and cohesion impact a mission's overall effectiveness, these two factors cannot be ignored while developing a framework for the evaluation of peace operations.

Diversity and social and cultural distances, when analysed in different dimensions, can affect the outcome of peace operations. For instance, after studying four peacekeeping operations, the authors observed that different levels of diversity and distance can be advantageous as well as create organisational challenges and coordination problems for peace operations. The different variables that have been considered in the concept are the same as the conflict-specific variables (discussed in Chapter 2) and are not applicable across the board to all the missions. For example, one of the observations of the authors' study is that the level of diversity within the mission affects the protection of civilians and significantly reduces the number of battle-related deaths.

In another observation, Bove, Ruffa, and Ruggeri mentioned that diversity can either enhance or hamper peacekeeping effectiveness. They reported that field diversity, depending on its level (high or low), can either enhance or reduce the effectiveness of peacekeeping. They observed that cultural (geography, language, and religion) and social (economy and institutions) distance between the peacekeepers and the local populations can either have positive or negative or both effects on a mission. They contended that interaction between the peacekeepers and the local population can lead to either a higher or lower level of effectiveness. It is because cultural and social distances, which could be shaped by each other's pre-existing ideas and differences, drive the beliefs, attitudes, values, and perceptions that are reflected in the peacekeepers' behaviour on the ground. They explained that when the social distance is more, it may improve cooperation because it signals the UN's commitment. To clarify, contingents from the Western countries are generally culturally and socially distant from the local population. However, the economic and political clout of these TCCs display the UN's commitment and act as a political deterrence. At the same time, it can have the opposite effect because of social disregard, lack of empathy, lack of local knowledge, and understanding of local cultural values. A wider distance means that trust between the Western peacekeepers and the local population is low and hence it undermines the mission's effectiveness. On the other hand, smaller distances can be a unifying factor between the peacekeepers and the local population. They cited the example of how the Qatari contingent was popular because of their religion and their speaking of the local language and how the French contingent could bond with LAF better than the other contingents. After comparing the key characteristics of UNIFIL with MINUSMA in terms of diversity, they observed that UNIFIL benefitted from both positive and negative effects. In Mali, MINUSMA and some of the contingents that came from the African region were considered partial, thereby undermining neutrality. As a result, since the major contribution is from the regional forces, national interests affect the mission. Overall, MINUSMA is perceived as biased and uncommitted. Troops comprise the bulk of the peacekeepers. In Central Africa, they found several instances that triggered relations that were negative for peacekeeping effectiveness.[41]

Even though the concept of 'mission composition' does not directly contribute to judging the effectiveness of peace operations, it helps to understand the reasons why a peace operation can be effective or not. Therefore, although the standardization of the assessment criteria for peace operations is a necessity, it cannot be used as a template for all peace operations, i.e., there is no 'one size that fits all'. Since the dynamics of peace operations will vary with each operation, the standard criteria should be used as general guidelines and appropriately modified to suit the uniqueness of each operation.

Framework for Evaluation

Defining success criteria for peace operations is not easy. Scholars, as well as practitioners, are at variance in their opinions on how to assess peace operations. The majority of the works lack any indicator or specification to assess peacekeeping.[42] Some scholars have reached conclusions on success or failure without identifying the criteria for assessment to develop such a concept.[43] A few authors, while trying to develop success criteria, have ended up only identifying some basic minimum criteria that a successful peace operation must meet. The conclusions that these authors arrive at are generally in consonance with the essential factors for a successful peace operation as listed in the 'United Nations Peacekeeping Operations: Principles and Guidelines', also known as the 'Capstone Doctrine':[44]

1. Strict adherence to the principles of peacekeeping, that is, consent, impartiality, and the non-use of force except for self-defence.
2. The local population perceiving the peace operation as legitimate and credible.
3. Emphasis on national and local ownership contribution to sustainable peace.
4. The presence of genuine commitment by stakeholders for the peace process to move forward.
5. The hope to recover the peace.
6. The peace operation has a clear, credible, and achievable mandate, well-trained and well-equipped peacekeepers, a strong logistical system, and adequate financial support.
7. The presence of a clearly visible unity of purpose among the members of the UNSC in support of UN peace operations.

8. The host country's commitment to unhindered freedom of movement and action for members of the UN peace operation.
9. The active engagement of both neighbouring countries and regional actors in the peace process.
10. The mission adopts an integrated operational approach by effectively coordinating with the host nation as well as other actors on the ground.
11. Peacekeepers maintain a high standard of professionalism and good conduct and are sensitive and respectful to local culture and tradition.

This list is not exhaustive. For instance, Ballard mentioned that the selection of individuals or units and the person to lead them is one of the most critical factors in determining the outcome of an operation.[45] Indeed, because of the diversity of opinions expressed by analysts, it is unlikely that a common analytical framework can guide all evaluations. That notwithstanding, by emphasising different aspects of the peace process, it should still be possible to get a better understanding of the diverse challenges and opportunities of peacekeeping.[46]

However, although all-encompassing work has been done by Bratt and Diehl and Druckman, standard criteria are absent.[47] In a later article, Bratt identified four factors that have affected the performance of peace operations: the role of the parties to the conflict; the existence of a Comprehensive Settlement Agreement; the role of the P5 members of the Security Council; the role of the USA and regional powers. Earlier, Bratt identified the following indicators to assess the success of peace operations: "Did the operation complete its mandate? Did the operation facilitate a resolution to the conflict? And did the operation limit the casualties of combatants, civilians, and peacekeepers?"[48] He explained that by using these indicators and weighing the four variables that he had identified, the performance of the UN peace operation could be categorised as either successful, moderately successful, or failed. He also noted that a peace operation that facilitates a resolution of conflict can be called a success. For any framework for evaluation to be logical and coherent, a few other essential factors that can influence the development of the concept for evaluation should also be considered. They are discussed in the following pages.

Factors Affecting the Evaluation Framework

Mandate

The easiest way to evaluate a peace operation would be to develop a scorecard and tick the boxes against mandated tasks.[49] There are, however, certain extra activities, such as infrastructure development, provision of medical care, and better education and humanitarian aid that contribute immensely towards the peace process. Lack of all or any of these would lead to dissatisfaction and may even compel a section of the populace to pick up arms against the administration. Unless the local population's basic rights are guaranteed, it cannot be said that sustainable peace has been restored at the end of the mission.[50] Therefore, answers to simple questions on mandate implementation will not be enough to comment on the effectiveness of a peace operation. The effectiveness of peace operations means much more than mandate implementation. Sigri and Basar recommended that an assessment process based on the end state of a mission which, in turn, is derived from the goals of the mission, will help to develop measures of effectiveness and measures of performance to identify the conditions for the success of peace operations.[51]

Also, while checking whether a peace operation has fulfilled its specific mandate or not, the contribution of peacekeeping to bigger issues such as limiting violent conflict, reduction of human suffering, preventing the spread of conflict and promoting conflict resolution, should be factored into the process of evaluation. This is because unless violent conflicts leading to human suffering are limited, a peace operation cannot be called a success regardless of whether they were specifically mandated or not. Using these criteria, Pushkina assessed 17 peace operations between 1945 and 1998. These missions have been classified as successful, partially successful and failed.[52]

Credibility

Assessing peace operations solely on mandate implementation or reduction of human suffering, however, seems too simplistic. Taking the argument forward, Newby argues that *'credibility'*, one of the basic conditions for a successful peace operation, has not been fully taken into consideration by scholars assessing peace operations. According to her, a peace operation gets credibility by demonstrating its ability to respond to the expectations of the local population. Credibility, however, is not available upfront. It has to be earned and supported by evidence over a period. While examining the role of credibility in a peace operation, Newby reported that the host-national population must have the confidence that the peacekeepers are not only able to deliver but also have the willingness to do so. She amplified that in addition to the need for providing material evidence, it is the 'assurance behaviour' of the peacekeepers that need to be continuously demonstrated in support of credibility. Assurance behaviour refers to the resolve and sincerity to fulfil the promises that they have made. She observed that provision of information that is transparent and honest, i.e., without withholding anything, repeated interactions, no matter how many times they have to be repeated, and displaying responsiveness and past behaviour are a few examples that indicate assurance behaviour.[53]

Credibility, however, is often confused with 'legitimacy.' Newby contended that "Credibility ultimately means delivering a promise."[54] She noted that it is a stand-alone concept and hence should not be confused with legitimacy. She mentioned that credibility must be constantly sustained by related activities that help to implement the mandate. On the other hand, legitimacy is based on ideas. Howard quoted Major General Luciano Portolano, the former UNIFIL Force Commander, stating that the relationship with the local population is UNIFIL's operational centre of gravity.[55] Therefore, ideas are something that should not be taken for granted but constantly nurtured to align with the ideas of the local population.

Local Legitimacy

According to Whalan, the legitimacy of a peace operation is achieved when the mission's deployment is endorsed by the UN Security Council. However, once it is deployed, the mission faces challenges of navigation in an unfamiliar domestic and political environment where ownership may lie with multiple actors with varying interests. It follows therefore that a peace operation that has international legitimacy need not be considered legitimate by the local population. Putting it differently, the mission may lack 'local legitimacy'. For example, in Lebanon, a few mandated tasks like the removal of unauthorised weapons from the Hezbollah (even though not specifically mentioned in the mandate but implied), was not considered legitimate task by the local population of South Lebanon.[56] That aside, since local legitimacy depends on how a mission is perceived, such perception may vary and change over time. Therefore, peacekeepers will have to continuously work to build a positive picture of what they are doing.[57]

When there is the presence of local legitimacy, even if it is not a hundred per cent, freedom of movement of the peacekeepers to undertake their basic mandated activities will be relatively easier than when there is no local legitimacy at all. Local legitimacy enables the peacekeepers to implement a large part of the mandate. Even though credibility and local legitimacy differ in concept, the common benefit is that both help to fulfil the mandate.[58] It, therefore, can be concluded that both are intricately linked in the mission area. Accordingly, even though it may be possible to earn credibility without local legitimacy or a contested local legitimacy, the chances of the success of peace operations are better when both credibility and local legitimacy are present. When compared with the framework for assessment based on mandate implementation, one can find commonality in the mandated tasks. However, the prism through which a peace operation is evaluated is slightly different. Scholars differ on the extent to which they deem a particular peace mission or peace missions in general, successful or not. As implied earlier, evaluations of peace missions are still far from being unequivocal.

Levels of Effectiveness

Another approach to measuring performance is by examining peace operations at three different levels, namely, strategic, operational, and tactical. At a strategic level, it will be difficult to quantify such performances. However, at operational and tactical levels, measuring the outcome of mandate implementation is possible by developing a comprehensive plan that synchronises the efforts of all the major players; the identification of key measures of effectiveness that measure all the aspects of the mission; and effective management and control of major events in the area of operations.[59]

The list of indicators or *Measures of Effectiveness* (MoE) to assess an operation in the field includes measures of security, humanitarian relief operations, governmental, infrastructure, public health, and agricultural and economic activities.[60] All these indicators, however, may not apply to peace operations across the board. For instance, details of humanitarian relief, the restoration of governmental machinery, the development of infrastructure and public health measures are actions taken by the international community to rebuild a society more in the context of intra-state conflicts and less in inter-state conflicts. However, some of the suggested security measures, such as recording weekly/monthly incidents of hostile fire, violent crimes, the number of patrols by the peacekeeping troops, and a total number of illegal weapons collected, will be more applicable to traditional UN peace operations.

Operational Outcome

While operational outcome/success is measured in terms of mandate implementation, the performance of the peace operation should also be judged by its ability to facilitate conflict management and limitation of casualties, as mentioned earlier. Even though rarely specified in the mandate, these are important inputs to evaluate the overall impact of the operation in the peace process.[61] Some of the criteria such as a limitation of casualties, even by timely humanitarian intervention, however, can be contested. It is because as illustrated by Weiss, "international military operations, under the rubric of 'humanitarian intervention' and more recently, 'the responsibility to protect' (R2P) are contested because they are governed by coercion, partiality, and overwhelming force."[62] As such, limiting casualties by humanitarian intervention may not be the correct input for assessing peace operations. Yet, combatant and civilian casualties, either directly due to the conflict, or indirectly because of a lack of timely humanitarian intervention, would provide better input to the process of assessment than by keeping it generic, like limiting armed conflict.[63] The logic for using 'limiting casualties' however makes sense in the case of a traditional peace operation where the local population has suffered due to hostilities between the warring nations and internal hostilities.[64]

After modifying the success criteria developed by other scholars, Bratt developed four success criteria based on: mandate performance, conflict resolution, conflict containment and reduction of casualties.[65] After applying these success criteria, the key questions that can be asked to judge the effectiveness of peace operations are:

1. Was the mandate fulfilled?
2. Did the operation lead to a resolution of the underlying dispute of the conflict?
3. Did the operation management prevent major powers or neighbouring states from interfering in the conflict (conflict containment)?
4. Was the operation able to reduce the number of civilian casualties?

In one of the very recent studies to assess the effectiveness of UNMISS, EPON applied a similar framework for its research in South Sudan.[66]

Bratt's success criteria, however, need some explanation. The first criteria, i.e., mandate implementation, can be judged by determining if the mandated tasks have been fulfilled or not. Similarly, the fourth criteria, i.e., whether the operation was able to reduce the number of casualties, can also be determined with the help of available statistics on the subject. The second and third criteria, i.e., conflict resolution and conflict containment, even though they can be determined as well, are much beyond the scope of the peacekeeping operation.

In this regard, Diehl and Druckman noted that "Peacekeepers can also promote violence abatement, but NOT settlement of underlying disagreements."[67] Conflict resolution, which implies the settlement of underlying disputes, therefore, can provide ways for positive and lasting peace. It includes conflict prevention, peace-making, peace-building and conflict termination. The role of peacekeepers is to create a secure environment for the peace process to move forward. However, peacekeeping operations have little or no role to prevent major powers or neighbouring states from interfering in the conflict.

Therefore, rather than resolving the underlying causes of the conflict, conflict containment or promoting conflict resolution and management, i.e., not allowing the conflict to get out of control, will be more appropriate criteria for judging the performance of peacekeeping operations.

Conflict-specific Variables

This criterion's questions should be answered in the context of factors that are beyond the control of both the mission and the peacekeepers but affect the performance of UN peace operations, nonetheless. To cite an example, as per the mandate of MONUSCO, Article 31 of Resolution 2409 explains that MONUSCO's priorities are: (i) protecting civilians; and (ii) supporting the implementation of the 31 December 2016 agreement to hold elections. The critical question that must be addressed now is: has MONUSCO been able to implement the mandate? On the one hand, the country had elections, which fulfilled one of the mandate's objectives, even though the polls were controversial, to say the least. Immediately after the election results were made public, the population took to the streets and violence recurred. On the other hand, there was also widespread evidence of the involvement of peacekeepers in sexual abuse, human rights violations, corruption, and failure to protect Congolese civilians.[68]

The peace process may also fall apart leading to the resumption of conflict due to an inconclusive peace agreement, dissension within the UNSC, and a lack of serious commitment on the part of the contributing nations to send well-trained and well-equipped troops. Rwanda is a clear example of such a paradox. To fulfil its mandate, General Dallaire, the FC, felt that the ideal option was 5,500 troops, but he had to manage with a small force of 2,600 troops.[69] The weakness in UNAMIR's structure, however, is not indicative of a lack of will on the part of the entire mission. Despite an inadequate force and lack of will on the part of a few contingents to go the extra mile to implement the mandate, the FC and a few other observers did not spare any effort when it came to saving innocent Tutsis and moderate Hutus. With a larger strength, there were reasonable chances of saving at least thousands, perhaps tens of thousands, of lives.

Conflict-specific variables, which will differ depending on the type of the conflict, can range from the role of the parties to the conflict, the nature of a settlement agreement, the role of the five Permanent Members of the UNSC, the role of the regional powers, the maintenance of the basic principles of peacekeeping, including consent, impartiality and neutrality, the use of force, the decision-making process, the mandate, the role of the UN Secretary-General, the selection of the mission leader and the peacekeepers, to planning for the operation.[70]

Goal Setting

The success or failure of a mission is directly proportional to what has been achieved about the objectives or goals that have been set. Therefore, answering the key or pillar questions, which are based on the overall aim of the peace operation, seems to be a practical method to assess it. It is similar to Bratt's idea of assessment by determining how a peace operation has performed against the indicators that he has identified.[71] The key questions and the sub-questions should be framed based on the peace operation's ability, or the lack of it, to achieve its goals. Setting a goal for performance evaluation has its benefits. Amongst others, it enhances the knowledge base and helps to take on additional responsibility. It is also a simple and easy method to plan and implement a project.

Therefore, the evaluation process should begin with the identification of goals. Out of them, some goals will be common to all peace operations and others will be mission-specific.[72] UN peace operations rely on a mandate which includes the mission structure. Thus, the goals for the missions should be derived from the mandate. However, as the mandates are often a product of ambiguous politicking processes, the essential part of the 'how' remains to be defined. This usually results in a lack of clarity in the instructions on the method of mandate implementation. It is difficult to state if such a lack of clarity is for either giving a latitude or an incentive to the main disputants in return for their consent to the peace agreement. It could also be for providing flexibility to the commanders on the ground to use the most appropriate method to implement the mandate.[73] Regardless of what the actual reason may be, the concerned peacekeepers have to be adequately geared in terms of operational capability, with reasonable clarity in the instructions for mandate implementation. Therefore, simply asking questions whether these goals were accomplished or not, would not provide a true assessment of any peace operation. An objective as given out in the mandate but without a framework (outlining the mode for implementation), will have implications for all components of the mission and the affected elements of the host nation. Accordingly, to make an objective assessment, the achievement of the peace operations will have to be analysed in the context of the challenges for fulfilling the goals.

Diehl and Druckman identified five core goals for peacekeeping operations. These are:[74]

1. Violence Abatement—Reduction or elimination of armed conflict.
2. Conflict Containment—Limiting violence between the original protagonists.
3. Conflict Settlement—Lowering the probability of recurrence of the conflict.
4. Good Relationship with the Local Population.
5. Organisational Values—Promoting good organisational values such as the protection of military peacekeepers and non-interference from national governments.

The similarity in the above five core goals and Bratt's set of criteria for determining success (as discussed earlier) can create confusion because the interpretation of the terminology may vary. Diehl and Druckman speak about core goals. On the other hand, Bratt used indicators of success (mandate performance, conflict resolution, conflict containment and reduction of casualties) for determining the attainment of 39 peace operations. Conflict containment is defined by Bratt as preventing outside powers or states from interfering in the conflict. But to Diehl, it is limiting the violence between the original protagonists. Likewise, despite several theoretical discussions to find a logical explanation to clear the confusion between success criteria and goals, scholars continue to differ in their opinion on the subject. Yet, at some level, the success criteria of Bratt or the core goals of Diehl and Druckman tend to overlap and become interchangeable in their usage.

In all peace operations, diffusing a conflict situation and bringing back normalcy are the primary objectives of stakeholders in the conflict zone. Given this as a precondition that is common to all peace operations, the five core goals of Diehl and Druckman appear to be practical and, hence, can be considered as common core goals for all peace operations. Their suggested table of detailed descriptions of the different dimensions of core peacekeeping goals brings clarity to this confusion. After appropriately modified, this format is a good example that can be used for the evaluation of all peace operations. At the same time, because of their determining influence, the success criteria or indicators of success that have been developed by Bratt, and Diehl and Druckman will also have to be factored in for evaluation for individual peace operations separately.

Besides, there are also certain mission-specific tasks for which separate goals will have to be formulated. For instance, a task like restoring international peace and security is an ambitious goal, the likes of which is rather impractical for any peace operation to achieve.[75] Mission leaders, therefore, must exercise caution in setting ambitious goals, which are difficult to achieve and likely to result in negative judgement. Similarly, a goal such as 'to complete disarmament, demobilization, and reintegration (DDR)', without adequate support in terms of strategy and adequate funding, would be a goal set for failure even before it is attempted. However, such a method of assessing a peace operation based on the goals is not without problems. For instance, first, the goals may not be related to each other and second, there can be more than one question related to each goal and similar or more measures of progress. Further, all indicators of the measures of progress may not always be available. Under these circumstances, it will be more practical to pass judgement on the success or failure of an operation after weighing its overall benefits against the limitations under which a peacekeeping mission must perform.

Base Line for Assessment

The framework for evaluation, however, should not be limited to goal setting and the consideration of conflict-specific variables and basic criteria for success. It should be comprehensive and part of a more general discourse that includes other factors with a direct bearing on the assessment. As stated by Diehl and Druckman, three major variables that relate to the question are stakeholders for whom the operation may be called a success and for whom it may not; the time of assessment; and whether or not to quantify the results of the operation.[76] Building on what scholars have suggested and putting it differently, these can be termed as essential baselines for assessment, and hence must be part of the overall framework for evaluation:

1. *Stakeholders and Success for Whom*: In the conflict zone, the local community which is the primary stakeholder of the peace process, may comprise heterogeneous people with different religions, occupations, living in different places and with different political leanings. Accordingly, expectations and perceptions of the population will rarely be uniform. Peacekeepers, therefore, will have to be careful not to offend any of the sections of the larger community. Some of the other common stakeholders are national, regional and local authorities in the host state; members of the peace operations (both uniformed and civilian); international and regional organisations; and UN and non-UN agencies, including NGOs and other experts who may be involved in work in the conflict zone. All stakeholders will have their perception of success depending on their national or organisational motives. Accordingly, answers to the same key questions will vary when seen from different perspectives. One illustration may suffice here. Those having the power to influence the opinion of the international community, like the Permanent Members of the Security Council or, for that matter, even the nations that do not participate in the operation with uniformed peacekeepers, may have strategic interests in supporting a peace operation because they could benefit from the victory of one or more parties to the conflict. As the distance from their homeland increases, their interests are often driven more by economic gain and less by security concerns. For example, the Middle East, on the one hand, is a major security concern for the European nations. On the other hand, it is a centre of tensions for the entire world because of its oil deposits. Similarly, both the Great

Lake regions and South Sudan are famous for rich mineral resources and oil, respectively. The hold of at least three Permanent Members (the USA, UK and France) on the unofficial tradition of the 'pen-holder' system in drafting UNSC resolutions is indicative of the extent to which the outcome of the conflict can be shaped and reshaped by powerful nations.[77] Such nations, therefore, tend to judge a mission's performance from the narrow prism of the peace operation's ability or inability to prevent the conflict from recurring. The local population, that suffers the most, on the contrary, will judge the performance of a PKO looking at *how* and *when* their misery can come to an end. For example, since UNPROFOR failed to save thousands of innocent lives in Bosnia, the mission was a highly tragic failure for the Bosnian Muslims. Yet, protecting the inhabitants was not explicitly formulated in SCR 819 and SCR 824. It is only the third resolution, SCR 836 that specifically mentions *acting in self-defence, to take all necessary measures, including the use of force for the protection of safe areas*.[78] All three resolutions were under Chapter VII mandates, and protection of safe areas means protecting the Bosnian Muslims in them. Yet, there were divergent positions of the members of the Security Council about the definition of 'safe areas' and how to implement the mandate. It was unclear whether force could be used for the protection of the enclaves or only for the self-defence of the peacekeepers.[79] As a result, the increment of the additional force of only 7,500, as opposed to the actual requirement of 35,000 to implement the mandate, was not adequate to protect innocent civilians in safe areas.[80] The motivation of the local population is simply to be able to survive the conflict and move ahead in their lives. Therefore, their opinions are likely to be more honest and forthright than that of the rest.

2. *Time of Assessment*: Assessment results will vary depending on what period has been selected. If the period of assessment covers that which begins with the peak of the violence until the ceasefire, it is likely to indicate success. On the other hand, if the period covered is from the time of the ceasefire to the end of the mission, it is likely to indicate a low success rate. At the same time, an assessment made during an operation would help to make the necessary mid-course corrections, if required. Similarly, an assessment made at the end of the operation would help to get a clearer perspective of the long-term impact on the peace process. Correspondingly, if the gap

between the end of the operation and the time of assessment is too long, it will be difficult to get a correct perspective.[81]

3. *Quantitative or Qualitative*: Both are accepted approaches used for research design, but the consideration of either of the two will be determined by who is being assessed. For example, as to the performance of profit organizations—judged by market value, that is, how much profit has been made—the input for assessment will be largely quantitative. Even for a classical military operation whose success or failure will be judged by the achievement of military goals, it will be quantitative. However, the mandate of peace operations is far more complex, relatively more abstract and its achievements difficult to quantify. Even then, statistics like the increase or reduction of civilian casualties, frequency of cross-border firing or military incidents will generally indicate the degree of effective control, or lack of it, of any peace operation in the conflict zone. Therefore, a combination of both quantitative and qualitative approaches would be better suited for a more objective assessment of peace operations.

Both the conflict-specific variables and the baseline for assessment are important and inseparable inputs for the evaluation of a peace operation. While the former affects the outcome of the peace operation, the latter influence the evaluation.

Success Criteria

There are two different but associated fundamentals that should be at the centre of any basic framework for evaluation. At the conceptual level, the indicators for success or failure and the basic conditions to be met for a peace operation to be successful are interlinked. The second fundamental is setting the mission objectives and goals at the operational level. These goals will be both political and operational. Framing key questions and determining whether these goals have been achieved or not will have to be examined in the context of meeting the basic conditions for a successful peace operation. As indicated earlier, a few important core goals that would be useful to evaluate a peace operation are:

1. Mandate implementation.
2. Contribution towards conflict resolution.
3. Contribution towards conflict management.
4. Limiting casualties.

5. Mitigating situations that have the potential to trigger a bigger conflict between warring factions/states.
6. Effect on the local population.
7. Restoration of law and order.
8. Return to normal functioning of the civil administration.
9. State of disarmament and demobilization of armed group/groups.
10. Freedom of movement of the peacekeepers.
11. Credibility and local legitimacy.

The next category of goals is mission-specific, which will have to be derived from the core goals as applicable to the mission. For example, tasks such as the protection of civilians in the context of an intra-state conflict will be implied, even though in some cases such a task is specified. Accordingly, peace operations like UNMISS and MONUSCO, which are always under criticism for failing to protect the lives of innocent civilians, will be generally judged for limiting civilian casualties. At the same time, in inter-state conflicts, civilian casualties can occur more as a result of collateral damage due to cross-border violence between the two countries. Thus, under the core goal of 'limiting casualties', the mission-specific goal for a traditional mission could be the *reduction of civilian casualties because of cross-border violence*. Each goal should be followed by a key question and a list of indicators. Answers to these questions, when analysed in the context of conflict-specific variables, the presence/absence of the basic criteria for a successful peace operation and different baselines for assessment, would help to make a substantiated assessment of the performance of the peace operation.

Assessment Report

Defining success and identifying criteria for the assessment of peace operations has never been easy. Therefore, it will not be appropriate to adhere rigidly to any format. What is important, however, is that the report should be comprehensive and make a coherent argument to support the assessment.

After spelling out the key elements of the established framework that have been considered at the beginning of the report, performance evaluation should be done across the critical dimensions as applicable to the mission. For example, in the case of a peace operation deployed in a high-intensity intra-state conflict, the analysis of dimensions like the incidence of intra-party clashes, the number of civilian casualties, and progress on DDR should be considered to assess the performance. Similarly, for a traditional peace operation like UNIFIL, the number of incidents along the Blue Line (BL),[82] the number of cross-border firings and landmine casualties will be the critical dimensions for evaluation. Essentially, these dimensions are the key questions to determine the progress of the key goals of the mission. Such analysis must consider the variables that can impact the output if they are corroborated by both primary and secondary sources. To derive the full benefit of the evaluation, the assessment should also end with an inventory of the major weaknesses and pointed recommendations for correction.

While presenting a conceptual framework for the assessment of traditional peace operations, the use of a fixed format is not the intention of what is advocated here. In the following section, as an example, the case of UNIFIL will be presented to highlight a few essentials for establishing the framework for the evaluation of a traditional peace operation. This can be appropriately modified for the performance evaluation of other complex intra-state conflicts.

Conclusion

Despite variance in opinions, there is a consensus to term a mission a failure if it has not been possible to adequately protect the innocent civilian population, whatever the reasons may be. While intra-state conflicts are often marked by extreme violence, it is relatively easy to assess such a peace operation's performance with the help of available statistics.

When it is difficult to pinpoint whether a peace operation is a success or not, it is better to understand how it has been able to gain control over the security situation so that there is no resumption of violence. Therefore, as described by Newby, rather than calling it either a success or failure, it will be fair to describe the mission as a shock absorber, which has earned the credibility for preventing a full-fledged conflict since 2006.[83] On similar lines, Bratt recommended that when a peace operation can facilitate a resolution to a conflict, it can be termed a success. If there has not been a resolution of the conflict but it has been able to limit casualties, it can be termed as moderately successful. The operation should be called a failure only when it has failed on all indicators or achieved only limited success in one of the indicators.[84] Categorization of the level of success however will vary from conflict to conflict.

In the end, it is the performance that matters. Evaluations are likely to fall short of a comprehensive, uncontested assessment. In this chapter, an attempt has been made to develop a conceptual framework and thereafter suggest an acceptable framework for the evaluation of traditional peace operations like UNIFIL. However, before applying the framework, a brief insight into the unique challenges of UNIFIL would help better follow the assessment of the mission in the final chapters. This will be discussed in Chapter 4 followed by the application of this framework of evaluation in Chapter 5 using generally available Operational and Primary Data. The final assessment and recommendations will be covered in Chapter 6.

ENDNOTES

1. This chapter is a revised and updated version of A.K. Bardalai, "A Conceptual Framework for Assessing Traditional Peace Operations," *Journal of Defence Studies* 13, no. 4 (October–December 2019): 71–101.
2. UN Security Council, Resolution S/PV.8349 (September 12, 2018).
3. UN Security Council, Resolution S/RES/2436 (September 21, 2018).
4. A.K. Bardalai, "United Nations Peacekeeping Operations: Causes for Failure and Continuing Relevance," *Journal of Defence Studies* 12, no. 4 (2018): 5–34 (Chapter 2 in this book).
5. A.B. Fetherston, *Towards a Theory of United Nations Peacekeeping* (Palgrave Macmillan Press: UK, 1994).
6. Paul F. Diehl and Daniel Druckman, *Evaluating Peace Operations* (New Delhi: Viva Books in arrangement with Lynne Rienner, 2011); Patricia M. Shields and Nandini Rangarajan, *A Playbook for Research Methods: Integrating Conceptual Frameworks and Project Management* (Stillwater: New Forum Press, 2013), 148–57.
7. UN Office of Internal Oversight Services (OIOS), accessed March 5, 2019, https://oios.un.org/what-we-inspect-evaluate
8. UN Office of Internal Oversight Services (OIOS), Inspection and Evaluation Division (IED), OIOS-IED, *Inspection and Evaluation Manual* (New York: September 2014), accessed March 5, 2019, https://oios.un.org/sites/oios.un.org/files/images/oios-ied_manual.pdf
9. Telephonic interview with Colonel K.B.S. Sirohi, September 25, 2019.
10. Cedric de Coning and Emery Brusset, "Towards a Comprehensive Results-based Reporting and Performance Assessment,' *Norwegian Institute of International Affairs (NUPI) Report*, no. 4 (2018), https://reliefweb.int/sites/reliefweb.int/files/resources/NUPI_Report_4_Towards%2Ba%2BComprehensive%2BRes.pdf
11. "Assessing the Effectiveness of the United Nations Mission in South Sudan/UNMISS," *EPON Report*, no. 2 (2019), 91, https://effectivepeaceops.net/unmiss/
12. "Assessing the Effectiveness of the United Nations Mission in the DRC/MONUC–MONUSCO," *EPON Report*, no. 3 (2019), https://effectivepeaceops.net/wp-content/uploads/2019/06/EPON-MONUSCO-LowRes.pdf
13. "Assessing the Effectiveness of the United Nations Mission in Mali/MINUSMA," *EPON Report*, no. 4, 2019, https://effectivepeaceops.net/wp-content/uploads/2019/05/EPON-MINUSMA-Report-Exec-Summary.pdf; Also see https://effectivepeaceops.net/wp-content/uploads/2019/11/EPON-MINUSMA-Report.pdf
14. Telephonic interview with Dr. Ali Ahmed, October 2, 2019.

15. UN, Situation in South Sudan, S/2019/722 (September 10, 2019).
16. UN Office of Rule of Law and Security Institutions of the United Nations Department of Peacekeeping Operations. Planning Toolkit, accessed July 10,2020, https://peacekeeping.un.org/sites/default/files/planning_toolkit_web_version_0.pdf
17. Fred Luthans, "Successful vs. Effective Real Managers," *The Academy of Management Executive* (1987), no. 2 (May 1988): 129, http://www.jstor.org/stable/4164814?origin=JSTOR-pdf
18. Barbara F. Walter, Lise Morje Howard, and Virginia Page Fortna, "The Extraordinary Relationship between Peacekeeping and Peace," *British Journal of Political Science* (2020): 12-14, doi:10.1017/S000712342000023X; Also see Kathleen M. Eisenhardt, "Building from Case Study Research," *The Academy of Management Review* 14, no. 4 (October 1989): 546–48.
19. Vincenzo Bove, Chiara Ruffa, and Andrea Ruggeri, *Composing Peace: Mission Composition in UN Peacekeeping* (New York: Oxford University Press, 2020), 183.
20. Lise Morje Howard, *Power in Peacekeeping* (New York: Cambridge University Press, 2019), 9, 100; Also see Joseph R. Matthews, "Assessing Organisational Effectiveness: The Role of Performance Measures," *The Library Quarterly* 8, no. 1 (2011): 83-110; J. Soeters, *Management and Military Studies. Classical and Current Foundations* (London/New York: Routledge), 2020.
21. The Social, Humanitarian and Cultural Affairs Committee of the UN General Assembly is also known as 'Third Committee'.
22. A. Parasuraman, V. Zeithaml, and L. L. Berry, "SERVQUAL: A Multiple-item Scale for Measuring Consumer Perceptions of Service Quality,"*Journal of Retailing* 62, no. 1 (1998): 12–40.
23. Ilona Bartuseviciene and Evelina Sakalyte, "Organisational Assessment: Effectiveness vs. Efficiency," *Social Transformation in Contemporary Society,* 1 (2013): 45–53.
24. George E. Mitchell, "The Construct of Organizational Effectiveness: Perspectives from Leaders of International Non-profits in the United States," *Non-profit and Voluntary Sector Quarterly* 42, no. 2 (2013): 324–45, http://journals.sagepub.com/doi/abs/10.1177/0899764011434589
25. Lise Morje Howard, "Power and United Nations Peacekeeping," *Power in Peacekeeping* (New York: Cambridge University Press, 2019), 1–3.
26. Tod Sandler, "International Peacekeeping Operations: Burden Sharing and Effectiveness," *Journal of Conflict Resolution* 61, no. 9 (2017): 1890, DOI: 10.1177/0022002717708601
27. Jorg Raab and Joseph Soeters, "Peace Operations as Temporary Network Organisations," in *The Management of Peacekeeping,* ed.Julian Junk, Francesco Mancini, Wolfgang Seibel and Till Blume (London: Lynne Rienner Publishers, 2017), 97.
28. Jessica di Salvatore and Andrea Ruggeri, "Effectiveness of Peacekeeping Operations", *Contentious Politics and Political Violence, World Politics* (September 2017), 23, DOI: 10.1093/acrefore/9780190228637.013.586
29. Aoi Chiyuki, Cedric de Coning, and Ramesh Thakur, "Unintended consequences, complex peace operations and peacebuilding systems" in *Unintended Consequences of PKO,* ed. Aoi Chiyuki, Cedric de Coning, and Ramesh Thakur (Tokyo: United Nations University, 2007),1–7.
30. Cedric de Coning, "Adaptive Peace Operations: Navigating the Complexity of Influencing Societal Change Without Causing Harm," *International Peacekeeping,* 27, no. 5 (2020): 836–858, DOI: 10.1080/13533312.2020.1797500

31. Johan Galtung, "Violence, Peace, and Peace Research." *Journal of Peace Research* 6, no. 3 (1969): 167–91. http://www.jstor.org/stable/422690
32. Vincenzo Bove, Chiara Ruffa, and Andrea Ruggeri, *Composing Peace: Mission Composition in UN Peacekeeping* (New York: Oxford University Press, 2020), 25; Annemarie Peen Rodt, "Successful Conflict Management by Military Means," *Ethnopolitics,* 11, no. 4 (2012): 376–91.
33. Lise Morje Howard, "Peacekeeping, Peace Enforcement and UN Reform." *Georgetown Journal of International Affairs* 16, no. 2 (Summer/Fall 2015): 9, http://www.jstor.org/stable/43773690
34. Oliver P. Richmond, "UN Peace Operations and Dilemmas of Peacebuilding Consensus," *International Peacekeeping* 11, no. 1 (March 2004): 91, DOI: 10.1080/1353331042000228403; Also see Severine Autesserre, "The Trouble with Congo: How Local Disputes Fuel Regional Conflicts," *Foreign Affairs* 87, no. 3 (May-June 2008): 95, https://www.jstor.org/stable/20032653; Severine Autesserre, *The Trouble with Congo: Local Violence and the Failure of International Peacekeeping* (New York: Cambridge University Press, 2010), 271.
35. Chiara Ruffa, "Force Employment, Unit Peace Operation Effectiveness, and Military Cultures," *Military Cultures in Peace and Stability Operations: Afghanistan and Lebanon* (Philadelphia: University of Pennsylvania Press, 2019), 21.
36. Ibid., 24–27.
37. Ibid., 88–89; Cornelius Friesendorf, "Military cultures in peace and stability operations: Afghanistan and Lebanon", *International Peacekeeping* 26, no. 2 (2019): 244–247, DOI: 10.1080/13533312.2018.1561187
38. Jan van der Meulen and Joseph Soeters, "Introduction", in *Cultural Diversity in Armed Forces: An international comparison*, ed. Jan van der Meulen and Joseph Soeters (New York: Routledge, 2007), 6.
39. Joseph Soeters and Phillip Manigart, "Epilogue," in *Military Cooperation in Multinational Peace Operations: Managing Cultural Diversity and Crisis Response*, ed. Joseph Soeters and Phillippe Manigart (New York: Routledge, 2008), 226; David C. Thomas, Efrat Elron, Gunter Stahl, Bjorn Z. Ekelund, Elizabeth C. Ravlin, Jean-Luc Cerdin, Steven Poelmans, Richard Brislin, Andre Pekerti, Zeynep Aycan, Martha Maznevski, Kevin Au, and Mila B. Lazarova, "Cultural Intelligence: Domain and Assessment," *International Journal of Cross-Cultural Management* 8, no.123 (August 2008), DOI: 10.1177/1470595808091787
40. Sebastian Rietjens and Chiara Ruffa, "Understanding Coherence in UN Peacekeeping: A Conceptual Framework," *International Peacekeeping* 26, no. 4 (March 3, 2019), 402, https://doi.org/10.1080/13533312.2019.1596742
41. Vincenzo Bove, Chiara Ruffa and Andrea Ruggeri, *Composing Peace: Mission Composition in UN Peacekeeping* (New York: Oxford University Press, 2020), 44, 153, 141–82; Also see Vincenzo Bove and Andrea Ruggeri, "Peacekeeping Effectiveness and Blue Helmets' Distance from Locals," *Journal of Conflict Resolution* 63, no. 7 (August 2019): 1630–55, https://doi.org/10.1177/0022002719826115
42. Paul F. Diehl and Daniel Druckman, "Evaluating Peace Operations" in *The Oxford Handbook of United Nations Peacekeeping Operations,* ed. Joachim A. Koops, Norrie Macqueen, Thierry Tardy, and Paul D. Williams (Oxford: Oxford University Press, 2015), 102.
43. Paul F. Diehl and Alexandru Balas, "The Success and Failure of Peace Operations", *Peace Operations* (Cambridge: Polity, 2014),141–42.

44. *United Nations Peacekeeping Operations: Principles and guidelines* (New York: UN Department of Public Information, 2008); Jair van der Lijn, "Success and Failure of UN Peacekeeping in UNMIS in Sudan," *Journal of International Peacekeeping,* 14, no. 1-2 (2010): 27–59.
45. John R. Ballard, "A Regional Recipe for Success: Multinational Peace Operations in East Timor," in *Military Cooperation in Multinational Peace Operations: Managing Cultural Diversity and Crisis Response*, ed. Joseph Soeters and Phillippe Manigart (New York: Routledge, 2008), 100–16.
46. Daniel Druckman and Paul Stern, "Perspectives on Evaluating Peacekeeping Missions," *International Journal of Peace Studies* 4, no. 1 (1999): 79–86.
47. Duane Bratt, "Assessing the Success of UN Peacekeeping Operations," *International Peacekeeping* 3, no. 4 (Winter 1996): 64–81; Paul F. Diehl and Daniel Druckman, *Evaluating Peace Operations* (New Delhi: Viva Books in arrangement with Lynne Rienner, 2011).
48. Duane Bratt, "Explaining Peacekeeping Performance: The UN in Internal Conflict," *International Peacekeeping* 4, no. 3 (2007), 46.
49. Christine M. Cervenak, "Lessons of the Past: Experiences in Peace Operations," in Antonia Handler Chayes and George T. Raach, ed. *Peace Operations: Developing in American Strategy* (Washington, DC: National Defence University Press, 1995), 39–65.
50. Eli Stamnes, "Critical Security Studies and the United Nations Preventive Deployment in Macedonia," *International Peacekeeping* 11, no. 1 (Spring 2004): 161–181; Alex J. Bellamy and Paul Williams, 'Peace Operations and Global Order Change,' *International Peacekeeping* 11, no. 1 (Spring 2004):1–15.
51. Unsal Sigri and Ufuk Basar, "An Analysis of Assessment of Peacekeeping Operations," *The Korean Journal of Defence Analysis* 26, no. 3 (September 2014): 393–99; Also see Todd Sandler, "International Peacekeeping Operations: Burden Sharing and Effectiveness," *Journal of Conflict Resolution* 61, no. 9 (2017):1875–1897, DOI: 10.1177/0022002717708601
52. Darya Pushkina, "A Recipe for Success? Ingredients of a Successful Peacekeeping Mission," *International Peacekeeping* 13, no. 2 (June 2006), 136.
53. Vanessa Frances Newby, "Between the carrot and the stick: Mapping the role of credibility in peace operation," (Unpublished article)
54. Vanessa Frances Newby, "The Role of Credibility in Peacekeeping," *Peacekeeping in South Lebanon: Credibility and Local Cooperation* (New York: Syracuse, 2018), 45.
55. Lise Morje Howard, *Power in Peacekeeping* (New York: Cambridge University Press, 2019), 114.
56. Vanessa Frances Newby, "The Role of Credibility in Peacekeeping," *Peacekeeping in South Lebanon: Credibility and Local Cooperation* (New York: Syracuse, 2018), 33.
57. Jeni Whalan, "The Local Legitimacy of Peacekeepers," *Journal of Intervention and Statebuilding* 11, no. 3 (2017): 314, https://doi.org/10.1080/17502977.2017.1353756.
58. Vanessa Frances Newby, *Peacekeeping in South Lebanon: Credibility and Local Cooperation* (New York: Syracuse, 2018), 47; Sophia Sabrow, "Local Perceptions of the Legitimacy of Peace Operations by the UN, Regional Organizations and Individual States: A Case Study of the Mali Conflict," *International Peacekeeping* 24, no. 1 (2017): 163.
59. Timothy Ford, "Determining Success in Peace Operations in The Challenges Project,"*Challenges of Peace Operations: Into the 21st Century—Concluding Report* 1997–2002 (Stockholm: Elanders Gotab, 2002), 253–72.
60. Ibid.

61. Duane Bratt, "Assessing the Success of UN Peacekeeping Operations," *International Peacekeeping* 3, no. 4 (Winter 1996): 68.
62. Thomas G. Weiss, "Peace Operations and Humanitarian Interventions," in *The Oxford Handbook of United Nations Peacekeeping Operations,* ed.Joachim A. Koops, Norrie Macqueen, Thierry Tardy, and Paul D. Williams (Oxford: Oxford University Press, 2015): 78.
63. Duane Bratt, "Assessing the Success of UN Peacekeeping Operations," *International Peacekeeping* 3, no. 4 (Winter 1996): 70.
64. Marrack Goulding, *Peacemonger* (London: Johns Hopkins University Press, 2003), 58. During the 2006 war, Israel used cluster bombs in Lebanon. According to the Landmine and Cluster Munitions Monitor, by the end of 2017, there had been at least 3,775 mine casualties including 913 killed and 2,862 injured (please see *Landmine and Cluster Munitions Monitor,* 2020, last modified November 19, 2018, http://www.the-monitor.org/en-gb/reports/2020/lebanon/casualties.aspx)
65. Duane Bratt, "Assessing the Success of UN Peacekeeping Operations," *International Peacekeeping* 3, no. 4 (Winter 1996): 64–81; Paul Diehl, *International Peacekeeping* (Baltimore: Johns Hopkins University Press, 1993).
66. Assessing the Effectiveness of the United Nations Mission in South Sudan/UNMISS', *EPON Report,* no. 2 (2019): 91, https://effectivepeaceops.net/unmiss/
67. Paul F. Diehl and Daniel Druckman, *Evaluating Peace Operations* (New Delhi: Viva Books in arrangement with Lynne Rienner, 2011), 43.
68. Chiyuki Aoi, Cedric de Coning, and R. Thakur, ed.*Unintended Consequences of Peacekeeping Operations* (Tokyo/New York/Paris: United Nations University Press, 2007), 7.
69. Romeo Dallaire, *Shake Hands with the Devil* (Cambridge: Da Capo Press, 2003); Donald C.F. Daniel and Bradd C. Hayes, *Beyond Traditional Peacekeeping* (London: Macmillan, 1995), 82.
70. Dennis C. Jett, *Why Peacekeeping Fails* (New York: Palgrave, 2001), 35–59.
71. Duane Bratt, "Explaining Peacekeeping Performance: The UN in Internal Conflict," *International Peacekeeping* 4, no. 3 (2007): 46.
72. Richard D. Bingham and Claire L. Felbinger, *Evaluation in Practice: A Methodological Approach* (New York: Chatham House Publisher of Seven Bridges, 2002); Ken Menkhaus, "Measuring Impact: Issues and Dilemmas", Occasional Paper Series Inter Peace (Geneva, 2003); Sebastiaan Rietjens, Joseph Soeters, and Willem Klumper, "Measuring the Immeasurable? The Effect-based Approach in Comprehensive Peace Operations," *International Journal of Public Administration* 34, no. 5 (April 2011): 329–38.
73. Beatrice Pouligny, *Peace Operations Seen from Below: UN Missions and Local People* (London: C. Hurst & Co., 2006), 104.
74. Paul F. Diehl and Daniel Druckman, *Evaluating Peace Operations* (New Delhi: Viva Books in arrangement with Lynne Rienner, 2011), 29–62.
75. UN Security Council, Resolutions 425 and 426 of 1978, Israel-Lebanon (March 19, 1978).
76. Paul F. Diehl and Daniel Druckman, *Evaluating Peace Operations* (New Delhi: Viva Books in arrangement with Lynne Rienner, 2011), 11–27.
77. UN Security Council, *The Pen Holder System,* no. 3, December 2018, https://www.securitycouncilreport.org/research-reports/the-penholder-system.php
78. UN Security Council, Resolutions S/RES/ 819 (April 16, 1993); S/RES/824 (May 6, 1993); S/RES/836 (June 3, 1993).

79. Human Rights Watch, "The Fall of Srebrenica and the Failure of UN Peacekeeping Bosnia and Herzegovina," 7, no. 13 (October 1995), 8. https://www.hrw.org/sites/default/files/reports/bosnia1095web.pdf
80. UN Security Council, Resolution S/RES/844 (June 18, 1993).
81. UNIFIL provides a good explanation of the impact of this parameter. When UNIFIL is evaluated for the period from 1978 (when the mission was first deployed) until just before the withdrawal of the IDF from South Lebanon in May 2000, UNIFIL will probably fall in the category of a failed mission. Please see Darya Pushkina, "A Recipe for Success? Ingredients of a Successful Peacekeeping Mission," *International Peacekeeping* 13, no. 2 (June 2006): 136.
82. The BL is the withdrawal line of the Israel Defence Forces demarcated in May 2000 based on certain geographical features between Lebanon and Israel. It is not the boundary between Lebanon and Israel.
83. Vanessa Frances Newby, "Walk the Line: An investigation of the Micro-Processes of a UN Peacekeeping Mission." Working Paper 37 (2016):19, DOI: 10.13140/RG.2.2.26928.76808
84. Duane Bratt, "Explaining Peacekeeping Performance: The UN in Internal Conflict," *International Peacekeeping* 4, no. 3 (2007): 46.

CHAPTER 4

UNIFIL: THE MANY CHALLENGES OF SUCCESSFUL PEACEKEEPING[1]

Introduction

A nation's decision to either participate in or support a UN-authorised peace operation is dependent on certain concerns such as national interests, the wish to serve humanity, commitment to UN policy, and love for global peace. The potential risk to peacekeepers has also been a major factor influencing a country's national policy towards peacekeeping missions. Elron observed that "TCCs are motivated to participate in peace operations for various reasons and if their specific goals are satisfied."[2] Bennis has argued that a government's foreign policy decision (in this case, to participate in a UN PKO) would be guided by the perceived interest of that government.[3] Gibbs has added that among other factors, economic and strategic considerations would also be taken into consideration while deciding to participate in PKO.[4] Weiss and Kuele also argue that regional interests and cooperation, as well as wider international recognition and prestige next to financial benefits, are reasons that drive the nations from the Global South to contribute to peace operations.[5] Generally, the self-interest of the states is the driver of the decision-making process. Yet, commitment to restoring global peace is likely to be cited as the main reason for participation in PKO by most nations. Meiske and Ruggeri observed that many governments use peacekeeping as a tool to pursue their foreign and security policies."[6] It is, however, difficult to pinpoint the exact reasons for a nation's decision to participate in PKO.

Post the end of the Cold War in 1989, PKO have changed in terms of type, concept, mandate, and the type of environment they have to operate in. There has also been a change in the pattern of participation in UN peace operations. Ambassador Samantha Power, the then United States (US) Permanent Representative at the UN, mentioned in her speech in Brussels on 9 March 2015, that 20 years ago European countries were the leaders in UN peacekeeping, but today European nations contribute less than 7 per cent of UN troops.[7] Currently, barring a few, maximum participation in the peace operations is from the TCCs from the Global South. UNIFIL however is an exception where three European TCCs have taken the lead since the invasion of Lebanon by Israel in 2006. Even though UNIFIL has its uniqueness and many challenges it faces in mandate implementation, because of the prolonged duration of relative peace, it does not get similar attention from the international community. Novosseloff describes such missions of the Cold War era as status quo missions as it suits the parties to the conflict to keep it that way to serve their political interests.[8] A look into what makes UNIFIL different from other traditional peace operations would help the readers to understand the way UNIFIL will be assessed. This will be discussed in the following sections from the perspective of the first-hand experience of the author.

UNIFIL and Many Challenges

UNIFIL is among the five oldest PKO and is a traditional one established to resolve inter-state conflicts. UNIFIL, with more than 10,000 personnel, is one of the largest existing missions.[9] It was established as a traditional mission to broker peace between Lebanon and Israel. The mission was established with three broadly defined purposes: confirming the withdrawal of Israeli forces; restoring international peace and security and assisting the Government of Lebanon in ensuring the return of its effective authority in the area.[10] As per the original mandate of UNIFIL, after the withdrawal of the Israeli Defence Forces (IDF) from Lebanon on 25 May 2000, the process of downsizing the mission had begun.[11] The Israel–Lebanon war of 2006, however, compelled the UN to deploy an expanded force under UNIFIL.[12]

Even though UNIFIL is a traditional peacekeeping mission, it is unique in several ways. Because of the geopolitically sensitive area of deployment of the mission and the possible recurrence of a major conflict between Israel and Lebanon, the scope of the violence is likely to expand beyond the geographic region of the Middle East. Even though the mission was established as a traditional PKO, the internal dynamics of Lebanon and its foreign policy have been greatly influenced by different stakeholders like the Hezbollah, Palestinian refugees, and inter-party competition on the ground. The Hezbollah, which is not even an official party to the conflict, is the main actor that cannot only decide the future course of the Israel-Lebanon relationship but also the internal stability of the country. The undercurrents of the domestic politics of Lebanon are so strong that they have pushed the country close to another major war with Israel several times. The instability in the adjoining countries also has a direct bearing on the functioning of UNIFIL as well as on the peace and stability in the Middle East. Unlike other missions, UNIFIL is hemmed in by the great regional power rivalries of Iran and Saudi Arabia, emerging in connection with Israel. This conflagration extends beyond the Middle East into the areas of interest of the five Permanent Members of the Security Council. The development of such an instrument will require the inputs of all the key stakeholders in the peace process. In turn, it will also provide a clear understanding of the way forward for UNIFIL to succeed in implementing its mandate. These complexities make UNIFIL an exclusive case to develop a reliable criterion to assess the outcome of PKO. A study of the performance of UNIFIL and how the mission has contributed toward peace for such a long duration will provide valuable takeaways for the UN and practitioners of UN peacekeeping in general.

Ever since 2006, the mission deployment numbers have remained around 10,000 personnel in contingents from three lead nations—Italy, France, and Spain. Although UNIFIL is based on military contingents from these three European nations, their combined strength is less than 50 per cent of the total strength of the mission; the mission predominantly relies on other, non-Western contingents. India has been one of the main troop-contributing nations to UNIFIL since 1999. It joined UNIFIL at a time when there was hardly any European contribution and remained even during the Israel–Lebanon War of 2006. Now, UNIFIL is a multinational peacekeeping mission and is unique in its own way.

In this context, Newby observed that since the changing aspects of the intra-state conflict within Lebanon impact the tensions between Israel and Lebanon with the potential to escalate into a wider regional conflict, "the UNIFIL mission sits on the crosshairs of a changing global political order".[13] While it is possibly the last of the traditional PKO, its complexities are far more challenging than many other contemporary missions. Elron believed that "UNIFIL II operates in an especially complex conflict theatre. Lebanon's frail democracy is constantly under threat from within and from neighbouring Syria and Iran," and "The complexity of the theatre compels the professional militaries involved in UNIFIL to adjust their doctrines and means in a coordinated manner to successfully cope with the dynamic and ever-changing challenges".[14] UNIFIL is a rare exception among the peacekeeping missions for several reasons.

First, despite being a traditional peacekeeping mission (inter-state conflict), rather than being deployed in a mutually accepted (both by Israel and Lebanon) neutral zone, it is deployed entirely in South Lebanon.

Second, UNIFIL has to grapple almost daily with some complex situational difficulties such as the unique political set-up of Lebanon and its impact on the mission. The Hezbollah, which was one of the main parties to the war of 2006, is a political party with a major say in crucial and important decision-making processes of the government and has a massive following amongst the masses.

Third, even though in terms of numbers, currently, troops from the South Asian region dominate the list of nations participating in UN peacekeeping missions, it is the only UN peace operation where peacekeepers from European nations have maximum participation, with peacekeepers from the North Atlantic Treaty Organization (NATO) and Western military involvement.[15]

Fourth, several troop-contributing countries (TCCs) of UNIFIL were or are deployed based on operational partnerships (when two or more military contingents combine to be deployed as part of a PKO). For example, 136 Finnish and 36 Estonian peacekeepers served alongside peacekeepers in the Irish contingent from 2012 to 2018 (The Finnish and Estonians later pulled out of UNIFIL because of their national commitments).[16] Even in this regard, UNIFIL can take the credit for housing more operational partnerships than any other peacekeeping mission since 2004.[17] Another current example is of a Hungarian platoon component of the Polish company and a company each from France and Finland comprising the Force Reserve of UNIFIL.[18]

Fifth, contingents from European nations have been deployed in UNIFIL with some heavy armaments and advanced military equipment, the like of which is an exception in traditional PKO (inter-state conflict) authorised under Chapter VI of the UN Charter.

Sixth, unlike any other traditional peacekeeping mission, where peacekeepers generally remain detached from the local population, UNIFIL peacekeepers have a challenging relationship with the populace of South

Lebanon. In Lebanon, the local population considers the Hezbollah as their only saviour against any Israeli invasion and does not like UNIFIL to search the Hezbollah's weapons arsenal. On the other hand, many in the local population expect UNIFIL to be a deterrent against Israel and not against the Hezbollah. Getting the cooperation of the local population is a challenge for UNIFIL. The relationship between deterrence and cooperation regularly reflects on the mindsets and conduct of the military peacekeepers from different parts of the world. Largely, a good understanding of this relationship helps the peacekeepers to discharge their responsibilities without hindrance. Newby also raised the question that "deterrence is an important aspect of a peacekeeping operation, but when the nature of deterrence is contested, how does cooperation accomplish this goal?"[19] She believed that it is the UNIFIL's credibility that wins cooperation.

Seventh, the consent of the parties to the conflict and their political agendas always has a profound effect on the progress of peace. In the case of Lebanon, the Hezbollah, even though officially not a signatory to the conflict, is the main actor that not only can decide on the future course of the Israel–Lebanon relationship but also the internal stability of the country. It is well entrenched politically and has an armed wing (they prefer to be called 'resistance'). As a result, the complexity of the political environment surrounding UNIFIL is rather peculiar and different from other contemporary missions.

Eighth, since immediately after the war in 2006, when the European nations began their participation, there has not been any major conflict between Israel and Lebanon. However, it cannot be stated if credit for this period of relative calm can be singularly attributed to the force structure of the mission comprising well-trained peacekeepers from a few developed nations from Europe. The answer to this will be available only if another war breaks out between Israel and Lebanon and the present structure of the mission remains intact then.

The professional skills and ability of military contingents from many non-Western nations to withstand the challenges of complex intra-state conflicts have been tested in contemporary missions like MONUSCO and UNMISS.[20] However, this cannot be stated in the case of the European nations, because they either have not got such an opportunity or have chosen not to participate in such difficult missions. These exceptions also pose some complicated challenges to the mission in fulfilling its mandate.

UNIFIL is a good mix of military peacekeepers from Western and non-Western nations, with differing operational philosophies, standards of training, equipment profile, and cultures, habits, and traditions. Despite these differences, contingents from Western and non-Western countries have been able to create synergy, thereby proving UNIFIL to be an effective peacekeeping mission in the Middle East. This chapter comments on the challenges faced by UNIFIL despite being a first-generation mission and the important role of peacekeepers from both Western and non-Western nations in the accomplishment of the mission's mandate. Much of the discussion is informed by the author's participation in PKO in general and UNIFIL in particular.

UNIFIL: A Robust Peacekeeping Mission

UNIFIL commenced its operations in 1978 with a strength of slightly more than 4,500 peacekeepers.[21] According to the initial mandate, that is, to oversee the withdrawal of the IDF from Lebanon, the mission was rightly deployed in South Lebanon.[22] However, the IDF pulled out voluntarily in May 2000. The strength went up by around an additional 1,500 peacekeepers to oversee this withdrawal. The strength was again reduced once the situation stabilised. However, after the war of 2006, UNIFIL's strength was augmented to more than 14,000 troops. Because of the strength and presence of well-equipped and well-trained contingents from three European nations, UNIFIL is also colloquially known as a 'robust mission'. Strictly going by the dictionary meaning, UNIFIL is indeed a robust mission. However, only time will tell whether it can truly deliver during a war-type crisis.

UNIFIL is the only UN PKO to employ medium tanks and artillery guns to provide the mission with a combat power that is among the highest in the world for a formation of this size. The current strength comprises staff officers, the Maritime Task Force (MTF) and certain specialised assets like engineering units, a helicopter unit, and the logistic unit. Also, inbuilt technical units and logistic support units of the sectors and contingents form part of this strength. This leaves the mission with insufficient combat troops to perform routine military tasks such as preventing the firing of rockets from Lebanon to Israel.

UNIFIL's force structure is based completely on the organisation of a NATO force.[23] It was not so earlier but took its present shape after the war of 2006 when NATO countries pledged their support. The given strength of a standard infantry battalion for a peacekeeping mission is 850 regular troops, with an inbuilt capacity to support the internal administrative requirement of the contingent. Except for a few, the organisational structures of the other contingents are different and have varying strengths. For instance, all the three lead nations from Europe—Italy, France and Spain—have their contingents structured (including equipment) in different ways based on their threat perception. While a composite battalion usually comprises three motorised companies and one mechanised company (wheeled armoured personnel carriers), the European contingents, over and above the UN-authorised organisation, include some specialised units such as a technical support unit, a logistic unit and a civil-military cooperation (CIMIC) unit. As for the equipment profile, while France has its army's main battle tanks and radar as part of its Quick Reaction Force (QRF), Italy has deployed wheeled armoured vehicles fitted with big bore main guns.

As stated, this organisational structure is akin to that of a NATO force. It can be argued that NATO countries are not very good at modifying their organizational structures, which are tailor-made for NATO operations, and adapt to a UN standard for a short period of four months.[24]

Combat troops are also employed for the protection of the contingent bases. The number of troops employed for such protection duties varies from contingent to contingent based on their (contingents') perceived threat from belligerents. The cumulative effect is that boots on the ground are less than even one-third of the overall deployed strength. Further, the involvement of NATO members has brought unusual structures and operational philosophies, which non-Western participants sometimes find problematic.

However, making use of the robustness of UNIFIL when it comes to the application of force at the tactical level is not without discussion. Robust peacekeeping is a new concept, but not unique to UNIFIL. After the tragedies of Rwanda and Srebrenica, where the peacekeepers failed to protect human lives, the need for stronger political back up and operational teeth to the peacekeepers was accepted across the world.[25] Accordingly, the doctrine on the use of force started to re-evolve. Peace operation mandates became stronger, peacekeeping forces became better equipped with the protection of civilians (PoC) as the core objective of their operations. The idea of robustness was enshrined in this new thinking. Robustness is to give operational capability while acting against spoilers. The 'Principles and Guidelines' define robust peacekeeping as follows:

> Robust peacekeeping involves the use of force at the tactical level with the authorization of the Security Council and the consent of the host nation and/or the main parties to the conflict. By contrast, peace enforcement does not require the consent of the main parties and may involve the use of military force at the strategic or international level, which is normally prohibited for the Member-States under Article 2(4) of the Charter, unless authorized by the Security Council.[26]

Clouded with ambiguity in the definition, the political acceptability and operational reliability of the concept has been actively contested. Hunt believed that the UN bureaucracy has spelt out the idea of robust peacekeeping as a defensive measure and ultimately an impartial activity. Citing the example of the Force Intervention Brigade (FIB) in MONUSCO, Hunt questioned the applicability of the principle of impartiality when the FIB had to use force against non-state actors; more specifically, when the FIB targets the M 23 rebel group on behalf of the DRC government armed forces.[27] Most of the TCCs that participate in complex peace operations are non-Western and believe that the concept of robustness is an agenda of Western nations who want to replace a lack of effectiveness by robust peacekeeping including the possible use of violence. Moreover, for a peace operation to be able to implement the mandate in a robust manner, the peacekeeping force, amongst other key elements, must have a robust structure comprising well-trained peacekeepers, and is logistically independent. Unfortunately, such a capability is rare with the major TCCs, particularly from non-Western countries. Even if it was possible to meet all the essential criteria of robustness, the need for a strong and lasting commitment by the Security Council and TCCs, which is another integral requirement of robust peacekeeping, can never be guaranteed.

Another question that comes up is acceptability in the host nation of the use of force by the peacekeepers at the tactical level when either the state itself is the perpetrator of the violence or one of the parties to the conflict is state-sponsored. In the context of Lebanon, it is difficult to even imagine getting consent from the Lebanese government to disarm the Hezbollah, whose legacy as the resistance force of Lebanon is seen as the only solution to defend the country against any aggression by Israel. Post the 2006 war, the European TCCs agreed to deploy their soldiers in Lebanon only after the structure of UNIFIL was redefined with a stronger mandate and rules of engagement.[28] As summed up by Tardy, "despite Western states' initial insistence on the robustness of UNIFIL II, such robustness is, in practice, peacekeeper centred rather than mandate centred, and Western states are extremely reluctant to take any action that could lead to escalation". To put it differently, the robustness of UNIFIL is not for the defence of the mandate but the protection of peacekeepers of Western nations.[29]

UNIFIL, Complex Politics of Lebanon and the Hezbollah

UN peacekeeping missions are the result of prolonged political processes that involve intense negotiations between parties to a conflict, various multinational players, and the international community at large. Therefore, military components in peacekeeping missions are only one of the players in the process of conflict resolution. Their role, however, is indispensable and crucial. This intricate relationship between politics and peacekeeping missions varies from region to region and according to the type of peacekeeping mission, with politics always retaining the upper hand. This picture becomes more complicated when other actors having indirect interests also join the conflict.

This is the case in the context of Lebanon–Israel conflicts. The Hezbollah fought a major war with the IDF in 2006 and today is one of the main political parties in Lebanon. Even after almost a decade of relative peace, both the Hezbollah and the IDF remain at loggerheads, with both sides frequently making accusations and counter-accusations. For Israel, the threat from its north (Lebanon) is real and with the Hezbollah acquiring more advanced weapons, this threat has become only larger. In the context of the Israel–Lebanon relationship, Israel is more worried about the Hezbollah than Lebanon. The Hezbollah's support base—the Shiites, the majority in South Lebanon—as well as many non-Shiite elements of Lebanese society also believe that Israel left Lebanon in 2000 and 2006 only because of a sustained effort by the Hezbollah. Newby observed that the "Hezbollah's legitimacy in Lebanon, particularly amongst the non-Shiite supporters, rests on its ability to keep Lebanon out of any further confrontation with Israel".[30]

The Hezbollah's survival as an organisation depends on support from its mentor, Iran, and the continuance of the Assad regime in Syria. Even though the Hezbollah has gone through a difficult phase and lost more than 1,300 fighters in the Syrian war, Israeli intelligence believes that the Hezbollah has not become weaker. On the contrary, it is preparing for the next conflict with Israel.[31] It is just that, presently, it is not interested in opening up another front with Israel. Therefore, the future shape of UNIFIL will largely be guided by the trajectory of the shifting security dynamics of the Middle East. This may undergo further changes as it will be difficult for the delicate regional power balance to escape from the influence of the dreaded COVID-19, which has given a blow to the global economy unleashing a geopolitical churn. There are signs of a realignment of the international and regional power balances and a change in the traditional friendship bond between nations. This is going to impact the security sector as well. It, however, is slightly early to predict the future relationship between Lebanon and Israel. The inter-state relationship of the regional countries, combined with their internal politics, affects the peace process. In the case of Lebanon and Israel, this is manifest in different forms generally near the Blue Line, at times almost pushing the region to the brink of a major war.[32]

Another factor that affects the functioning of UNIFIL is the unique nature of Lebanon's parliamentary system. No peacekeeping mission can deliver unless there is support from the host government and the parties to the conflict. In Lebanon, political power is shared following a confessional system. Essentially, it is shared between the Maronite Christians, the Sunnis and the Shiites, without any unanimous power or authority in the hands of any party.[33] It was a compromised and weak political order, allowing the elites of Lebanese society to drain the country's economy for their personal use. As reported by Cook in the wake of the current internal turmoil of the country, "The country's confessional political order that was intended to create a rough, but uneven, balance to ensure a modicum of stability was little more than a system of spoils for Maronite, Sunni, and Shiite leaders, who plundered the country".[34] Therefore, support from one single political party, which should have been derived after forming the government at the centre, seems not possible in Lebanon. Consequently, any support that might come has to be the result of a consensus among the political factions of the three confessions.

The religious diversity also makes Lebanon an easy target for external interference.[35] To explain, the port of Beirut was shocked by a massive explosion on 4 August 2020 killing hundreds of people and devastating thousands of lives. So far, there has been no evidence to pinpoint culpability for the disaster. But as observed by Rahman, this crisis can be used by interested external powers, because of Lebanon's dependence on its neighbouring countries for economic and political stability. He reported that, for instance, it will be an opportune moment for both the USA (a key ally of Israel) and Saudi Arabia, who are anti-Hezbollah and support the 'March 14 movement' (the Sunni Muslim political party), to pursue their regional agenda.[36] Hence, unlike in other peacekeeping missions, the relationship between peacekeeping and politics is more intertwined and complicated in UNIFIL.

Rise of Non-Western Peacekeepers

The rise in the contribution of non-Western nations to UN peacekeeping has been gradual over a period. Many like to refer to this trend as the result of the evolution of the global power system, a shift in power politics and the use of peacekeeping as an important tool for profile enhancement.[37] For India, it matches its regional profile of wanting to be a regional leader by setting an example in the field of peacekeeping. This, however, should not be misinterpreted as a regional hegemony. According to Carvalho and Coning of the Norwegian Peacebuilding Resource Centre, this phenomenon of the rising powers in general, and Brazil, Russia, India, China and South Africa (BRICS) in particular, can be understood as a bloc of countries that seek to counter what they perceive as the unfair advantage that the Western bloc has gained from the current architecture.[38] While it will be difficult to counter this argument, the rising powers, however, share a common perspective to assert themselves as regional emerging powers, as well as, for some of them, to make a legitimate claim for permanent seats in the Security Council. The question thus arises: will the emergence of rising powers significantly shift the landscape of PKO; and is there a clash of the philosophy of peacekeeping within the mission?

UNIFIL is the only PKO where there could be a clash of such ideas, as in this mission, troops from both the so-called developed and the developing world meet. Troops from the developed world barely participate in complex and difficult peacekeeping missions. As reported by Karlsrud and Smith, there was a comeback by the European nations to participate in difficult peacekeeping missions like MINUSMA.[39] Except for the Special Forces, technically, the actual boots on the ground are not yet there. Since these specialised troops are located centrally as quick response teams and not for holding posts, the overall low troop density in the Area of Operations remains unchanged. This is the case in all peacekeeping missions. The major European contribution to MINUSMA, however, has now reduced to only 15 peacekeepers from Germany (as learnt from media reports, after France terminating its military Operation Barkhane, and pulling out its soldiers from Mali in August 2022, even Germany is likely to suspend its contribution to the peacekeeping mission soon). There are however a few other European nations that have contributed less than 100 troops.[40]

In UNIFIL, the total contribution from Western nations with well-trained and well-equipped troops is the largest among all current UN peacekeeping missions. India and Ghana were the two major non-Western TCCs during the 2006 war. When it ended, the mission's strength was augmented and peacekeepers from three European nations—France, Spain, and Italy—were quickly deployed to provide much-needed immediate stability to the mission. Simultaneously, troops from other non-Western nations also started getting deployed, albeit slowly.

While there is no misunderstanding amongst the military contingents in UNIFIL, there are certainly functional problems. Competing bilateral interests, combined with strict adherence to national military protocols, result in rigidity and inflexible handling of even the smallest of incidents. However, despite different ethnicities, religious faiths, traditions and cultures, there is something common amongst the non-Western national contingents. Social adjustment comes with ease amongst these nations. For instance, hosting peacekeepers from different contingents for a meal without any prior information or invitation is quite common amongst non-Western contingents. Yet, there are differences, stemming from inside and outside of the troops.

Newby noted that in the case of Lebanon, as the countries of the European contingents have diplomatic relations with Israel, the Hezbollah and civilians are extremely sensitive about foreigners taking photographs in the area of operations. Since such photographs with important terrain information may fall into the hands of Israel, photography by foreigners is considered a security risk and spying for Israel. She further noted that the local population seems to have a relatively negative perception of European peacekeepers. In this regard, Newby commented, "In general, the personal characteristics of Asian battalions were more popular than the Europeans".[41] According to her, there are two primary reasons for such a perception. One, the invasions of Afghanistan and Iraq led the local Lebanese population to believe that the deployment of peacekeepers from NATO member-states in Lebanon is another invasion of the Muslim world by Western nations. Two, the interests and foreign policy of some of the European nations are more aligned towards Israel. Because of such a perception, taking photographs in even their area of operations by European peacekeepers is regarded as more problematic than by the non-European peacekeepers.[42]

There is also a distinct difference in the force protection measures between the Western and non-Western contingents. While those from

European nations appear robust and hence are likely to be perceived as arrogant (because of peacekeepers moving around in heavily protected armoured vehicles and wearing full battle gear), the other group (the non-Western national contingents) seems to find better acceptability in Lebanese society. This probably stems from the tradition of setting aside bilateral differences to work as comrades when it comes to striving for a common goal. For instance, peacekeepers from India and Pakistan, known to be sworn enemies otherwise, have been regularly fighting side by side in the Democratic Republic of Congo (DRC).

Peacekeeping operations differ from conventional military operations in many ways unless it is an intervention by force. Accustomed to the NATO environment in fighting terrorists in places like Afghanistan, peacekeepers from Western nations, who are rotated quite frequently, find it difficult to adjust to UN peacekeeping, which is more traditional and bureaucratic. Even the past institutional memory of many Western TCCs, who participated in UN peacekeeping before 1996, has been lost.[43] As a result, there is a tendency to import the NATO philosophy to UN PKO. Well-trained and well-equipped peacekeepers from these countries tend to look at every incident in the mission through a military prism and try to separate the black from the white. However, there are many different shades of grey between black and white.

For the successful implementation of peace deals, a clear understanding of the underlying differences between the processes of mediation and verification is especially important. For, while assessing the performance of the UN peacekeeping mission in El Salvador, Howard explained that in the process of mediating peace deals, the mediator learned of many politically sensitive acts that should not be subjected to verification standards.[44] For example, the Hezbollah is officially not a signatory to the peace agreement leading to the adoption of SCR 1701. However, unless the Hezbollah—considered to be a resistance movement in Lebanon—consented, SCR 1701 would not have been adopted. Moreover, its presence in South Lebanon is widely known. Yet, the removal of either the Hezbollah or its arsenals cannot be part of the mandate. Therefore, the inability of the UN to disarm it cannot be considered a verification standard. Otherwise, the mission will be doomed even before it starts functioning.

During this author's tenure in UNIFIL, the way how incidents related to the discovery of unauthorised arms were handled led a large part of the local community to suspect the underlying motives of the TCCs that executed the operations. So much so that the local population obstructed routine investigations of a few incidents by UN teams. There have been at least three incidents (these will be separately covered in Chapter 5) of serious violations of SCR 1701 by the Hezbollah in South Lebanon, in which the local population prevented UNIFIL and LAF teams from investigating the unauthorised presence of arms and ammunition.

At the same time, such obstructions were rare in the eastern sector of UNIFIL, which was predominantly held by peacekeepers from non-Western nations. This was probably because military peacekeepers from the non-Western nations have special skills—that is, the ability to deliver more by their positive attitude and less by use of force—complex challenges of UN PKO in these parts of the area of operation are handled more efficiently. Even isolated incidents of obstruction of freedom of movement of peacekeepers generally took place in areas that were outside the area of operation of the non-Western nations.

It was noted by Ruffa that some of the contingents from Western nations were there more for political reasons and less for peace. She quoted an Italian officer, "Our presence is for sure political presence for us; for the military, it is not easy: we can never intervene at first, we have to wait until the political authorities decide, but it makes us look good".[45] Essentially, there was a trust deficit vis-à-vis such contingents. In this regard, very often the Deputy Force Commander (DFC)—who in some cases was a non-Westerner—had to personally lead some of the sensitive investigations. One can always attribute such acceptance by the host government to the position and rank of the DFC, but other factors, such as the DFC's nationality, may play a role as well. Once, an armoured tank of one of the European nations accidentally rolled backwards from its carrier (when the chain securing it suddenly snapped) and crushed the private car following it immediately behind. A Lebanese man and his daughter—occupants of the car—died on the spot. Following this event, the DFC was unanimously nominated to visit the mourning family to pay condolences on behalf of UNIFIL. Whether this was because of the official position of the DFC or his nationality, it cannot be stated. Such decisions are best left to the judgement of the senior leaders of the mission at that time and the population at large.

Were the military contingents of the non-Western nations soft-pedalling when it came to implementing the mandate? The answer to this is evident from one of the biggest recoveries of illegal arsenals by the then Indian contingent in the eastern sector of UNIFIL in South Lebanon on 9 January

2009.[46] It was not possible to verify whether these belonged to the Hezbollah or some other Palestinian armed group. However, given the quantity and type of arsenals, it was reasonable to believe this cache belonged to the Hezbollah. There were no repercussions from anywhere whatsoever. It was the result of a professional search of a suspected cache of illegal weapons and not because of any attempt to enter a suspect's house/premises of local Lebanese citizens in search of illegal arms. Similar parallel examples exhibiting professionalism and unique skills, which are especially suited for PKO, can be drawn from other contemporary peacekeeping missions. For example, Indian peacekeepers regularly resort to coercive action against the spoilers in DRC.[47]

Peacekeeping contingents from most of the Western nations are backed by their national logistic support systems over and above what the mission provides. To explain, to manage the national logistic backup, additional strength is deployed in the mission area, which is over and above the UN authorised strength for each contingent (as agreed to in the MoU between the TCC and the UN). The costs of the maintenance of this additional strength as well as the extra expenditure for their daily maintenance, which can be anything up to 8 Euro per peacekeeper per day, are borne by the respective national governments.

Such a national support system, however, will find it difficult to work when there is a break in the supply chain because of the resurgence of conflict. On the other hand, such luxury is absent in the case of almost all the non-Western contingents, who are used to managing what they get from the UN. The UN provided a scale of rations and other allied support services that are more than adequate for the peacekeepers to discharge their duties during their tour of duty in the mission area. On the flip side, despite being bereft of such national extravagance, non-Western contingents like India and Ghana did not find it difficult to undertake their peacekeeping duties even when South Lebanon continuously came under IDF bombardment during the peak of the 2006 war. The tales of bravery of these two contingents during the war are still recounted by the local Lebanese people. Whenever there was talk of the 2006 war, the local population proudly cited tales of bravery of Indian and Ghanaian peacekeepers. Peacekeepers from these two nations put their own lives in the line of fire and saved the lives of many innocent Lebanese civilians of South Lebanon. Even during the war in 2006, without caring for their safety, peacekeepers from India and Ghana used to move out of their posts to pick up and transport stranded civilians to safe places. The peacekeepers from these two nations thus put their own lives in the line of fire and saved the lives of many innocent Lebanese civilians of South Lebanon.[48]

This is not a judgement of the professional skills, or lack of it, of the military peacekeepers of Western nations. Uniformed peacekeepers from Western nations in UNIFIL are highly trained professionals, with sophisticated communications systems and advanced weaponry like artillery, radars, unmanned aerial vehicles (UAVs; though never used for lack of permission from the host government) and armoured tanks; and also, some economic disparity.

The UN reimburses the TCCs both for personnel and equipment (number and category of both as agreed in the Memorandum of Understanding [MoU] before deployment in the mission), based on a fixed standard rate of the UN. No payment is made for any additional deployment of personnel over and above what was agreed to in the MoU. As mentioned earlier, in addition to the UN entitlement, all three European nations (plus probably a few small European contingents), first deploy additional manpower as an administrative backup, and second, spend a substantial amount of their own money to provide better boarding and lodging for their contingents. This has created an apparent economic disparity, though without any overt/visible impact on the operational efficiency of the contingents of non-Western nations. However, it is too early to predict the usefulness of such assets during a full-fledged conflict.

Yet, despite these differences, there is a convergence of goals and commitment amongst Western and non-Western peacekeepers. Political clout and military muscle of the developed world combined with the unique peacekeeping skills of the non-Western nations have helped to delicately balance UNIFIL in South Lebanon to provide the much-needed stability and succour. It has been almost a decade since the last major war of 2006. Undoubtedly, this has been the longest era without a major conflict between Israel and Lebanon.

UNIFIL: Local Legitimacy and Credibility

Unless there is a secure situation, making progress on any task, whether mandated or not, will be difficult. Therefore, amongst others, the credibility that is earned in providing security will take priority. In Lebanon, building credibility particularly pertains to UNIFIL maintaining peace along the BL, because occurrences of BL violations could trigger a resumption of hostilities. As also mentioned by Newby, these violations could be:[49]

- Accidental violations by shepherds, livestock, farmers, and visitors.
- Deliberate violations by throwing stones at IDF personnel by Lebanese citizens.
- Organised demonstrations by Palestinians every year on 30 March, as a sign of protest against either forced Israeli land appropriation or Israel's declaration of Independence on 14 May (eight hours before the end of the British Mandate of Palestine) or commemoration of the who were displaced following Israel's victory in the Six-Day War on 5 June.
- Violation of Lebanese air space by Israel.
- Weapon pointing either by the LAF or IDF at each other.
- Rocket attacks on Israel.

Taking prompt control of sensitive situations along the BL is just the first step towards ironing out the doubts and apprehensions of both sides. This has to be later followed up by UNIFIL through its liaison and coordination mechanism, exchange of information, marking of the BL to avoid inadvertent crossing and building the capacity of security institutions like the LAF for it to take over the security responsibility of South Lebanon. The institution of tripartite meetings is one such forum where both the IDF and LAF get an opportunity to air their grievances and remove misunderstandings.

Even though it is a traditional peace operation and not specifically tasked, some of the activities of UNIFIL can be called peacebuilding activities. Working with the local administration to undertake developmental activities, which can be funded either by UNIFIL or out of the national fund of some of the contingents, helps to establish a line of communications between UNIFIL and the civilian population. It, in turn, helps to get cooperation from them. Similarly, the capacity building of the LAF in terms of its training, and lobbying with the international community to build its military equipment profile is something that helps to strengthen the security institution of Lebanon.

Assisting the LAF to establish its authority in South Lebanon is one of the mandated tasks of UNIFIL. Most of the Lebanese population including the Shiite base in South Lebanon shares the opinion that the LAF should take responsibility for their security. They are, however, conscious of the reality that the LAF does not have the capability to take on this responsibility. Post withdrawal of the IDF after the 2006 war, the LAF only slowly and with difficulty attempted to re-establish its authority in South Lebanon. That is where the Hezbollah stepped in. Such a challenge has been further compounded by a lack of a stable political system, the Hezbollah's role in Lebanese politics and the people's belief that the Hezbollah can manage Lebanon's national security. Accordingly, the capacity building of the LAF has been one of the priorities for UNIFIL. Yet, given the Hezbollah's almost unquestionable writ over South Lebanon, UNIFIL and LAF have to carefully navigate in the delicate landscape without upsetting the balance of power in society. It amounts to accommodating both the Hezbollah and its supporters and recognize and respect its legacy in the confrontation between Lebanon and Israel. Newby described the Hezbollah's heavy footprint in South Lebanon as, "If UNIFIL had strictly enforced its mandate, it might have rid the area of weapons briefly, but it would have been expelled by the local community".[50]

Under such circumstances, even though the growth of the LAF in South Lebanon has been slow, its capability as the guarantor of security has improved manifold. Joint activities like joint patrolling and joint training, exchange of liaison officers, and encouraging the LAF to take the lead role in either searching for illegal weapons or removing misunderstandings between UNIFIL and the local civilian population are a few confidence-building measures. These not only improve UNIFIL-LAF cooperation but also strengthen the latter's role in South Lebanon. UNIFIL also continuously lobbies to arrange external funding for the modernisation of the LAF. The long-term objective of UNIFIL is to gradually transfer the responsibilities (currently carried out by the mission) to the LAF and have it assume effective security control over UNIFIL's area of operations and Lebanese territorial waters. LAF's primary missions include defending Lebanon and its citizens against external aggression, maintaining internal stability and security, confronting threats against the country's vital interests, engaging in social development activities and undertaking relief operations in coordination with public and humanitarian institutions.

A lack of capacity in terms of strength and equipment hinders UNIFIL–LAF coordinated operational activities. The LAF finds it difficult to keep up with UNIFIL troops as it lacks the requisite equipment and infrastructure. Newby noted that there is, however, suspicion in the minds of the potential donor countries that their financial assistance may be used to equip the LAF to wage war against Israel. Therefore, to allay such fears, UNIFIL seeks funding for LAF battalions that are based throughout Lebanon, not just south of the Litani River. Also, UNIFIL successfully lobbied in the UN General Assembly for a sum of money, estimated to be around US$ 500,000, for the specific purpose of assisting the LAF to purchase essential supplies.[51] Such a justification, however, does not seem to be easily accepted by the donor countries, because, even if funding is made based on the assurance of UNIFIL, the LAF always has the luxury to rotate its units throughout Lebanon. The donor nations may not voice their opinions in public, but Israel continues to protest any financial aid to the LAF.[52]

Earning credibility from the population, however, is challenging because the expectations of the civilian population will vary depending on their political and religious affiliations. Local knowledge, being sensitive to local culture and traditions, and always reaching out to the needy population with a helping hand help to gain their confidence and cooperation. One of the main differences between traditional and complex peacekeeping operations is that the civilian population becomes the primary objective of war and violence. Since a peacekeeping force has to mingle with the population, peacekeepers must maintain impartiality and empathy towards the local citizens to accomplish the mandate. However, peacekeepers are not saints. They are soldiers, but first, humans with their prejudices. At times, these prejudices affect their judgments and actions, and their presence may add fuel to the existing conflagration. At times, prejudices arise from the perception that members of a group pose a threat to another group. It is and will be normal for the host population to look at all outsiders with suspicion until the peacekeepers find acceptability in society.

In Lebanon, UNIFIL often becomes the victim of the coloured perception of the local population. The very people they are mandated to protect have stoned peacekeepers. Whenever a peacekeeping mission is established, initially, the local population of the host nation welcomes it and looks at them with respect, as if they were a sort of *angels of peace*. But gradually, such respect turns into dislike, if not outright hatred, when the same peacekeepers start disregarding local mores and fail to assimilate into local society. It will be common for the host nation to expect TCCs to use their forces diligently and not to turn the same guns towards the population. Inability to understand and speak the local language also contributes towards negative perceptions. For example, a routine complaint by a

Lebanese citizen, if construed and projected as unfriendly behaviour, will have the cumulative effect of being perceived as the unfriendly attitude of the local community at large towards the peacekeepers. Subsequently, such perceived feelings begin to send negative vibes increasing the gap between peacekeepers and the population. These can be called "vicious circles of peacekeeping".

Often, the operational reports of the contingents (who do not have a good command of the English language) that pour into the HQs daily only add to the complications. Children on the roadside pointing toy guns and young people making unfavourable gestures at the peacekeepers are only a few such incidents, which fall in this category. More than the intention, the inability of the peacekeepers to appropriately describe these incidents (because of a lack of command over the local vernacular) often results in labelling them as unfriendly behaviour. This kind of misunderstanding often takes place while corresponding with the LAF, whose official language is Arabic. When correspondences between UNIFIL and LAF are translated into their respective official languages, the real meaning of the events tends to get distorted.

In Lebanon, people from the south have suffered the most in all the wars and almost remained separated from the rest of the country for more than 22 years until the IDF made the final withdrawal in May 2000. It is understandable that after being isolated for so many years, the thinking of the common people has changed. Therefore, in the context of such cultural differences, what is required from the TCCs while operating outside their countries is the willingness to understand and accept the genuine grievances of the host population because the norms that apply in the peacekeepers' native countries seldom hold the same meaning in another country. To forge a good relationship, the first step to be taken by peacekeepers is changing one's social norms and appealing to people's values, learning about, and respecting the local culture and traditions before induction. It is also true that the outlook of the military contingents varies from TCC to TCC, based on national perceptions. As stated earlier, observations show that those coming from NATO countries are more inclined towards security. As a result, some of the troops from these countries have to make special efforts to come closer to the population.

To reach out to the public and extend a helping hand with developmental Quick Impact Projects (QUIP) are recent and commonly used approaches in peacekeeping missions. Regrettably, the amount of money available to meet the expenditure of all the projects is negligible. This often results in adjusting the fund allocation and changes in the priority of work. This may be perceived as partiality by the faction of society that could not benefit from such a program.[53] Howard described QUIP as a type of inducement (one form of power in peacekeeping) that is used to convince unwilling warring groups or even the government to behave in a particular manner. Inducement is different from the other two forms of power of peacekeeping—*coercion* and *persuasion*. Coercion is about limiting choice and persuasion is about ideas. In UNIFIL, this power is generally exercised through inducement.[54]

Since the advantages of successful projects are tremendous, many rich TCCs spend huge amounts of additional national funds to finance projects in their respective areas of operations. Such generosity helps in filling the gaps created by the limited funds of the UN. At the same time, it may lead to disparity in the overall distribution of such funds and an apparent feeling of being neglected in areas where less wealthy contingents are deployed. Moreover, national contributions are contingent upon the continued participation of such troops from other nations. The moment any nation decides to pull out of the mission, such funds will dry up. This notwithstanding, the combined resources of UNIFIL and the contingents are judiciously used in close coordination with each other and the CIMIC section of the force HQ. Besides, the programs and projects by and large are oriented towards the all-round development of society, which is normally not coming forward from the state administration.

Educational programs, medical camps (for health check-ups), the building of roads and infrastructure, the provision of alternative sources of power and drinking water and creating environmental awareness are some of the policies that have found favour among the local populace. On the flip side, many TCCs and their contingents consider developmental projects as a good way to ensure, or for that matter to buy, security for their contingents. As observed by Gordon, "CIMIC teams often simply deliver projects (largely out of unsubstantiated claims that it fosters force protection) and rarely engage communities".[55] CIMIC helps to earn material credibility. However, despite spending huge amounts of money on developmental projects, there has not been a big change in the attitude of the local people of South Lebanon. Newby noted that a positive relationship towards UNIFIL does not, however, extend to trust. The same local population will close ranks to support the Hezbollah when it comes to Hezbollah-related activities. She mentioned, "Material credibility wins cooperation that enables the mission to patrol. But it does not win trust or legitimacy".[56] Even in those areas where some of the TCCs have invested extensively, instances displaying anguish are not uncommon. Spending on CIMIC projects, if perceived by the local community as a means to buy force protection by the peacekeepers, may turn out to be counterproductive and result in a negative unintended consequence of CIMIC activities in peace operations.[57]

If peace operations gain credibility, the local population believes in the peacekeepers and trusts them. UNIFIL tries to do that by bringing about an attitudinal change, empathizing with their grievances and becoming a part of society. The Civil Affairs (CA) officers of mission HQs act as the interface between the peacekeepers and the local population. CA officers are generally local civilians employed by UNIFIL. Being local, they can easily spend time with the locals and attend local ceremonies. Because of their knowledge of the local language, culture and traditions and even though being employees of UNIFIL and generally looked at with suspicion, CA officers find better acceptability. The role of the CA officers can be compared to unarmed civilian peacekeepers, who work for international NGOs with independent agendas. Rejecting the idea that peacekeeping requires military personnel and weapons, Julian and Gasser observed that civilian peacekeepers can make an equally good contribution to the peace process by undertaking several peacekeeping tasks such as monitoring human rights situations, influencing the behaviour of the local population, investigating, negotiating and collaborating, etc.[58] That aside, CA officers, even though they work for the military mission, use the same power of communication as the civilian peacekeepers to influence the behaviour of the armed actors without using force or the threat thereof. They support CIMIC officers with advice and recommendations and can act as an effective tool for damage control.

For example, during their routine operational patrolling, UNIFIL patrols may come across unfriendly behaviour on the part of the local population. This could happen in the form of denying freedom of movement by temporarily blocking the patrols' routes, making arrogant and offensive gestures, or pelting stones at them. At times, the locals forcefully bring the patrols to a halt, surround them, and snatch away their cameras if it is suspected of having taken photographs, which is considered an act of spying for Israel. Regardless of the reason, the situation can turn ugly. It can become worse if, by chance, the patrol happens to get involved in an accident resulting in injuries to civilians. Under such circumstances, UNIFIL patrols, always take care to remain calm and are prepared to defend themselves against unruly mobs. The best option for the patrol at such a point in time will be to summon a CA officer as quickly as possible to intervene and defuse the situation. Interventions of CA officers along with LAF support are part of the daily life of UNIFIL.

Similarly, at the operational level, the most effective mechanism to iron out differences in perception between the LAF and IDF is the Tripartite Meetings. These meetings, which are held periodically, are attended by representatives of the LAF and IDF and chaired by the UNIFIL FC. Disagreements/disputes in BL marking, major BL violations or firing of rockets into Israel and retaliation by IDF are the common agendas of the tripartite meetings. Essentially, all issues that cannot be resolved at the tactical level are discussed to find a mutually acceptable solution. Tripartite meetings, in addition to an exchange of information by the UNIFIL liaison team and personal interactions by the FC with both sides, has been the most effective mechanism in building confidence and trust and, above all, to gain credibility by UNIFIL.[59]

Conclusion

It is difficult to measure the success of any peacekeeping mission. So far, UNIFIL has generally been able to maintain a stable environment in the region. However, it was not successful in preventing the war of 2006. Despite its size and composition, the ability of UNIFIL to prevent another war by force cannot be stated with certainty because there is no history of peacekeepers from Western and/or non-Western nations achieving a similar feat. Moreover, let alone ensuring a permanent ceasefire, even the cessation of hostilities cannot be ensured by using force. As observed by Bove, Ruffa and Ruggeri, the presence of well-trained and well-equipped peacekeepers from the European nations is a deterrent to Israel for reasons that are different from their robust composition. They quoted Goksel, a former political adviser to UNIFIL, who stated, "the Europeans have the political clout that certainly the third world troop-contributing countries don't have and even the UN as an institution does not have".[60] The robust structure of UNIFIL is more for the protection of the peacekeepers and less for the defence of the mandate. Therefore, rather than expecting UNIFIL to prevent another war, it will be safe to assume UNIFIL's ability to create suitable conditions for a cessation of hostilities, and nothing more. As long as there is hostility between the Hezbollah and Israel, there will be some organisation that will be needed to help cease hostilities, as they are not going to end soon. If at all, the situation is only going to become more complicated. In this regard, the sheer absence of war is a success that UNIFIL can boast of. For Israel too, it will remain a security buffer as long as UNIFIL can undertake its basic peacekeeping duties and manage to prevent an escalation of conflicts with quick responses to any incident near the BL that has the potential to spiral out of control. As concluded by Newby, "UNIFIL mission has acted as a shock absorber for local tensions and maintained a negative peace, that is, it has prevented the escalation of minor incidents into large-scale conflict".[61]

As for the international community, UNIFIL provides legitimacy for maintaining at least the status quo. Therefore, the existence and presence of UNIFIL is a necessity in the larger interests of the international community and the Middle East. The present structure of UNIFIL is unique in the sense that it is a multinational organisation comprising a good mix of well-trained and well-equipped military peacekeepers from the developed world and non-Western military contingents (more than half the strength of UNIFIL). Despite the differences in training, equipment, culture and tradition between the Western and non-Western national contingents, UNIFIL's contribution to maintaining peace in the region is noteworthy. The Western and non-Western contingents have been able to create synergy, and thus UNIFIL has proved to be an effective and credible peacekeeping mission in the Middle East.

Military peacekeepers from non-Western nations have special skills, which are probably more in demand than the others. Apart from professional skills, modesty, restraint, decency, sensitivity to local customs and more, humility and being accommodative are traits that can be easily identified with military peacekeepers from non-Western nations. Despite the economic disparity between Western and non-Western nations, the commitment of the military peacekeepers from the latter is worth special mention. Bridging the economic gap will be an additional source of motivation for them to embolden their commitment to the cause of world peace. For UNIFIL to be more effective, the international community at large, and the TCCs in particular, will have to work hand in hand and side by side, to face the challenges that are associated with a multinational organisation. Until now, UNIFIL can boast of having saved the region from more wars for more than one decade with its mere presence. However, given the current vitiated situation in the Middle East, it will be difficult to predict the source as well as the trajectory of the next regional war. If it happens, UNIFIL will possibly remain a mute spectator, with many TCCs, barring a few, leaving the mission hastily, as it happened in 2006.

UNIFIL is generally criticised for what it has not been able to achieve. Israel, the main party to the conflict, and its allies, always highlight UNIFIL's inability to rein in the Hezbollah even though this task is not part of the mandate of UNIFIL. The Hezbollah is still around and not likely to go away any time soon, primarily for two reasons. One, it is deeply entrenched in Lebanese politics and discussion about it as part of the national resistance is not going to gain favour in the present political set up. Two, the survival of the Hezbollah is based on the ever-growing hatred between Israel and Lebanon. It never lets go of any aggressive action by Israel whether it is inside Lebanon or not, without a strong military response.

For instance, on 28 January 2015, the Hezbollah launched several anti-tank guided missiles from a UNIFIL area of operation at an Israeli convoy that was driving south of the BL. The Hezbollah claimed responsibility for this attack as retaliation for Israeli airstrikes on Golan Heights on 18 January killing six Hezbollah members and one high-ranking Iranian military officer.[62] Therefore, unless there is an alternative to the Hezbollah to defend Lebanon against any aggression from Israel and unless there is a decline in popular support for it, this will be the status quo in the relations between Lebanon and Israel.

To conclude, as observed by Newby, what UNIFIL has been able to manage so far is to create conditions so that the present status quo is not altered, and people can live their daily lives with minimum disruption. It will not be unfair to hope that as time passes there will be a loss of appetite for war. According to her, in close to two decades, UNIFIL has been able to earn credibility by creating a predictable security environment that is less dangerous than an unpredictable security environment. Therefore, rather than calling it either a success or failure, it will be fair to describe UNIFIL as a 'shock absorber'.[63] The same credibility, however, has pushed UNIFIL into a credibility trap, which is not likely to end until there is a full ceasefire between Israel and Lebanon. The relationship between Israel and Lebanon is still based on considerable animosity and is badly intertwined with the internal dynamics of Lebanon. In such a situation, it is difficult for UNIFIL to even plan an exit from Lebanon. Applying the conceptual framework developed in the preceding Chapter 3, it is possible to develop and generate a few essentials that can form the core of the framework for evaluation of UNIFIL:

1. *Key Goals*: The key goals for UNIFIL derived from the mandate are:
   (i) Restoration of peace and security.
   (ii) Creating conditions to prevent the resumption of hostilities between Lebanon and Israel.
   (iii) Ensuring South Lebanon is free of armed personnel, assets, and weapons other than those of the Lebanese government and UNIFIL.
   (iv) Assistance to Lebanese Armed Forces (LAF) in fulfilling their security responsibilities.
   (v) Ensuring support from the local population.
   (vi) Maintaining operational effectiveness of the mission.
2. *Key Questions*: The key question to ask against a key goal like *restoration of peace and security* will be: 'is violence still present?' Some of the indicators to find an answer to the key questions can be: what is the duration without clashes/war; details of face-offs of rival factions; and cross-border shooting in the case of a traditional peace operation. While statistical data will be available to support answers to some of the questions, analysis of other responses will have to be qualitative. For instance, one of the tasks of UNIFIL is to 'assist the LAF in establishing an area between the Litani River and the Blue Line (BL), free of any armed personnel, assets and weapons other than those of the Government of Lebanon and UNIFIL'.[64] Such a task can never be quantified because there is no parameter to judge if it is UNIFIL that has failed to assist the LAF or it is the LAF that has failed to fulfil its part of the mandate despite the sincere commitment and best efforts on the part of UNIFIL. Hence, quantitative criteria will not be appropriate for evaluation. The criteria for such a task will perforce have to be qualitative, based on the stakeholders' perceptions of success.
3. *Stakeholders*: There are many stakeholders in UNIFIL with varying interests. It is not only Israel, Lebanon, the Hezbollah, the Palestinian refugees, or the outside powers that take sides in this conflict. An apt account of the complexity was given by Marrack Goulding, the then USG of UN in charge of peacekeeping, in his book, *Peacemonger*. To understand it well, a word-by-word description is necessary. He stated:

> Think of Lebanon as a cockpit. But it's not a normal cockpit. The fights are not single combats between two cocks; they are fights between teams of cocks, in ever-changing alliances. And the floor of the cockpit is strewn with brightly coloured beads. They are called 'assets' and they come in various colours—blue for political assets, yellow for economic assets, khaki for strategic assets, white for ideological and religious assets, red for criminal assets. Inside the cockpit, there are several resident teams of cocks. The four principal ones are the Maronite Christians, the Sunni Muslims, the Shiite Muslims and the Druze, a heretical Islamic sect. There are other lesser teams of cocks. Each team includes some fighting cocks, called 'militias.' The teams fight with each other to accumulate and control as many of the assets as possible. Alliances between teams are frequently formed and frequently dissolved. Sometimes, teams fight within themselves and split into two or smaller teams. The fights are violent and cruel; many team leaders are assassinated, sometimes by members of their own teams. Around the cockpit, there are several gamblers. The principal ones are Israel, Syria, Iran, and the Palestine Liberation Organisation (PLO). Lesser ones are Egypt, Iraq and Jordan. Like the resident teams, the gamblers' objective is to accumulate and control assets in the Lebanese cockpit. Three of them (Israel, Syria and the PLO) have, or have had, their fighting cocks in the cockpit. But all of them also hire the services of *one or more of the resident teams, as does Iran and the lesser gamblers* (emphasis in original).[65]

Even though it is far away, a nation like the USA has a large stake in the shape of Israel–Lebanon relations. It even ignored the existence and political motives of other players in the region at the time of the establishment of UNIFIL in 1978.[66] It hurriedly pushed for the deployment of the peace operation without understanding the intricacies of the bi- and multi-lateral relations in the area. This, in turn, created a flawed image of the mission in Lebanon and led to the perception that UNIFIL was unable to fulfil its mandate. This image has not changed even after so many years. For the USA and Israel, the inability to disarm the Hezbollah is the biggest failure on the part of UNIFIL because it has deliberately ignored the growing capacity of the Hezbollah. The USA simply wants UNIFIL to rein in the Hezbollah, regardless of whether disarming it is mandated to UNIFIL or not. To illustrate, even though there has not been a major conflict between Israel and Lebanon after 2006, both the USA and Israel are highly critical of UNIFIL.[67] On the other hand, Iran looks at UNIFIL through the prism of the Hezbollah's survival and its dominance over Lebanese politics. Thus, picking up the most appropriate stakeholder for evaluation will always be a challenge. However, as explained earlier, the perception of the Lebanese local population and, to some extent, also the population of Israel, must play a dominant role in assessing UNIFIL's performance.

4. *Timing of Assessment*: For evaluation, based on the mandate and the timing, UNIFIL can be divided into two distinct phases. During the period from 1978 until when the Israeli Defence Forces (IDF) voluntarily pulled out from South Lebanon in 2000, UNIFIL was considered a failed mission.[68] Before 2006, UNIFIL could never meet the conditions essential for it to be effective. All that it achieved was only a secondary contribution to the maintenance of peace.[69] After the war of 2006, as approved by Security Council Resolution (SCR) 1701 (2006), UNIFIL was given a different and stronger mandate, with a different organisational structure and larger capabilities than before. Therefore, the period covering the adoption of SCR 1701 to date will be more appropriate to evaluate the performance of UNIFIL.

While some of the evaluation criteria, which have been identified are common, they cannot be applied to UNIFIL as a template. The dynamics of UNIFIL are peculiar. Hence, to be fair to the mission, the evaluation process must consider the distinctiveness of UNIFIL. The most appropriate and practical method to judge UNIFIL will be by determining the extent to which the mission has been able to achieve its goals. A Table with suggested key goals, key questions, and measures of progress that can be used for evaluation of UNIFIL post-2006 is given in Appendix A (for details using UNIFIL as a case study in the context and history, please see Appendix B). Similar tables for evaluation of other traditional peace operations can be made on similar lines. In the next chapter, an assessment of UNIFIL will be made using generally available operational and primary data.

ENDNOTES

1. This chapter is a revised and updated version of A.K. Bardalai, "UN Peacekeeping Operations: perspective of an Indian Peacekeeper," in *The United Nations Interim Force in Lebanon: Multiple Perspectives on a Multinational Peace Operation*, ed. Elena Aoun (Brussels: Peter Lang, 2018), 263–301.
2. Efrat Elron, "UNIFIL II, Israel, Lebanon, The United Nations and the International Community: New and Renewed Partnerships and Implications for Mission Effectiveness," in *Cultural Challenges in Military Operations,* ed.Cees M. Coops and Tibor Szvircsev Tresch, (NATO Defence College, 2007), 97, https://www.jstor.org/stable/resrep10333
3. Bennis Phyllis, *Calling the Shots: How Washington Dominates Today's U.N.* (New York: Olive Branch Press, 1996), 272.
4. David N. Gibbs, "Is Peacekeeping a New Form of Imperialism?" *International Peacekeeping* 4, no. 1 (Spring 1997): 122–28.
5. Thomas G. Weiss and Giovanna Kuele, "The Global South and UN Peace Operations, "*International Relations,* February 3, 2019, https://www.e-ir.info/2019/02/03/the-global-south-and-un-peace-operations/
6. Maline Meiske and Andrea Ruggeri, "Peacekeeping as a Tool of Foreign Policy," *Oxford Research Encyclopedias, Politics,* September 26. 2017, https://doi.org/10.1093/acrefore/9780190228637.013.462
7. Samantha Power, "Come Back to UN Peacekeeping," http://www.undispatch.com
8. Alexandra Novosseloff, A comparative study of older one-dimensional UN Peace Operations: Is the Future of UN Peacekeeping its Past?, EPON and FES Cyprus (2022), https://effectivepeaceops.net/publication/a-comparative-study-of- older-one-dimensional-un-peace-operations/
9. UN Department of Peace Operations, Peacekeeping Operations Fact Sheet (November 2021), https://peacekeeping.un.org/sites/default/files/peacekeeping_missions_factsheet_246_nov2021_en.pdf
10. UN Department of Peace Operations, UNIFIL Background, accessed November 10, 2020, https://unifil.unmissions.org/unifil-background
11. UN Security Council, Resolutions 425 and 426 of 1978, Israel-Lebanon (March 19, 1978).
12. UN Security Council, Resolution S/RES/1701(August 11, 2006).
13. Vanessa Frances Newby, "Introduction," *Peacekeeping in South Lebanon: Credibility and Local Cooperation* (New York: Syracuse, 2018), 9.
14. Efrat Elron, "UNIFIL II, Israel, Lebanon, The United Nations and the International Community: New and Renewed Partnerships and Implications for Mission Effectiveness," in *Cultural Challenges in Military Operations,*(Report), ed. Cees M. Coops and Tibor Szvircsev Tresch, (NATO Defence College, 2007), 96, accessed December 4, 2018, https://www.jstor.org/stable/resrep10333
15. The trend in the rise in participation by countries from the South Asian region can be attributed to the desire of emerging powers to gain prestige and international recognition by participating in peacekeeping missions far away from their homeland even if there is no specific motivation to do so.
16. "Review of the 113th Infantry Battalion leaving for service with UNIFIL," (Speech), last updated October 8, 2019, https://www.gov.ie/en/speech/08fd43-review-of-the-113th-infantry-battalion-leaving-for-service-with-unif/

17. Donald C. F. Daniel, Paul D. Williams, and Adam C. Smith, "Deploying Combined Teams: Lessons Learned from Operational Partnership in UN Peacekeeping," *Providing for Peacekeeping*, Report no. 12, *International Peace Institute*, August 2015, www.ipinst.org
18. Tony Lawrence, "Estonia has announced that it will shortly discontinue its deployment of peacekeepers to the UNIFIL mission in Lebanon," *International Centre for Defence and Security*, https://icds.ee/estonia-leaves-unifil/, last modified October 8, 2018. Also, see https://polandin.com/52327766/polish-hungarian-def-mins-discuss-bilateral-cooperation-in-2021.
19. Vanessa Frances Newby, "The Role of Credibility in Peacekeeping," *Peacekeeping in South Lebanon: Credibility and Local Cooperation* (New York: Syracuse, 2018), 52–53.
20. UNMISS is considered contemporary as it has generally been in the limelight because of the violent conflict resulting in increasing number of civilian casualties.
21. UN Security Council, Resolutions 425 and 426 of 1978, Israel-Lebanon (March 19, 1978).
22. At the time of formulation of the mandate, the drafters of the resolution could not have foreseen the future trajectory of the conflict and its implications on the functioning of the mission—in principle, it is a violation of one of the basic principles of UN peacekeeping, that is, impartiality. UNIFIL is deployed inside Lebanon. In principle, it should have been in a neutral area between Israel and Lebanon. Since it is in Lebanon, often, UNIFIL's actions are perceived as biased by Israel. It is a different matter that Israel will never agree to deploy UNIFIL in a separated zone between both countries. Hence, partiality has been inbuilt from the beginning.
23. The organisation of UNIFIL is based on the NATO military organisation. Even the non-NATO members have to adapt to this organisation.
24. J. Soeters, *Management and Military Studies. Classical and Current Foundations*, (London/New York: Routledge, 2020),18–22.
25. UN General Assembly, *Report of the Panel on United Nations Peace Operations*, A/55/305-S/2000/809 (August 21, 2000); UN Department of Peacekeeping Operations and Department of Field Operations, A New Partnership Agenda: Charting a New Horizon for UN Peacekeeping (July 2009).
26. *United Nations Peacekeeping Operations: Principles and guidelines* (New York: UN Department of Public Information, 2008).
27. Charles T. Hunt, "All Necessary Means to what Ends? The Unintended Consequences of the 'Robust Turn' in UN Peace Operations," *International Peacekeeping* 24, no. 1 (2017): 111–13.
28. Elena Aoun, "The European Involvement in post 2006 UNIFIL: The Art of the Possible," in *The United Nations Interim Force in Lebanon*, ed. Elena Aoun (Brussels: Peter Lang, 2018),115–39.
29. Thierry Tardy, "A Critique of Robust Peacekeeping in Contemporary Peace Operations," *International Peacekeeping* 18, no. 2 (2011): 165, DOI:10.1080/13533312.2011.546089
30. Vanessa Frances Newby, "Playing with Fire: Understanding the Sunni-Shiite Sectarian Lifecycle," *Griffith Asia Quarterly* 1, no. 2/3(2013): 84.
31. Ronen Bergman, "Hezbollah 3.0: How Israel's No. 1 Enemy is Preparing for the Next Lebanon War," 2015, http://www.ynetnews.com/articles/
32. The Blue Line is the withdrawal line of the IDF in May 2000, based on certain

geographical features between Lebanon and Israel. It is not the boundary between Lebanon and Israel.

33. In the Lebanese political framework, at the very head of the government, the President of the Republic is always a Maronite Christian, the Prime Minister a Sunni Muslim and the Speaker of the Parliament a Shiite Muslim. Christians and Muslims are also granted a 50:50 representation in the legislature. Further, key positions such as the head of the armed forces, the central bank and the national university are allocated according to sectarian affiliations.
34. Steven A. Cook, "The End of Hope in the Middle East," *Foreign Policy,* September 5, 2020, https://foreignpolicy.com/2020/09/05/middle-east-end-hope-recovery-yemen-lebanon/
35. "Lebanon: Why the country is in crisis," *BBC News,* August 5, 2020, https://www.bbc.com/news/world-middle-east-5339010
36. Abdul Rahman, "Beirut blasts intensify economic and political crisis in Lebanon," *Peoples Dispatch,* August 5, 2020, https://peoplesdispatch.org/2020/08/08/beirut-blasts-intensify-economic-and-political-crisis-in-lebanon/
37. Thierry Tardy, "Emerging Powers and Peacekeeping: An Unlikely Normative Clash," *GCSP Policy Paper* (2012-13), http://www.operationspaix.net; https://www.files.ethz.ch/isn/141118/Emerging%20Powers%20and%20Peacekeeping.pdf
38. Benjamin de Carvalho and Cedric de Coning, "Rising Power and Future of Peacekeeping and Peace Building," *Norwegian Resource Centre,* Report (November 14, 2013), http://peacebuilding.no
39. John Karlsrud and A. C. Smith, "Europe's Return to UN Peacekeeping? Lessons from Mali," *Providing for Peacekeeping,* Report no. 11 (International Peace Institute, July 2015), http://www.ipinst.org
40. UN Peace Operations, MINUSMA Factsheet, accessed August 25, 2022, https://peacekeeping.un.org/en/mission/minusma
41. Vanessa Frances Newby, "Credibility through Aid," *Peacekeeping in South Lebanon: Credibility and Local Cooperation* (New York: Syracuse University Press, 2018), 158.
42. Vanessa Frances Newby, "Power, politics and perception: the impact of foreign policy on civilian-peacekeeper relations," *Third World Quarterly* (2017): 7, DOI: 10.1080/01436597.2017.1334542
43. John Karlsrud and A. C. Smith, "Europe's Return to UN Peacekeeping? Lessons from Mali," *Providing for Peacekeeping,* Report no. 11 (International Peace Institute, July 2015), http://www.ipinst.org
44. Lise Morje Howard, *UN Peacekeeping in Civil Wars* (New York: Cambridge University, 2008), 99.
45. Chiara Ruffa, "French and Italian Units in Lebanon," *Military Cultures in Peace and Stability Operations: Afghanistan and Lebanon* (Philadelphia: University of Pennsylvania Press, 2019), 84.
46. Author's personal experience—had they been soft peddling, the contingents would not have been able to recover such a large quantity of arms. It means that they were doing their jobs as mandated. Also see UN Security Council, *Report of the UN Secretary General on the Implementation of the Security Council Resolution 1701* (2006), S/2009/119 (March 3, 2009).
47. Thierry Tardy, "Emerging Powers and Peacekeeping: An Unlikely Normative Clash," *GCSP Policy Paper* (2012–13), https://www.files.ethz.ch/isn/141118/Emerging%20Powers%20and%20Peacekeeping.pdf

48. I heard such tales of bravery while informally interacting with the local population of South Lebanon. Gen J. P. Nehra, who was the DFC during the war, had also narrated them earlier during his operational brief to me on his relief.
49. Vanessa Frances Newby, *Peacekeeping in South Lebanon: Credibility and Local Cooperation* (New York: Syracuse, 2018), 83–94.
50. Vanessa Frances Newby, "Positive hybridity? Unpacking UN security sector reform in South Lebanon," *Contemporary Politics* (2016), 15, DOI: 10.1080/13569775.2016.1233756
51. Ibid., 14.
52. Arie Egozi, "Israel asks Trump to Withhold TOWs, Drones from Lebanese Military Aid," *Breaking Defence* (December 3, 2019), https://breakingdefense.com/2019/12/israel-asks-trump-to-withhold-tows-drones-from-lebanese-military-aid/
53. List of UNIFIL Quick Impact Projects 2018-2019, last modified September 13, 2019, https://unifil.unmissions.org/sites/default/files/quick_impact_project_18-19_0.pdf
54. Lise Morje Howard, *Power in Peacekeeping* (New York: Cambridge University Press, 2019), 1, 81.
55. Stuart Gordon, "Unintended consequences of Civil-Military Cooperation in Peace Operations," in *Unintended Consequences in Peacekeeping Operations,* ed. Chiyuki Aoi, Cedric de Conning, and Ramesh Thakur (Tokyo/New York/Paris: United Nations University Press, 2007), 122.
56. Vanessa Frances Newby, "Credibility through Aid," *Peacekeeping in South Lebanon: Credibility and Local Cooperation* (New York: Syracuse, 2018), 152–53.
57. Stuart Gordon, "Unintended consequences of Civil-Military Cooperation in Peace Operations," in *Unintended Consequences in Peacekeeping Operations,* ed. Chiyuki Aoi, Cedric de Conning, and Ramesh Thakur (Tokyo/New York/Paris: United Nations University Press, 2007), 109.
58. Rachel Julian and Russell Gasser, "Soldiers, civilians and peacekeeping–evidence and false assumptions," *International Peacekeeping* 26, no. 1 (2019): 22–54, https://doi.org/10.1080/13533312.2018.1503933
59. Vanessa Frances Newby, "Credibility in Interstate Conflict," *Peacekeeping in South Lebanon: Credibility and Local Cooperation* (New York: Syracuse University Press, 2018), 95–97.
60. Vincenzo Bove, Chiara Ruffa, and Andrea Ruggeri, *Composing Peace: Mission Composition in UN Peacekeeping* (New York: Oxford University Press, 2020), 157.
61. Vanessa Frances Newby, "Walk the Line: An investigation of the Micro-Processes of a UN Peacekeeping Mission," *Working Paper* 34 (2016): 19, DOI:10.13140/RG.2.2.26928.76808
62. UN Security Council, *Report of the Secretary-General on the implementation of Security Council Resolution 1701 (2006),* S/2015/147 (February 27, 2015).
63. Vanessa Frances Newby, "Walk the Line: An investigation of the Micro-Processes of a UN Peacekeeping Mission," *Working Paper* 37 (2016): 19.
64. UN Security Council, Resolution S/RES/1701 (August 11, 2006).
65. Marrack Goulding, *Peacemonger* (London: Johns Hopkins University Press, 2003), 58.
66. Grant T. Hammond, "The Perils of Peacekeeping for the US: Relearning Lessons from Beirut to Bosnia," in *A Future for Peacekeeping,* ed. Edward Moxon Browne (London: Macmillan Press, 1998), 74–75.
67. Benn Avni, "UN Failure is Leading to Another Lebanon War," *New York Post,* 29

August 2017, https://nypost-com.cdn.ampproject.org/c/nypost.com/2017/08/29/un-failure-is-leading-to-another-lebanon-war/amp

68. Indar Jit Rikhye, *The Theory and Practice of Peacekeeping* (London: C. Hurst & Co., 1984), 109.
69. Alxandra Novosseloff, "United Nations Interim Force in Lebanon (UNIFIL I)," in *The Oxford Handbook of United Nations Peacekeeping Operations*, ed. Joachim A. Koops, Norrie Macqueen, Thierry Tardy, and Paul D. Williams (Oxford: Oxford University Press, 2015), 254.

CHAPTER 5

Assessment of UNIFIL Using Empirical Data

Introduction

This chapter seeks to synthesise information about the operational activities that UNIFIL has carried out since 2006 when the new UNIFIL was set up after Israel had withdrawn its troops from South Lebanon. Following up on the conceptual framework that was developed in Chapter 3, this part of the study aims to present information based on the data and records available in open sources and primary data. In doing so, UNIFIL's concept of operations, its internal reports, the reports of the Secretary-General to the Security Council, opinions of scholars and subject matter experts as well as the personal experiences of the author have been considered.

The personal experiences of the author are presented here because they provide additional in-depth information from an (acting) commander of a UN mission (in the period from March 2008 to March 2010), who sincerely tried to understand what was happening around him, to improve his performance and that of the mission in general. Personal data from people with managerial or commanding responsibilities, for instance in diaries or autobiographies, have been used before in management and organization studies, particularly to provide a kind of triangulation in research design.[1] To keep these personal experiences and views separate from official data, the observations of the author have been inserted in the form of text boxes.

SECTION I: ASSESSING UNIFIL USING GENERALLY AVAILABLE OPERATIONAL DATA

Operating Environment, Concept, and Operational Strategy

Among all UN's peacekeeping operations today, UNIFIL seems to be one of the most complex and sensitive missions. Though classically a traditional PKO, i.e., operating in a post inter-state conflict environment, it has many similarities with the characteristics of PKO in an intra-state conflict scenario. To understand the operational dynamics of UNIFIL, it is important to first study relevant factors that impact the operational activities and functioning of UNIFIL, such as the geography and demography of the country.

When the mandate of a PKO, operating in an environment intermeshed with complex politics, security, and intricate external influence, is translated into distinct tasks, it essentially aims at the prevention of the resumption of hostilities. Many reasons could lead to a resumption of hostilities between Israel and Lebanon. These can range from purely bilateral reasons and the spillover of a regional conflict to delays in solving the Palestinian and border issues that keep surfacing in different forms close to UNIFIL's area of operations.

Preventing another war, which, for example, could result from possible changes in the bilateral relationship between Israel and Iran, will, however, be beyond the control of UNIFIL. At the same time, to prevent a war from recurring because of trivial incidents near the BL should be within the reach of UNIFIL. The launching of rockets by both Lebanese and non-Lebanese armed groups, the throwing of stones by Lebanese at the IDF and Lebanese crossing the BL are viewed as minor incidents. Even if these are minor issues, Newby mentioned, "These minor issues present significant risks to the region, as they are the sparks that can light the fire of a larger existential conflict".[2]

Therefore, the Military Strategic Concept of UNIFIL is to create a space for the political process to move forward by having effective control of the Litani River, the BL, and the hinterland by creating a military buffer. This includes multifarious activities such as mitigating potential causes of conflict by dominating the entire area of operation along with and in close coordination with the LAF; making an all-out effort to pre-empt and speedily react to crises near the BL; mediation and negotiation; and keeping the international community engaged for their support. These activities can cut across the entire spectrum of strategic, operational, and tactical levels. Accordingly, the strategic objectives of UNIFIL are to:[3]

- Rapidly contribute to the restoration of peace and security in South Lebanon.
- Create the necessary conditions to prevent the resumption of hostilities.
- Assist the Lebanese authorities to fulfil their security responsibilities in South Lebanon plus Lebanese territorial waters.
- Create the necessary conditions required for the implementation of previously adopted agreements between the parties and the UN Security Council resolutions.
- Ensure that the area is not used for hostile activities of any kind.
- Establish an area free of any armed personnel, assets and weapons other than those of the Government of Lebanon and UNIFIL, between the BL and Litani River, thus, assisting the Government of Lebanon to remove all foreign fighters from its soil.
- Develop a security force that can respond rapidly, within means and capabilities, to deal with any degradation of security conditions.

Accordingly, it was envisaged that the desired strategic end state of UNIFIL would be a situation on the ground, in which:

- The Government of Lebanon exercises its sovereign authority within its internationally recognised borders.
- The full implementation of the relevant provisions of the Taif Accords has been achieved.[4]
- No weapons or authority exists in Lebanon other than that of the Lebanese State.
- Conditions are established to support lasting peace in the region.

To accomplish the above, the operation has been divided into five consecutive phases:[5]

- **The First Phase** (Cessation of Hostilities): This stage consists of operations to reinforce existing military capabilities and pay special attention to rear area security and security of lines of communications.
- **The Second Phase** (IDF Disengagement): This involves handing over the IDF-occupied locations of South Lebanon and Lebanese territorial waters to the LAF via UN interface where applicable.

- **The Third Phase** (Transition Phase): Assistance to the LAF to achieve its full operational capacity. This would be possible only by assisting the LAF in maintaining effective control over the entire area of South Lebanon.
- **The Fourth Phase** (Stabilization Phase): This phase would commence after a formal cease-fire agreement and would be followed by monitoring the activities of the parties and ensuring compliance with the agreement.
- **The Fifth Phase** (UNIFIL's Drawdown and Closure): This phase will depend on the transfer of operational responsibilities to the LAF and Lebanese authorities in South Lebanon.

The phases, however, are a mere description of the broad outline plan of UNIFIL without any clear-cut divisions between them. Currently, UNIFIL is going through the second and third Phases. This is because the IDF is yet to vacate the northern part of the village of Ghajar, which it occupied during the war in 2006, as well as several smaller disputed areas near the BL, which Lebanon considers to be illegal occupation by Israel. Ghajar, inhabited by Alawite Syrians, is divided into two parts by the BL passing through almost the centre of the village.[6] Control over Ghajar has changed hands many times. When Israel captured the Golan Heights from Syria in 1967, Ghajar remained a no man's land for two-and-a-half months. Later, Ghajar expanded northward into Lebanese territory, subsuming the Wazzani settlement north of the border. However, the PLO, active at that time in the region, repeatedly violated the cease-fire and carried out terrorist attacks in Israel in which dozens of Israelis were killed and hundreds injured. In June 1982, Israel launched Operation Peace for Galilee and occupied the northern part of Ghajar. The people of the village hold Israeli citizenship. However, according to Lebanon, this area belongs to it. Israel says they do not have any objection to handing over the village, but the border issue between Lebanon and Syria must be resolved first. Therefore, even though formally UNIFIL has not entered the Fourth Phase, its operational activities are primarily geared towards stabilizing the security situation in the area of operation.

UNIFIL Operational Activities

To operationalise its concept, the resources at the disposal of UNIFIL come from a large number of different countries in the form of military contingents, including an MTF, engineering companies, helicopter units, hospitals, a maintenance company, and a QRF.

This force is deployed in the area of operation in a balanced manner to cover the entire area, maintain a strict vigil on both the Litani River and the BL, and react immediately and effectively to any given situation. Essentially, the area of operation is divided into two sectors based on HQ and troops provided by Italy and Spain. The operational activities of UNIFIL include the establishment of Observation Points (OPs), Check Points (CPs), BL patrolling, village patrols and Counter Rocket Launching Operations (CRLO) to prevent the firing of rockets by armed groups into Israel. Patrolling is both on foot and vehicle-based.

On an average, a total of 450 operational activities are undertaken every day. Essentially, the entire Area of Operations (AO) is saturated with UNIFIL operations combined with humanitarian activities to instil a sense of confidence among the population. While undertaking these operations, care is taken to ensure that the sensitivity of the local populations is not hurt. Most of these activities are carried out in close coordination with the LAF.

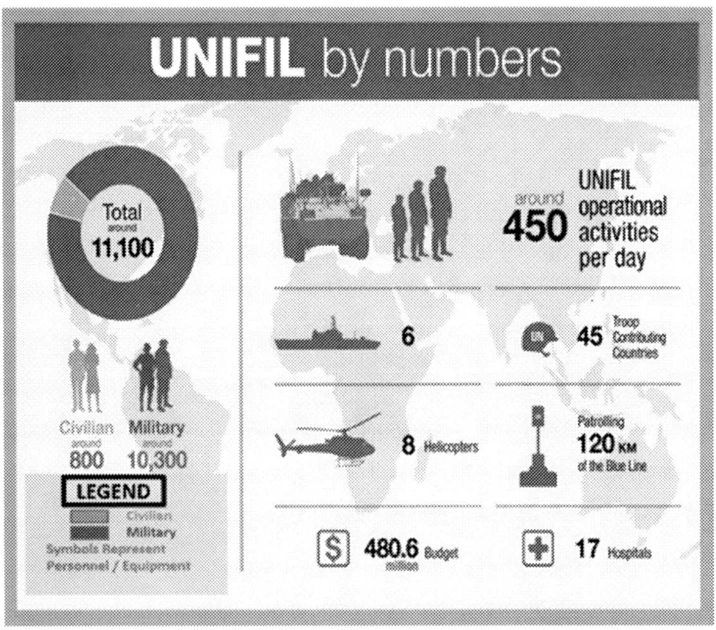

The adjoining infographic of April 2021 provides an impression of UNIFIL's resources and activities. The Area of Maritime Operation (AMO) spans about 110 nautical miles from north to south, and some 43 nautical miles from the Lebanese coastline to its western edge. The Maritime Task Force was deployed at the behest of the Lebanese Government to the UN within the mandate of SCR 1701 in October 2006. Since its deployment, it has supported the Lebanese Navy in monitoring its territorial waters, securing the Lebanese coastline, and preventing the unauthorised entry of arms or related material by sea into Lebanon.[7]

De-mining is another essential activity of UNIFIL, which is a joint venture of the UN Mine Action Coordination Centre in South Lebanon (UNMACC SL) and the LAF (represented by the Lebanon Mine Action Centre and known as LMAC). This set-up was established in 2007, after the withdrawal of the IDF from South Lebanon to clear the contaminated land and remove cluster bombs from the South Lebanese region. Even though the responsibility for clearance operations in South Lebanon has been with LMAC since 31 December 2008, UNMACC continues to coordinate the activities of UNIFIL teams and units of international NGOs, comprising Battle Area Clearance Teams, Explosive Ordinance Disposal (EOD) teams and mechanical de-mining teams. The number of civilian casualties from mine/UXO/cluster munitions, which increased immediately after the 2006 conflict, has gradually decreased as work on the de-mining progressed.

Next to monitoring the cessation of hostilities as well as the prevention of hostile activities, the protection of both UN and civilian personnel and ensuring their freedom of movement, UNIFIL has the role to support the Government of Lebanon. All other security-related tasks are the responsibility of the LAF. Yet, the subject of mandate implementation by UNIFIL continues to be a rallying point, mostly for the parties to the conflict, in their accusation that UNIFIL is not doing enough to implement it. These allegations emerge when there is evidence of Hezbollah arms and ammunition in the area of operations, or when the Israeli Air Force violates Lebanese air space or when some rogue elements start firing rockets from South Lebanon into Israel. Israel also never refrains from criticizing UNIFIL for failing to disarm the Hezbollah, which, however, is not its responsibility. As for the local population of Lebanon, either they are unaware of the provisions of the mandate or they expect too much from UNIFIL in terms of influencing Israel or the international community for the restoration of peace. We will now discuss in more detail what UNIFIL does at the operational level to cope with the various challenges that face it. (Figure 5.1 shows UNIFIL's current deployment as of November 2021.)[8]

Figure 5.1: UNIFIL Area of Operations (As of November 2021)

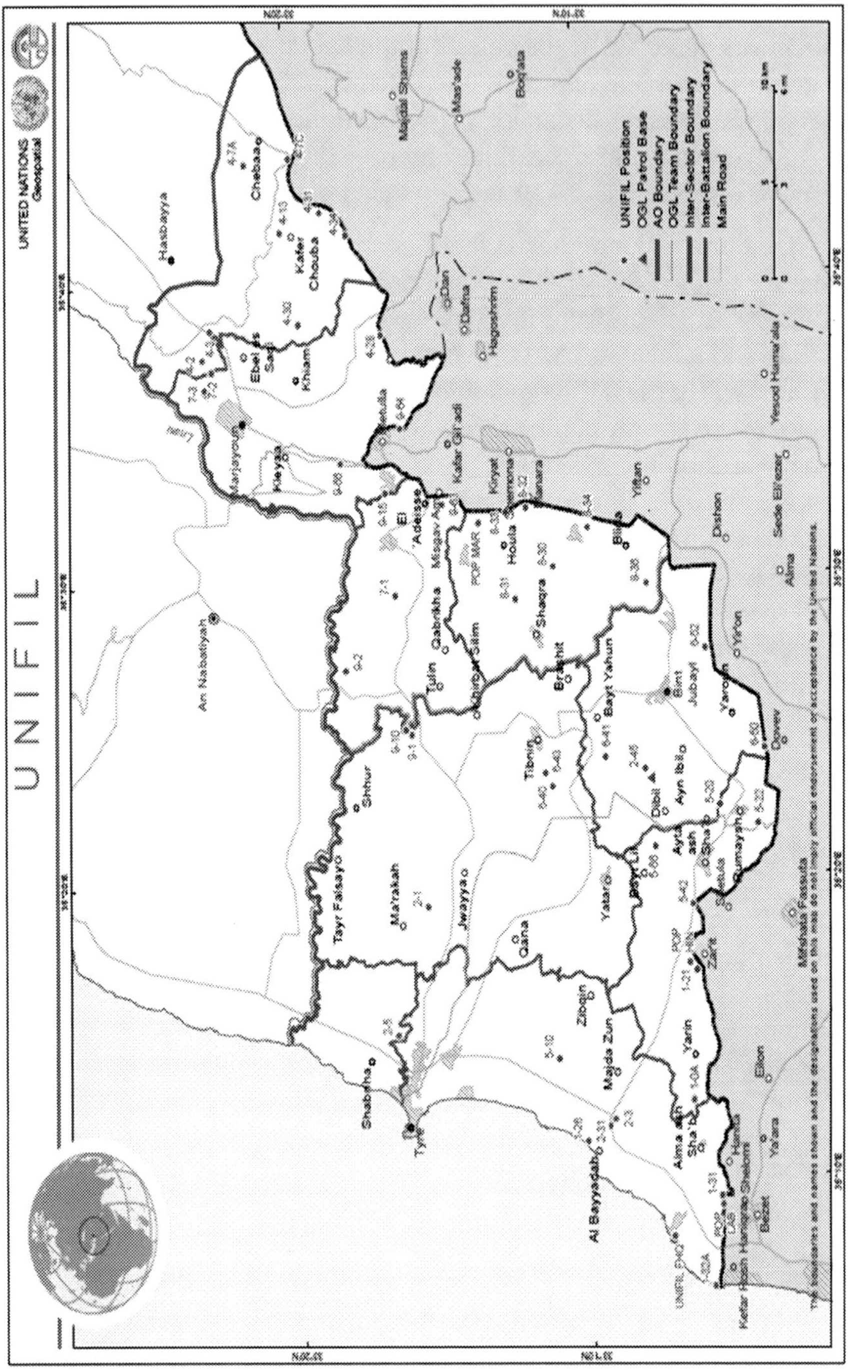

Monitoring the Cessation of Hostilities

The cessation of hostilities, which must precede a permanent ceasefire, is possible when both sides agree to cooperate with the confidence-building measures initiated by UNIFIL. The current absence of war for more than a decade can be attributed to several factors: *firstly,* the gradual assertion of authority by the LAF in South Lebanon; *secondly,* the development of domestic politics in Lebanon; *thirdly,* the changing security dynamics in the region and *finally,* an effective liaison, i.e., a confidence and credibility building mechanism.

A possible resumption of hostilities could occur for several reasons. The main challenge for UNIFIL is to control and de-escalate potentially violent situations arising out of seemingly small and routine incidents. These could vary from BL violations either because of accidental or deliberate land crossings to the firing of a rocket by armed elements from South Lebanon into Israel; hunting by local Lebanese near the BL possibly provoking IDF soldiers on duty; smuggling of arms and other arsenals into South Lebanon; an attack on IDF posts near the BL by Hezbollah operatives; protests by Lebanese near the BL against the Israeli occupation of Palestine; and provocative actions by either side near disputed areas like Ghajar. Even the straying of cattle across the BL from Israel in search of water at times has become a rallying point for Lebanese citizens to stage protests and force UNIFIL to block the entry of animals into Lebanon (see text box). Kneissl stated that the local Lebanese population perceives this as a deliberate attempt by Israel to send trained animals to drink water in Lebanese territory.[9]

> *Towards the extreme eastern side of the UNIFIL's area of operations in the UN positions 4–31 in Shebaa Farms area, there is a pond on the Lebanese side of the BL. During summer, almost every day, there is a stream of unattended cattle that comes from Israel to drink water at this pond. Almost every day, following a beaten path, the cattle cross over to Lebanon through the broken technical fence of the IDF, drink water and return by a different route. UNIFIL tried innovative methods to block the entry of the cattle.*

The violation of Lebanese air space by the Israeli Air Force on an almost daily basis is regarded as a deliberate act of provocation by the Lebanese. Although UNIFIL's role is only to monitor the cessation of hostilities, it takes the extra mile to defuse volatile situations by occupying posts all along the BL, positioning liaison teams in Israel and the HoM/FC constantly engaging the governments of Lebanon and Israel at strategic and operational levels.[10]

Transgressions of the BL

Accidental transgressions of the BL sometimes take place because of a lack of knowledge of the exact alignment of the unmarked BL. It frequently occurs that Lebanese shepherds tend their animals and farmers try to till their land falling on the other side of the BL. One reason for an incorrect understanding of the BL alignment is that there is a technical fence built by Israel that runs almost parallel but at a varying distance to and from the BL, at times by a couple of metres, to the south. The marked portion of the BL is indicated by blue coloured barrels placed at close intervals making it easy to have a clear understanding of the alignment. However, the harsh terrain on the eastern side of Lebanon sometimes makes it difficult to place the barrels at standard intervals. Violations of the BL by farmers, who are generally perceived by Israel as spies of Lebanon, are taken very seriously by UNIFIL to prevent further transgressions.

A quick de-escalation of the situation that may arise because of such transgressions is more important than following agreed protocols. There are times when it is not possible for UNIFIL to directly observe some of the transgression sites because the terrain is not easily accessible or where the marking of the BL has not commenced. In such cases, information about transgressions is communicated by the IDF.

Whenever the persuasion and negotiation techniques of UNIFIL patrols do not work and owners insist on tilling their land across the BL, UNIFIL involves local government officials to intervene on its behalf. UNIFIL's approach to controlling the BL generally works except for the hunting by the locals near the BL, which tends to become a real nuisance. The hunters travel either alone or in pairs in their self-driven vehicles. By the time, the sound of the hunters' gunshots is heard by UNIFIL posts or patrols and is reacted to, the hunters have generally proceeded to the next hunting site. There is, however, no fixed pattern of such violations of the BL. Yet, according to UN reports, from August 2006 to June 2020, there has been a sharp increase in BL violations by Lebanese armed hunters over the last couple of years (Figure 5.2).[11]

Figure 5.2: Number of BL Violations from Lebanese Side

Deliberate Violations and Protests

The occurrence of protestors and armed groups causing confrontations between the LAF and IDF (because of provocation from either side) can be termed as a deliberate violation. Protests generally take place in areas where the Lebanese road is close to the BL and Israel's technical fence. These manifestations are considered serious because of the high possibility of a simple protest going out of control. In an event like this, UNIFIL and LAF work hand in hand, with the latter taking the lead role to maintain a vigil. UNIFIL, representing the international community, acts as deterrence to unruly crowds.

Throwing stones at IDF soldiers on duty, especially in disputed areas on the BL, is another serious violation of the BL. Sheikh Abbad's tomb, which is located near the Lebanese village of Houla, is one such contested spot. Bisected by the BL, this tomb is viewed differently by Lebanon and Israel. Israelis believe that it is the tomb of a fifth-century rabbi, but Lebanese citizens consider it the tomb of a local sheikh. With an IDF post almost overlooking the tomb, Sheikh Abbad hill is a flashpoint on the BL. Lebanese youths regularly visit the hill and throw stones at the IDF posts and at times dangle Hezbollah flags on the technical fence. However, after some strict visitor control measures imposed by the new post of UNIFIL, Sheikh Abbad hill has become completely peaceful. Blandford attributes this drop in the probability of a resumption of violence in such hot spots to the operational activities of UNIFIL.[12]

The firing of rockets by unknown and unorganised armed groups from South Lebanon into Israel inviting instant IDF retaliation is viewed as another deliberate and serious violation of the BL. However, the IDF takes care to see that its retaliatory firing does not kill/damage either innocent people or infrastructure. The moment a rocket is launched, it is either picked up by UNIFIL's sensors or informed by the IDF through the hotline.

Immediately on receipt of the information, the first thing UNIFIL does is to convince the IDF to refrain from retaliation, which however rarely succeeds. It invariably retaliates but warns UNIFIL before commencing firing. Once the firing stops and this has been confirmed by the IDF, UNIFIL investigation and liaison teams positioned in Israel rush to the launch and strike sites for a detailed investigation. Besides, as a precaution and to achieve deterrence, joint patrols of UNIFIL and LAF also regularly patrol and inspect possible rocket launching sites in South Lebanon.

There is, however, no clear evidence of any prominent group responsible for the launching of such rockets. The Hezbollah has claimed responsibility only once for a rocket attack on an Israeli convoy in the Shebaa Farm area as retaliation to an IDF attack on it in Syria in January 2015.[13] The rudimentary nature of such launch systems and the inaccuracy in firing also indicate that such firing incidents are the handiwork of armed groups other than the Hezbollah.

The number of incidents of firing rockets by armed groups other than the Hezbollah from March 2007 to February 2013, i.e., for six years, was 20. While there were 23 incidents from June 2013 to February 2015, there have been only six in 2016.[14] Over the most recent years, the number of these incidents has come close to zero. It is difficult to deduce the exact reasons, but the effectiveness of the LAF and its close operational coordination with UNIFIL can be attributed to the decrease in such incidents (Figure 5.3).[15]

Pointing of weapons at each other by either side (IDF and LAF), which occur regularly and in broad daylight, has the potential to escalate into a full-fledged conflict. However, the frequency of such weapon pointing has also gradually gone down. UNIFIL is, however, straddled with and has not been able to do anything about the regular violation of Lebanese air space by unarmed vehicles (UAVs) and fighter aircraft of the IDF. Its justifies its action of maintaining surveillance on the Hezbollah's activities for the defence of their motherland. Until the beginning of 2020, these violations in the air have occurred frequently, often more than once per day.[16]

BL Marking

As said earlier, most of the incidents of violation of the BL are due to inadequate knowledge of the correct alignment of the BL. Therefore, its marking has become the top priority for UNIFIL. It is a technical and painstaking process, which includes the identification of the exact alignment on the map and coordination between both the LAF and IDF. It is, thereafter, followed up by identifying the exact location on the ground and finally marking the points with blue barrels. The actual marking is a time-consuming process since it depends on many factors such as the type of terrain, level of cooperation from either side to agree to the alignment, and time needed to prepare and lug the barrels to the marking site. Substantial progress has indeed been made since the first barrel was placed on 26 September 2007. As of 9 February 2017, of 527 assessed markers, access to 326 points (because of de-mining) has been cleared; 278 points have been

Figure 5.3: Number of Rocket Launches

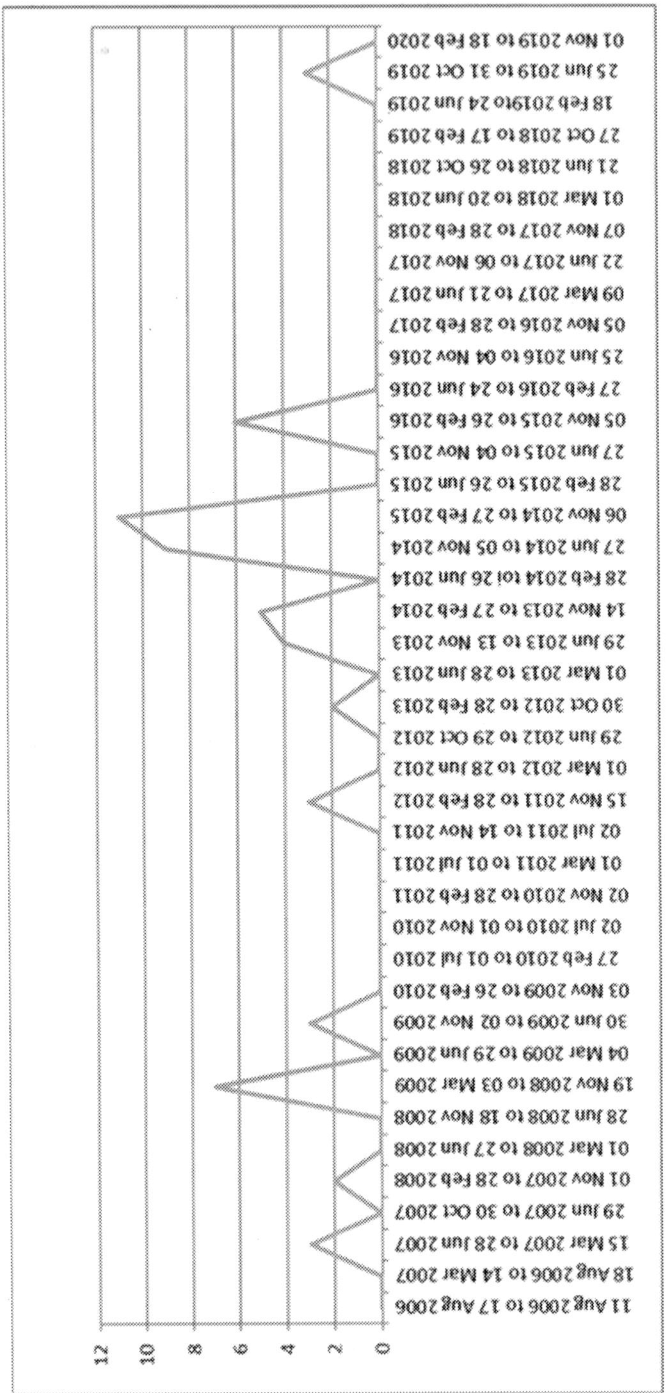

measured; 263 markers have been constructed and 246 others verified.[17] However, the marking of the BL that has been stalled since 2017 pending discussion on 13 technical observations of Lebanon in tripartite meetings has now resumed on 16 November 2021.[18]

Response Mechanism

UNIFIL has a multi-layered response mechanism to mitigate crises, which simultaneously works at all levels and in coordination with its strategic partner—the LAF. Within the organization, it is well coordinated with the civil affairs staff of the political adviser to the HoM/FC. It is generally the civil affairs staff that interfaces with the civilian population when it comes to addressing challenges associated with the local population. This, however, does not prevent the military peacekeepers from directly interacting with the civilian population. On the contrary, it is important and beneficial that such well-coordinated interactions take place regularly at all levels. For the response mechanism to work well, every member of the mission must be aware of the mandate, the operational concept, and the strategic vision to bring back normalcy.

As a result, the first responder to any critical situation, which may occur either near the BL or in the hinterland, is generally a military peacekeeper of the rank of corporal or, at best, a sergeant. The dissemination of information normally follows the channel of command, which implies that information about an incident and the response thereof is rapidly passed to mission HQs. At HQs, they can work out a response strategy in advance, in case this incident could take a political turn at a later stage.

The liaison team of UNIFIL, which works directly under the HoM/FC, is the interface between IDF and UNIFIL, both at the operational and tactical levels. The liaison team (one detachment is positioned in Israel) is the first to be activated the moment there is either a confrontation or a confrontation-like situation. Newby calls it a 'micro security arrangement'. She observed that timely management of the incident is the most nerve-racking. That is where the role of the first responder comes in, which, if not supported by the higher levels, may trigger a major conflict.[19] Newby reported that the liaison and response mechanism and measures applied by UNIFIL under difficult conditions appear to have been able to make an invaluable contribution to the prevention of the outbreak of another war since 2006.[20]

Tripartite meetings are another instrument for conflict management between Israel and Lebanon. These meetings, chaired by the HoM/FC, are held almost once a month at a UNIFIL outpost near Naqura (near UNIFIL HQs) to address and resolve complicated issues. The discussions are about issues that necessitate intervention by senior members of the IDF and LAF, who are given reasonable authority to take decisions to de-escalate delicate situations. This forum is not limited by any specific agendas. All sensitive issues like the unintentional violation of the BL, waterlogging of Lebanese territory as a result of construction work in Israel and ironing out issues that may hinder progress in the marking of the BL can be, and are, in fact, discussed. The UN Secretary-General noted that tripartite meetings are the most stabilizing factor in the framework of SCR 1701 to build confidence between Israel and Lebanon and to defuse tensions in potential flashpoints.[21]

The Presence of Unauthorized Armed Personnel, Assets, and Weapons

This is one of the most controversial mandated tasks. UNIFIL assists the LAF to ensure that the area south of Litani River is free of all armed personnel, assets, and weapons other than those authorized by the Lebanese government and UNIFIL. However, the execution of this task has come under severe criticism because of the presence of unauthorized elements and arms in South Lebanon. There are more than 450,000 Palestinian refugees in different camps in Lebanon. In the south of Lebanon too, there are designated camps for refugees and their entry and exit is strictly controlled by the LAF. In the past decades, innumerable militias and terrorists have been taking shelter in these camps.[22] According to Chararah, al-Qaeda affiliated terrorist groups try to exploit the refugee camps to expand their support base in South Lebanon.[23] What, however, worries Israel more is the presence of the Hezbollah and its arsenals in South Lebanon. So far, however, there have been only 10 known instances of the Hezbollah violating the terms of SCR 1701. Of these, on two occasions, the Hezbollah fired missiles at IDF patrols across the BL and on four, attacked IDF soldiers by exploding IEDs. In response, the IDF responded with fire from both direct and indirect firing weapons.[24] There have been five serious instances of either the presence of unauthorised armed personnel or the Hezbollah's military-like infrastructures in South Lebanon.

In the first incident that took place during the night of 30/31 March 2008, a UNIFIL patrol came across a truck towing a trailer near a village within its area of operation. When the patrol tried to follow it, two cars with five armed elements suddenly arrived on the scene and blocked the road. Though the patrol challenged the armed elements, they did not respond and left after a couple of minutes. The truck and the trailer also moved away and could never be traced. This was a clear violation of the mandate and looked like a transfer of armaments. UNIFIL had all the right to use force to prevent this. However, the quick turn of events probably took the patrol leader by surprise. It was later learnt from reliable sources that the Hezbollah had undertaken this activity.

The second incident took place when a series of explosions took place in a building on 14 July 2009, in the vicinity of village Khirbat Silim, in the UNIFIL area of operations. The explosions were caused by the deflagration of ammunition stored in the building. The building was under the control of the Hezbollah and turned out to be an 'arms and ammunition' depot. It was a clear violation of SCR 1701 (2006). Following the explosion, people known to be affiliated with the Hezbollah removed a substantial quantity of remnants from the site in civilian vehicles to an unknown location. The following day, when the UNIFIL team went to the site for investigation, it was met with stiff public opposition and display of rude behaviour by not granting the patrol access to the explosion site. Some of the civilians even resorted to a physical confrontation resulting in a minor injury to one of the members of the investigating team and the destruction of a UN camera. On 18 July, when the UNIFIL team went for further inspection of the suspicious house in the vicinity of the explosion site, it was subjected to stone-throwing by agitated civilians resulting in injuries to 14 UNIFIL personnel and damage to 18 UNIFIL vehicles.[25] In hindsight, since the explosion was clear evidence of the presence of illegal arms and ammunition south of the Litani River, the peacekeepers trying to force their way through the hostile crowd would have undoubtedly resulted in crossing the red line in the eyes of the Hezbollah. Any attempt to either search for the Hezbollah cache of arms and ammunition or disarm the group when confronted by UNIFIL and the LAF is considered as crossing the red line by the Hezbollah.

The third incident took place on 12 October 2009 in Tayr Falsay, with a residential building caught fire, probably owing to an explosion inside its garage. This house was owned by a local municipal official of the Hezbollah. Unfortunately, even before the arrival of the joint UNIFIL and LAF investigation team, all signs of evidence were removed from the site by unknown persons and reportedly taken to the nearby village of Deir Qanun an-Nahr. A visit to the second site in the village too revealed nothing. Someone had managed to remove the evidence from there as well.[26] In all the three incidents, UNIFIL investigation teams faced a dead end because of the Hezbollah's influence in the government and South Lebanon.

The fourth incident took place on 20 April 2017, when the Hezbollah organised a tour for Lebanese and international media in the UNIFIL area of operation. The LAF informed UNIFIL of the tour just an hour before it started. When a UNIFIL patrol tried to stop the convoy, the LAF intervened and informed UNIFIL that the tour had been cleared by the government. Although there was no evidence of any unauthorised armed personnel, UNIFIL believed that media reports citing unauthorised armed personnel as part of the tour were credible.[27]

When it comes to confronting the Hezbollah, the LAF either feigns ignorance or follows the rule book. It is less because of its lack of military capability and more due to its (political) powerlessness to ensure that there are no unauthorised armed personnel in South Lebanon. It is the LAF that should serve as the locomotive for the security of South Lebanon. However, like the local population, the LAF's tacit acceptance of the Hezbollah as the symbol of resistance against Israel makes it impossible to ensure that South Lebanon is free of unauthorised armed groups.

The fifth incident was between 4 December 2018 and 13 January 2019 when the IDF informed UNIFIL that it had discovered six tunnels across the BL. UNIFIL was able to verify five of them near Kfar Kila village. A technical assessment by UNIFIL confirmed at least two tunnels crossing the BL to the South. Later, on 22 December, UNIFIL and the Observer Group Lebanon (OGL) observed liquid cement seeping out of the premises of a building (formerly a concrete factory and then a poultry farm) in the same village of Kfar Kila around 100 metres from the BL. Local civilians blocked entry to the premises and prevented UNIFIL from undertaking any investigations. Even the LAF supported them stating that it was private property and stipulated that the LAF did not have any jurisdiction over it. On 29 December, UNIFIL confirmed that the factory had an opening to a tunnel that crossed the BL.[28] An investigation by Lebanese authorities of all such incidents, even if a clear violation of SCR 1701 is apparent, is never conclusive (except for the basic formality of filing a report by UNIFIL to the Secretary-General and by the Secretary-General to the Security Council.

The lack of reports of any serious incident related to unauthorised armed personnel or the Hezbollah's military-like infrastructures in South Lebanon for a long period from July 2009 to March 2017, however, does not imply that the Hezbollah is absent from South Lebanon, as demonstrated by several incidents. The first incident was encountered by UNIFIL during patrolling. The second and third incidents were discovered by accident. A fifth one was also an accidental discovery and was notified by the IDF. The fourth incident of 20 April 2017, however, was a blatant display of the Hezbollah's influence in South Lebanon.

While all the five incidents were verified by UNIFIL, there were other incidents, which were either suspected by UNIFIL or notified by the IDF but could not be verified by UNIFIL. Besides, such incidents do not take place only from the Lebanon side. The discovery of tunnels on 4 December 2018 and 13 January 2019 by the IDF could not have been by chance. Being conscious of the Hezbollah's tunnel construction effort, the IDF is always on the lookout for such activities. In December 2018, the IDF entered a tunnel from the Israeli side. During Operation Northern Shield, Brigadier General Rafi Milo, the Galilee Division Commander, along with a select group, entered a tunnel, and crossed over to Lebanon. Israel will always justify such action as defensive just as the violation of Lebanese airspace by Israeli aircraft. However, this is also a violation of the BL. If the IDF team had been detected and kidnapped or killed, the temporary state of calm between Israel and Lebanon would have vanished immediately in the Middle East. UNIFIL was not informed by the IDF about this.[29]

Besides, there were three incidents in 2018 wherein the Hezbollah publicly displayed its alliance with Iran, its mentor, near the BL. On 28 January 2018, a senior Iranian military officer, Ebrahim Raisi, visited the UNIFIL area of operation.[30] Later, in early December, there was video footage of Qais-al-Khazali of the Iraqi Shi'ite militia Asa'ib Ahl al-Haq, visiting South Lebanon in military uniform in the company of a Hezbollah representative. Again, on 26 December, a photo of Haz Hamza, the commander of an Aleppo-based pro-Syrian government militia, the Imam al-Baqir Brigade, standing near the BL appeared on social media.[31] These incidents were a clear and outright display of the Hezbollah's power in South Lebanon and a public display of its alliance with its mentors.

The Hezbollah's role in Lebanese politics and influence in the government was reinforced by the Lebanese government's policy statement of as early as 2 December 2009, which reads as follows: *"It is the right of the Lebanese people, Army and the (Hezbollah-led) Resistance to liberate the Shebaa Farms, the Kfar Shuba Hills and the northern part of the village of Ghajar as well as to defend Lebanon and its territorial waters in the face of any enemy by all available and legal means"*. Therefore, when it comes to disarming the

Hezbollah, the matter is controversial at the highest political level and a no-go even for the LAF.

According to Sayyed Hassan Nasrallah, Hezbollah's Secretary-General stated in an interview on TV on 27 August 2006 that there was a commitment on the Hezbollah's part to avoid armed manifestations in South Lebanon. Therefore, if the Lebanese army finds any person carrying a weapon on a road or in a town, the army's natural right and duty is to confiscate it and apply the law of the land on that person. However, at the same time, he also contradicted his statement by stating that it was not the task of the Lebanese army to disarm resistance or spy on its weapons or plans.[32] Naturally, any attempt to strengthen the LAF and expect it to fight the Hezbollah will fail. Therefore, the Hezbollah's lack of visibility in South Lebanon can be interpreted more as its indirect cooperation for the PKO to succeed and less due to the LAF succeeding and ensuring (with assistance from UNIFIL) the freeing of South Lebanon of unauthorised arms and weapons.

Assistance to the LAF in South Lebanon

The LAF's support is crucial to implement the mandate of UNSCR 1701 (2006), and the Security Council has identified UNIFIL-LAF cooperation as being at the heart of the implementation of the mandate. As a strategic partner, a strong LAF is bound to have a positive and direct influence on UNIFIL's operational activities. The biggest achievement in this regard is that today, the LAF is deployed in South Lebanon, albeit not in full strength, and operating in close cooperation with UNIFIL.

According to the International Centre for Defence and Security (ICDS), the LAF is constrained by its involvement in fighting many terrorist groups inside Lebanon, whereas its attention is more focused on the north and east of the country to ensure the integrity of the Lebanese-Syrian border. In the ICDS report, Lawrence, Jermalavicius, and Bulakh described the southern region of Lebanon as a calm and resting place for the LAF.[33] Paradoxically, the LAF's inability to fully deploy or commit more troops in South Lebanon hinders the scope and the number of its operational activities in UNIFIL's area of operations as well as in Lebanese territorial waters. This in turn impedes UNIFIL's efforts to gradually hand over the security responsibility of the area of operations and maritime entry points to the LAF in the future. Much as the LAF would like to take on the full responsibility of the security of Lebanon, currently, it lacks that capability. Moreover, the unique architecture of Lebanon's internal security has stretched the LAF to its outer limit. The LAF, therefore, has to be content with UNIFIL's efforts to broker peace in the years' long conflict between Israel and Lebanon.

The LAF's deployment in South Lebanon would mean exercising its authority in its area of deployment. It would, therefore, necessitate building its capability not only in troop strength but also in equipment and training. While making available the required strength is the responsibility of the Government of Lebanon (with support of the international community), the best support that UNIFIL could provide is by sharing its operational expertise during joint training. One of the missions of the LAF is "cooperation and coordination" with UNIFIL to implement Resolution 1701. This includes dealing with Israeli violations and performing joint military manoeuvres to raise the level of preparedness and readiness to face any emergency".[34]

Ensuring the Area of Operations is free of Hostile Activities

One of the reasons cited in the Report of the Panel (2002) for the Failure of UN Peacekeeping Missions, in general, is the vague and unclear mandate. Post-2000, mandates of the PKO, therefore, have become clearer. To this end, paragraph 12 of UNSCR 1701 (2006) makes it explicit that it "authorises UNIFIL to take all necessary action in areas of deployment of its forces and as it deems within its capabilities, to ensure that its area of operations is not utilized for hostile activities of any kind".

> *Taking action against hostile activities imply, among others, having a clear understanding of the definition 'hostile act', having a well-trained and well-equipped peacekeeping force with rapid deployment capability to respond immediately and having a clear set of robust RoE. These three elements are intractably connected. Ambiguity in the definition or lack of understanding of any of the three elements could result in mission paralysis. Improving this should be an ambition for UNIFIL.*

A controversy arose when it came to define "hostile acts" or "hostile intent". According to Kneissl, both Israel and Lebanon had different interpretations but finally agreed to interpretation on a case-by-case approach.[35] For instance, can the incident described earlier during the night of 30/31 March 2008—when a UNIFIL patrol detected and wanted to follow a truck with a trailer, but was prevented from doing so by five armed people—be considered a hostile act?[36] Yukin considered such acts as a demonstration of "UNIFIL's inability to use force effectively despite its rules of engagement allowing it to do so when facing violations of its mandate".[37] However, since the armed elements only blocked the UNIFIL patrol and did not threaten it, their hostile intent is open to debate. Similarly, can the regular violation of Lebanese air space by IDF fighter aircraft be interpreted as hostile intent? Such ambiguity in the interpretation of the meaning of 'hostile act' results in inaction by UNIFIL and is labelled as a failure for not being able to implement the mandate.

Force Structure and Rules of Engagement

UNIFIL is often referred to as a robust mission. Military contingents from a few European nations have been deployed with their heavy armaments and equipment, which one is not likely to be found in traditional PKO. Also, around half of the military contingents come from non-Western nations. While most of the European contingents operate along the lines of the NATO doctrine and tactics, there is no such similarity in the modus operandi of non-Western national contingents. If at all, there is a huge diversity within the contingents of the non-Western nations and also within all the contingents of UNIFIL. The complexity of the differences amongst the military has been elaborated by Elron in one of her articles on the subject.[38]

First and foremost, the professional and national pride of each contingent, including their reluctance to submit to the command of a different nationality, plays a role. Each national contingent also maintains dual lines of command owing to suspicion of each other's motives. Every aspect of mission activity is reported through national channels. On important operational matters, where either the interests of the nation or the security of the troops is likely to be affected, the national defence authorities promptly intervene through their permanent missions. Going by the poor track record of the UN in providing security to the peacekeepers against attacks by rogue adversaries, most of the European TCCs have set up their parallel intelligence channels, albeit unofficially.

Another complexity is the dividing line created by differences in power and wealth. Elron frames this as 'Developed/Developing' and 'First/Third World' categories. This in turn may lead to tensions amongst the peacekeepers.[39] One of the unique features of UNIFIL is that it is one of the PKO where partnership arrangements amongst the contingents of a few countries exist. Such arrangements may include a division of labour, bilateral

> *Relations between national contingents can be affected by ethnic, religious, cultural, institutional, and political factors. The diversity in national culture does influence the way the force is structured, the functioning of the HQ as well as the modus operandi of the contingents. I observed that the feeling of being second-grade militaries affected the operational efficiency of a few non-NATO military contingents. In addition, despite being well trained, different operating procedures posed major challenges for contingents from India, Ghana and Nepal to adapt to the operational orders and Standing Operating Procedures (SOPs) from the sector HQs which were commanded and dominated by the Italian and Spanish peacekeepers. At the same time, cultural and regional affinities helped achieve better operational interoperability between Indian, Indonesian, and Nepalese contingents. On the other hand, contingents from the TCCs of the NATO are, highly influenced by their experiences in Afghanistan. Their national RoE, which are generally force protection-centric, inhibited the peacekeepers from interacting with the local population. In contrast, Indian contingents sparingly use their Armoured Personnel Carriers with due caution to avoid being aggressive.*

command and control mechanism or, for that matter, a generally bigger and capable TCC taking on the responsibility to equip the smaller TCC with major equipment.

While such arrangements provide good interoperability and cooperation amongst different contingents, it comes with its share of problems. Normally, contingents that are part of the same partnership program are generally located as one operational unit. However, at times, there may be an operational necessity to break such a composition and employ these contingents separately, which is generally met with stiff resistance. UNIFIL has a distinct advantage over some of the contemporary complex peace operations in terms of infrastructures, other allied facilities, and road communications networks. However, some areas of the eastern sector of the UNIFIL area of operation are still relatively inaccessible. As a result, once established in their bases, contingents that are deployed in the western sector are hesitant to move out of their comfort zone to the eastern sector even if such moves are needed for operational reasons and are of short duration.

As noted many times earlier, organised on the lines of a NATO force, the present structure of UNIFIL is the only peacekeeping operation to employ medium tanks and artillery, which makes it the most heavily armed PKO of this size in the world. Also, it has a QRF based on main battle tanks, a military helicopter unit and a Maritime Task Force—the first of its kind in a PKO.

Yet, despite being a robust force, UNIFIL has always been blamed for its failure in either disarming the Hezbollah in confrontational situations or preventing its supporters from obstructing UNIFIL in implementing the mandate. Yukin noted that it was futile for even such a robust force to hope to disarm the Hezbollah, as it was not an option.[40] Therefore, disarming or even an attempt at disarming the Hezbollah would invite the wrath of the local population and displeasure of the Lebanese government of which, the Hezbollah is an integral part. It has also been stated that the presence of the Hezbollah in South Lebanon is well known and disarming it by UNIFIL with or without the support of the LAF would only end in the mission's failure even before it would have begun.[41]

An example of the Hezbollah's actual power play manifested in the form of public anger by a small group of civilians and the inability of the LAF to firmly deal with a flash mob that had blocked UNIFIL from going near the explosion site in Khirbat Silim on 15 July 2009 and subsequently to the second suspected location on 18 July 2009.

The MTF is another unique component of UNIFIL. Since its activation on 15 October 2006, it continues to detect and hail vessels and inspect those that were classified as "suspect". The MTF has been able to carry out its primary mandate, as requested in the Lebanese Prime Minister's letter, by working closely with the LAF and Navy. The LAF-Navy's capability has been constantly improving over the last three years to the point where its personnel and naval assets have become close partners in the conduct of MTF operational activities. As the LAF-Navy's capabilities have increased, they have taken on an increasing role in planning and conducting training with the UNIFIL MTF providing an oversight and evaluation role. To a considerable extent, this has been possible because of their training.

Assuming that the Lebanese authorities are sincerely implementing Security Council Resolution SCR 1701, the absence of evidence of smuggled arms into Lebanese ports signifies that the MTF's presence and Lebanese inspections of suspicious vessels has had a strong deterring effect.

However, the LAF-Navy has still not developed a capability to maintain a sustained presence in the outer areas of the area of operations. Additional maritime vessels capable of staying at sea for prolonged periods, even during unfavourable weather and sea conditions, are urgently required by the LAF-Navy. This lack of capacity has a direct impact on determining a timeline for the future transfer of responsibilities from UNIFIL to the LAF-Navy. Another limitation affecting the impact of training by UNIFIL's MTF is the regular rotation of LAF-Navy personnel. In the LAF, there are no dedicated naval personnel. On numerous occasions, LAF-Navy personnel trained by MTF have been temporarily assigned roles that are otherwise primarily meant for army personnel. As a result, the LAF-Navy has not been able to derive the full benefit of the training imparted by MTF. The LAF-Navy remains severely restricted by its lack of adequate vessels.

The next related issue relates to the RoE, which is formulated by the mission and approved by UN HQ. Israel hoped and expected the UN to give more teeth to UNIFIL with a robust RoE to help the LAF to be deployed in South Lebanon and UNIFIL to open fire on the Hezbollah when needed. For instance, for situations in which the Hezbollah would launch rockets into into Israel, it (Israel) hoped that the UN Secretary-General would give clear authorization to UNIFIL to open fire. According to Keinon, "this is to date the most explicit expression of the upgrade to the UNIFIL force that has yet been received".[42] This was more because UNIFIL, after 2006, was well armed and equipped. Therefore, it was even more surprising that in a series of incidents UNIFIL did not intervene when confronting armed elements. This put a question mark on its willingness or ability to implement the mandate. There could be many reasons for this.

> *RoE are generic by necessity since no two situations can be similar where an approved RoE can be used as a template. Therefore, it is the commander on the spot who has to take a call on how to interpret the RoE. Invariably, it is the directive from the national government of the contingent that influences the commander's decision on application of the RoE. Using the RoE is not simply applying a mathematical formula. On the contrary, it is the wisdom to use force for a just reason depending on the way the situation develops.*

Nations participate in peace operations primarily because of their national interests. Using force to implement the mandate will be responded to with violent means, which may, in turn, result in casualties of their peacekeepers. This is a chance that TCCs do not easily want to take. A robust structure of the peacekeeping force, therefore, is more for their protection and less for implementing the mandate. In Lebanon, given the type of population support for the Hezbollah, most of the TCCs believe that the costs of alienating such a support base far outweigh that of disarming a few unauthorised armed elements, which primarily is the responsibility of the LAF.

Another incident that demonstrated UNIFIL's lack of willingness to maintain an assertive posture was the incident of 12 May 2008 in South Eastern Lebanon. During a routine patrol, a UNIFIL team came across some suspiciously looking cables in a construction site. When UNIFIL took photographs of the cables, they were confronted by the local people, presumably Hezbollah supporters, who pelted stones and snatched their cameras.[43] It was certainly a violation of UNSCR 1701 and obstruction to the freedom of movement of UNIFIL. This was like the earlier mentioned incident of Khirbat Silim on 14 July 2009 wherein an ammunition dump belonging to the Hezbollah had caught fire and the local Lebanese population prevented a UNIFIL investigation team from carrying out its work.[44]

Yukin reported that UNIFIL's inability to use force despite being heavily armed and having the requisite RoE is probably because of the Hezbollah's strong support base in South Lebanon and the fear of losing the trust of the common people. Moreover, with the Hezbollah being well entrenched in Lebanese politics, the cost of the resultant animosity with the Hezbollah would not be worth the effort.

As stated above, RoE is a set of rules specifying the general circumstances for use of force. However, since no two situations can be similar, the rules ought to be generic leaving their interpretation to the commander on the spot on a case-by-case basis. Commenting on UNIFIL's operations, Yukin mentioned, "Unclear rules of engagement and an unclear chain of command is another problem that continues to plague UNIFIL operations."[45] His observations are not limited to UNIFIL alone. As put forward by Findlay, the chief concern of the commanders in UN peace missions has been not to exacerbate the situation and to prevent losing the consent of the parties to the conflict at the tactical, operational, and strategic levels. They fear that this would create the risk of hostilities getting out of control again. Instances of use of force are quoted more for not using it than using it.[46]

In a study of four contingents from different nations in UNIFIL, Ruffa concluded that within the same mission, four different contingents interpreted the rules differently. The Ghanaian unit would use force in self-defence and protect civilians as well as other UNIFIL personnel against the Hezbollah and Israel. The Korean contingent would use force against the

Hezbollah only in defence of Korean soldiers. Even though not clear, the Italian contingent stated that like the Koreans, they too would use force only in defence of Italian soldiers against the Hezbollah. On the other hand, the understanding of the French contingent was limited to the use of force only in the context of the Hezbollah and the IDF. It was, however, not clear from the answer of the French contingent if the use of force against the Hezbollah and IDF was allowed in defence of only French soldiers or other peacekeepers as well. Even though there were different views, the use of force in self-defence was the common line that cut across all four contingents. However, none of the contingents mentioned anything about the use of force to implement the mandate.[47] It is difficult to know the exact national positions of the respective contingents. However, based on the personal experience of the researcher, barring a few, most of the contingents will use force only for their protection and not for either defence of the mandate or the protection of civilians.

Ensuring Freedom of Movement

Denying freedom of movement includes preventing either the peacekeepers or other civilian staff of UNIFIL from moving around freely in the AO. UNIFIL terms these situations as "unfriendly behaviour vis-à-vis UNIFIL peace-keepers". Ensuring freedom of movement to UNIFIL is the responsibility of the Government of Lebanon and the LAF. There is, however, no set pattern or frequency of incidents of the denial of freedom of movement. Nor is there any major incident of denying freedom of movement for a protracted period except in the case of the explosion of the arms depot on 14 July 2009 and the discovery of the Hezbollah's tunnel construction factory on 26 December 2018. However, incidents of unfriendly behaviour do occur in spurts and are generally triggered by either an intentional act or, most of the time, unintentionally hurting the sensitivity of the local population. Since

> *Villagers do not like UNIFIL patrols trespassing through the narrow roads of their villages and damaging their property, hence, they sometimes attempt to prevent their movement by placing stones on the patrol routes. But when the patrol insists on moving on that route, a crowd immediately gathers to protest and at times resorts to pelting stones at them. The denial of freedom of movement or unfriendly behaviour also depends on the way the peace-keepers operate. High-speed driving by armoured vehicles through the narrow roads/lanes of the villages by fully attired (in battle dress and weapons ready to use) peacekeepers is perceived as arrogance by the locals.*

2017, there has been, however, an increase in the number of incidents of obstruction to UNIFIL's freedom of movement (Figure 5.4).[48] As noted earlier, suspicious of passing intelligence to Israel, the Lebanese are averse to UNIFIL taking photographs in South Lebanon and at times have forcibly snatched photographic equipment from UNIFIL patrols. On receipt information of such incidents, the LAF intervenes to resolve such issues.

The battle profile of the peacekeepers and their operating patterns vary from contingent to contingent depending on the way they perceive the threat which, in turn, influences the perception of the local population. Normally, peacekeepers from Western nations are better equipped and lay higher priority on force protection. From her study of perceptions and behaviour of peacekeepers in Lebanon, Ruffa pointed out two different styles of behaviour. She concluded that "the French and the Korean contingents seem to be more 'deterrence oriented,' while the Italian and Ghanaian are 'more humanitarian oriented".[49] During the period from August 2006 to February 2020, there has been a total of 216 incidents of unfriendly behaviour towards UNIFIL peacekeepers.[50] The frequency of acts of unfriendly behaviour towards UNIFIL, which is as low as one per month for the same period, is an indication of UNIFIL's establishing credibility and local legitimacy in Lebanese society. At the same time, a similar conclusion can be drawn from only two incidents of denial of freedom of movement to UNIFIL for a protracted period. It just so happened that by not being able to discover the Hezbollah's infrastructure, UNIFIL did not cross the red line of the Hezbollah. Therefore, such acceptance should not be taken for granted and needs to be carefully nurtured by continuously forging a good relationship with the local populace.

Population and Perception

> *In the final reckoning, it boils down to the general attitude of the peacekeepers while interacting with the Lebanese in the course of the mandated tasks. Therefore, respect for and understanding of the local culture and tradition must be a major element during the pre-mission training of peacekeepers.*

To accomplish their mandate, peacekeepers have to mingle with the local population of the host country and, hence, they have to behave properly with the them. With specific reference to UNIFIL, Rubinstein emphasized the need for a good relationship with the local population.[51] Even though a peacekeeping force such as UNIFIL is deployed only after the consent of the host government,

Figure 5.4 Number of Unfriendly Behaviour with UNIFIL TPS

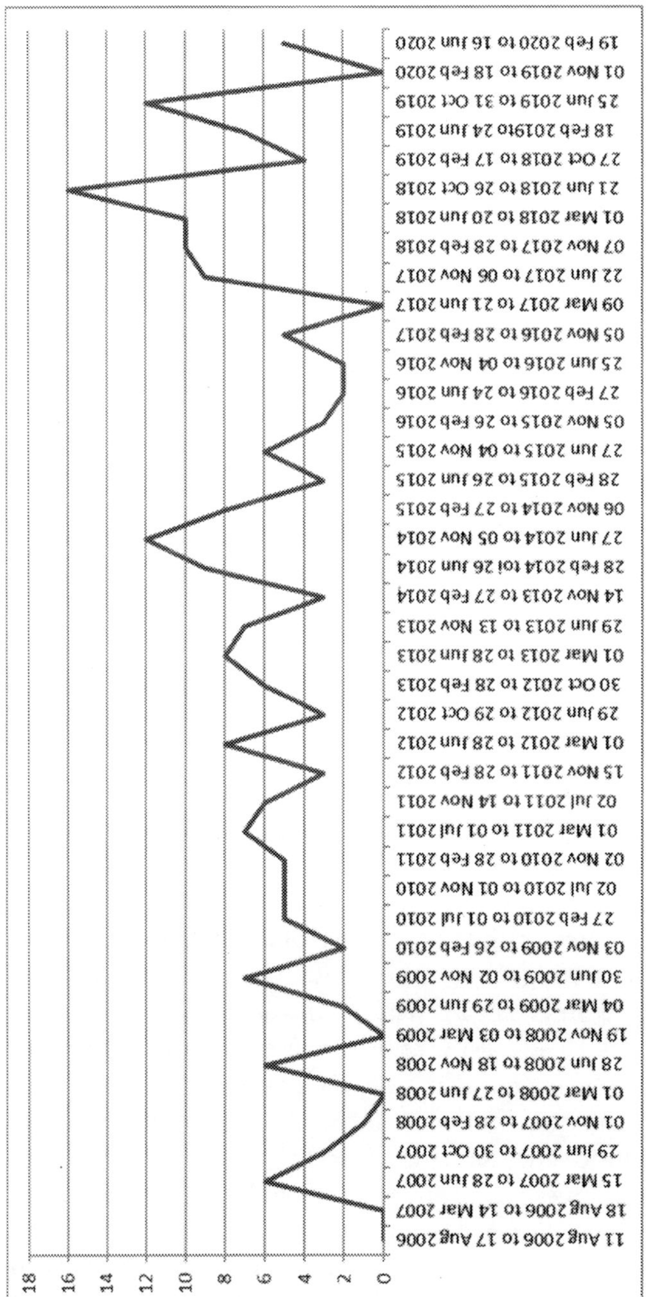

peacekeepers are often seen as 'outsiders' and are not always welcome. This is because the host-national population is unfamiliar with the new situation and often tends to be prejudiced. What is more, aberrations in the behaviour of peacekeepers tend to render the local population resentful against them. In social psychology, prejudice is typically defined as a negative evaluation of an entire social group.[52] The theory suggests that prejudice results from the perception that the members of a group pose a threat to another group. Applying this theory, it is normal for the local Lebanese to look at the 'outsiders' with suspicion until they prove themselves worthy of acceptance by them. As aptly put by a Brigadier General of the LAF during his interaction with a delegation of DPO at LAF HQ on 10 December 2009, "The face of Lebanon, which is the popular support base for the Hezbollah, has changed from warmongers to a respectable society since the war of 2006. And the population wants everyone to see them this way and not be pushed around with a show of big military display".[53]

UNIFIL always tries to influence such a perception by reaching out to the public with a good code of conduct and by extending a helping hand in various developmental projects, the so-called QUIP.[54] Howard mentioned that QUIP, which is one type of inducement that peacekeepers use to exercise power over the population, is "geared towards improving local relations between peacekeepers and civilians in the communities they serve."[55] This concept was first tried out by the UN Missions in Ethiopia and Eretria (UNMEE) and found success.[56] QUIPs are one of the many tools used for Civil-Military Cooperation (CIMIC). Knight reported that CIMIC and human security are related but the definition of this relationship varies according to the main actors of the concept, i.e., the military and the civilians. It is designed to support the achievement of military goals. In the conflict zone, it entails protecting the local population and individuals working with the civilian humanitarian agencies.[57] In the context of a peace operation, Conning described CIMIC as the security and developmental interface in the link between military and civilian components.[58] Knight further narrowed the definition as "CIMIC can be considered as an operational tool that can advance human security."[59] In UNIFIL, contingents spend their national resources for CIMIC, which entails the same activities as the QUIP with the only difference that the QUIP relies on UN funding and CIMIC activities are based on national funding. The kind of CIMIC activities varies from contingent to contingent depending on how much priority is given to CIMIC. For instance, CIMIC is a high priority for the Korean contingent in the UNIFIL mission. Ruffa observed that there are also contingents that do not have the luxury of national funding for CIMIC activities. Such contingents use innovative ways to extend a helping hand by, for instance, providing veterinary care to the animals of the local population. On the other hand, contingents from wealthier nations indulge more in resource incentive projects, such as solar lights.[60]

Newby however is of the opinion that the local population has understood the limitations of UNIFIL whose presence in Lebanon is temporary and therefore, any sign or semblance of peace is not real peace but only a *feeling of peace*. She carefully observed UNIFIL for many years and interacted with the local community, as well as with international peacekeepers and Lebanese civilians working with UNIFIL. Using the prism of credibility and legitimacy (one of the basic conditions for successful peace operations), i.e., how much or what kind of credibility has been earned by the mission and if the mission has earned legitimacy in the area of operation, Newby concluded that UNIFIL cannot restore peace.

She observed that a peace operation gets credibility by demonstrating its ability to rise to the expectations of the local population. Credibility, however, is not available upfront. It must be earned and supported by evidence over a period. This comes along with its local legitimacy. Local legitimacy is different from strategic legitimacy, which is obtained by the approval of the peace operation by the Security Council. Simply put, it is the acceptance of the peace operation at the grassroots level in the area of operation. When there is the presence of local legitimacy, even if it is not a hundred per cent, freedom of movement of the peacekeepers to undertake their basic mandated activities will be relatively easier than when there is no local legitimacy at all. Because of its strong relationship with trust, local legitimacy helps peacekeepers to win it and thereby implement the mandate.[61]

In the context of UNIFIL, the range of activities to earn credibility in peace operations can include anything and everything, such as quick response to security incidents along the BL, assistance to LAF to build its capability so that it can assume its primary responsibility of security in South Lebanon, financial assistance to local municipalities for developmental work or, for that matter, providing the services of UNIFIL to remove mistrust between the LAF and IDF. All this will help UNIFIL to improve its credibility. Newby concluded that post-2006, by demonstrating credibility and achieving local legitimacy, UNIFIL so far has been able to take control of the potential triggers of violence and prevent escalation of the conflict.

UNIFIL therefore has been acting as a security buffer between Lebanon and Israel.

Security of UN Personnel and Humanitarian Workers

The host government is primarily responsible for the security and protection of UN peacekeeping personnel and assets. It is the host government's responsibility to maintain law and order, and protect persons and property within its jurisdiction including the special privileges and immunity enjoyed by the UN in international crises as per UN Article 109 of the Charter.[62] In this connection, the UN gets into a Status of Forces Agreement (SOFA) with the host government outlining the details of privileges and responsibility for the provision of security. However, in a crisis, not all the elements in the country will be in the control of the government and despite its best efforts, it would not always be possible for the host government to ensure proper protection to UN personnel. Further, peacekeepers continue to be targets of violence. It, therefore, becomes the responsibility of the PKO to ensure the protection and security of its personnel. This includes both military and civilian staff.

For the military, this is relatively easy and based on a SOP issued by mission HQs. 'Force Protection' measures are both active and passive such as mobile patrolling (aerial, vehicle-mounted and on foot) and the defence of the contingent base. Military peacekeepers in UNIFIL have also become targets of violence, even though there have been only five such major incidents post the 2006 war. This low rate can be attributed to a combination of factors such as the adoption of effective force protection measures and a general decline of violence because of the growing effectiveness of the LAF in South Lebanon.

The biggest attack post-2006 was on a Spanish APC on 24 June 2007, killing six peacekeepers when a bomb exploded under it. The next attack took place in January 2008, when a roadside bomb targeted a UN vehicle in South Lebanon, slightly wounding two peacekeepers. The third attack took place on 27 May 2011 leading to the injuring of six Italian peacekeepers when a bomb targeting their vehicle exploded on the highway leading to the South Lebanon coastal city of Sidon. The fourth incident took place on 26 July 2011 when a bomb blast on a UNIFIL logistic convoy injured six French peacekeepers. The fifth incident took place on 9 December 2011, when another bomb blast injured five French peacekeepers and two Lebanese civilians.[63] Since then, there were no more such attacks on peacekeepers. The Lebanese security forces being able to exercise better control on the internal security situation of the country as well as UNIFIL peacekeepers finding acceptability in Lebanese society could be probable reasons for the improvement in the situation.

The real problem, however, is the security of the civilian peacekeepers. Providing security is the responsibility of the host nation, based on the SOFA and the Status of Mission Agreement (SOMA). At the same time, it very much remains the responsibility of the UN to provide security to its civilian staff members so that they can perform their duties in line with the execution of the mandate. The UN Security Management System (UNSMS) is designed to enable the delivery of UN projects and programs by ensuring a safe working environment for UN staff who deliver these programs. As per the policies developed and promulgated by the UN Department of Safety and Security (UNDSS), UNIFIL security staff follow an analytical process (in close coordination with the military staff) to identify the risk level in the area of operations. Security cover is accordingly provided to civilian staff at the UN premises, facilities, road movements, etc.[64] The UNIFIL HoM/FC, who is also the Designated Official (DO), is responsible for the safety and security of the UN civilian staff in the area south of the Litani River. Despite the challenges in providing security to the civilian staff, so far, there has not been any incident of threat or perceived threat to their lives. This is probably because of the strict adherence to the security protocol, the cooperation by all members of the mission, the civilian staff being perceived as harmless, as well as the level of acceptance of UNIFIL in Lebanon.

UNIFIL and Conflict Containment

Deployed in a land of contradictions and political complexities, UNIFIL faces unique challenges that are unlike the tasks that other PKO have. After its initial withdrawal from half of the occupied territory by April 1978, the IDF handed over the area to Major Hadad's militia instead of UNIFIL. Although UNIFIL took over the positions/checkpoints to prevent infiltration by any armed group, it could never function properly since neither the PLO nor Major Hadad cooperated. Major Saad Hadad, who was a deserter of the Lebanese National Army, was the commander of the *de facto forces* in South Lebanon. This *de facto force* comprised mainly Christian militias and had been trained and armed by Israel. In essence, even though IDF finally withdrew from Lebanon by June 1978, it continued to control South Lebanon by its proxy—the *de facto force*. Major Hadad's force never cooperated with

UNIFIL. On the contrary, its activities became a kind of harassment to UNIFIL's operations in South Lebanon.[65] For UNIFIL, it was something like operating within Israeli-occupied territory and hence almost amounted to recognition of the IDF's legitimate right over South Lebanon as an occupation army. On the other hand, it also gave a reason for the Lebanese to resist. Sitkowski observed that UNIFIL was sidelined by Hadad's force from the very beginning. He further noted that since it violated its mandate, UNIFIL was as good as a spent force. After the Israeli *Operation Peace for Galilee* against the Palestinians in Lebanon in 1982, the Hezbollah, which already existed, came on stage. It became more active and attacked all Israelis and civilians whenever there was an opportunity. Given its strong fundamentalist position, the Hezbollah's relations with Hadad could not have been anything other than bad.[66]

After the 2006 war, the dynamics in the relationship between Israel and Lebanon changed slightly. The IDF continued to intrude into Lebanese air space with its fighter aircraft and the Hezbollah continued its unauthorised activities completely unchecked. Yet, from 2006 until now, it is the longest period of history during which there has not been any major conflict between Lebanon and Israel. Sobleman observed that the mutual deterrence between the Hezbollah and Israel has also prevented the recurrence of another major conflict. According to him, to achieve a state of mutual deterrence, both sides framed their rules of the game and conveyed them to each other.[67] For instance, the Hezbollah's Secretary-General, Nasrallah, has always maintained a position that "We do not want war. Our strategy as resistance is not an open war. That is well known".[68] With this communication, Nasrallah managed to convince Israel not to use its strategic assets like the air force and artillery and limit the conflict. Israel's acceptance of these rules is probably to save its citizens residing near the BL. Nasrallah, however, stated that the rules of the game are a function of deterrence and based on how it is communicated and the way it is perceived. At the same time, communications can fail, and an all-out war could still break out like it did in 2006. The presence of mutual deterrence is evident from statements of the IDF's Northern Command Chief, Gadi Eisenkot, in November 2010 and subsequently by his successor, Yair Golan, late in 2014. Both spoke of the presence of a sort of mutual deterrence between the Hezbollah and Israel.[69] Sobelman noted that the Hezbollah was more vocal in accepting mutual deterrence. According to him, "Nasrallah claimed in early 2016 that it was the Hezbollah that was preventing the outbreak of another war."[70]

At the same time, the quick responses of UNIFIL to take control of hot spots that have the potential to trigger a major conflict have a major role in the current state of peace and tranquillity in South Lebanon.[71] Therefore, the credit for the absence of war in Lebanon must go to all the stakeholders, including UNIFIL, who make it happen. Despite infrequent interruptions in its operational activities, such as obstructions to the freedom of movement, UNIFIL has found a better acceptance by Lebanese society. Having made substantial progress in marking the BL and with an effective liaison and coordination mechanism in place, UNIFIL has been able to withstand the pressure over time and give a boost to the effort to restore calm and peace in the region.

Whether it is a preoccupation of the Hezbollah in Syria or the control of incidents at the tactical level by UNIFIL or, for that matter, the presence of mutual deterrence between the Hezbollah and Israel, in the end, there has been no war for close to one-and-a-half decades. Shields calls such absence of war 'negative peace.' This, however, is not enough. Shields stated that 'positive peace might be lacking in a city or a community even when a nation is not at war.'[72] Rissler and Shields describe positive peace as follows: "It is not simply the absence of violent conflict but the management and sometimes transformation of the myriad conflicts that emerge in any society with diverse value systems to allow for continued prosperity and justice".[73] Shields also observed that there are limits to negative peace. She reported that even though the absence of war is negative peace, it does not happen automatically. The military will have to be prepared to enforce it if required. She further stated that the term 'negative peace' also implies that the underlying conditions of disputes should have been resolved and hence the tension may remain.[74] Howard explained positive peace on similar lines as moving towards normalising political, social, and economic relations between previously warring groups.[75] Putting these explanations together in the context of Israel and Lebanon, *firstly*, for continued prosperity and justice, a country should be able to first fully recover from the conflict. *Secondly*, the cessation of hostilities and the establishment of normal bilateral relations between both nations will be a prerequisite. Therefore, when Lebanon and Israel are in a state of war, the absence of war for a protracted period—strictly speaking, 'negative peace'—is the initial but essential step towards positive peace.

As concluded earlier, this negative peace would not have been possible without the active contribution of UNIFIL. As for implementing the mandate, Rikhye's comment on the UN operation in Congo can be compared to what UNIFIL had achieved prior to the 2006 war. Rikhye reported that the UN did not entirely succeed in implementing its mandate to oversee the withdrawal of Belgian troops and assist in restoring law and order in Congo in 1960. But "UN peacekeeping forces can only prove effective if their mandates and resources are tailored to the needs of their missions for which they depend on the decision of the Security Council and mandates that it provides."[76] Likewise, UNIFIL has been able to at least make a substantial contribution to the absence of war for a long period.

Summary and Analysis

This section covered an assessment of UNIFIL's performance during the period from 2006 (post the Israel-Lebanon war) to March 2020, by collating the observations made from publicly available reports of the UN and UNIFIL, opinions of subject matter experts found in peacekeeping-related books and articles combined with the personal observations of the author. The section began with a brief overview of the operational concept and strategy of UNIFIL followed by a detailed description of the various operational activities of the mission. This period is the longest in the history of UNIFIL without a major conflict between Israel and Lebanon. Even though it is difficult to predict the future, the practitioners would like to attribute this absence of war to UNIFIL.

One could of course always argue that this is more because of Israel and Lebanon (in specific, the Hezbollah in the case of Lebanon) not wanting or not yet being ready for another conflict, and less because of UNIFIL's contribution. Mutual deterrence between the Hezbollah and Israel, the preoccupation of the former in Syria or the current relatively lower profile of the Hezbollah in Lebanese society because of the internal instability of Lebanon, however, can change as quickly as a shift in the wind. While UNIFIL has no control in this context, by undertaking various operational activities and using different types of liaison and coordination mechanisms, it has been effective in monitoring and preventing hot spots near and along the BL from spiralling out of control. Such hot spots have the potential to trigger violence with little or without any warning resulting in a full-fledged conflict. Therefore, the counter-argument is that the bilateral relationship between Israel and Lebanon could plummet if it were not for UNIFIL. Except for the 10 incidents of the unauthorised presence of arms and weapons in South Lebanon from August 2006 to February 2020 and despite the frequent violations of Lebanese air space by IDF aircraft, UNIFIL has so far made some notable contributions.

The marking of the BL has made good progress and incidents of the inadvertent crossing of the BL by either side have come down. Even protests like stone-throwing in and around hot spots along the BL have decreased substantially. In the case of de-mining, good progress has been made after UNIFIL's intervention to persuade Israel to hand over the record of cluster bombs dropped in South Lebanon during the war of 2006. The decrease in the number of incidents of denial of freedom of movement of UNIFIL within the area of operations is an indication of better acceptability of UNIFIL in Lebanese society. Overall, there is a sense of calm and increased confidence in UNIFIL.

Even though credit for the present situation must be given to all the stakeholders, it is evident that the contribution of UNIFIL is noteworthy. At the same time, reports and statistics do not reveal the true picture unless the observations made from such official reports and statistics are corroborated by the views of the stakeholders. In the next section of this chapter, observations made in this section will be analysed from the stakeholders' perspective of how UNIFIL is performing.

SECTION II: ASSESSING UNIFIL THROUGH PRIMARY DATA

Introduction

The previous section attempted to find out how far UNIFIL has achieved its goals based on available records and data of the UN and UNIFIL. To corroborate this assessment and enrich the results that have been obtained so far, the current section aims to utilize primary data. Perceptive responses of three different segments of stakeholders were used to gather primary data for this study. The data collection and analysis again follow the framework for the assessment of peacekeeping operations as developed in Chapter 3. In text boxes here and there, I have added some personal reflections.

This section contains some results of the quantitative responses from the UNIFIL contingents, next to the descriptive findings of the online answers of the 41 operational leaders and, in particular, the qualitative interviews. Questions to the contingent members were given in two parts. As mentioned earlier at the beginning of this book, the data of the UNIFIL contingents, however, did not prove to be useful because of similarity in the responses (see Appendix E for the summary of data and analysis of responses).

Violence between Israel and Lebanon

The first question related to the occurrence of incidents in the area of operations that have, however, not led to a major conflict since 2006. Analysing the reasons for this, the former UNIFIL Deputy Chief of Integrated Staff (DCIS) and former FC of UNDOF, who were interviewed, felt that the potential cost of a major conflict was a deterrent to Israel and Lebanon. Similarly, the former LAF General and former senior adviser and official spokesman of UNIFIL, who was interviewed, believed that both sides fear the destructive consequences of another war. A former Swedish senior-level civilian employee of UNIFIL in the interview sample underscored these views by emphasising the negative impact on the economy a new war would have on both countries. A former IDF officer in the interview sample argued that while it was the Hezbollah that feared the consequences of the next war most, the mutual deterrence by both IDF and the Hezbollah has been a restraining factor in the current stability. Moreover, the Hezbollah is stretched by its involvement in Syria and is afraid of simultaneously opening up a second front. He, however, thought that the conflict was likely to recur when stability in Syria returns. The likelihood of a possible war will also depend on the bilateral relations between the USA and Iran. A Lebanese local staff member at UNIFIL HQs agreed that the level of deterrence between Israel and Lebanon has helped to maintain the balance of power between these two nations. As also noted in an academic article by Sobelman, it is the mutual deterrence between the Hezbollah and Israel that has prevented the recurrence of another major conflict. Sobelman argued that despite the vast military disparity between IDF and the Hezbollah, the latter has been able to coerce the IDF by the threat of being able to hit important urban areas of Israel with thousands of rockets.[77] According to Sobelman, "Israel

> *The absence of major violence between Israel and Lebanon is more because of the preoccupation of the interested parties with the deteriorating situation in the Middle East in general and less of their desire to find a permanent solution to the conflict in South Lebanon. Based on my ground experience of two years, the Middle East is a tinderbox waiting to be ignited. It is only a matter of time before it happens.*

and the Hezbollah have in recent years come to view their conflict as being characterised by mutual deterrence".[78]

A former Military Advisor at UNDPO agreed with the former IDF officer who was interviewed that the Hezbollah, apart from being involved in Syria, is afraid of overwhelming retaliation by the IDF in the next war. However, a former civilian senior mission leader of UNIFIL thought the reason for not going to war again is simply to avoid casualties on both sides. He also highlighted the positive role of UNIFIL in drawing the attention of the international community to the conflict. A former DFC of UNIFIL and a former Deputy Director of Political and Civil Affairs (DDPCA) observed that unless the root cause of the problem was addressed, no matter what is done, violence in the region will recur.

Similarly, a former Indian senior staff officer of UNIFIL stated that "*the situation is characterized by an absence of open hostilities but marked by underlying tension with the potential to escalate*". A former senior French General and Chief of Staff at UNIFIL HQs believed that the absence of war was due to the enhanced efficiency of UNIFIL. UNIFIL should not be judged by the recurrence of occasional recurrences of violence since this is generally the handiwork of the Hezbollah or Palestinian terrorists. Others felt that essentially, neither side is interested in another war and neither do they attribute the current stability to the role of the UNIFIL and its rapid response to the crisis (via efficient monitoring, liaison, and conflict mechanisms) that is in place. A former Italian DDPCA of UNIFIL however, disagreed and described "*UNIFIL as an interim solution*". He stated that unless the root cause of the problem is addressed, no matter how long UNIFIL continues, there will be no change in the current state of Israel-Lebanon relations. UNIFIL is not there to provide a permanent solution but to maintain the *status quo*. However, the fear of the *status quo* ending in a stalemate does frustrate many TCCs.

The 41 operational leaders who filled questionnaires indicated that there have been occasional incidents with the potential to trigger major conflicts since 2006. In their views, the presence of UNIFIL, however, has prevented the escalation of violence. A majority of 29 respondents expressed the view that UNIFIL has been able to take effective control of such incidents in time.

Violence against Peacekeepers

Violence against peacekeepers, by and large, is a common phenomenon. Many peacekeepers, military and civilian, have died worldwide because of

> *Violence against peacekeepers is a common phenomenon in intra-state conflicts. While use of force by peacekeepers is always retaliated, there are other reasons for violence that however are difficult to pinpoint. In UNIFIL, there have not been too many such incidents. For this, the acceptability of the peacekeepers by both the local population and the main warring group, in this case, the Hezbollah, is an important factor. Some of the contingents, namely, from the non-Western regions and a few senior mission leaders, have found a reasonable degree of acceptability. While the HoM/FC always moved around with a heavily armed personal protection group, I, as the Deputy HoM/DFC always felt safe in the entire South Lebanon with only a single escort. Whether it was either a false sense of confidence or because I was not that an important target, will remain an enigma.*

their work in such missions. Peacekeepers routinely become targets of either party to the conflict or others while fulfilling their duties. While the level of violence generally is more explicit in intra-state conflicts, even in a traditional PKO like UNIFIL, violence is no exception. UNIFIL peacekeepers have been victims of numerous attacks by unauthorised armed groups in Lebanon. Such attacks on peacekeepers are covered under "Malicious Acts" by the UN, which are defined as fatalities that occur as a result of "war; invasion; hostilities; acts of foreign enemies, whether war be declared or not; civil war; revolution; rebellion; insurrection; military or usurped power; riots or civil commotion; sabotage; the explosion of war weapons; or terrorist activities".[79]

According to UN statistics, after 2006, there have been only five major incidents including the one of June 2007, which took the lives of six Spanish peacekeepers, until February 2020.[80] In this incident, the former IDF officer who was interviewed concluded that it was the Hezbollah that had attacked the Spanish contingent for its active role in the Shiite-dominated area. Other than this incident, there were, however, a few incidents of unfriendly behaviour by the locals, such as posing restrictions on freedom of movement of UNIFIL patrols. The decline in incidents is corroborated by the online answers of the operational leaders on the ground. Most of the respondents (85%) expressed their (strong) agreement with the idea that the overall violence against peacekeepers has declined since the attack on the Spanish peacekeepers in 2007.

Whenever peacekeepers were targets of violence, the majority opinion, including that of online respondents (62%), was that these peacekeepers offered coincidental, opportune targets to perpetrators of violence. Contrary to this majority opinion, an Indian senior staff officer in the interview sample who was posted to the Force HQs noted that the demeanour of the European contingents was responsible for earning the hatred of the Lebanese population. Concurringly, a former Indian contingent commander felt that the contingents from Western nations are deliberately singled out and prevented from moving around freely. These views are supported by more than one-third of the online responses (38%) who (strongly) disagreed with the idea that there is no fixed pattern of malicious acts or unfriendly behaviour by the host-nationals vis-à-vis peacekeepers. They believe there are patterns to be distinguished, just like the two Indian respondents declared.

A Lebanese local staff member added that "there won't be violence as long as UNIFIL restricts itself to its mandate". Similarly, a former UNIFIL liaison officer, a senior mission leader of UNIFIL and a Belgian subject matter expert, attributed the occurrence of incidental violence to crossing the Hezbollah's red line. The former DCIS and former FC of UNDOF pointed to the presence of an external hand to drive a wedge between UNIFIL and the local populace. The French QRF Commander who was interviewed stated that the reduction of violence occurred because of the non-aggressive posture of UNIFIL. He commented that the kind of RoE that is used to fight the Taliban in Afghanistan is not possible to be applied in Lebanon. On the other hand, this high-ranking French General thought that the drastic reduction in violence against peacekeepers was due to the robust structure of UNIFIL. The Italian DDPCA, however, had a completely different view on the subject. According to him, the tolerance level of the local population is reciprocal to the presence of a threat from Israel. In other words, a protest against UNIFIL is an indication of its failure to stop the aggressive stance of Israel.

Essentially, it was a consensus among the interviewees that post 2007 there has been a decrease in the number of malicious acts and there is no fixed pattern of either malicious acts or unfriendly behaviour of the local population. If at all, often, these are generally triggered by inappropriate conduct of the peacekeepers. A large minority of the online respondents (as well as some interviewees) indicated, however, that violence against specific peacekeepers is not that coincidental.

Humanitarian De-mining

Cluster Munitions Remnants (CMR) contaminated Lebanon partially because of the earlier conflicts of 1978 and 1982 and largely due to the war of 2006. Even though humanitarian de-mining is widely appreciated as one of the most popular tasks undertaken by UNIFIL, it is difficult to put a figure to the results of de-mining. The uncertainty of its effectiveness relates to the fact that the overview of contaminated areas is continuously revised following the discovery of previously unrecorded contaminated areas. Further, no permission to clear mined areas in proximity to the BL has been given. For example, after the war of 2006, the contaminated area was estimated to be 55 square kilometres. The new estimate made at the end of 2016, resulted in the identification of a contaminated area of 60 square kilometres. After clearing an area of approximately 44 square kilometres, the area left for clearance was around 16.3 square kilometres.[81]

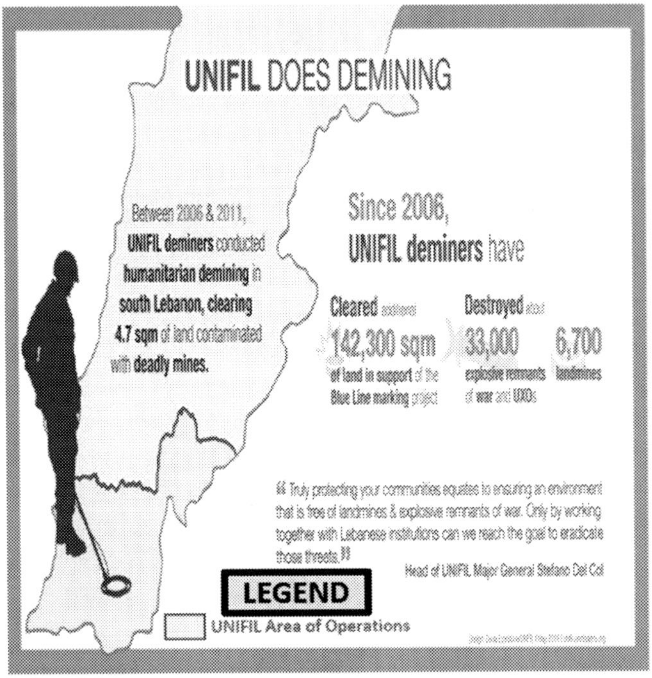

Given the fact that around 85 per cent of the cleared area has been used for socio-economic purposes, the clearance of 44 square kilometres in ten years is regarded by the population at large as one of the most important activities of UNIFIL. Until 2019, 6,700 mines and 33,000 explosive remnants of war and UXOs have been destroyed by UNIFIL (see the infographic that pertains to 2019). A Lebanese citizen and a former LAF General, as well as the former DFC and the French DDPCA of UNIFIL who were interviewed, expressed similar views in their appreciation of UNIFIL's role in humanitarian de-mining. Since 2006, UNIFIL teams alone have cleared around 4,000,000 square metres (4 square kilometres) of contaminated areas in Lebanon. Among the online respondents, 83 per cent regard the overall effect of humanitarian de-mining to be (very) good. To illustrate the importance of this task: by the end of 2012, more than 3,000 people were killed in Lebanon by the remnants of cluster bombs that were used by Israel during the war of 2006.

At the same time, while acknowledging the importance of humanitarian de-mining, the senior Indian staff officer and the junior staff officer at UNIFIL HQ who were interviewed, commented that the progress of de-mining has been slow due to lack of resources among the Lebanese Mine Action Services. The high ranking French General in the interview sample, on the contrary, observed that even though humanitarian de-mining is not the responsibility of UNIFIL (except for a supervisory role), the progress made is rather encouraging. To derive full benefit, he recommended that UNIFIL should be mandated to do humanitarian de-mining. Perhaps, not so surprisingly, the security expert from Israel who was interviewed, stated that Israel is not much concerned with this subject since it has not affected the Israeli population.

Mechanisms to Prevent Hostilities

While all the respondents acknowledged that the existing mechanisms are extremely productive, the Italian DDPCA felt that the prevention of hostilities by UNIFIL was wishful thinking. However, a Lebanese local employee, a student, a citizen, the UNIFIL liaison officer, the two Indian contingent commanders and the French DDPCA in the interview sample attributed the present state of stability to UNIFIL's liaison and coordination mechanism. Others emphasised that it was mostly the tripartite meetings that worked out to be the most effective mechanism of all. In this context, the IDF officer highlighted that the tripartite meeting was a mechanism that was not mentioned in the mandate but had developed into a new tool to discuss important issues that needed immediate attention and higher priority.[82] Discussing important subjects across the table in the same room has helped to better understand each other's position and problems. The French General and the French QRF Commander maintained that the tripartite meetings and liaison and coordination mechanism of UNIFIL are of immense help to prevent the recurrence of hostilities. The QRF Commander who was interviewed added that in this regard, the Standing Operating Procedures of UNIFIL, which are regularly updated, have also contributed to the maintenance of peace.

The Lebanese student observed that monitoring by UNIFIL and diplomatic pressure on Lebanon and Israel compels the two nations to exercise restraint. The Lebanese local employee believed liaison and communication become effective only when the mission reaches out and communicates with the right person/s; by reaching out to people, one does not lose dignity.

The online survey looked at the available mechanisms for effective management of conflicts. The general picture conveyed in the interviews was confirmed in the online survey that there was a consensus on the effective role of the current mechanism, in maintaining peace and tranquillity between Israel and Lebanon. Generally, most of the interviewees considered tripartite meetings to have proved to be the best mechanism of all in the prevention of hostilities. However, the opinion of those who responded online was at a slight variance to this outcome. It is probably because the short tenure of the online respondents (who are in the junior military ranks) did not give them adequate opportunities to develop a deeper understanding of how third-party mediation in the form of tripartite meetings can help the parties to understand the benefit of the absence of conflict as a better alternative to the continuation of the conflict. The online respondents were more familiar with the impact of the mechanisms that are regularly used at the tactical level such as 'quick response and control', and 'the liaison and coordination section of the Force HQs'.

Conflict Management

The subject of conflict management drew mixed responses. The former DCIS and UNFOF FC who were interviewed stated that the delicate bilateral relations between Israel and Lebanon depend on the regional security environment. The French DDPCA and the Lebanese local employee underscored the point of view of the former DCIS and UNDOF FC. He, however, emphasised the role of UNIFIL in maintaining this balance. Even though other respondents also harped on the importance of UNIFIL, the comments of the Lebanese local employee were explicit and concurred with what Zartman had explained about the role of a third party to help the conflict to move from conflict to reconciliation.[83] Third-party mediation between Israel and Lebanon by UNIFIL aptly explains the theory of Zartman.

Commenting on the way the process of conflict management is affected by the regional security situation, the senior civilian mission leader observed that the Hezbollah's involvement in Syria and the interest of other Islamic countries of the region in defeating Israel, has helped to contain the conflict. This situation however has changed with the UAE and Bahrain's recent decision to establish diplomatic relations with Israel, as will be briefly explained in the next chapter.

The two contingent commanders, the former FC, the liaison officer, the Israeli security expert, and the Swedish civilian staff member in the interview sample gave credit to UNIFIL's effort in expediting the marking of the BL, which helped to define its exact alignment and act as a mitigating factor in handling avoidable crises in and around the disputed areas. While the former DFC pointed out that UNIFIL helps to contain the conflict at an acceptable level, the Belgian Lebanese expert stated that *"UNIFIL is a good vehicle for peace"*. The Belgian subject matter expert felt that it is the tripartite meetings that have helped and are still helping to manage the conflict. The senior Indian logistic staff officer felt that the spilling over of the Syrian war is a big threat to the region. However, the former senior advisor and official spokesman of UNIFIL was optimistic and believed that the likelihood of the Syrian war spilling over to Lebanon is minimal. At the same time, immediate interventions by UNIFIL in response to crises with cooperation from the LAF are seen as particularly good management techniques. The senior Indian staff officer believed that despite the impact of the Syrian war, UNIFIL has been able to provide real-time communication to avoid the recurrence of violence. On the other hand, the junior staff officer noted that the already fragile relationship marred by regional political instability, in turn, has questioned the credibility of UNIFIL.

The Israeli security expert who was interviewed stated that while the relationship between both countries depends on the regional situation, it reached a deadlock because of the weak Lebanese government. The IDF officer had a similar view of the Lebanese government. According to him, *"Lebanon is a weak state because even though it has a constitution, it is without a state"*. He also brought in a different perspective to the application of the concept of conflict management. According to him, before 2005, the presence of the Syrian Army in Lebanon was a restraining factor for the Hezbollah. After its withdrawal from Lebanon, it enabled the Hezbollah to grow stronger with support from Iran. Presently, with the power of the Syrian regime dwindling, Iran will probably call the final shots in a possible war between Israel and Lebanon. Susser's views in a historical overview are similar to the IDF officer who was interviewed. He assessed that despite being surrounded by the most complex internal conflicts in the Middle East,

Israel's present security threat is more from non-Arab states like Iran and its protégé—the Hezbollah. Coupled with a continuous shift in the regional power balance because of the unbridled conflict between Shiites and Sunnis, and Iran's pursuit of the nuclear weapons program, Iran poses the most serious threat to Israel.[84]

The French General, who was interviewed, believed that despite the apparent calm in the region, the bilateral relationship between Israel and Lebanon continues to remain fragile and can deteriorate any time due to the regional security dynamics. He further maintained that the established conflict management mechanisms have helped to make good progress in the marking of the BL. The French QRF Commander was of the view that the threat of violence between the Hezbollah and IDF is always high near the BL. However, the robust structure of UNIFIL and its quick response capability have been deterrents to both the IDF and the Hezbollah. According to the IDF officer, even though the outcome of the Syrian war will probably decide the future trajectory of the delicate bilateral relations between Israel and Lebanon, the contours of conflict management in this context are more complicated than the simple narrative of a dispute over territory. Therefore, the future of Lebanon depends on its choice of alignment with either the Arab nations or Iran.

Notwithstanding these analyses, the former operational leaders who responded online, agreed that the marking of the BL has seriously helped to resolve existing disputes, and they think completing this marking should be expedited.

There are several disputed areas—big and small—near the BL. There has been a general lack of knowledge of the exact layout and alignment of most of the disputed areas resulting in confusion and hostility amongst the populace on either side of the BL. Seventy per cent of the online respondents felt that marking of the BL has helped to clear such misunderstandings to a great extent with a consequent decline in violence.

Presence of Unauthorised Armed Groups in South Lebanon

One of the elements of the mandate of SCR 1701 is that the area south of the Litani River must be free of Lebanese and non-Lebanese militias other than those from the Government of Lebanon and UNIFIL. Dealing with unauthorized armed groups is the direct responsibility of the Government of Lebanon—principally the LAF—with UNIFIL only in an assistance role.

Even though not specifically mentioned in the mandate, unauthorised armed groups essentially refer to the Hezbollah and non-Lebanese armed groups such as Palestinian terrorists. Barring a few, most of the interviewees mentioned the Hezbollah as the principal actor in South Lebanon. Without making any reference to it, the Lebanese local employee at UNIFIL HQs who was interviewed stated that it is a part of South Lebanon and is there to fight Israel.

Therefore, UNIFIL disarming the Hezbollah amounts to taking up arms against its people. Hence, he pointed out, that without a cessation of hostilities between Israel and Lebanon, it is not possible to remove unauthorised arms from South Lebanon. The QRF Commander stated that there has been no progress at all because of the Hezbollah's growing strength in South Lebanon and the reluctance on the part of the major stakeholders, except for Israel, to disarm the Hezbollah. The French General who was interviewed observed that while UNIFIL has been able to take control of a large area because of extensive patrolling, the presence of the Hezbollah and Palestinian terrorists always has been a real threat. He believed there was a lack of commitment on the part of the LAF to disarm the Hezbollah because it considers it to be an instrument of resistance against Israel. The former Spanish FC in the interview sample maintained there was no visible presence of uniformed militias in the UNIFIL area of operation, and the former senior civilian mission leader noted that removing illegal arms and unauthorised armed groups from South Lebanon is not doable for two reasons. *One*, it is difficult to make a clear distinction between Lebanese and non-Lebanese militia. *Two*, the Hezbollah is not only well entrenched in society but also part of the Lebanese political structure. Except for the Israeli security expert and the IDF officer, who in the interviews held slightly different opinions, all respondents believe that with the Hezbollah being part of the political structure, the LAF cannot even attempt to disarm it. The Israeli security expert called the Hezbollah a 'cancer' in Lebanese society, which is of no use to anyone in the Middle East. Makdisi, during his interview with Pass Blue, the independent journalism site that extensively covers the UN, commented similarly. He also believed that the sectarian politics of Lebanon would not allow the LAF to disarm the Hezbollah. If any attempt was made to do that, "the army would split along political and sectarian lines as it did during Lebanon's civil war from 1975 to 1990".[85]

According to the IDF officer in his interview, expecting UNIFIL to assist the LAF is putting the task too simplistically. The Hezbollah is part of the

The presence of unauthorized arms and weapons has always been an extremely sensitive subject for UNIFIL. While UNIFIL was not responsible for the removal of unauthorized arms and weapons, it always hoped that there were no unauthorized arms in its area of operations. Israel always believed and had proof that the Hezbollah moved around South Lebanon with impunity. It was therefore particularly important for UNIFIL to carefully investigate all incidents that violate SCR 1701 resulting in reports of the presence of unauthorized arms and weapons to DPO without causing any embarrassment to itself. Being the Deputy HoM and DFC, I was specially deputed to carry out a one-man investigation (like most of the other sensitive investigations) of the explosion of the Hezbollah's ammunition dump at Khirbat Silim that took place on 15 July 2009. During the investigation, it was established that Hezbollah armed operatives were present at the site and prevented the UNIFIL investigation team from carrying out its duties. My draft report to the HoM/FC had to be honest and included every detail of the incident. At the same time, any mention of the presence of Hezbollah operatives in the six-monthly report of the Secretary-General would have appeased Israel and its supporters. On the other hand, it would not have found favour with either the Lebanese government or the Hezbollah. Such reports, even though they do not in any way alter the ground situation; do influence the behaviour and cooperation of the host government and other non-governmental parties to the conflict. The final decision on the content of the official report, therefore, had to be taken by the HoM in consultation with his political advisors, considering what was best in the interest of both UNIFIL and the region. It was a paradox which is best compared to the reasons for deliberate moderation of the mandate to get one or more adversarial parties on board for a peace process. The final report mentioned that the presence of arms and ammunition in South Lebanon is a violation of SCR 1701. But the report left out much of the details like armed civilians preventing UNFIL from visiting the incident site.

government and has a major say even in the appointment of the President of the country. Under such circumstances, disarming the Hezbollah by the LAF is not possible. At the same time, since there are still unauthorised arms and armed groups in South Lebanon, technically, UNIFIL has failed in its duty to assist the LAF to disarm the armed groups. That notwithstanding, the least UNIFIL can do is to make an accurate reporting of violations of SCR 1701.

The online respondents (90%) also indicated that in their perception unauthorized groups were active in South Lebanon, particularly pointing to the presence of the Hezbollah.

All the interviewees believe that the Hezbollah, which is part of the Shiite majority in South Lebanon, is well entrenched in society (with a sort of "Robin Hood image" as described by the French DDPCA in his interview), and is part of Lebanese politics and the government. Hence, disarming the armed units of this movement is not a practical task. Interestingly, no interviewee mentioned Palestinian terrorists while referring to unauthorised armed groups or elements. However, the opinions of the respondents in the online survey about the Hezbollah's military strength in South Lebanon were at variance, and there was no general agreement among them on the lasting character of the Hezbollah's dominance.

Disputes over Occupied Areas

The former DCIS and UNDOF FC, the Lebanese citizen, the senior advisor and UNIFIL spokesman, the senior Indian staff officer and the IDF officer who were interviewed were all of the view that BL marking helped to bring down the number of flashpoints in the disputed areas. The UNIFIL spokesman, however, qualified that resolution of the dispute of Shebaa Farm was possible only after consultation with Syria because Israel claims to have captured the land from the Syrians. The Lebanese civilian local employee insisted that the marking of the BL is only a technical process and unless the BL is respected by both the Lebanese and the Israelis, many Lebanese villagers will continue to pluck the products of their orchards that fall on the other side of the BL. According to him, if the frequency of incidents near the disputed areas has reduced, it is only because of the presence of UNIFIL and not because of the BL, as suggested by others. The QRF Commander's view was somewhat similar to the Lebanese local employee. He observed that while the marking of the BL helps to resolve disputes to some extent, the difference between the BL and the actual border negates the benefits of progress in the marking. The French General reported that the marking of the BL has progressed only in the undisputed areas. Lack of political will on the part of both Israel and Lebanon is the only stumbling block in BL marking. The Indian contingent commander was of the view that since the root cause of the Israel-Lebanon problem is the support of the citizens for their respective countries' differences will remain unless it is resolved. He agrees that marking the BL has helped to resolve a lot of disputes except for the Shebaa Farm area, which is located at the base of the three countries and is strategically important to Israel, Lebanon, and Syria.

The Lebanese student and the UNIFIL liaison officer in the interview sample commented that there is either no progress or only negligible progress in resolving disputes. Other respondents had varying views on the subject. For instance, the senior civilian mission leader felt that the resolution has to be part of a bigger regional package including Palestine and Syria, and the Military Advisor saw no solution soon. Both the former DFC and the French DDPCA stated that it is in the interest of both Israel and Lebanon to maintain the *status quo* because of the larger political gains of the current situation. In their opinion, the current state of tension between Israel and Lebanon provides a reason for both Israel and the Hezbollah to survive. In the name of fighting the Hezbollah, Israel gets support from the West. Similarly, most of the Islamic countries of the Middle East exploit the situation to support their fight against Israel. At the same time, waging a full-fledged war and expecting it to terminate the conflict, does not benefit those who are fighting or their supporters. It is therefore not in the interests of either Israel or the Hezbollah or their supporters to find a permanent solution to the state of conflict. For similar reasons, it will be difficult to find a solution to the problems arising out of a few hot spots along or near the BL and that indirectly help both Israel and Hezbollah to keep the issue alive. Shebaa Farm, located in the eastern sector of the UNIFIL area of operations and bordering Lebanon, Syria and Israel, is one such area. This is a contested area between Lebanon and Israel, and will remain that way until there is a general understanding between Israel, Lebanon, and Syria. However, BL marking has helped to reduce the number of incidents near the disputed areas and hence the completion of this process must be expedited.

Capability Building of the LAF

Almost all the interviewees responded that relations between UNIFIL and the LAF are incredibly good in terms of training and operational activities. However, more is needed to be done in terms of supporting the LAF with financial assistance. The senior civilian mission leader observed that the kind of cooperation between UNIFIL and the LAF is one of the best examples amongst all PKO. The QRF Commander in the interview sample commented that the LAF is poorly equipped and hence any kind of assistance, whether in the form of equipment or training or advice, will be helpful to augment the capacity of the LAF. The French General who was interviewed felt that the LAF is very well trained and can face any internal situation except for disarming the Hezbollah. Commenting on the occasional restriction of freedom of movement of UNIFIL, the LAF General stated that such restriction is not due to a lack of cooperation between the LAF and UNIFIL, but because of the suspicion that a few contingents are trying to collect intelligence on behalf of their governments. The collection of intelligence in UN peacekeeping is a sensitive subject. In UNIFIL, the local population generally suspects the European peacekeeping contingents of collecting intelligence on behalf of their governments under the guise of patrolling and other operational activities.

The Israeli security expert and the IDF officer, however, had a different perspective on the capability building of the LAF. According to the security expert, its close relationship with the Hezbollah poses a dilemma for it. On the other hand, the IDF officer felt that with the Hezbollah amassing more and more rockets, the capability building of the LAF becomes irrelevant. He pointed out that while a better dialogue and joint training will help to improve the cooperation between UNIFIL and LAF, it contributes little to enforce the mandate. He observed that, on the one hand, there is an improvement in the cooperation between UNIFIL and the LAF, but on the other hand, there is a drop in UNIFIL's efficiency. Similarly, the junior staff officer also observed that the intertwined involvement of the militias in domestic politics hinders the LAF to exercise its authority. Essentially, while the LAF has turned out to be a capable organisation with the ability to stand up to the internal threat, it currently is still not able to take full control of South Lebanon as implied in the objectives of the peace mission and defend Lebanon against external threat. The views of the online respondents generally corroborated this assessment.

Relations with Local Population

The need to forge a good relationship with the host-national population was emphasised by all the respondents as a means of success for the mission. The interviewees as well as the online respondents agreed that UNIFIL's relationship with the local population is 'good' to 'very good'. However, they also highlighted different aspects of the relationship between the peacekeepers and the local

> *Innocent civilians, mostlywomen and children, who suffer the most in complex intra-state conflicts, should be the centre of gravity in peace processes. Unfortunately, not much emphasis has been paid to this subject both by academics and practitioners. Inability to recognize this, combined with a lack of sensitivity to the local culture and tradition distances the population from the peacekeepers. Such gaps can never be bridged by CIMIC activities unless there is an attributional change in the peacekeepers, and they reach out to the population with a helping hand and a genuine smile on their faces.*

population. The QRF Commander observed that the relationship of UNIFIL with the local population was always good until UNIFIL brought in heavy armaments and equipment. He stated that the local population prefers a UNIFIL that helps in infrastructure development under CIMIC activities, rather than moving around with a thick armoured shield. Regarding infrastructure development, the French General, on the other hand, commented that CIMIC activities are good but should not be undertaken at the cost of operational preparedness. The IDF officer in his interview commended UNIFIL for finding innovative ways to teach the local populace how to benefit from peaceful co-existence with their neighbours. The Lebanese citizen pointed out that good relations between the peacekeepers and the local population is crucial for the success of UNIFIL. In this regard, the Lebanese local staff stated that UNIFIL's presence is acceptable to the local population in South Lebanon. The Belgian Lebanese expert, however, commented such acceptance does not guarantee unconditional support to UNIFIL from the local population.

The UNIFIL liaison officer in his interview observed that the Hezbollah is a wedge between UNIFIL and the local population. Several respondents stated that the attitude and conduct of peacekeepers during their routine interaction with the population and while undertaking operational activities like patrolling, can either improve or spoil the relationship. According to the online respondents, respecting local culture and traditions, for instance, helps to develop and maintain good relations. Connected to this was the statement by the Belgian subject matter expert, that an overemphasis on force protection is detrimental to a good relationship with the host-national population. The senior civilian mission leader pointed out that aggressive patrolling by UNIFIL troops and occasionally transgressing Lebanese sensitivity points such as attempting to collect intelligence on behalf of their respective nations have resulted in stone-pelting by the locals at UNIFIL patrols. The Military Advisor observed that social ills and societal differences between peacekeepers and local society also contribute to the problem.

The contingent commander in the interview sample described UNIFIL as an organisation that is not so good at 'people contact.' But the senior advisor and the UNIFIL spokesman were more specific in singling out the European contingents and European politicians for lacking public diplomacy. The former DFC pointed out that there is a difference in the way various national contingents behave in PKO and that peacekeepers from Asian regions, such as India, generally find better acceptance in

Lebanon. Even among the European troops, there are differences in operational style.

According to Ruffa, military culture, which she defined as "the core set of beliefs, attitudes, norms, and values that become deeply embedded at the national army level" explains the behavioural differences of different contingents.[86] Such differences are visible in the behaviour of peacekeepers when they reach out to people for humanitarian work and also in their operational activities. Drawing from observations of UNIFIL, she highlighted varying behaviours of Italian and French contingents. For instance, following their military culture, Italian soldiers want to be good humanitarians and accordingly consider CIMIC a top priority and prefer to maintain a low profile for force protection. On the other hand, to the French, CIMIC is not a priority, and they would rather lay more emphasis on force protection. Peacekeepers of the French contingent are generally attired in helmets and bulletproof jackets even when inside their vehicles.[87] From her study, she earlier concluded that the varying operational styles is taken advantage of by hostile parties such as Israeli media reporting the Hezbollah hiding arms and weapons in Italian area of operations and Italians generally overlooking such activities. From her engagement with the local population, she reported that the local population was not convinced by the general effectiveness of UNIFIL II (post-2006). She concluded that overall, UNIFIL II was well perceived by the local population and seen as a tool for the US initiative to support Israel.[88]

The Italian DDPCA in his interview observed that UNIFIL had boosted the local economy. He stated that depending on their capacity to spend, some contingents use their national funds to improve the livelihood of locals. He, however, noted that on the flip side, a decline in such investment is always accompanied by unhappiness amongst the locals. As noted by Ruffa, a contribution to developmental work also depends on national military culture. For instance, for the Italian soldiers, CIMIC is a good way to make a positive contribution and an opportunity to improve the army's reputation. On the other hand, for the French contingent, operational activity is the priority.[89]

The online respondents also highlighted that financial contributions, respect for local culture and tradition, the presence/absence of suspicion in the motive of the peacekeeping contingents and presence/absence of aggressive attitudes during operational activities shape the perception of the local population. As revealed earlier, the online respondents believed the local population distinguished between the nationalities of the various contingents, giving preference to non-Western troops. The general feeling was that the number of obstructions of UNIFIL activities had decreased over the years. There has been, however, a spike in the number of obstructions to UNIFIL's freedom of movement during the period from 2017 to 2019. In this regard, the views of the online respondents, which predates 2017, corroborates with the official data of the UN.[90]

In PKO, there often seems a contradiction between operational tasks and the need to forge a good relationship with the local population. Often, peacekeepers end up either doing nothing out of fear of hurting local sentiments or distancing themselves from the local populace because of an overemphasis on force protection. To overcome the challenges of the latter, some of the contingents from non-Western nations (such as India and others), find innovative methods to delicately balance the need for force protection and respond to the crisis on one hand and the necessity to reach out to the population on the other. This concept is described as organizational ambidexterity by Shields and Travis, which refers to being simultaneously good at two things that seem unrelated or even contradictory.[91]

The Mandate

Questions on the mandate evoked three different kinds of responses. *One*, opinion on the lack of clarity on mandate formulation was unanimous. *Two*, UNIFIL has been able to fulfil its direct responsibility part of the mandate. *Three*, some of the mandated tasks are far-fetched and not achievable.

Commenting on UNIFIL's ability to fulfil its part of the responsibility, the former IDF officer stated during his interview that since the Hezbollah is still around in South Lebanon, it can be concluded that UNIFIL had failed to even provide the required assistance to the LAF to disarm it. He added that it was difficult to translate the mandate into an actionable plan. Even though the relative stability in South Lebanon is an indication of the political support to UNIFIL, Israel expects much more from UNIFIL. As for lack of clarity in the mandate, this is often cited as one of the most important reasons for the failure of PKO. Political scientist Diehl stated that the initial mandate of UNIFIL (SCR 425 and 426) created difficulties since it did not specify some details necessary for operational deployment. However, post the 2006 war, the current mandate of UNIFIL, as given out in SCR 1701 (2006), is clearer than what it was earlier. This notwithstanding, even before 2006, he felt that to attribute all the problems of UNIFIL to a vague mandate would be unfair.[92]

Pouligny considered vagueness as a political necessity. According to her, "maintaining this element of vagueness is often considered by negotiators a condition for the signing of an agreement; if everything was made clear, the parties would never sign."[93] Juxtaposed with the mandate of UNIFIL, there is no mention of the Hezbollah in SCR 1701 while referring to the removal of unauthorized and non-Lebanese armed groups from South Lebanon. Even Guehenno pointed out that "if UNIFIL had more authority, it could find itself in a collision course with the Lebanese government and the Hezbollah."[94] The relevance of Guehenno's remark can be better understood by the events leading to the attack on the Spanish armoured car in South Lebanon on 24 June 2007. Encouraged by the strong mandate, when the Spanish contingent started taking photographs of the hostile activities, their armoured car was blown up by a bomb on a road near village Khiam that resulted in the deaths of six Spanish peacekeepers. About a possible next war, the Indian contingent commander in his interview stated that UNIFIL is not capable of preventing any full-fledged war. Both, the French General and the QRF Commander mentioned that the mandate is clear except for the part that expects UNIFIL to assist the LAF to disarm all non-Lebanese armed groups. The online respondents agree that UNIFIL has only been able to fulfil its mandate partially.

> *UNIFIL is commonly known as a robust PKO not because of the number of peacekeepers but because of the armaments and equipment held by some of the military contingents that no other PKO has. It therefore is natural for members of the international community, who are favourably disposed towards Israel, like the USA, to expect that disarming the Hezbollah should be within its capability and is the responsibility of UNIFIL.*

The absence of a clear and achievable mandate has been cited as one of the main reasons for the failure of many PKO in the past. In the case of UNIFIL, there is a part of the mandate, which is its direct responsibility. Otherwise, in most cases, UNIFIL is supposed to be only in an assistance role. As to the part of the mandate for which UNIFIL is solely responsible, UNIFIL has been able to implement its mandate. The French General added that the reduction of violence and the absence of war for more than a decade is an indication of UNIFIL's success in implementing the mandate. The

Spanish FC, without commenting on the feasibility of implementing the mandate, however, stated that UNIFIL does at least provide an opportunity to the parties to talk of a permanent ceasefire. The UNIFIL senior advisor and the spokesman drew a comparison and stated that SCR 1701, however, is relatively clearer than the original mandate of UNIFIL—SCRs 425 and 426. In this regard, according to Rikhye, "It has to be recognised that the resolutions have often papered over ambiguities that have to be preserved for political reasons".[95] It is the general opinion of the interviewees that while UNIFIL enjoys political support, it is not practical to expect them to assist the LAF in disarming the Hezbollah.

UNIFIL Structure

This question pertains to the capabilities of UNIFIL to prevent another conflict and the relevance of the RoE. It is the general hope that UNIFIL will be able to prevent the outbreak of another major conflict between Israel and Lebanon. In this regard, even though the opinions of the interviewees differed slightly, everybody concurred that UNIFIL is not capable of preventing a major conflict because there is a lack of political will in the TCCs, who do not want to risk casualties to their soldiers. For instance, the Indian contingent commander in the interview sample observed that the use of force can never guarantee the cessation of hostilities while the UNIFIL liaison officer believed that UNIFIL is not capable of either preventing the outbreak of another war or dissuading an Israeli invasion. The views of the online respondents, however, are at variance. Eighty per cent of the respondents considered that the effectiveness of UNIFIL was because of its robust structure and not because of the political influence of the TCCs from Europe.

The QRF Commander commented that UNIFIL can gather operational intelligence but lacks the military capability to either disarm the Hezbollah or prevent another full-fledged war because of the different operational capabilities of the military contingents. He added that the RoEs are exhaustive but limited by national caveats. The French General had a slightly different view on the subject. He believed that the multi-national structure of UNIFIL, in addition to providing legitimacy to the mission, also helped to curtail the activities of the Hezbollah. As for the RoE, the French General observed that the rules are exhaustive, but several military contingents lack the will to use force fearing casualties to the peacekeepers. The Italian DDPCA commented that Israel always considers UNIFIL biased towards Lebanon.

The senior civilian mission leader, the UNIFIL spokesman, the Swedish civilian staff member, the Belgian expert, the UNDOF FC and the Military Advisor, all felt that the use of force for the prevention of war is not an option. The IDF officer also commented that a big PKO like UNIFIL is not at all cost-effective since it is not capable of preventing another war. He pointed out the new challenges that Israel would face in the next war because of a bigger and stronger UNIFIL, a stronger Hezbollah and a professionally more capable LAF. Concurrently, once the war commences, there will be no pause in the battle, leaving either a small or no window at all for UNIFIL to pull out from Lebanon until the war ends. On this subject, Guehenno commented that "a strong UNIFIL in the South would not prevent a resumption of war by the Hezbollah or by the Israelis if they so decided, but would certainly complicate their strategic calculations and that was the best a PKO could achieve in Lebanon".[96]

Accordingly, the interviewees felt that the robust multi-national structure of UNIFIL was a signal of the political commitment of the international community. On the question of the relevance of RoE, the respondents stated that RoEs are quite exhaustive. However, while some observed that RoEs are prone to different interpretations, the LAF General felt that these RoEs are suitable only for no-war conditions and hence, a different set of RoEs will be necessary in case of a full-fledged conflict. The Military Advisor in his interview commented that while the RoEs are meant to avoid the abuse of force, it has become an excuse not to use force even when required. Since RoEs are related to the use of force, the UNIFIL spokesman observed that no contingent will use force even if it is ordered. However, only 45 per cent of the online respondents agreed with the Military Advisor and the UNIFIL spokesman.

The operational leaders in the online survey agreed that creating operational synergy among the TCCs from Western and non-Western countries is generally possible with regular training, although a large minority sees difficulties in this. As to the usefulness of the RoEs, opinions vary a lot. There is not a lot of convergence on the topic of RoEs. The opposing views on it are also almost equally large. Clearly, there is more than one view about RoEs. Contingents from Western nations lay high priority on force protection. Consequently, these nations set aside more combat troops for the protection of the base. On the other hand, a lower priority on force protection by the non-Western contingents enables them to employ maximum troops for operational activities. At the same time, to some of the non-Western contingents, RoE becomes an excuse to avoid using force fearing retaliation against their peacekeepers. Even within the Western nations, there are opposing views based on the military culture of the contingents. For example, as previously mentioned in Chapter 3, Ruffa noted that the French contingents considered that force can be used against anyone who comes in their way of implementing the mandate. This includes the Hezbollah, Islamist terrorists, the IDF and even local Lebanese citizens. On the other hand, the Italians considered UNIFIL as a traditional peacekeeping operation and hence they use force only if the Hezbollah attacks them.[97]

Summary and Analysis

The opinions of almost all the respondents, i.e., the stakeholders who were interviewed and those who responded online, are generally in line with the observations of the previous chapters. All of them agreed with the general opinion that the level of violence or potential for violence between Israel and Lebanon had reduced drastically. They attributed this to the confidence-building mechanisms with special reference to the tripartite meetings, the expeditious marking of the BL and other proactive measures taken by UNIFIL.[98] They believed that BL marking had helped to remove most of the irritants near the BL even though Shebaa Farm is going to remain a controversial point for quite some time. The liaison and coordination mechanisms are well entrenched (with a detachment permanently located in Israel) and can quickly respond to clear any confusion or misunderstanding between the IDF and LAF. Howard believed that "UNIFIL has proven effective at reducing conflict primarily by inducing cooperation". She further mentioned that "It is impossible to argue decisively that UNIFIL has been either a success or a failure. On the whole, the evidence indicates important positive effects, but with significant caveats".[99] However, most respondents believed that the conflict management measures that have been instituted by UNIFIL have helped to instil a great sense of confidence among the major disputants. Building on what Howard and the respondents commented as well as from the personal experience of the researcher, it can be concluded that UNIFIL has proven effective by using a combination of approaches like inducement and well-tested conflict management measures. Even though the future of the bilateral relationship between Israel and Lebanon cannot be predicted, the crisis in Syria has made the overall situation more complicated. One of the tasks of UNIFIL is to assist the LAF in its deployment and exercise its authority in South Lebanon. Over the years, although the LAF has grown to be a very responsible and capable organisation, able to stand up to the country's internal threats, it is still far from fully taking control of South Lebanon.

Opinions on the centrality of the local population in the peace process and the imperative to respect the local culture and tradition, as well as the view on the efficacy of the implementation of the mandate and UNIFIL's robust structure has been more or less unanimous. The presence of tensions between the operational tasks of the PKO and the requirement to forge a good relationship with the local populace and, hence, the need for a delicate balancing act has come out very clearly. It is also the general opinion that UNIFIL has been able to fulfil the better part of the mandate, which is much clearer now than it was in 2006 and for which it has direct responsibility. Even though UNIFIL is considered a robust PKO, disarming the Hezbollah is not a practical option. UNIFIL's earlier attempts to use a robust RoE to forcibly search for suspected arms and equipment of the Hezbollah heightened the tension between the peacekeepers, the Hezbollah and the local population.[100] In this regard, Howard also observed that the use of compelling force, one of the techniques of the coercive power of peacekeeping, may achieve only temporary compliance. On the other hand, it may trigger sustained resistance unless it is considered by those who are compelled as legitimate.[101] Secondly, despite an exhaustive set of RoEs, UNIFIL is not able to prevent the possibility of a full-fledged war because of lack of political will and the fear of casualties among TCCs. The robust structure of UNIFIL, therefore, is only a signal of the political commitment of the international community in support of UNIFIL's continued presence to bring back normalcy and help in the cessation of hostilities and establishment of a permanent ceasefire.

Summary of Key Goals and Extent of Progress

As mentioned in Chapter 3, the assessment of a peace operation can be more unequivocal by evaluating the extent of progress of the goals that have been set, based on the mission mandate. From the preceding sections, it is clear that UNIFIL has so far been able to implement a large part of the mandate, find better acceptability in Lebanese society and, most importantly, contribute to the absence of a major conflict between Israel and Lebanon for close to two decades after the 2006 war. A summary of the key goals and extent of progress as presented in this chapter is given in the table in Appendix F. It follows the conceptual framework that was developed in Chapter 3. The results of the table are analysed in the next chapter.

ENDNOTES

1. Blake D. Mathias and Anne D. Smith, "Autobiographies in organizational research: using leaders' life stories in a triangulated research design," *Organizational Research Methods* 19, no. 2 (2016): 204–30.
2. Vanessa Frances Newby, "The UNIFIL Mission in Context," *Peacekeeping in South Lebanon: Credibility and Local Cooperation* (New York: Syracuse University Press, 2018), 81.
3. UNIFIL, *Military Strategic Concept of Operations for UNIFIL 001/06* (September 11, 2006).
4. In October 1989, the Lebanese National Assembly met in Taif, Saudi Arabia, to ratify a "National Reconciliation Accord" under Syrian and Saudi tutelage. The Accord was designed to end the Lebanese civil war that had been raging for decades, to reassert Lebanese authority in South Lebanon, which was then occupied by Israel, and to legitimize and perpetuate the Syrian occupation of Lebanon.
5. UNIFIL, *Military Strategic Concept of Operations for UNIFIL 001/06* (September 11, 2006).
6. Alawites are an offshoot of Shiites. There are disagreements whether Alawites are Muslims or not. The Alawites claim to follow the essential teachings of Islam, but there are wide differences in interpretation. Presently, three-and-half millionAlawites control Syria.
7. UNIFIL Maritime Task Force, accessed October 22, 2019, https://unifil.unmissions.org/unifil-maritime-task-force
8. UN Department of Peace Operations, UNIFIL Maps as of November 2021, accessed July 29, 2022, https://unifil.unmissions.org/unifil-maps
9. Karin Kneissl, "An analysis on UNIFIL II: Three Years after UNIFIL: How and until when will the "interim" continue?" *Report by Friedrich Ebert Stiftung*, November 2009, accessed September 20, 2018, https://library.fes.de/pdf-files/bueros/beirut/07161.pdf
10. UN Security Council, *Report of the UN Secretary-General on the Implementation of Security Council Resolution1701 (2006)*, S/2013/381 (June 26, 2013).
11. Also see Appendix C.
12. Nicholas Blandford, "Why peace is prevailing, for now, in south Lebanon," *The Christian Science Monitor*, August 23, 2016, http://www.csmonitor.com/World/Middle-East/2016/0823/Why-peace-is-prevailing-for-now-in-south-Lebanon
13. "Two Israeli soldiers killed as Hezbollah missile hits vehicle on Lebanon border," *The Guardian*, January 28, 2015, https://www.theguardian.com/world/2015/jan/28/israel-missile-lebanon-syria-hezbollah
14. Also see Appendix C.
15. Also see Appendix C.
16. Appendix C.
17. UN Security Council, *Report of the UN Secretary-General on the Implementation of Security Council Resolution 1701 (2006)*, S/2017/201 (March 8, 2017).
18. UN Security Council, *Report of the UN Secretary-General*, S/2020/473 (June 1, 2020); UN Security Council, *Report of the UN Secretary-General*, S/2021/240 (March 9, 2021).
19. Vanessa Frances Newby, "The Pieces that Make the Peace: Micro-Processes of International Security," *International Peacekeeping* 23, no. 1 (November 2015): 148, http://www.tandfonline.com/doi/full/10.1080/13533312.2015.1110790
20. Ibid.
21. UN Security Council, *Report of the UN Secretary-General on the Implementation of Security Council Resolution 1701 (2006)*, S/2013/381 (June 26, 2013), 7.

22. Khaled Abu Toameh, "The Palestinians: Refugee Camps or Terrorist Bases?" *Gatestone Institute International Political Council,* July 21, 2016, https://www.gatestoneinstitute.org/8511/palestinians-refugee-camps
23. Nasser Chararah, "Terrorist Groups Exploit Palestinians in South Lebanon," *Al-Monitor,* September 20, 2013, http://www.al-monitor.com/pulse/originals/2013/09/lebanon-ain-hilweh-takfiri-groups-influence.html
24. Appendix C.
25. UN Security Council, *Eleventh Report of the Secretary-General on the Implementation of Security Council Resolution 1701 (2006),* S/2009/566 (November 2, 2009).
26. Ibid.
27. UN Security Council, *Report of the Secretary-General on the Implementation of Security Council Resolution 1701 (2006),* S/2017/59 (July 11, 2017).
28. UN Security Council, *Report of the Secretary-General on the Implementation of Security Council Resolution 1701 (2006),* S/2019/237 (March 14, 2019).
29. Nehemia Stern, Uzi Ben-Shalom, Niv Gold, Corinne Berger, Avishai Antonovsky, and Dvir Peleg,"Tunnel Operations in the Israel Defence Forces: Adapting the Warrior Ethos to Post-Heroic Conflict," *Armed Forces & Society,* (June 2020): 2, https://doi.org/10.1177/0095327X20924040
30. UN Security Council, *Report of the Secretary-General on the Implementation of Security Council Resolution 1701 (2006),* S/2018/210 (March 8, 2018).
31. UN Security Council, *Report of the Secretary-General on the Implementation of Security Council Resolution 1701 (2006),* S/2018/210 (March 8, 2018).
32. Nicholas Noe, ed. *Voice of Hezbollah: statements of Sayyed Hassan Nasrallah* (London: Verso,2007), 386–87.
33. Tony Lawrence, Tomas Jermalavicius, and Anna Bulakh, "Soldiers for Peace: Estonia, Finland and Ireland in UNIFIL," *ICDS Report,* December 2016: 33.
34. Lebanese Armed Forces, "Missions of the Lebanese Army," last modified 2017, https://www.lebarmy.gov.lb/en/content/mission-lebanese-army
35. Karin Kneissl, "An Analysis on UNIFIL Three Years after: How and until when will the "interim" continue?" November 2009, *Friedrich Ebert Stiftung,* http://library.fes.de/pdf-files/bueros/beirut/07161.pdf
36. UN Security Council, *Report of the Secretary-General on the Implementation of Security Council Resolution 1701 (2006),*S/2008/425 (June 27, 2008), 5–6.
37. Eugene Yukin, "UNIFIL's Mandate and Rules of Engagement," *Middle East Policy and Security* 1 (2009): 8, ttps://www.aub.edu.lb/ifi/ifi_saj/Documents/saj2009/unifil_mandate_rules_of_engagement_yukin.pdf
38. Efrat Elron, "The interplay between the transnational and multinational: Intercultural integrating mechanism in UN peace operations," in *Military Cooperation in Multinational Peace Operations: Managing cultural diversity and crisis response,* ed. Joseph Sorters and Philippe Manigart (London: Routledge, 2008), 28–48; Eyal Ben-Ari and E. Elron, "Blue helmets and white armour: Multi-nationalism and multi-culturalism among UN peacekeeping forces," *City & Society* 13, no. 2 (2008): 271–302.
39. Efrat Elron, "The interplay between the transnational and multinational: Intercultural integrating mechanism in UN peace operations," in *Military Cooperation in Multinational Peace Operations: Managing cultural diversity and crisis response,* ed. Joseph Sorters and Philippe Manigart (London: Routledge, 2008), 32.
40. Eugene Yukin, "UNIFIL's Mandate and Rules of Engagement," *Middle East Policy and Security* 1(2009): 6, https://www.aub.edu.lb/ifi/ifi_saj/Documents/saj2009/unifil_mandate_rules_of_engagement_yukin.pdf

41. A.K. Bardalai, "UNIFIL: The many challenges of successful peacekeeping," *Journal of Defence Studies*10, no. 3 (July-September 2016): 74–75.
42. Herb Keinon, "Annan to give UNIFIL 'teeth'," *Jerusalem Post,* August 21, 2006, http://www.jpost.com/Opinion/Letters/August-21-No-free-lunch
43. UN Security Council, *Report of the Secretary-General on the Implementation of Security Council Resolution 1701 (2006), S/2008/425* (June 27, 2008), 6.
44. UN Security Council, *Eleventh Report of the Secretary-General on the Implementation of Security Council Resolution 1701 (2006),* S/2009/566 (November 2, 2009).
45. EugeneYukin, "UNIFIL's Mandate and Rules of Engagement," *Middle East Policy and Security* 1(2009): 10, https://www.aub.edu.lb/ifi/ifi_saj/Documents/saj2009/unifil_mandate_rules_of_engagement_yukin.pdf
46. Trevor Findlay, *The Use of Force in UN Peace Operations* (Stockholm: Oxford University Press, 2002).
47. Chiara Ruffa, "What Peacekeepers Think and Do: An Exploratory Study of French, Ghanaian, Italian, and South Korean Armies in the United Nations Interim Force in Lebanon," *Armed Forces & Society,* 40, no. 2 (2014): 215.
48. UN Security Council, United Nations Interim Force in Lebanon, *Report of the Secretary-General,* S/2020/473 (June 1, 2020); Also see Appendix C.
49. Chiara Ruffa, "What Peacekeepers Think and Do: An Exploratory Study of French, Ghanaian, Italian, and South Korean Armies in the United Nations Interim Force in Lebanon," *Armed Forces & Society,* 40, no. 2 (2014): 217.
50. Appendix C.
51. R. Rubinstein, *Peacekeeping Under Fire: Culture and Intervention* (London: Paradigm Publishers, 2008), 38.
52. Kurt A. Boniecki and Thomas W. Britt, "Prejudice and the Peacekeeper" in *Psychology of the Peacekeepers: Lessons from the Field,* ed.Thomas W. Britt and Amy B. Alder (London: Praeger, 2003).
53. Brigadier General Abdul Rahman Shehaitly, who was the Deputy Chief of Operations of the LAF, made this statement in my presence.
54. Vanessa Newby, "Credibility through Aid," *Peacekeeping in South Lebanon: Credibility and Local Cooperation* (New York: Syracuse University Press, 2018), 145–147.
55. Lise Morje Howard, *Power in Peacekeeping* (New York: Cambridge University Press, 2019), 85, 117.
56. UN Security Council, *Progress report of the Secretary-General on Ethiopia and Eritrea,* S/2001/1194 (December 13, 2001).
57. Andy Knight, "Civil-Military cooperation and human security," in *Civil Military Cooperation in Post-Conflict Operations: Emerging theory and practice,* ed. Christopher Ankersen (London/New York: Routledge, 2008), 15–30.
58. Cedric de Coning, "Civil-military coordination and complex peace building systems," in *Civil Military Cooperation in Post-Conflict Operations: Emerging theory and practice,* ed. Christopher Ankersen (London/New York: Routledge, 2008), 63.
59. Andy Knight, "Civil-Military cooperation and human security," in *Civil Military Cooperation in Post-Conflict Operations: Emerging theory and practice,* ed. Christopher Ankersen (London/New York: Routledge, 2008), 20.
60. Chiara Ruffa, "What Peacekeepers Think and Do: An Exploratory Study of French, Ghanaian, Italian, and South Korean Armies in the United Nations Interim Force in Lebanon," *Armed Forces & Society,* 40, no. 2 (2014): 208; Vanessa Newby, "Credibility through Aid," *Peacekeeping in South Lebanon: Credibility and Local Cooperation* (New York: Syracuse University Press, 2018), 145.

61. Vanessa Frances Newby, "The Role of Credibility in Peacekeeping," *Peacekeeping in South Lebanon: Credibility and Local Cooperation* (New York: Syracuse, 2018), 53–55.
62. UN Department of Public Information, *Charter of the United Nations* (New York: UN Department of Public Information, 1945).
63. Appendix D.
64. UN Department of Safety and Security, accessed October 20,2020, https://www.un.org/en/safety-and-security
65. UN, *The Blue Helmets: A Review of United Nations Peacekeeping* (New York: United Nations, 1996), 93–95.
66. Andrej Sitkowski, *Peacekeeping: Myth and Reality* (London: Praeger Security International, 2006), 55–60.
67. Daniel Sobelman, "Learning to Deter: Deterrence Failure and Success in the Israel-Hezbollah Conflict, 2006-16," *International Security*, 41, no. 3 (Winter 2016/17): 153–55.
68. Sayed Nasarallah, "Hezbollah Stronger, Gold will Always Remain Gold" (speech, Beirut, March 29, 2014), Al Manar, http://archive.almanar.com.lb/english/article.php?id=143208
69. Gadi Eisenkot, "Northern Command Chief: No Interest in Launching Another Confrontation," in "Learning to Deter," Daniel Sobelman, *International Security* 41, no. 3 (winter 2016/17): 151–95.
70. Sayyed Nasrallah,"Martyr Leaders' Anniversary" (speech, February 16, 2016), Al Manar, http://archive.almanar.com.lb/english/article.php?id=255297
71. Vanessa Newby, "Credibility in Interstate Conflict," *Peacekeeping in South Lebanon: Credibility and Local Cooperation* (New York: Syracuse University Press, 2018), 82; Severine Autesserre, "Going Micro: Emerging and Future Peacekeeping Research," *International Peacekeeping* 21, no. 4 (2014): 492–500.
72. Patricia M. Shields, "Jane Addams: Peace Activist and Peace Theorist," *Jane Addams: Progressive Pioneer of Peace, Philosophy, Sociology, Social Work and Public Administration* (Texas: Springer International Publishing, 2017), 37.
73. Grant E. Rissler and Patricia M. Shields, "Positive Peace—A Necessary Touchstone for Public Administration," *Administrative Theory & Praxis*, 41, no.1 (2019): 60–78, https://doi.org/10.1080/10841806.2018.1479549
74. Patricia Shields, (2017). "Limits of Negative Peace, Faces of Positive Peace," *Parameters*: Journal of the US Army War College, 47 (2017): 5–12.
75. Lise Morje Howard, "Peacekeeping, Peace Enforcement and UN Reform," *Georgetown International Affairs*, 16, no. 2 (Summer/Fall, 2015): 9, http://www.jstor.org/stable/43773690
76. Indar Jit Rikhye, "The United Nations Operation in the Congo: Peacekeeping, Peacemaking and Peacebuilding," in *Beyond Traditional Peacekeeping*, ed. Donald C. F. Daniel and Bradd C. Hayes (London: Macmillan, 1995), 226; Indar Jit Rikhye, *Military Adviser to the Secretary General: UN Peacekeeping and Congo Crisis* (New York: St. Martin Press, 1993), 318.
77. Daniel Sobelman, "Learning to Deter: Deterrence Failure and Success in the Israel-Hezbollah Conflict, 2006–16," *International Security*, 41, no. 3 (Winter 2016/17): 151.
78. Ibid., 153.
79. Appendix D.
80. UN Security Council, *Report of the Secretary-General on the Implementation of Security Council Resolution 1701 (2006)*, S/2015/147 (February 27, 2015).

81. "Clearing Cluster Munition Remnants 2016," last modified 2018, http://www.mineactionreview.org/assets/downloads/Clearing_Cluster_Munition_Remnants_2016_WEB.pdf
82. Vanessa Frances Newby, "Credibility in Interstate Conflict," *Peacekeeping in South Lebanon: Credibility and Local Cooperation* (New York: Syracuse University Press, 2018), 95–97.
83. William Zartman, "Towards the Resolution of International Conflicts," in Peacemaking in International Conflict: Methods & Techniques, ed. William Zartman and J. Lewis Ramussen (Washington DC: United States Institute of Peace Press, 2001), 9.
84. Asher Susser, "Fifty Years since the Six Day War," *The Rusi Journal*162, no. 3 (June/July 2017): 40–48.
85. Karim Makdisi, "The UNIFIL Peacekeeping Mandate: Kicking the Southern Lebanon Can Down the Road," *PassBlue,* September 3, 2020, https://www.passblue.com/2020/09/03/the-unifil-peacekeeping-mandate-kicking-the-southern-lebanon-can-down-the-road/
86. Chiara Ruffa, "Military Cultures and Force Employment in Peace Operations," *Security Studies* 26, no. 3 (2017), 397.
87. Ibid.
88. Chiara Ruffa, "What Peacekeepers Think and Do: An Exploratory Study of French, Ghanaian, Italian, and South Korean Armies in the United Nations Interim Force in Lebanon," *Armed Forces & Society* 40, no. 2 (2014): 199–225.
89. Chiara Ruffa and Pascal Vennesson, "Fighting and Helping? A Historical - Institutionalist Explanation of NGO–Military Relations," *Security Studies* 23, no. 3 (2014): 599.
90. Appendix C.
91. Patricia M. Shields and Donald S. Travis, "Innovations in Warfare Strategy: Achieving Organisational Flexibility Through Ambidexterity," *Parameters* 47, no. 2 (Spring 2017): 65–76; Patricia M. Shields and Joseph Soeters, "Peaceweaving: Jane Addams, Positive Peace, and Public Administration", *American Review of Public Administration* 47, no. 3 (April 2017): 323–39, https://doi.org/10.1177%2F0275074015589629
92. Paul F. Diehl, *International Peacekeeping: With a new epilogue on Somalia, Bosnia and Cambodia* (Baltimore: Johns Hopkins Press, 1993), 74.
93. Beatric Pouligny, *Peace Operations Seen from Below: UN Missions and Local People* (London: C. Hurst & Co. Publishers, 2006), 104.
94. Jean-Marie Guehenno, "How to End War," *The Fog of Peace* (Washington: Brookings Institution, 2005), 229.
95. Indar Jit Rikhye, *The Theory and Practice of Peacekeeping* (London: C. Hurst & Company, 1984), 109; Jean-Marie Guehenno, "How to End War," *The Fog of Peace* (Washington: Brookings Institution, 2015), 212–231.
96. Jean-Marie Guehenno, "How to End War," *The Fog of Peace* (Washington: Brookings Institution, 2015), 230.
97. Chiara Ruffa, "French and Italian Units in Lebanon," *Military Cultures in Peace and Stability Operations: Afghanistan and Lebanon* (Philadelphia: University of Pennsylvania Press, 2019), 88–89.
98. Vanessa Frances Newby, "Credibility in Interstate Conflict," *Peacekeeping in South Lebanon: Credibility and Local Cooperation* (New York: Syracuse University Press, 2018), 95–97.

99. Lise Morje Howard, "Inducement in Lebanon, *Power in Peacekeeping* (New York: Cambridge University Press, 2019), 81, 100.
100. Karim Makdisi, "Reconsidering the struggle over UNIFIL in Southern Lebanon," *Journal of Palestine Studies* 43, no. 2 (February 2014): 37, https://doi.org/10.1525/jps.2014.43.2.24
101. Lise Morje Howard, *Power in Peacekeeping* (New York: Cambridge University Press, 2019), 137.

CHAPTER 6

FINAL ASSESSMENT AND RECOMMENDATIONS

Discussion

Defining the success and identifying criteria for the assessment of PKO has never been easy for any mission leadership or, for that matter, for the UN. Scholars and practitioners are at variance in their opinions on how to assess PKO. Most of the work in this field has been limited to a comprehensive study of selected PKO to analyse the reasons for success and failure but fell short of identifying the criteria for evaluation of PKO. Cameron suggested that "different models of effectiveness are useful for research in different circumstances. Their usefulness depends on the purposes and constraints placed on the organizational effectiveness investigation".[1] After analysing the varying definitions of success, what has emerged is that a practical and logical method to assess a PKO will be by measuring its performance against the set goals. Success and failure predominantly depend on the goals that are set to be achieved at the beginning of the mission. These goals, after considering the factors/variables that can impact the outcome of the PKO, will be largely determined by the mission's mandate.

Some of the generic goals will be the core goals and applicable across all PKO. Such core goals are reduction of violence; conflict management including mitigating or control of triggers for recurrence of violence leading to a full-fledged war; conflict resolution; alleviating the misery of the local populations, etc. The other category of goals will be mission-specific but derived from the core goals. The first step of the evaluation process, therefore, should be to identify the key goals based on the mandate.

Some of the key goals that would be useful to evaluate UNIFIL can be stated as follows:

- Restoration of peace and security.
- Creating conditions for prevention of resumption of hostilities between Lebanon and Israel.
- Ensuring that South Lebanon is free of armed personnel, assets and weapons other than those of the Lebanese government and UNIFIL.
- Assistance to the LAF in fulfilling its security responsibilities.
- Ensuring support from the local population.
- Maintaining the operational effectiveness of the mission.
- Achieving credibility and local legitimacy.

The second step is to formulate a few pillar questions and answers to ascertain whether the goals have been achieved or not. Accordingly (based on the purpose of this study), to establish a model of assessment of traditional peace operation, many UNIFIL-related key questions have been developed to obtain data for analysis. Based on the inputs received from stakeholders (collected via interviews and online answers from experts and contingent members) and available documents, it is possible to summarize how UNIFIL has performed to achieve its goals.

Any assessment based on such a framework will be both quantitative and qualitative. For example, while institution-related and survey data provide a quantitative result, the perception of the local population regarding the centre of gravity of the effectiveness of a peace operation will usually be qualitative. Accordingly, Newby dwells on the perception of the local population's perception of the credibility and legitimacy of the peace operation. Newby's concept, however, is based on qualitative inputs, which provides a good insight into what people think. Perception can provide an important insight into observations and understanding of the human mind. At the same time, if not supported by evidence, the assessment so formed, can be misleading. Therefore, observations (qualitative) that are supported by quantitative evidence help to arrive at a logical conclusion of the judgement. Accordingly, performance evaluation of UNIFIL using the conceptual framework that combines goal setting and ground level perception is discussed in the following sections.

Peace and Security

For more than a decade, since the last Israel-Lebanon war of 2006, there has not been a major conflict in the region. Even though there may have been many occasions or flashpoints for the resumption of hostilities, the absence of war for such a long duration is indeed noteworthy. Except for the regular violation of Lebanese air space by the Israeli air force, UNIFIL can take the credit for controlling potentially volatile situations along the BL combined with an effective liaison and coordination mechanism with both the IDF and LAF. Protests against air violation, as and when they take place, are regularly reported to the UN by both UNIFIL and Lebanon. Israel, however, dismisses the protests justifying the violations as being their standard defensive measures.

At the same time, it is also true that neither the Hezbollah nor Israel showed any interest in fighting another war, probably because of the prohibitive costs. Undoubtedly, tension is palpable in the region with the potential to blow up at the slightest provocation. Even though UNIFIL cannot be compared with other complex PKO, when it comes to violence against peacekeepers, there have been instances, albeit far and few, when its peacekeepers have been targeted. In the pattern of the unfriendly behaviour against UNIFIL and BL violations, there was however a spike for a short period around June-July 2014.

Such short spikes are deliberately manipulated announcing to the international community, and more specifically to UNIFIL, the continued relevance of the interested actors in South Lebanon. The period during which ceasefire violations occurred was chosen probably because the conflict in Syria was at its peak around that time as also because General Portolano assumed responsibility as the HoM and FC on 24 July 2014. Protagonists of all movements have their ways of reminding peace brokers that they are there to stay until there is a complete cessation of hostility. On 20 April 2017, the Hezbollah organised a media tour of the border between Israel and Lebanon. As stated by Karam, "The tour, under the gaze of the UN peacekeepers based in the border town of Naqoura, sometimes took on a theatrical nature". "The Hezbollah wanted to send a message by the tour in case Israel was preparing for war. The message is 'I see you, and I have another scenario for you'."[2] An incident like this can be problematic and has the potential to blow up without much warning. For events like this, the LAF is the contact point for UNIFIL. If it ever failed to inform UNIFIL in advance, it was because of a lack of coordination or because it deliberately did not inform UNIFIL of the impending visit. Given the kind of writ that the Hezbollah runs on the Lebanese government, it is most unlikely for the LAF not to receive instructions from the government of Lebanon to coordinate the tour in South Lebanon. Pretending ignorance by the LAF of the impending tour probably was to avoid embarrassment to both UNIFIL and LAF, which would have come if UNIFIL was given this information in advance.

It is difficult to establish a specific pattern of violence against peacekeepers. However, since violent acts are generally triggered by inappropriate conduct of the peacekeepers, the decrease in the violence can be considered an indication of gradual improvement in the personal conduct of the peacekeepers and their acceptance in Lebanese society. The act of de-mining, although not in the mandate of UNIFIL, has gone down well with the local population.

Creating Conditions for the Prevention of Conflict

The prevention of hostilities by UNIFIL is wishful thinking for several reasons such as both the Hezbollah and Israel not wanting to get lured into another large-sized conflict. At the same time, because of UNIFIL's quick response in defusing crises and the Hezbollah's involvement in Syria, there has neither been any conflict nor has it expanded beyond the geographical borders of Israel and Lebanon. However, the present stability is temporary and the bilateral relations between Lebanon and Israel are much more than a simple narrative of animosity between two states. In this regard, a lot will depend on the future trajectory of the ever-shifting regional power balance in the Middle East.

To a great extent, stability in South Lebanon is guaranteed by the positions taken by Israel and Lebanon and their armies, other armed groups, and the ability of UNIFIL to delicately balance the challenges of mandate and environment. For instance, the Hezbollah, with its massive following in South Lebanon and now part of the government, is officially not a party to the conflict. Yet, it has an important say in the future of the Israel-Lebanon relationship. There have been times when simply because of lack of coordination, both Israel and the Hezbollah were close to tipping the balance. For that matter, any military action by the IDF against the Hezbollah, even in Syria, will reverberate in the disputed area between Israel and Lebanon. Aoun observed that despite UNIFIL's contribution, the unprecedented quiet on the Lebanese Israeli border is prone to destruction by the burgeoning threatening environment of the Middle East as rivalry amongst the uncontrollable actors intensifies.[3]

UNIFIL's sincere efforts in marking the BL, the existing liaison and coordination mechanisms, and the periodical UNIFIL tripartite meetings have also helped to remove many misunderstanding and contributed to preventing the resumption of hostilities. Despite this, the continued prevailing tension provides an opportunity to Israel and other critics of UNIFIL, who deliberately choose to overlook the stability that has been achieved for more than a decade and instead criticize it for not doing anything about the non-mandated tasks, such as disarming the Hezbollah.

Ensuring South Lebanon is Free of Unauthorised Armed Groups

This is one of the most controversial mandated tasks. UNIFIL has only an assistance role to the LAF in removing unauthorised armed groups from South Lebanon. Taking this into account and given the political dynamics of Lebanon, including the Hezbollah's growing clout and the presence of a majority Shiite community in South Lebanon, disarming the Hezbollah is neither an option nor is it doable. Besides, as there is no visible presence of the Hezbollah in UNIFIL's area of operations, it makes it more difficult to fulfil this task. Therefore, to castigate UNIFIL for a task, which is neither its responsibility nor practical, is rather unfair to the mission.

Assistance to the LAF

There are several disputed areas along the BL. UNIFIL's painstaking efforts to expeditiously place clear and visible markings along the BL has helped to remove misunderstandings in a few disputed areas. Consequently, incidents of inadvertent crossing of the BL by the villagers, which was earlier relatively high, has also come down. However, the contentious dispute over the Shebaa Farm area remains unresolved and continues to be a sticking point in the triangular relationship between Israel, Syria, and Lebanon. As for cooperation between UNIFIL and the LAF, this aspect of the mission has made considerable progress. Unfortunately, the Hezbollah's position in the government, its relationship with the LAF and the fear of such military assistance finally falling into the hands of the Hezbollah is something that has not been taken very lightly by the international community. Notwithstanding the Hezbollah factor, the operational cooperation and coordination, as well as joint training of UNIFIL and the LAF, is widely acknowledged and appreciated.

Relationship with the Local Population

The UN High-Level Independent Panel Report enunciated that as locals can immensely contribute with information and possible solution/s to the conflict, engagement with local communities is considered a core element for a mission's success.[4] Since the local population is the most affected section of society, they tend to perceive different types of PKO through their own prism and rally around that perspective. However, people's perception is also formed by the systematic feeding of information by those who gain from a specific perception. In Lebanon, the identity of UNIFIL is regularly shaped and reshaped by the local population, which in turn, is formed based on inputs from the various political parties. For instance, to the Hezbollah, the presence of UNIFIL is mainly for disarming them and weaken it, and its affiliate's—the "8 March movement"—influence over the local populace in South Lebanon by undertaking various social welfare projects.

The continued relevance of the Hezbollah and its ally in South Lebanon, therefore, impacts on a strategic narrative that is built upon a discourse that portrays UNIFIL as a pro-Israeli force and disseminating the same information to the local population. The Hezbollah's strategy is aimed at restricting UNIFIL's freedom of movement in South Lebanon on the ground that UNIFIL patrols are collecting intelligence on behalf of Israel. This helped the Hezbollah to stay alive in South Lebanon. Such discourse, however, slightly changed around the year 2011 because of the Syrian conflict in which the Hezbollah was actively involved. A possible escalation of violence with Israel in the south certainly did not help its cause. Gradually, UNIFIL found more acceptance in society and there was no hesitation to use it as a mediator. For instance, when Spanish Corporal Francisco Javier Soria Toledo was killed during an exchange of fire between the IDF and the Hezbollah on 28 January 2015, the Hezbollah quickly blamed the IDF but refrained from describing the death as UNIFIL's failure to prevent violence. A shift in the position of the Hezbollah and the 8 March movement, however, is and will only be temporary. Those groups will always consider UNIFIL as an unwelcome guest in Lebanon.[5]

Accordingly, there is a growing understanding of the necessity to forge a good relationship with the local population for shaping a better perception of the peacekeeping force. The present relationship is quite good and UNIFIL peacekeepers have found better acceptance in Lebanese society. The support of the population is reflected in UNIFIL's ability to carry out its operational activities unhindered except in those areas that are sensitive to the population and the Hezbollah. More importantly, unbecoming conduct and arrogance in the form of overemphasis on force protection measures distances the population from UNIFIL. Monetary contribution by a few contingents of the Western nations for developmental activities, on the other hand, has at least helped to navigate within the mission area with ease. To be able to navigate with ease, hence, implies freedom of movement with less difficulty, but not with impunity. Should the peacekeepers commit a mistake, the local population will not refrain from displaying their anger. On the contrary, many contingents hailing from non-Western nations seem to have found better ways to win the hearts of the population simply by being sensitive to Lebanese culture and tradition. In this regard, Meulen and Soeters observed that "the general point that armed forces stand a better chance of success when to some degree their own diversity matches the culture and diversity of host nations is very plausible indeed".[6] Overall, despite the criticism and periodical complaints about the conduct of the peacekeepers, since its inception in 1978, UNIFIL has become a part of the life of Lebanese society, which is difficult to sever. As Ruffa wrote, Italian peacekeepers are slightly more diverse in their outlook than the other Western nations. They understand the close relationship between the local population of South Lebanon and the Hezbollah, and at the same time want to be loved by the population. To avoid earning displeasure from either of them, Italian peacekeepers would use force strictly in self-defence.[7] This was Ruffa's belief, which she reconfirmed after studying the variation in the behaviour of French and Italian contingents in multinational operations in both Lebanon and Afghanistan. At the end of her study to explore the impact of military culture on the ground, she concluded that "While French troops emphasized operational activities and displayed high force protection levels, Italian troops focused on humanitarian activities". In the UPOE concept, she termed this variation "combat/security effectiveness and humanitarian effectiveness".[8]

Mandate and Operational Effectiveness

Like any other PKO, some aspects of the mandate of UNIFIL are not clear since the mandate is the function of political adjustment and, hence, not an independent factor for success and failure. In the case of UNIFIL, vagueness is prominent where it is in the assistance role such as in helping the LAF to remove unauthorised arms and armed groups from Lebanon. At the same time, being one of the oldest PKO, UNIFIL has become synonymous with ensuring peace and tranquillity in South Lebanon. Accordingly, anything more than this would simply not be acceptable to the international community and, more specifically, to Israel. Consequently, the handful of limited tasks for which UNIFIL has direct responsibility, lose their relevance in the face of the rising expectations of the outside world.

A robust structure of the peacekeeping force is equally important for operational effectiveness. UNIFIL is unique because of its multinational configuration of the well-trained and well-equipped European contingents operating alongside lesser equipped (and some less trained) non-Western troops from Asia and Africa. The RoEs are also quite exhaustive. However, fearing casualties because of retaliation, the use of force to enforce the mandate is not an option for the TCCs. The net result oftentimes is inaction or measured actions by the military contingents in case of the occurrence of violence.[9]

What complicates the matter is the growing strength of the Hezbollah and its rapid response capability, which Israel has pledged to meet with appropriate countermeasures, and the uncertainty of the shape of the next conflict that looms large in the region. Under these circumstances, despite its robust structure, UNIFIL is not able to either prevent or possibly halt the outbreak of another possible full-fledged war between Israel and Lebanon. Hence, the present structure of UNIFIL at best can be considered as nothing more than an indication of the international community's commitment and political support to UNIFIL.

Analysis and Final Assessment

UNIFIL was established in 1978 with the primary task of ensuring IDF withdrawal from Lebanon. Even after 40 years of its deployment in Lebanon and more than a decade without a major conflict, not too many studies and analyses of UNIFIL have been done so far. *Peacekeeping in South Lebanon* by Vanessa Newby, however, is a new and different contribution to the scholarly work in the field of peacekeeping.[10]

The IDF stayed in the region until it unilaterally decided to withdraw in May 2000. Given that UNIFIL was not able to implement the mandate as per SCRs 425 and 426, UNIFIL has often been considered a failure. The role of UNIFIL post-2006, however, is different than what it was earlier. Initially established with a force of around 4,000 peacekeepers, as of 30 June 2022, the troop strength now is 9,995 the spike in the right half of the infographic explains how the force level went up after the adoption of SCR 1701 post the 2006 war.[11] Even though UNIFIL cannot claim to have achieved complete

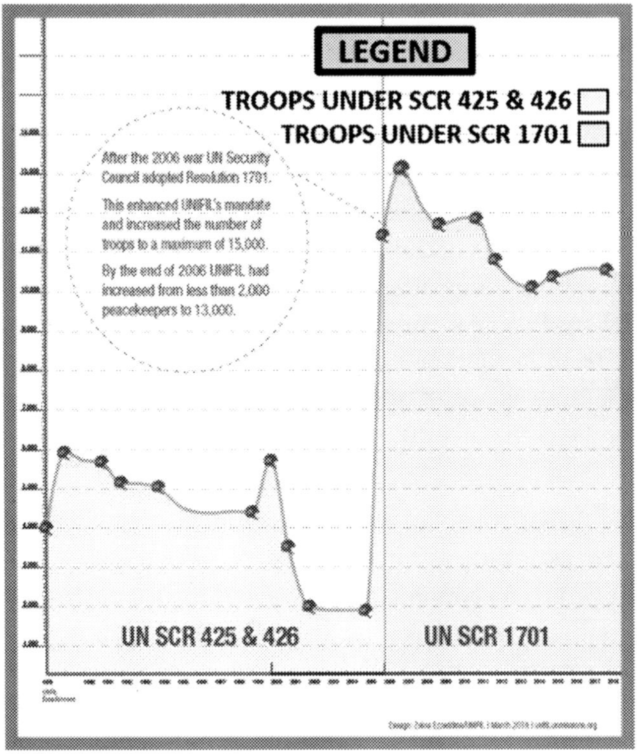

cessation of hostilities with such a big force, the period of more than a decade without a major conflict is the longest in the history of UNIFIL, although the animosity between the parties to the conflict still runs deep. While it is difficult to pinpoint the exact reasons for this period of stability, UNIFIL's contribution has been significant and widely acknowledged.

To a large extent, peacekeeping by UNIFIL is attributable to the political support of the international community at the strategic level, the physical presence of some European nations in the mission, effective liaison and coordination mechanism, good inter-personal relations with the local populace, expeditious marking of the BL, extra humanitarian efforts taken by UNIFIL in many areas, effective control on activities along the BL, both by observation and quick response, as well as dynamic mission leaders. However, there will be times when the initiative of the mission leaders can come under severe criticism because of the host nation's political motives or conflict of interests of the main disputants.

Contrary to the general perception of many Western TCCs, the robust capabilities of the mission's set-up seem to have made little contribution to the present state of stability in the region. If at all, advanced weaponry combined with an aggressive attitude on the part of the peacekeepers of certain Western nations only adds to the occasional estranged relations between UNIFIL and the local populace. As noted by Novosseloff, military robustness is unlikely to produce tangible results when a robust force is deployed as a substitute for the political process.[12]

The mandate under SCR 1701 is relatively clearer than the one under SCRs 425 and 426. A portion of the mandate, which is deliberately vague, is viewed as an unavoidable political necessity to accommodate and obtain the consent of one of the major non-state parties to the conflict. Immediately after the war of 2006, the structure of UNIFIL as it exists today was considered a strategic and operational necessity. However, given the precarious nature of the regional instability and its likely effect on the future of bilateral relations between Israel and Lebanon, even a much bigger force than what exists today is unlikely to be able to prevent an outbreak of a major conflict. UNIFIL is part of a larger strategic chessboard in the sense that any regional instability, especially in Syria, is bound to spill over to Lebanon. Therefore, an assessment of UNIFIL will be incomplete if this parameter is disregarded. The limitations of UNIFIL were reflected even in the very first report of the Secretary-General soon after the adoption of SCR 1701.[13] At the same time, the presence of a peacekeeping force in Lebanon has become a way of life for the Lebanese population, which provides legitimacy to the stand taken by Lebanon and Israel. Within the modicum of a forced standoff, convinced with what UNIFIL is doing, both the countries seem to agree to disagree with each other, although tentative for the time being.

As observed by Sitkowski, soon after the IDF withdrawal from South Lebanon in 2000, despite the UN wanting to cut down the size and finally close down the ill-conceived operations in Lebanon, UNIFIL continues to be in place.[14] In this regard, some of the UN's main financial contributors, in particular the USA, are unhappy over the growing clout of the Hezbollah and are determined to reduce the budget for all UN PKO. As quoted by the *New York Post*, UN Ambassador Nikki Haley also conveyed the fact that automatic renewal of UNIFIL, which takes place annually, will not be accepted by the USA anymore.[15] In this connection, it is important to realize that the US Administration's proposal of $ 1.07 billion for UN peacekeeping for Financial Year 2020-21 is a sharp decrease of its contribution by 29 per cent from the enacted budget of $ 1.52 billion for 2019-20.[16]

For Israel, UNIFIL is more cost-effective than having to occupy the land itself. Rikhye's observation, made in 1984, that UNIFIL was a 'Salami in a Sandwich' caught in the political quagmire, holds good even today.[17] Bosco also pointed out, "if any one of a number of players—the Hezbollah, Israel, anti-Assad forces in Syria or opponents of the Hezbollah inside Lebanon—decides to escalate the fragile situation, the UN can do very little to stop them".[18] Therefore, the question is if UNIFIL is not in a position to prevent a major conflict between Israel and Lebanon, and if it is not able to assist in disarming the Hezbollah, then why should UNIFIL continue. The answer to this question lies in the political necessity of continuing UNFIL and understanding the likely shape of the regional security given the volatility in Syria in the event of a new front opening up along the Lebanon-Israel border.

UNIFIL is called a robust PKO, comprising well-trained and well-equipped peacekeepers from the developed countries in the West. Whether such an organisation has been able to contribute to restoring order or would be able to do that in the event of another major conflict, purely because of its robust structure, should best be decided by the environment. As observed by Aoun and Efrat, "Like all peace operations, UNIFIL is not a solution but a conflict management tool that serves as a means to an end".[19] UNIFIL, which is more than four decades old and has weathered major storms in the past, is still without an exit strategy. Even if the situation in Lebanon deteriorates, the mission may still be there to pick up the pieces afterwards.[20] As resonated by Soeters, even though UNIFIL can be considered a 'frozen conflict' and problematic to many Westerners, its continuation is inevitable under current conditions. Hence, closing the mission would amount to the international community abdicating its responsibility of providing a semblance of hope and stability to the people of Lebanon and Israel in particular and the region in general.[21]

UNIFIL suffers from challenges that peacekeeping operations face in general today. One of the challenges, amongst many, is the gradually shrinking budget for peacekeeping operations, as we just indicated.[22] For FY 2020-21, as the Trump Administration is proposing to cut the US share by at least 26 per cent, UN peacekeeping is bound to feel the heat in the years to come. Shendruk, Hillard, and Roy of the Council on Foreign Relations, however, observed that the "U.S. contributions often represent a significant percentage of an entity's revenue".[23] They may imply that this will not drastically impact the peacekeeping operations, but with the trend of the shrinking budget and the impact of the global COVID-19 recession on the way, the UN may have to think of a fresh look at international peace and security. It is something the Security Council should be worried about. While a reduced budget may affect a mission in many ways, it will also be one of the factors for deciding the total number of missions or putting a cap on the total number of troops in individual missions. Either way, the UN may not be present where its presence is required, or it may compromise on the operational effectiveness of individual missions. Post the 2006 war, the new UNIFIL structure was based on the saturation model, i.e., saturate the area of operation with a greater density of troops. According to Security Council Resolution 2845 of 2019, a review of UNIFIL was undertaken in coordination with the TCCs and the government of Lebanon. The review proposed to restructure UNIFIL with reduced strength and more reliance on new and advanced equipment. As a first step, the troop ceiling went down from 10,600 to its current strength of 9,995.[24] Restructuring of UNIFIL though was due as early as in 2010 when the troop strength was almost at its peak. Even at that time, it would have been possible to make optimum use of troops (without compromising on the security of the base) by using advanced surveillance technology and quick mobility while responding to the developing situation.

That aside, even while it becomes more difficult to sustain the existing peace operations, the fear of the peacekeepers spreading the COVID-19 virus is likely to make the local public suspicious leading to more hostility towards them as was seen in the DRC when Ebola health workers were attacked in 2019.[25] Recognizing the challenge of post-COVID-19 to peacekeeping, UN Secretary-General Guterres commented:

> Our peacekeeping operations and special political missions will continue to be guided by four key objectives: "First, to support national authorities in their response to COVID-19". Second, to protect our personnel and their capacity to continue critical operations. Third, to ensure that our own personnel are not a contagion vector. And fourth, to help protect vulnerable communities and continue to implement mission mandates (UN Secretary-General Guterres, 20 April 2020).[26]

In keeping with the UNSG's remarks on the impact of the pandemic on peacekeeping operations, Razza observed that the protection of civilians will remain the core objective of the peacekeeping mandate, but the very concept of protection strategy is likely to be contested and hence will have to change. He believed that as hostility towards the peacekeepers increases, there will be a need to re-examine the way they can be employed to provide protection. Razza remarked that the UN may think of more ways to support the host states to take on the ownership of the protection strategies.[27] The senior advisor to the International Peace Institute, Mahmoud, reported that as a consequence of a reduction of UN peace operations, that part of the protection mandate, which requires military intervention, will need to be undertaken by a non-UN-led force, however, under the mandate of the UN. In such cases, where the host nations are trying to recover from an authoritarian rule, special political missions can help them towards a smooth transition to democracy. Even in these cases, peacebuilding activities will have to be more localized with the states taking on national ownership.[28] The observations of Raza and Mahmoud, however, are more relevant to complex peace operations such as MONUSCO and UNMISS, where peacekeepers have been mandated to protect civilians and required to intermingle with the local population more closely than in the UNIFIL mission.

Despite the absence of conflict for close to two decades, for UNIFIL, challenges remain. One of them is UNIFIL's lack of control over the consequences of the ever-changing regional power balance in the Middle East. One of the views is that the intent of the Islamic countries to defeat Israel and the Hezbollah's involvement in Syria perhaps were reasons for the absence of conflict for a long period. This could have been a logical assessment, however, only until the recent turn of events when the UAE and Bahrain signed the Abraham Accord on 15 September to forge diplomatic relations with Israel.[29] Bohl observed that the fear of the threat of Pan-Islamism to regional stability has pushed Saudi Arabia and the UAE to nationalism.[30] Kedar reported that the impression of the Arab world's hatred for Israel to rally around the Palestinian cause is ill-founded. According to him, the Arab world dislikes the Palestinians more than they revile Israel. He believes that the Arab nations dislike being cheated by their people or community and look at Israel as one of the most prospering democracies.[31] Khashan also commented that the Gulf States are afraid of Iran, particularly when the USA is becoming a less reliable partner. Fearing stronger Israeli-Iranian ties, when conflicts between them end, the Gulf States want to be more proactive. It is a simple geopolitical sum that may need recalculation.[32] Improving a bilateral relationship with Israel will be economically more beneficial than supporting the Palestinian cause. As the momentum of nationalism picks up speed, more and more nations from the Middle East are likely to follow the UAE and Bahrain. After the UAE and Bahrain, countries like Africa and Sudan has also agreed to recognize Israel.[33] Left with a shared feeling of abandonment, both Fatah and Hamas, although on opposing sides, maybe pushed to join hands and be further caught in the sphere of other nations such as Turkey and Iran. The

Palestinians, who provided common cause to the Middle East nations to oppose the West and Israel, may feel betrayed by the Abraham Accord. However, it could also encourage the Hezbollah because, even in the past, it has never failed to exploit the Palestinian card when it came to confronting Israel.

According to the Secretary General's report of June 2020, even though the current structure of UNIFIL has been a deterrence to the resumption of hostilities, the violations of Lebanese air space by the IDF have not decreased. In Lebanon, the report stresses that there is an increasing number of cases of obstruction to freedom of movement to UNIFIL by the population of South Lebanon. This questions more and more the impartial stand of the peacekeepers, as a gradually increasing number of areas is being made inaccessible to UNIFIL, more specifically near the BL, and permission to visit the sites of incidents that were reported to be connected to violations of SCR 1701 is being denied progressively. The good point, however, is that the population seems to be recognising the LAF as the sole security provider of Lebanon. Illustrating the empirical evidence that was drawn from UNIFIL, Newby, as explained earlier in Chapter 3, concluded that "assurance behaviours have built UNIFIL a positive reputation that enables them to function". She further states that "the relationships built with local institutions are based on the confidence UNIFIL will continue to deliver on its promises and little more".[34]

As such, the report of the Secretary-General is somewhat contrary to Newby's claims that the UNIFIL has been able to prove its credibility and has received local legitimacy.[35] Another way of looking at the new attitude of both the government of Lebanon and the population of South Lebanon is that UNIFIL has been able to achieve whatever it could, and it is now time to reduce its footprint in Lebanon. These, however, do not point to the end of the resumption of violence. The risk of full-fledged violence either due to changes in the regional geopolitics like a new relationship between nations of the Arab world and Israel or a local incident along the BL remains. For that matter, even the recently concluded first round of direct talks between Lebanon and Israel on 14 October 2020 to solve the disputed maritime boundary may raise too much optimism concerning their bilateral relations. While both the Hezbollah and its ally, the Amal party, did not discourage any direct discussion, they did not like any politician to be part of the Lebanese team for the talks.[36]

Azhari questioned the timing of the talks as the Trump Administration increased sanctions on Lebanese individuals and the Hezbollah's ally including former finance minister Ali Hasan Khalil, who is the Hezbollah's main Lebanese ally and Lebanese Parliament Speaker Nabih Berri's top aide. It, therefore, left the Hezbollah with no option other than to agree reluctantly to the US-brokered plan. If it were so, the evolving relationship is likely to change again with President Joe Biden's foreign policy. Biden had mentioned the way he would like to deal with Iran as early as in March 2020: "But there is a smart way to counter the threat that Iran poses to our interests and a self-defeating way—and Trump has chosen the latter. The killing of Qasem Soleimani, the commander of Iran's Quds Force, removed a dangerous actor, but also raised the prospect of an ever-escalating cycle of violence in the region, and it has prompted Tehran to jettison the nuclear limits established under the nuclear deal".[37] Even though the President did not refer to the Hezbollah directly as being the proxy arm of Iran, Biden's comment would have placed implicit reliance on diplomacy to make a meaningful contribution to the way Israel and Lebanon may like to take forward their bilateral relationship. Therefore, even though Rose, an author at *Geopolitical Future* believed that the talks looked like Israel extending an olive branch to Lebanon which may melt the frozen relations between Israel and Lebanon, it is too early to predict the future trajectory in their relations.[38]

UNIFIL is in no position to influence the outcome of any of these developments. What, however, is possible for UNIFIL is to keep a close tag on the BL and prevent small incidents from blowing up into full-fledged conflicts. Therefore, the presence of UNIFIL, even in the form of a smaller force but with inbuilt capability for good observation and good information analysis coupled with quick response capabilities both at the tactical and operational level, will be a necessity. Such a force, which can connect with the local population and is led by able and effective leaders, should be able to accomplish a larger part of the mandate. In this regard, Howard noted that more than a large-sized formation, armed with a mandate to use force, peacekeepers who have the freedom to learn from the locals in a society that is either recovering or has already recovered from conflict would be able to contribute better to make a peace operation successful.[39]

In the final analysis, the assessment of a UN peace operation is complex and full of contradictions and hence necessarily subject to discussion and debate. Doyle and Sambanis had concluded that the UN is what it makes out of it. The Secretary-General's Secretariat does not have a standing force to intervene but has to rely on the decision of the Security Council and troop contributions from the member-states for deployment of a peace operation. Therefore, if things go wrong, it is not necessarily, first, the fault of the UN but that of those member-states who choose not to act or act inadequately. Doyle and Sambanis believe that even though peacekeeping cannot solve every conflict, within the constraints, no one does the job better than the UN. As said before, a meta-review of a wide range of studies of the impact of UN peacekeeping comes to a similar conclusion.[40] In ordinary military operations, success and failure can be measured by using parameters like territorial gain or loss, own and enemy casualties, and destruction of war equipment. However, it is not possible to use the same parameters to evaluate the performance of a peace operation. As seen from the extent of the progress (see Appendix F) made on the key goals, except for Goal 4 and partly Goal 6, UNIFIL so far has fared well.

UNIFIL's achievements in fulfilling Goals 1 and 2, i.e., 'restoration of peace security and creating conditions for prevention of resumption of hostilities between Lebanon and Israel have been creditable. As for Goal 3, despite the challenges of the presence of unauthorised armed groups in South Lebanon, UNIFIL has made notable success. The local population supports UNIFIL, and it has achieved credibility as well as local legitimacy (Goals 5 and 7). However, since local support and legitimacy are not unconditional, UNIFIL needs to continue its work to provide evidence in support of credibility and local legitimacy.

Fulfilling Goal 4, i.e., 'assistance to LAF in fulfilling its security responsibilities', however, is complex and challenging. It is a political compulsion for the Government of Lebanon and the LAF not to act against the Hezbollah. Therefore, regardless of how strong the LAF becomes militarily, there is an extremely low probability of UNIFIL's ability to fulfil this goal. As brought out earlier, is it not possible for UNIFIL to directly challenge the Hezbollah even if the mission was under Chapter VII of the UN. Under the current circumstances, to expect the LAF to remove unauthorised arms and armed groups including the Hezbollah from South Lebanon is not workable. Therefore, instead of failure, it will be reasonable to categorise UNIFIL's achievement of Goal 4 as a moderate success. UNIFIL must continue its efforts to build the LAF's professional capability by organising joint training and engaging with the international community for external financial aid for it. Side by side, a revised resolution that mandates UNIFIL in an assistance role that is limited to only building the LAF's professional capability and NOT for the security of South Lebanon is an option worth considering. Such a revision will help to improve UNIFIL's image as an effective peace broker.

For Goal 6, i.e., 'maintaining the operational effectiveness of the mission,' UNIFIL can be assessed as operationally fit. But the contingents are generally shy of using force, which is perceived similarly by the local population. However, UNIFIL's ability and will power to enforce the mandate and use force is yet to be tested on the ground. There were occasions when UNIFIL could have used force in self-defence, but it chose to exercise restraint so as not to upset the delicate status of UNIFIL in Lebanese society. Hence, it will be premature to label UNIFIL as a failure in fulfilling this part of Goal 6. On an average, UNIFIL's overall achievement in fulfilling all the six goals has been significant.

Pursuing the indicators formulated by Walter, Howard, and Fortna—reducing and preventing violence from recurring, containing its spread within and across the borders, reducing civilian and military deaths, and making post-conflict settlement easier—UNIFIL has proved to be an effective peacekeeping mission.[41] Therefore, UNIFIL can be placed in the category of 'satisfactorily successful' UN peace operations.

It will be, however, beyond the control of UNIFIL to prevent a possible future major conflict between Israel and Lebanon if it happens because of the spilling over of a larger regional conflict. Until then, as Newby concluded, "at the subnational level, UNIFIL can influence its security environment and hence contribute to the maintenance of international peace and security".[42] It is not difficult to imagine a situation with UNIFIL not in it. In close to the past two decades, not many days have passed without any incident that had the potential to result in another possible full-fledged conflict between Lebanon and Israel. That aside, the decision on the future of UNIFIL should be considered on the lines of what Sambanis remarked on sustainable peace, "UN missions have a robust positive effect on peacebuilding outcomes, particularly participatory peace, but the effect occurs mainly in the short run and is stronger when peacekeepers remain".[43] UNIFIL's contribution towards negative peace is likely to be more noticeable if the mission continues to operate the way it is doing now as long as possible.

Future Scope of Research

The main objective of the study was to formulate a conceptual framework for the evaluation of UN Peace Operations and apply that to assess the performance of a traditional peace operation. Subsequently, the evaluation of UNIFIL gave rise to other related subjects. Walter, Howard, and Fortna had recommended a new design of research that would help to make peacekeeping more effective.[44] The future study, which should be in similar lines, can be further validated and corroborated by the following proposals:

- By conducting a quantitative study on the success criteria in other missions under the UN or regional organisations. This will validate and develop success criteria for future use.
- By conducting a field survey on the success factors at the tactical level in all four UN peace operations in the Middle East/ Mediterranean area, which will include UNIFIL (Lebanon), UNDOF (Golan Heights) and UNTSO (Palestine-Jerusalem).
- There are many moderating and mediating variables, which further influence the outcomes of UN peace operations. These include the political philosophy of ruling parties in the conflict zone, the relationship with the warring parties, religious legacies of conflict and strategic importance of the geographical areas. Further quantitative studies can be carried out on the role of these variables on the outcomes of missions.
- Success criteria can be further employed after any major event or a lapse of time in UNIFIL to update its validity and find the way forward for its success.

Implications and Major Takeaways

Evaluations of UN peace operations are important to understand whether they are a success or a failure to be able to make mid-course corrections and also to apply lessons learned for the benefit of future peace operations. Further, unless there is a good comprehension of the reasons for success and failure, evaluations of peace operations, purely based on a template, will not only be inaccurate but will fail to make a positive contribution in the field of peace operations. To that extent, some of the implications and major takeaways for enhancing the operational effectiveness of peace operations are given in the following sections.

Implications

From the empirical research based on a case study combining qualitative and quantitative data, major takeaways are: *one,* since the factors/variables affecting the performance vary from conflict to conflict, there is no single way to assess the effectiveness or performance of UN peacekeeping operations. The instrument used to assess the performance of UNIFIL should not be use as a template but can be used for the assessment of other traditional UN peace operations after being suitably modified; *Two,* the relevance and necessity of UN peacekeeping operations will depend on the prevailing geopolitical environment; *Three,* in the absence of any other alternative conflict management tool, the role of UN peacekeeping operations is not likely to change soon. Therefore, the benefits of the financial burden of maintaining a peacekeeping operation far outweigh the cost of a war that may occur because of the absence of a peacekeeping mission; *Finally,* empirical research based on a case study combining qualitative and quantitative data is advantageous to produce a more reliable analysis.

Major Takeaways

There will always be varying interpretations of the principles of peacekeeping which will influence the outcome of any UN peace operation. Therefore, organised training for peacekeepers in the deployment area in the form of debates and discussion would help to limit the scope of the misinterpretation of the nuances of principles of peacekeeping. The current structure of UNIFIL comprising peacekeepers from a few Western as well as non-Western nations is a good and rare combination. It provides political deterrence to antagonists with a more "human" face. Therefore, for the sake of maintaining the current state of 'negative peace', UNIFIL should remain in its current form and further strengthen its conflict management measures. The institutionalisation of a mechanism for periodical collation and analysis of disaggregated data in terms of opinion surveys and operational statistics by the mission HQs would also help to make continuous improvement and mid-course correction in the operational activities of UNIFIL.

UNIFIL is one of the older missions established in an inter-state conflict setting. Missions like UNIFIL, in the words of Novosseloff, are status quo missions and do not lend to conflict resolution. Yet, the importance of such status quo missions that manage to keep the lid on instability and can usher in negative peace in some cases cannot be overlooked. However, for UNIFIL even though its effectiveness is mainly due to its quick response to the flash points and the effective liaison and coordination mechanism, the probability of escalation of violence into a regional conflict is very high. In the light of the danger of the consequences of the post Cold War inter-state conflicts, the subject of preventive deployment and the relevance of the role of an observer mission to oversee a ceasefire agreement between two warring nations calls for a revisit. Depending on the final outcome of the Ukraine conflict, the lessons learned thereof can provide valuable inputs for such a study.[45]

Final Conclusion

After the deployment of UNIFIL post the 2006 war, despite the prevailing security situation of the region and a delicate bilateral relation between Israel and Lebanon, there has not been any major conflict between them for close to two decades. This made UNIFIL an exclusive case to develop a reliable criterion to assess the outcome of a PKO. In accordance with what Walter, Howard, and Fortna reported that "almost every large study finds a strong statistically significant relationship between peacekeeping and reduced bloodshed", UNIFIL has, until now been effective in preventing bloodshed since the 2006 war.[46] Therefore, the major finding of this research is that UNIFIL can be assessed as a satisfactorily successful UN peace operation. This is an important and final conclusion as this research has been based on the perceptions and practices of practitioners, subject matter experts at the operational and tactical levels, and contains valuable takeaways for the UN for future reform and best practices for those who are active on an every-day basis in UN peacekeeping.

ENDNOTES

1. Kim S. Cameron, "Effectiveness as Paradox: Consensus and Conflict in Conceptions of Organizational Effectiveness," *Management Science* 32, no. 5 (May 1986): 541.
2. Zeina Karam, *Associated Press*, April 20, 2017.
3. Elena Aoun, "The Evolving Environment of UNIFIL: Old Challenges and New Threats," in *The United Nations Interim Force in Lebanon: Multiple Perspectives on a Multinational Peace Operation*, ed. Elena Aoun (Brussels: Peter Lang, 2018), 76.
4. UN General Assembly Security Council, *Report of The Independent High-Level Panel on Peace Operations*, A/70/95–S/2015/446 (June 17, 2015).
5. Matthieu Cimino and Nadim Farhat, "Lebanese Perceptions of the UNIFIL: Views from the South," in *The United Nations Interim Force in Lebanon: Multiple Perspectives on a Multinational Peace Operation*, ed. Elena Aoun (Brussels: Peter Lang, 2018), 81–113.

6. Jan van der Meulen and Joseph Soeters, "Introduction", in *Cultural Diversity in Armed Forces: An international comparison*, ed. Jan van der Meulen and Joseph Soeters (New York: Routledge, 2007), 6.
7. Chiara Ruffa, "What Peacekeepers Think and Do: An Exploratory Study of French, Ghanaian, Italian, and South Korean Armies in the United Nations Interim Force in Lebanon," *Armed Forces and Society* 40, no. 2 (2014), 213–15.
8. Chiara Ruffa, "Conclusion," *Military Cultures in Peace and Stability Operations: Afghanistan and Lebanon* (Philadelphia: University of Pennsylvania Press, 2019), 125–26.
9. A.K. Bardalai, "UNPKO and Military Contributions: Challenges and Opportunities for Asia-Pacific Governments," *Journal of the United Service Institution of India*, CXLVII, no. 607 (2017): 26–34.
10. Vanessa Frances Newby, *Peacekeeping in South Lebanon: Credibility and Local Cooperation* (New York: Syracuse University Press, 2018).
11. UN Security Council, *Report of the Secretary-General on the Implementation of Security Council Resolution 1701 (2006)*, S/2022/556 (July 14, 2022). Also, see United Nations Interim Force in Lebanon, https://unifil.unmissions.org/unifil-troop-contributing-countries, accessed July 29, 2022
12. Alexandra Novosseloff, "Expanded United Nations Interim Force in Lebanon (UNFIL II)" in *The Oxford Handbook of United Nations Peacekeeping Operations*, ed. Joachim A. Koops, Norrie Macqueen, Thierry Tardy, and Paul D. Williams (Oxford: Oxford University, 2015), 776.
13. UN Security Council, *Report of the Secretary-General on the Implementation of Security Council Resolution 1701 (2006)*, S/2006/670 (August 18, 2006).
14. Andrej Sitkowski, *Peacekeeping: Myth and Reality* (London: Praeger Security International, 2006), 60.
15. Avni, Benny, "UN failure is leading to another Lebanon war," *New York Post*, August 29, 2017, https://nypostcom.cdn.ampproject.org/c/nypost.com/2017/08/29/un-failure-is-leading-to-another-lebanon-war/amp
16. "United Nations Issues: U.S. Funding of U.N. Peacekeeping," *Congressional Research Service (CRS)*, last modified March 23, 2020, https://fas.org/sgp/crs/row/IF10597.pdf, accessed June 25, 2020.
17. Indar Jit Rikhye, *The Theory and Practice of Peacekeeping* (London: C. Hurst & Company,1984), 109.
18. David Bosco. "The Multilateralist: The UN's troubled Lebanon peacekeepers," *Foreign Policy*, March 25, 2013, https://foreignpolicy.com/2013/03/25/the-uns-troubled-lebanon-peacekeepers/, accessed June 26, 2020.
19. Elena Aoun and Efrat Elron, "The UNIFIL: Multiple Perspectives on a Peace Operation's Challenges and Effectiveness," in *The United Nations Interim Force in Lebanon: Multiple Perspectives on a Multinational Peace Operation*, ed. Elena Aoun (Brussels: Peter Lang, 2018), 36.
20. Richard Gowan, "Diplomatic Fallout: For UN and Europe, a Peacekeeping Crisis in Lebanon," *World Political Review*, March 25, 2013.
21. Joseph Soeters, *Sociology and Military Studies. Classical and Current Foundations* (New York: Routledge, 2008), 71.
22. Please see UN General Assembly, *Press Release*, GA/11927 (June 30, 2017); GA/AB/4287 (July 5, 2028); *Approved resources for peacekeeping operations for the period from 1*

July 2019 to 30 June 2020, A/C.5/73/21 (July 3, 2019); UN General Assembly, *Press Release*, GA/11927 (June 30, 2017); GA/AB/4287 (July 5, 2028); *Approved resources for peacekeeping operations for the period from 1 July 2019 to 30 June 2020*, A/C.5/73/21 (July 3, 2019) and *United Nations News*, "How we are funded," https://peacekeeping.un.org/en/how-we-are-funded, accessed June 7, 2022.

23. Amanda Shendruk, Laura Hillard, and Diana Roy, "Funding the United Nations: What Impact Do U.S. Contributions Have on UN Agencies and Programs?" *Council on Foreign Relations*, last modified June 8, 2020, https://www.cfr.org/article/funding-united-nations-what-impact-do-us-contributions-have-un-agencies-and-programs
24. UN Security Council, Resolution S/RES/2485 (2019) (August 29, 2019), https://undocs.org/s/res/2485(2019); United Nations Interim Force in Lebanon, *Report of the Secretary-General*, S/2020/473 (June 1, 2020) and UN Security Council, *Report of the Secretary-General on the Implementation of Security Council Resolution 1701 (2006)*, S/2022/556 (July 14, 2022). Also, see United Nations Interim Force in Lebanon, https://unifil.unmissions.org/unifil-troop-contributing-countries, accessed July 29, 2022
25. Karen McVeigh, "Ebola staff in Congo on Lockdown after angry residents storm UN camp," *The Guardian*, November 27, 2019, https://www.theguardian.com/global-development/2019/nov/27/ebola-staff-in-congo-on-lockdown-after-angry-residents-storm-un-camp and Han Dorussen, "Peacekeeping after COVID-19," *Peace Economics, Peace Science and Public Policy* 26, no. 3 (July 13, 2020), https://doi.org/10.1515/peps-2020-0022
26. UN Department of Peace Operations, *The UNSG's Remarks to The Security Council on The Covid-19 Pandemic* (April 10, 2020), accessed 17 May 2020, https://peacekeeping.un.org/en/unsgs-remarks-to-security-council-covid-19-pandemic.
27. Namie di Razza, "What to Expect for the Future of Protection in UN Peace Operations." *IPI Global Observatory*, September 24, 2020, https://theglobalobservatory.org/2020/09/what-to-expect-for-future-of-protection-in-un-peace-operations/
28. Youssef Mahmoud, "Whatever Future Holds for Peace Operations, Peacebuilding must be more Local and Plural," IPI Global Observatory, September 25, 2020, https://theglobalobservatory.org/2020/09/whatever-future-holds-peace-operations-peacebuilding-must-be-more-local-plural/; UN, "Policy: The Protection of Civilians in United Nations Peacekeeping," November 2019, https://peacekeeping.un.org/sites/default/files/poc_policy_2019_.pdf
29. "Abraham Accords," *CNN Politics*, September 15, 2020, https://edition.cnn.com/2020/09/15/politics/israel-uae-abraham-accords-documents/index.html. Last updated September 15, 2020.
30. Ryan Bohl, "A New Brand of Nationalism Takes Root in the Middle East," *Stratfor*, September 4, 2020, https://worldview.stratfor.com/article/new-brand-nationalism-takes-root-middle-east.
31. Lt Col (retd) Mordechai Kedar, "Why Do the Arabs Hate the Palestinians?", *The Begin-Sadat Centre for Strategic Studies*, September 24, 2020, https://besacenter.org/perspectives-papers/do-arabs-hate-palestinians/
32. Hilal Khashan, "The Middle East Alliance," *Geopolitical Futures*, September 22, 2020, https://geopoliticalfutures.com/the-new-middle-east-alliance/
33. "Sudan-Israel relations agreed, Donald Trump announces," *BBC News*, October 24, 2020, accessed November 21, 2020, https://www.bbc.com/news/world-africa-54554286

34. Vanessa Frances Newby, "Between the carrot and the stick: Mapping the role of credibility in peace operation," (Unpublished article).
35. UN Security Council, *Report of the Secretary-General*, S/2020/473 (June 1, 2020).
36. "Hezbollah, Amal oppose Lebanon border talks with Israel," *Middle East Monitor*, October 15, 2020, https://www.middleeastmonitor.com/20201014-hezbollah-amal-oppose-lebanon-border-talks-with-israel/; Also see Timour Azhari, "Analysis: The politics behind the Lebanon-Israel border talks," *Al Jazeera*, October 12, 2020, last updated October 14, 2020, https://www.aljazeera.com/news/2020/10/12/analysis-the-politics-of-the-lebanon-israel-border-talks
37. Joseph R. Biden, Jr, "Why America Must Lead Again: Rescuing U.S. Foreign Policy After Trump" *Foreign Affairs*, March/April 2020, https://www.foreignaffairs.com/articles/united-states/2020-01-23/why-america-must-lead-again
38. Caroline D. Rose, "Not Quite a Lebanese-Israeli Entente," *Geopolitical Future*, October 19,2020, https://geopoliticalfutures.com/not-quite-a-lebanese-israeli-entente/
39. Lise Morje Howard, "Peacekeeping, Peace Enforcement and UN Reform," *Georgetown International Affairs* 16, no. 2 (Summer/Fall, 2015): 6–13, http://www.jstor.org/stable/43773690
40. Michael W. Doyle and Nicholas Sambanis, *Making War and Building Peace: United Nations Peace Operations* (Princeton: Princeton University Press, 2006), 350–51; Also see Barbara F. Walter, Lise Morje Howard, and Virginia Page Fortna, "The Extraordinary Relationship between Peacekeeping and Peace," *British Journal of Political Science* (2020): 1-18, doi:10.1017/S000712342000023X and Paul D. Williams, "A Decade of Developments in Peace Operations," *IPI Global Observatory*, April, 14, 2021, https://theglobalobservatory.org/2021/04/decade-developments-peace-operations/
41. Barbara F. Walter, Lise Morje Howard and Virginia Page Fortna, "The Extraordinary Relationship between Peacekeeping and Peace," *British Journal of Political Science* (2020): 1,8, doi:10.1017/S000712342000023X
42. Vanessa Frances Newby, "Walk the line: An Investigation into the Micro-processes of a UN Peacekeeping Mission," *Working paper, AUB Policy Institute* (2016), DOI: 10.13140/rg.2.2.26928.76808
43. Nicholas Sambanis, "Short- and Long-Term Effects of United Nations Peace Operations," *The World Bank Economic Review* 22, no.1 (2008), 30.
44. Barbara F. Walter, Lise Morje Howard, and Virginia Page Fortna, "The Extraordinary Relationship between Peacekeeping and Peace," *British Journal of Political Science* (2020): 12-14, doi:10.1017/S000712342000023X
45. Alexandra Novosseloff, A comparative study of older one-dimensional UN Peace Operations: Is the Future of UN Peacekeeping its Past? EPON and FES Cyprus (2022), https://effectivepeaceops.net/publication/a-comparative-study-of- older-one-dimensional-un-peace-operations/
46. Barbara F. Walter, Lise Morje Howard, and Virginia Page Fortna, "The Extraordinary Relationship between Peacekeeping and Peace," *British Journal of Political Science* (2020): 14, doi:10.1017/S000712342000023X

APPENDIX A
KEY GOALS AND QUESTIONS FOR ASSESSMENT OF UNIFIL

Key Goals	*Sub-Goals*	*Key Questions*	*Measures of Progress*	*Data Source*
1. Restoration of peace and security.	(a) Violence between Israel and Lebanon.	(a) Has the violence between Israel and Lebanon reduced?	(i) Duration without clashes/war in the past 10 years. (ii) Details of IDF and LAF face-offs near BL. (iii) Cross-border shootings and air space violations.	• UN documents • Mission reports • Interviews
	(b) Violence against peacekeepers.	(b.1) Has the violence against peacekeepers reduced?	(i) Number of incidents of attack or threat or attempt to attack peacekeepers. (ii) Details of peacekeeper casualties (fatal and non-fatal).	• UN documents • Mission reports
	(c) Humanitarian de-mining.	(c.1) What have been the activities around and response to humanitarian de-mining?	(i) Total area cleared of cluster bombs/unexploded ordnance (UXO). (ii) Details of total arsenals destroyed. (iii) Number of civilian casualties because of landmines.	• UN documents • Mission reports
		(c.2) Has Israel handed over maps to Lebanon?	(i) Details of maps handed over.	• UN documents • Reports from LAF
2. Creating conditions for the prevention of resumption of hostilities between Lebanon and Israel.	(a) Mechanism is available for the prevention of hostilities.	(a) How have the available mechanisms helped in the prevention of resumption of hostilities?	(i) Periodical meetings, like tripartite meetings, chaired by UNIFIL. (ii) Exchange of liaison teams. (iii) Interactions between HoM/FC of UNIFIL with the appropriate authority in Israel and Lebanon.	• UN documents • Mission reports • Interviews • Articles in professional journals, local Lebanese and Israeli media reports

Key Goals	*Sub-Goals*	*Key Questions*	*Measures of Progress*	*Data Source*
			(iv) Rapid/quick investigation of incidents/ complaints of incidents reported by Israel and Lebanon. (v) Progress of BL marking.	
	(b) Conflict management.	(b) Has UNIFIL contributed to preventing the conflict from expanding geographically?	Comparative state of violent incidents in the area of operations. (AO).	
3. Ensuring South Lebanon is free of armed personnel, assets and weapons other than that with the Lebanese government and UNIFIL.	(a) Prevent the presence of Lebanese and non-Lebanese militias other than the Government of Lebanon and UNIFIL in South Lebanon.	(a.1) Are there unauthorised armed personnel in South Lebanon?	(i) Details of incidents—reports involving armed elements other than the Lebanese security force (LAF). (ii) Reports/evidence received from IDF.	• UN documents • Mission reports • Interviews • Opinions in local, regional and international newspapers
		(a.2) Are the measures to ensure assistance provided by UNIFIL for the removal of this armed personnel effective?	(i) Details of armed groups operating in Lebanon and South Lebanon. (ii) Influence of the armed groups in the governance of Lebanon by the elected body. (iii) Role of the armed groups, including the Hezbollah and Palestinian refugees, in the internal policy and internal security of Lebanon and Israel–Lebanon relationship.	• UN documents • Mission reports • Interviews • Opinions in local, regional and international newspapers
4. Assistance to LAF in fulfilling its security responsibilities.	(a) Resolving disputes of occupied areas.	(a.1) Have Lebanon and Israel resolved their major disagreements?	(i) Vacation state of occupied areas. (ii) Progress of BL marking.	• UN documents • Mission reports • Interviews
		(a.2) Has the marking of BL helped in resolving disputes?	(i) Progress of BL marking. (ii) Details of hotspots along BL.	• UN documents • Mission reports • Interviews

Key Goals	*Sub-Goals*	*Key Questions*	*Measures of Progress*	*Data Source*
	(b) Capability building of LAF.	(b.1) Has the capability of LAF in fulfilling its responsibilities been enhanced?	(i) Total strength of LAF and troops-to-task ratio of LAF deployment in the AO. (ii) Operation reliability in terms of strength, training, and equipment. (iii) Area under the effective control of LAF.	• UN documents • Mission reports • Interviews • Reports from LAF • Reports from IDF
		(b.2) Is there freedom of movement for locals and UNIFIL in the AO? What are the reasons for the restriction of movement and does the pattern of restriction on movement vary from contingent to contingent?	(i) Number of available primary roads available for movement in the AO. (ii) Number of incidents of restriction of freedom of movement by the local population. (iii) Perception of the local population about freedom of movement.	• UN documents • Mission reports
		(b.3) Has LAF's cooperation with UNIFIL improved? Has UNIFIL helped LAF get external financial aid?	(i) Mechanism available to improve cooperation. (ii) Details of joint patrolling and operations. (iii) Details of joint training activities. (iv) Details of external aid to LAF (money, equipment, and training). (v) Progress of operational response from LAF to UNIFIL's requests.	• UN documents • Mission reports • Interviews • Reports from LAF • Published materials
5. Ensure support from the local population.	(a) Good relations and support from the local population.	(a.1) Does the local population support UNIFIL?	(i) Data on the extent of peacekeepers' knowledge of the local population. (ii) Data on the extent of population support for the operation. (iii) Data on the contribution by the mission for infrastructure development of the AO in support of the locals. (iv) Number of attacks on UNIFIL personnel.	• Mission reports • Opinion poll, if available • Interviews • Published material

Key Goals	Sub-Goals	Key Questions	Measures of Progress	Data Source
			(v) Number of incidents on the restriction of movement of peacekeepers in the AO.	
		(a.2) Are there social ills created by peacekeepers?	(i) Incidents of rape and prostitution associated with the mission. (ii) Incidents of local crimes associated with the mission.	• UN documents • Mission reports • Interviews
6. Maintain the operational effectiveness of the mission.	(a) Clear and achievable mission mandate.	(a.1) Is the mission mandate clear and achievable?	(i) Feasibility of implementing the operational tasks. (ii) Adequacy of the strength of the peacekeepers. (iii) Standard of training and state of equipment of the military contingents.	• UN documents • Mission reports • Interviews
		(a.2) Is the mission operationally prepared to effectively execute the mandated tasks?	(i) Level of peacekeepers' awareness of the mission, local culture and tradition and other sensitivities. (ii) State of support to the military contingents from their respective national governments. (iii) Adequacy of the budget in support of the mission. (iv) Availability of administrative support for mission sustainment.	• UN documents • Mission reports • Interviews
		(a.3) Is there adequate support from the parties to the conflict of the mission for mandate implementation?	(i) Political support to Lebanese security forces and IDF for mandate implementation. (ii) Cooperation to resolve pending disputes and investigation of incidents by the mission.	• UN documents • Mission reports • Interviews • Published materials

Key Goals	*Sub-Goals*	*Key Questions*	*Measures of Progress*	*Data Source*
	(b) Organisational structure for mandate implementation.	(b.1) How is the multinational force structure responding and adapting to challenges?	(i) Interoperability amongst the contingents in terms of operational ethos, training and equipment. (ii) Diversity in the philosophy of UN peacekeeping and culture—its effect on the operations.	• Interviews • Media reports and published materials • (interviews only)
		(b.2) Are the rules of engagement (RoE) adequate to meet the operational needs of the mission?	(i) Understanding and interpretation of RoE by contingents of different nations. (ii) Presence/lack of national directives on the interpretation of RoE.	• Interviews • Media reports and published materials
7. Credibility and Local Legitimacy	Adherence to principles of peacekeeping and people-centric operational activities.	(a.1) Is the operation credible in the eyes of the parties to the conflict and the local population? (a.2) Has the operation found local legitimacy?	(i) Ability to implement a larger part of the mandate. (ii) Freedom of movement to peacekeepers to undertake operational activities. (iii) No negative feedback in the vernacular.	• Media reports and published materials • Interviews

APPENDIX B
UNIFIL: CONTEXT AND HISTORY OF THE CASE STUDY

UNIFIL is the result of Israel's first major invasion of Lebanon on 14-15 March 1978, termed *"Operation Litani"*, as a response to Palestinian gunmen launching an attack on Israeli territory on 11 March 1978, leaving over 30 civilians dead.[1] Before this, the Lebanese civil war of 1975 led to a power vacuum and confrontation between Israel and its Lebanese proxies on one side and the "Joint Forces" of the PLO and Progressive Lebanese Movement on the other. It, in turn, resulted in a series of offensive actions by militias supported by Israel along the Lebanon-Israel border. This continued for almost two years and ended with the US-backed (and Israeli approved) deployment of the Arab Deterrent Force (ADF), a peacekeeping force mostly comprising troops from the Syrian army.[2] However, later, Egypt under President Anwar Sadat broke away from its Arab allies and made a separate peace with Israel on 26 March 1979, becoming the first Arab nation to forge a diplomatic relationship with Israel. Soon after, Israel also increased its cross-border raids on Lebanon.[3]

On 19 March 1978, the UNSC adopted UN SC Resolutions 425 and 426 calling for the immediate withdrawal of Israeli forces and authorising the establishment of UNIFIL. The initial contributions to UNIFIL came from France, Nepal, Norway, Iran, Senegal, Nigeria, Ireland, and Fiji. UNIFIL was established in haste due to the USA's desire to resolve this new crisis quickly before the commencement of negotiations between Egypt and Israel at Camp David. SCR 425 mandated UNIFIL to *confirm the withdrawal of Israeli forces from Lebanese territory, restore international peace and security in the border area*, and *assist the Government of Lebanon in ensuring the return of its effective authority in the area.*

UNIFIL was established as a traditional mission to broker peace between Lebanon and Israel.[4] Goulding described the background of the policy to establish UNIFIL thus:

> It is an operation about whose viability the then Secretary-General and his senior advisers had doubts. It was nevertheless pushed through the Security Council by the USA for pressing, if passing, political reasons. President Carter was launching the negotiations, which were to lead to the Camp David Accords, and did not want the process derailed by the Israeli invasion of Lebanon, which had just taken place.[5]

According to Rikhye, UNIFIL's presence promoted the achievement of other political objectives in the region. More importantly, UNIFIL was a symbol of the belief of some of the UN members that techniques of traditional PKO were not dead yet and that they could still be applied to situations that demanded enforcement actions.[6] Skogmo similarly reported that for the USA, sending a peacekeeping force to Lebanon would help avoid further damage to the peace process in the Middle East.[7] Similarly, Hammond described it as Lebanon being caught in the middle of the competition for turf between the USA and the Soviet Union. The warlord factions controlling their mini-states grew in strength pursuing their political agendas leaving the international community hardly any option for conflict resolution. The situation did not change and, if at all, it worsened. The USA, which neither knew much nor was interested to know, pushed for SCRs 425 and 426.

The mandate was based on the assumptions that Israel would entrust the responsibility of its border security to the UN, that the PLO would accept the Security Council resolution and stop attacks on Israel, and that the Lebanese government would be able to exercise its authority in South Lebanon. These assumptions were wrong because *firstly,* the PLO had hardly been involved in the negotiations and it had no intention of giving up its fight against Israel. *Secondly,* the IDF did withdraw from Lebanese territory in June 1978 but after handing over all its positions in the vicinity of the border to the South Lebanese Army (SLA) under Major Haddad, whose paymaster was Israel.[8] Kaufman stated that in any case the withdrawal to the international border could not have been verified because the formal process of demarcation of the border by the UN had not commenced. As for Lebanon, it was burning because of the civil war. Israel continued to criticize UN SCR 425 and invaded Lebanon once again in 1982. Later though, the IDF pulled out of Beirut but remained in South Lebanon.

Judging from the point of mandate implementation, UNIFIL at the time was a good example of a failed PKO. When the IDF unilaterally pulled out at last in May 2000, the other two parts of the mandate, i.e., restoring international peace and security and assisting the Government of Lebanon in ensuring the return of its effective authority in the area, remained to be fulfilled. According to Rikhye, "UNIFIL has some successes to its credit, although it is popularly regarded as a failed mission".[9] He noted, "A comparison with the mandate of the mission and its performance is a clear indication of the extent that the UN has failed in Lebanon."[10] Rikhye's comment, however, pre-dates the Israel-Lebanon war of 2006 and the IDF's withdrawal from South Lebanon in May 2000. Given that UNIFIL was tasked to ensure the withdrawal of IDF vide SCRs 425 and 426, and IDF continued to stay in South Lebanon and UNIFIL was viewed as a failure.

However, some factors were beyond the control of either the Security Council or the mission HQs. The situation that existed in Lebanon post the 1975 civil war was different and UNIFIL was caught in a paradox. The Lebanese administration collapsed and the Arab League peacekeeping force, i.e., the ADF, predominantly comprising Syrians and a few Arabs, was brought in to keep the peace in Lebanon. After some time when the Arabs left, only the Syrians remained. The presence of the ADF in Bekka Valley was a threat to Israel. It wanted the Syrians to remain north of the Litani River and accordingly assisted the Christian forces under the command of Major Haddad to stay in South Lebanon. To that extent, since Israel always considered UNIFIL as pro-PLO, and their troops drawn from neutral and non-aligned nations would favour the PLO cause, it wanted UNIFIL to control South Lebanon except for the Christian enclave that was under the control of Major Haddad. On the other hand, the PLO felt that SCR 425 was biased towards Israel. At the same time, it considered operating from South Lebanon as its legitimate right under the Cairo Agreement. As a result, UNIFIL's authority in South Lebanon was challenged by the PLO by restricting its freedom of movement from the beginning.[11]

Historical Background to the Crisis

The various historical facts and events, which led to the genesis of this crisis, can be broadly divided into five distinct stages: the division of the Ottoman Empire and the demarcation of the boundary, the Arab Israeli wars and Palestinian refugees, the Palestine Liberation Organisation, the Lebanese civil war and the emergence of the Hezbollah.[12]

Division of Ottoman Empire

The area of what would later be called the states of Lebanon and Israel once formed part of the Ottoman Empire (1299–1924). During World War I, the Allies made several agreements for the partition of the Ottoman Empire, of which the most prominent was the Sykes-Picot Agreement between the British and the French in 1916. The Sykes-Picot Agreement was a secret Anglo-French memorandum, which laid the basis for the partition of the Middle East. This agreement between the governments of the UK and France, with the rise of imperial Russia, defined their respective spheres of influence and control in West Asia after the expected downfall of the Ottoman Empire. The terms were negotiated by the French and British diplomats, François Georges-Picot and Sir Mark Sykes.[13]

This was followed by the Balfour Declaration in 1917 by the British, enabling the international Zionist movement to strive for the establishment of a Jewish homeland in the Palestine region, which had a significant Jewish minority population but with a majority Arab-Muslim population.[14] Davison noted that at the end of World War I, Britain took full control of Palestine. This triggered the established military-run Occupied Enemy Territorial Administrations (OETA) between the British and the French covering Syria and Palestine. OETA South roughly corresponded to Palestine while OETA North extended northwards into modern-day Lebanon. The line separating the OETA North under French control from OETA South under British control was an amended version of the Sykes-Picot proposal of 1916. The OETA line began at the Mediterranean, midway between Tyre and Acre, at Ras Naqoura, but ran more or less horizontally eastward to the northern end of Lake Huleh in the Galilee panhandle, *thus granting Britain a slice of territory previously allocated to France under the Sykes-Picot Agreement*.[15]

On 24 July 1922, the League of Nations approved the terms of the British Mandate over Palestine and Transjordan. On 16 September 1922, the League formally approved a memorandum from Lord Balfour confirming the exemption of Transjordan from the clauses of the mandate and from the mandate's responsibility to facilitate Jewish immigration and land settlement.[16] However, since a permanent frontier between Syria and Palestine was never drawn, Lt Col M. Pulet of France and Lt Col Mark Stuart from Britain led a joint Franco-British military commission to complete this task.[17]

Demarcation of Boundary

Competing interests greatly added to the complications. For instance, Christianson noted that the Zionists always gazed with envious eyes at the water-rich land to the north of Palestine and sought to secure access to the lower reaches of the Litani River and the waters of the Hasbani River in Mount Hermon. To advance their argument, the Zionists pointed out that the waters of the Litani River were more beneficial to the people in the south than to those in the north.[18] Since the agreement was concluded without due consideration to any geographic, economic or demographic reality, it was always resisted by the Arab nationalists.[19]

In the process of demarcation of the boundary, the commission made a few mistakes. The first mistake was the discovery of the incorrect placement of Border Post (BP) 22 during the survey in August 1940 without any corrective action being taken. It was located 500 metres northwest of the Saliha police station in Palestine, while it should have been sited 400 metres south of the building. This effectively resulted in 500 metres of the present territory of Lebanon going under Israeli control. Rather than correcting it, the French decided to leave the BP where it was but instead shifted BP 33 on Sheikh Abbad hill near Houla a little to the east so that a gravel road would remain in Lebanon. Israeli historians suggested that the commission also made a mistake at Ras Naqoura and that the border should have terminated on the Mediterranean at Naqoura village two kilometres north of the present location.[20]

As Biger stated, the second major mistake was shifting the jurisdiction of around 24 villages and farms that were earlier in the north of the OETA line to the south of the new border from Greater Lebanon to Palestine—a total land area of 2,729 hectares (now under the effective control of Israel).[21] Of these, 12 were Sunni, two were Maronite, one was Greek Catholic, two were Jewish, six were Shiite and one was divided between Shiite and Greek Catholics. The six Shiite villages were Terbikha, Saliha, Malkiyeh, Nabi Yusha, Kades and Hunin. The mixed Shiite-Greek Catholic village was Ibl Qamh. Collectively, these villages today form what is known as the Seven Villages. All the residents lost their Lebanese nationality and were granted Palestinian citizenship.[22] These mistakes became some of the major bones of contention between Lebanon and Israel and are still regular hot spots.

By 1931, when the Jewish population jumped from 17 per cent to 32 per cent within nine years, hostility between both the countries grew.[23] With the Nazis coming to power and because of the growing persecution of Jews in Nazi Germany, the number of Jewish immigrants to Palestine increased in 1935. The British administration considered this as too high a figure. Consequently, in 1936, Britain imposed restrictions on the immigration of Jews to Palestine.[24] These processes created annoyances on all sides, resulting in violence breaking out between Arabs and Jews. The first violent incident occurred in Tel Hai followed by riots in Jerusalem. In August 1929, Arabs murdered 67 Jews in the city of Hebron, in what became known as the Hebron Massacre. By 1936, escalating tensions led to the 1936–1939 Arab revolt in Palestine.[25] British efforts to block immigration led to more violent resistance and an all-out armed rebellion by underground Zionist groups, perpetrating hundreds of attacks against British installations and posts, citing that the British had defaulted on their original promise in the Balfour Declaration and that restricting Jewish immigration was a pro-Arab policy.[26] In November 1947, the UN adopted the Partition Plan for Palestine and Israel declared its independence on 14 May 1948. On the expiry of the British Mandate on 15 May1948, Britain announced its plans to fully withdraw from Palestine.[27]

Arab-Israeli Wars and Palestine Refugees

The trouble did not end there. Egypt, Lebanon, Transjordan, and Iraq joined and attacked Israel at the beginning of 1948.[28] The war ended with the signing of the Armistice Agreements (Green Line) on 23 March 1949.[29] As part of the agreement with Lebanon, Israeli forces withdrew to the international border, which should have coincided with the Lebanon-Palestine boundary of 1922, but the actual area occupied by Israel was much larger than what was allocated under the United Nations Partition Plan. It was probably presumed by all the parties at that time that the armistice agreements were neither peace treaties nor the final resolution of the conflict, including the borders with Israel.[30] Israel fought two more wars with its Arab neighbours—the 1967 Six-Day War and the Yom Kippur War 1973. A disengagement agreement after the Yom Kippur war in 1973 resulted in the establishment of a UN buffer zone and UNDOF was established on Golan Heights in 1974.

PLO

After it was founded in May 1964 in Jerusalem, the PLO became the centre of hope for the Palestinian communities and remained at the heart of the Arab-Israeli conflict.[31] Although Lebanon did not take part in these two wars, their results have affected the geopolitics of the region to this day.

The wars ended but the influx of Palestinian refugees turned out to be an eternal problem for Lebanon. Even though they were housed in different camps, Lebanese Christians feared the loss of their political dominance because of the growing Muslim population and the corresponding change in the country's demography. Accordingly, they imposed restrictions on the status of the Palestinian refugees.[32] The additional influx of refugees turned the Palestinian camps throughout the Middle East into centres of terrorist activity.[33] Side by side, because of the growing frustration as a result of discrimination, the Palestinian refugees who had left Israel in 1948 became vulnerable and started being recruited by the PLO.[34]

In March 1968, when Yasser Arafat took over the leadership of the PLO with his HQs in Beirut, the PLO fighters rapidly took over South Lebanon, launching a cross-border terrorist attack into northern Israel. The situation became too complicated in 1970 when the PLO attempted to overthrow the reigning monarch, King Hussein of Jordan. Later, when the Jordanian authorities retaliated, the PLO leadership and their troops were forced to flee from Jordan to Syria and finally to Lebanon increasing the cross-border violence.[35]

With HQs now in Beirut, PLO factions recruited new members from the Palestinian refugee camps.[36] South Lebanon was nicknamed "Fatah land" due to the predominance there of Yasser Arafat's Fatah organization. With its army operating freely in Lebanon, the PLO managed to create a state within a state.[37] In reaction to the 1972 Munich massacre of 9 April 1973, members of Israel's elite Special Forces landed in Lebanon by boat and infiltrated the PLO HQs in Beirut and assassinated several members of its leadership.[38]

Beirut was unable to control the PLO fighters and the Popular Front for the Liberation of Palestine, General Command (PFLP–GC) split from the PLO in 1974.[39] On 15 May 1974, when the Popular Democratic Front for the Liberation of Palestine (PDFLP), the breakaway faction of PFLP–GC, attacked the Israeli border town of Ma'alot killing 10 adults and eight children, the Israeli Air Force was called in to attack Palestinian terrorist camps in Lebanon.[40]

Lebanese Civil War

By 1975, more than 300,000 displaced Palestinians were living in Lebanon.[41] The Phalangists, a Christian militia organisation of Lebanon, with support from Israel, clashed with the Palestinians over the latter's armed struggle with Israel from Lebanese territory. On 13 April 1975, a civil war broke out. However, the causes of the civil war are much more than merely the outcome of clashes between the Phalangists and the Palestinians. It was the manifestation of long pent-up feelings of anger and frustration, beginning with the support of the international community for the creation of a Jewish state in Palestine, division of territory, boundary agreements, Arab-Israeli wars, the influx of Palestinian refugees and Palestinians losing faith in Lebanon when it came to supporting their cause. It got further complicated when Syria decided to intervene militarily and positioned 40,000 troops in Lebanon. Later, it intervened in the civil war of Lebanon in June 1976 to support the Maronite-dominated government of Lebanese President Suleiman Frangieh.[42] The civil war continued until 1990, which cost 150,000 lives, injured 300,000, and displaced almost a million people. By the time the war ended, Lebanon was completely devastated. It was a complex conflict in the form of shifting alliances between and among Lebanese Maronite Christians, Lebanese Muslims (Sunnis and Shiites), Palestinian Muslims, Lebanese Druze, and other non sectarian groups.[43]

Taking advantage of the internal turmoil of Lebanon and in retaliation to cross-border raids by PLO militants, which killed 37 Israeli civilians on 11 March 1978, Israel invaded Lebanon on 14 March 1978. Israel occupied the whole of South Lebanon with 25,000 troops except for the city of Tyre.[44] As stated earlier, on 19 March 1978, the UN adopted resolutions 425 and 426 calling upon Israel to withdraw from Lebanon and establishing UNIFIL on 23 March 1978. Though Israel withdrew its troops later in 1978, it handed over the occupied territory to its proxy, the SLA. Israel invaded Lebanon again in 1982 to attack the PLO and this time moved right up to Beirut.[45] Though the war ended with the intervention of the USA, Israel made only a partial withdrawal in January 1985.

Hezbollah—the Resistance

The partial withdrawal of the IDF from Lebanon should have restored normalcy in Lebanon and also gradually initiated the process for closure of UNIFIL even though the most important part of the mandate under SCRs 425 and 426 (to ensure IDF withdrawal from Lebanon) had not been fulfilled by then. However, within a month of the IDF's partial pullback in January 1985, Shiite Sheik Ibrahim al-Amin declared a manifesto in Lebanon announcing a resistance movement called the Hezbollah. Its goal included combating the Israeli occupation.[46] The Hezbollah's announcement of the resistance movement was preceded by its attack on the US Embassy in Beirut in April 1983, which killed 63 people and injured more than 63 others. Within a few months, the Hezbollah simultaneously bombed the French and the US Marine barracks in Beirut in October 1983 killing 241 US Marines and 58 French soldiers. It was followed by another attack on French soldiers in South Lebanon in December 1983. French and US troops finally left Lebanon in 1984.[47] The Israeli army, however, stayed back in Lebanon, even though UNIFIL had already been deployed, until it decided to unilaterally pull out from Lebanon on 25 May 2000. However, Major Hadad's Christian militia often interfered with UNIFIL's operations.[48] Diehl stated that during the intervening period from 1985 to 2000, the PLO always claimed that it was its right to operate from South Lebanon. Consequently, they smuggled weapons and attacked Israeli positions. Such attacks in the form of firing rockets into Israel continue. Diehl observed, however, that the Lebanese Sunni Muslims of the area did not hinder the activities of UNIFIL.[49]

Side by side, Hezbollah militia groups had waged a guerrilla campaign against Israeli forces occupying South Lebanon and their SLA allies. The Hezbollah, which had, and still has a unique relationship with the PLO never failed to exploit the cause of Palestine when it came to confronting Israel. Despite having different religious orientations (the Hezbollah are Shiites, and the Palestinians are Sunnis), they continue to share their common positions of anti-Western and anti-Israeli. The Hezbollah and Hamas, the militant Palestinian faction, get support from Iran and are independent. As described by Koss, the relationship between the Hezbollah and Palestinians is "a mutually beneficial, cross-sectarian alliance".[50]

The period between Israel's invasions in 1982 and May 2000, when the IDF fully withdrew from Lebanon, was marred by attacks on the multinational force comprising troops from Britain, Italy, France, and the USA, with attacks on the IDF by the Shiite militias and a change in alliances in various groups/parties operating in and outside Lebanon.[51] After the IDF's withdrawal, relative calm prevailed for the next couple of years. However, both sides remained at loggerheads with the Hezbollah virtually taking control of the territory south of the Litani River. The long-standing boundary dispute and ill-fated Palestinian refugees contributed to this standoff. The Hezbollah continued its fight with Israel. When in a trans-border raid on 12 July 2006, it kidnapped two Israeli soldiers, killed three others, and fired rockets on Israeli cities, the IDF mounted its third major attack on Lebanon on 14 July 2006. The war lasted for 34 days. It destroyed the country's infrastructure, displaced one million people, and killed more than 1,000 Lebanese, the majority of them civilians. The Hezbollah, in turn, fired nearly 4,000 rockets at Israel, killing 43 civilians and 120 Israeli soldiers.[52] Finally, amidst immense public outcry and with full support from the USA and France, on 11 August 2006, the Security Council unanimously adopted Resolution 1701 (co-drafted by the USA and France) and, thus, gave shape to the present structure of UNIFIL.[53]

With a maximum strength of 15,000 troops, in addition to its mandate under resolutions 425 and 426, the UNIFIL mandate under resolution 1701 included the following tasks:

- Monitoring the cessation of hostilities.
- Assisting and supporting the deployment of the LAF throughout South Lebanon, including along the BL as Israel withdraws from Lebanon.
- Assisting the LAF in establishing an area between the Litani River and the BL free of any armed personnel, assets, and weapons other than those of the Government of Lebanon and UNIFIL.
- Assisting the Government of Lebanon, at its request, to secure its borders/entry points to prevent unauthorised entry of arms.
- Extending assistance to help ensure humanitarian access to civilian populations and the voluntary and safe return of displaced persons.
- Ensuring that the Area of Operations (AO) is not utilized for hostile activities of any kind.
- Protecting UN personnel, facilities, installations, and equipment.
- Ensuring the security and freedom of movement of UN personnel and humanitarian workers.
- Protecting civilians under imminent threat of physical violence.

ENDNOTES

1. UN, "UNIFIL Background," accessed November 18, 2020, https://unifil.unmissions.org/unifil-background
2. Laurie Zittrain Eisenberg, "From benign to malign: Israeli-Lebanese relations, 1948-78," in *Israel and Hezbollah: An asymmetric conflict in historical and comparative perspective*, ed. Clive Jones and Sergio Catignani (New York: Routledge, 2010), 21; Imad Salamey, *The Government and Politics of Lebanon* (New York: Routledge, 2013).
3. Imad Salamey, The *Government and Politics of Lebanon* (New York: Routledge, 2013).
4. Grant T. Hammond, "The Perils of Peacekeeping for the US: Relearning Lessons from Beirut to Bosnia," in *A Future for Peacekeeping*, ed. Edward Moxon Browne (London: Macmillan Press, 1998), 74–75.
5. Marrack Goulding "The Evolution of United Nations Peacekeeping," *International Affairs* 69, no. 3 (1993), 453.

6. Indar Jit Rikhye, *The Politics and Practice of UN Peacekeeping: Past, Present and Future* (Clementsport: The Lester B. Pearson Canadian International Peacekeeping Training Centre, 2000), 85.
7. Bjorn Skogmo, *UNIFIL: International Peacekeeping in Lebanon, 1978–1988* (Colorado: Lynne Rienner, 1989), 9.
8. Asher Kaufman, "From Litani to Beirut–Israel's invasions of Lebanon 1978-85: causes and consequences," in *Israel and Hezbollah: An asymmetric conflict in historical and comparative perspective*, ed. Clive Jones and Sergio Catignani (New York: Routledge, 2010), 37.
9. Indar Jit Rikhye, *The Theory and Practice of Peacekeeping* (London: C. Hurst & Company, 1984), 109.
10. Indar Jit Rikhye, *The Politics and Practice of UN Peacekeeping: Past, Present and Future* (Clementsport: The Lester B. Pearson Canadian International Peacekeeping Training Centre, 2000), 85.
11. Indar Jit Rikhye, *The Theory and Practice of Peacekeeping* (London: C. Hurst & Company, 1984), 101–109, 246.
12. Henry Asquith Herbert, *The genesis of the war* (London: Cassell & Company, 1972), 82.
13. David Fromkin, *A Peace to End All Peace: The Fall of the Ottoman Empire and the Creation of the Modern Middle East* (New York: Holt Paperbacks, 1989), 286–88.
14. Paul C. Helmrich, "*From Paris to Sèvres: The Partition of the Ottoman Empire at the Peace Conference of 1919-1920*," review by Roderic H. Davison, *Slavic Review* 34, no. 1 (1975), 186-87, DOI:10.2307/2495927.
15. Nicholas Blandford, "Seven Villages: Origins and Implications," accessed September 21, 2020, https://now.mmedia.me/Library/Files/EnglishDocumentation/Other%20Documents/The_Seven_Villages-paper-final2.pdf
16. Martin Sicker, *Reshaping Palestine* (Praeger Publishers,1999), 164.
17. Scott Christianson, "The Origins of the World War I Agreement that Carved up the Middle East: How Great Britain and France secretly negotiated the Sykes–Picot Agreement," 16 November 2015, http://www.smithsonianmag.com/history/sykes-picot-agreement. [Also excerpted from Scott Christianson, *100 Documents That Changed the World: Magna Carta to Wikileaks*, (Batsford Ltd.), 2015].
18. Wadith el Khazen, "The Litani river of Lebanon and the desire of Israel to obtain additional water sources," *Khazen.org*, December 15, 2001, accessed September 21, 2020, https://www.khazen.org/index.php/archive/92-de-khazen-members/cheikh-wadih-el-khazen/97-blank-78510489
19. James Parker, *A History of Palestine from 135 AD to Modern Times* (Victor Gollancz: London, 1949), 285.
20. Aiko Nishikida, "Palestinians from Seven Villages: their legal status and social conditions," *Kyoto Bulletin of Islamic Area Studies*,3-1(July 2009), 220–231, www.asafas.kyoto-u.ac.jp/kias/1st_period/contents/pdf/kb3_1/15nishikida.pdf
21. Gideon Biger, "The Boundaries of Israel-Palestine Past, Present and Future: A Critical Geographical View," *Israel Studies* 13, no. 1 (Spring 2008), 68–93.
22. Nicholas Blandford, "Seven Villages: Origins and Implications," accessed September 21, 2020, https://now.mmedia.me/Library/Files/EnglishDocumentation/Other%20Documents/The_Seven_Villages-paper-final2.pdf
23. Ann M. Lesch and Dan Tschirgi, *Origins and Development of the Arab-Israeli Conflict* (West Port, Connecticut: Greenwood Press, 1998), 47.

24. "Immigration to Israel: British Restrictions on Jewish Immigration to Palestine," Jews Virtual Library, accessed October 8, 2020, https://www.jewishvirtuallibrary.org/british-restrictions-on-jewish-immigration-to-palestine. Also see Charles D. Smith, *Palestine and the Arab Israeli Conflict: A History with Documents* (Bedford/St. Martin's: Boston, 2004),129.
25. Ann M. Lesch and Dan Tschirgi, *Origins and Development of the Arab-Israeli Conflict* (West Port, Connecticut: Greenwood Press, 1998).
26. Mike Konrad, "The White Paper of 1939," *The American Thinker,* 2 June 2013, accessed May 15, 2015, http://www.americanthinker.com/articles/2013/06/the_white_paper_of_1939.html
27. UN *General Assembly Resolution 181*, November 29, 1947.
28. The USA Ministry of Foreign Affairs, accessed July 17, 2019, https://history.state.gov/milestones/1945-1952/arab-israeli-war
29. Israel Ministry of Foreign Affairs, accessed July 17, 2018, https://mfa.gov.il/MFA/ForeignPolicy/MFADocuments/Yearbook1/Pages/THE%20ARMISTICE%20AGREEMENTS.aspx
30. Andrew Humphreys, Lara Dunston, and Terry Carter, *Lonely Planet Syria & Lebanon* (Footscray, Victoria: Lonely Planet Publications, 2004), 31; Robert Fisk, *Pity the Nation: The Abduction of Lebanon* (New York: Thunder's Mouth Press/Nation's Books, 2002), 74; United Nations, *Report of the Secretary-General on the United Nations Interim Force in Lebanon*, S/2006/560.
31. Cheryl A. Rubenberg, *The Palestinians, A Search of a Just Peace* (London: Lynne Rienner Publishers, 2003), 14–16.
32. Devon Woznack, "Institutionalization in the Palestinian Refugee Camps of Lebanon," *Anthós*, 6, no. 1 (2014), DOI 10.15760/anthos.2014.19714.197
33. Andrew Humphreys, Lara Dunston, and Terry Carter, *Lonely Planet Syria & Lebanon* (Footscray, Victoria: Lonely Planet Publications, 2004), 31.
34. Laura Zittrain Eisenberg, "Do Good Fences Make Good Neighbours? Israel and Lebanon After the Withdrawal," *Middle East Review of International Affairs* 4, no. 3 (September 2000).
35. Asher Kaufman, "From Litani to Beirut–Israel's invasions of Lebanon 1978-85: causes and consequences" in *Israel and Hezbollah: An asymmetric conflict in historical and comparative perspective,* ed. Jones Clive and Catignani Sergio (New York: Routledge, 2010), 26.
36. Laura Zittrain Eisenberg, "Do Good Fences Make Good Neighbours? Israel and Lebanon After the Withdrawal," *Middle East Review of International Affairs* 4, no. 3 (September 2000).
37. Mordechai Nisan, *The Conscience of Lebanon: A Political Biography of Etienne Sakr (Abu-Arz)* (London, New York: Routledge, 2003), 20.
38. Laurie Zittrain Eisenberg, "From benign to malign Israeli-Lebanese relations, 1948-78," in *Israel and Hezbollah: An asymmetric conflict in historical and comparative perspective,* ed. Clive Jones and Sergio Catignani (New York: Routledge, 2010), 10–24.
39. Ibid., 18.
40. Alex P. Schmid, and A.J. Jongman, *Political Terrorism: A New Guide to Actors, Authors, Concepts, Data Bases, Theories & Literature* (New York: Routledge, 2017).
41. The USA Central Intelligence Agency, "Lebanon: Refugees and internally displaced persons," *The CIA World Factbook* (Skyhorse Publishing, 2006).
42. Laurie Zittrain Eisenberg, "From benign to malign Israeli-Lebanese relations, 1948-

78," in *Israel and Hezbollah: An asymmetric conflict in historical and comparative perspective,* ed. Clive Jones and SergioCatignani (New York: Routledge, 2010), 21.

43. Ben D. Mor and Zeev Maoz, *Bound by Struggle: The Strategic Evolution of Enduring International Rivalries* (University of Michigan Press, 2002), 192.
44. Cheryl A. Rubenberg, *Israel and the American National Interest: A Critical Examination* (Illinois: University of Illinois Press, 1989), 227.
45. Cheryl A. Rubenberg, *The Palestinians, A search of a Just Peace* (London: Lynne Rienner Publishers, 2003), 23.
46. Hussain Sirriyeh, "The emergence of Hezbollah and the beginning of resistance, 1982-85", in *Israel and Hezbollah: An asymmetric conflict in historical and comparative perspective,* ed. Clive Jones and Sergio Catignani (New York: Routledge, 2010), 39–48.
47. Olivier Guitta, "France and Hizbullah: The End of the Affair," *U.S.-Europe Analysis Series*, November 2005, accessed November 21, 2020, https://www.brookings.edu/wp-content/uploads/2016/06/guitta20051103.pdf
48. Ray Murphy, "UN Peacekeeping in Lebanon and the use of force", *International Peacekeeping* 6, no. 2 (1999): 38–63, DOI: 10.1080/13533319908413771
49. Paul F. Diehl, *International Peacekeeping: With a new epilogue on Somalia, Bosnia and Cambodia* (Baltimore: The Johns Hopkins University Press, 1993), 83–85.
50. Maren Koss, "Flexible Resistance: How Hezbollah and Hamas Are Mending Ties", *Carnegie Middle East Centre,* July 11, 2018, https://carnegie-mec.org/2018/07/11/flexible-resistance-how-hezbollah-and-hamas-are-mending-ties-pub-76782
51. The multinational Force in Lebanon was created and deployed in Beirut in 1982 to oversee the withdrawal of the PLO after the IDF's pull out. On 18 April 1983, the US embassy in West Beirut was bombed, killing 63 people. It was followed by another attack on US marines and French paratroopers on 23 October 1983, when two car bombs driven by suicide bombers hit the barracks of the Western troops killing 243 US and 58 French soldiers instantly. Responsibility for these two attacks has not been defined as yet. But the USA blames the Hezbollah and Iran for them.
52. Mohamad Bazzi, "Lebanon's Shadow Government," *Foreign Affairs*, September 11, 2009, http://www.foreignaffairs.com
53. Raffaella A. Deal Sarto, *Israel Under Siege: The Politics of Insecurity and the Rise of the Israeli Neo-Revisionist Right (*Washington DC: Georgetown University Press, 2017).

APPENDIX C
TRIGGERS OF VIOLENCE BETWEEN LEBANON AND ISRAEL

Sl. No.	*Report of the UN SG on UNIFIL*	*Period Covered*	*No. of Major Instances of BL Violations*	*Violations of Lebanese Air Space by Israeli Air Force*	*No. of Unfriendly Behaviours towards UNIFIL Peace-keepers and Obstruction of Freedom of Movement*	*No. of Rockets/ Missiles fired (from South Lebanon)*	*No. of Lebanese Armed Hunters*	*No. of unauthorised arms carrying instances within the Area of Operations*	*No. of serious incidents (Hezbollah/ LAF/IDF) near/across BL*
1	2	3	4	5	6	7	8	9	10
1.	S/2006/670	11 August 2006 to 17 August 2006	04		-	-	Data not available	Data not available	
2.	-	18 August 2006 to 14 March 2007	-		-	-	-do-	-do-	
3.	S/2007/392	15 March 2007 to 28 June 2007	04	Daily (900 violations)	06	03	-do-	-do-	
4.	S/2007/641	29 June 2007 to 30 October 2007	-	do-	03	-	-do-	-do-	
5.	S/2008/135	01 November 2007 to 28 February 2008	36	do-	01	02	-do-	-do-	
6.	S/2008/425	01 March 2008 to 27 June 2008	-		-	-	-do-	-do-	Night of 30/31 March 2008. Five armed elements in two cars prevented UNIFIL patrol from following a suspicious-looking truck with a trailer.

1	2	3	4	5	6	7	8	9	10
7.	S/2008/715	28 June 2008 to 18 November 2008	04	do-	06	-	-do-	-do-	
8.	S/2009/119	19 November 2008 to 03 March 2009	10	-do-		07	-do-	-do-	
9.	S/2009/330	04 March 2009 to 29 June 2009	02	-do-	02		-do-	-do-	
10.	S/2009/566	30 June 2009 to 02 November 2009	02	-do-	07	03	-do-	-do-	1. 14 July 2009. Actively maintained ammunition dump of Hezbollah exploded. Local civilians assaulted and prevented UNIFIL investigating team from entering the site of the incident. It resulted in injuries to 14 UNIFIL personnel and damage to property. 2. 12 October 2009. One residential building owned by a local municipality of Hezbollah went up in flames due to an explosion in it. Evidence removed and taken away to an unknown location before the arrival of UNIFIL and the LAF investigating team.

1	2	3	4	5	6	7	8	9	10
11.	S/2010/105	03 November 2009 to 26 February 2010	03	-do-	02		-do-	-do-	
12.	S/2010/352	27 February 2010 to 01 July 2010	08	-do-	05		-do-	-do-	
13.	S/2010/565	02 July 2010 to 01 November 2010	Occasional	-do-	05		-do-	-do-	
14.	S/2011/91	02 November 2010 to 28 February 2011	04		05		-do-	-do-	
15.	S/2011/406	01 March 2011 to 01 July 2011	02	do-	07		02	-do-	
16.	S/2011/715	02 July 2011 to 14 November 2011	03	-do-	06		Data not available	-do-	
17.	S/2012/124	15 November 2011 to 28 February 2012	02	-do-	03	03	-do-	-do-	
18.	S/2012/502	1 March 2012 to 28 June 2012	05	-do-	08		03		
19.	S/2012/837	29 June 2012 to 29 October 2012	04	-do-	03		Data not available	-do-	
20.	S/2013/120	30 October 2012 to 28 February 2013	03	-do-	06	02	-do-	-do-	
21.	S/2013/381	01 March 2013 to 28 June 2013	02	-do-	08		27	-do-	
22.	S/2013/650	29 June 2013 to 13 November 2013	06	-do-	07	04	Data not available	-do-	7 August. Activation of IEDs by Hezbollah in the South of BL. Four IDF soldiers injured.

1	2	3	4	5	6	7	8	9	10
23.	S/2014/130	14 November 2013 to 27 February 2014	05	-do-	03	05	-do-	-do-	15 December. One LAF soldier shot and one IDF soldier killed south of the BL.
24.	S/2014/438	28 February 2014 to 26 June 2014	04	-do-	09		100	-do-	14 March. IDF patrol vehicle hit by roadside explosives south of the BL.
25.	S/2014/784	27 June 2014 to 05 November 2014	10	-do-	12	09	Data not available	-do-	5 October. LAF soldier injured by IDF fire.7 October. IDF vehicle hit by IED south of the BL injuring two IDF soldiers.
26.	S/2015/147	06 November 2014 to 27 February 2015	11	-do-	08	11 (including 06 missiles) by the Hezbollah	-do-	05	28 January. Two IDF soldiers were killed by missile fire and one UNIFIL peacekeeper killed by IDF firing.
27.	S/2015/475	28 February 2015 to 26 June 2015	02	-do-	03		-do-	06	
28.	S/2015/837	27 June 2015 to 04 November 2016	02	-do-	06		-do-	03	
29.	S/2016/189	05 November 2015 to 26 February 2016	06	-do-	03	06 (including 03 IEDs by the Hezbollah)	-do-	Data not available	4 January. 3 IED attack by the Hezbollah on two IDF vehicles across the BL.
30.	S/2016/572	27 February 2016 to 24 June 2016	08	-do-	02	-	-do-	-do-	
31.	S/2016/931	25 June 2016 to 04 November 2016	03 (100 men)	-do-	02		02	-do-	
32.	S/2017/201	5 November 2016 to 28 February 2017	Notable increase (Data NA)	-do-	05		Data not available	-do-	

1	2	3	4	5	6	7	8	9	10
33.	S/2017/591	9 March 2017 to 21 June 2017	Data NA	-do-	Marginal (data NA)		-do-	-do-	20 April. The Hezbollah conducts a tour of the BL for Lebanese and international media.
34.	S/2017/964	22 June 2017 to 6 November 2017	420	-do-	09		240	11	
35.	S/2018/210	7 November 2017 to 28 February 2018	204	458	10		439	03	
36.	S/2018/703	1 March 2018 to 20 June 2018	475	456	10		189	03	
37.	S/2018/1029	21 June 2018 to 26 October 2018	319	550	16		195	01	
38.	S/2019/237	27 October 2018 to 17 February 2019	175	386	04				4 December. IDF discovers Hezbollah tunnels across BL26 December. UNIFIL and OGL discover Hezbollah's tunnel construction factory
39.	S/2019/574	18 February 2019 to 24 June 2019	333	400	07		93	04	
40.	S/2019/889	25 June 2019 to 31 October 2019	421	787	12	03 missiles fired by the Hezbollah	256	04	
41.	S/2020/195	1 November 2019 to 18 February 2020	313	291			348	02	
42.	S/2020/710	19 February to 16 June 2020	518 including 4 incidents of Sudanese citizens, and 2 by IDF	Daily basis (average of 11 hours flying)	5	-	3	165	2 (1 incident of face-off by 47 IDF and 26 LAF soldiers near the BL and 1 incident of cutting of technical fence at 3 locations

APPENDIX D
INCIDENTS OF TERRORIST ATTACKS ON UNIFIL

Sl. No.	*Report of UN SG on UNIFIL*	*Period Covered*	*Attacks by Terrorists*
1.	S/2007/392	15 March 2007 to 28 June 2007	24 June. A bomb blast killed 06 Spanish peacekeepers.
2.	S/2007/641	29 June 2007 to 30 October 2007	16 July. Bomb blast at Tanzanian checkpoint - No casualty.
3.	S/2011/406	01 March 2011 to 01 July 2011	27 May. Bomb blast north of Saida. Six peacekeepers injured.
4.	S/2011/715	02 July 2011 to 14 November 2011	26 July. A bomb blast on logistic convoy on UNIFIL – 06 French peacekeepers injured.
5.	S/2012/124	15 November 2011 to 28 February 2012	09 December. Bomb blast outside Tyre – 05 French soldiers and 02 Lebanese civilians injured.

APPENDIX E
RESPONSES FROM UNIFIL CONTINGENTS: PART A

1. Participants (n)

S. No.	Category	Code	Total (n)
1	Soldiers (Sepoys)	1	126
2	Non-Commissioned Officers/ Junior Commissioned Officers	2	102
3	Officers	3	09
	Total		237

2. Responses and Constructs

S. No.	Construct	Sub Construct or Item	Strongly Disagree	Disagree	Agree	Strongly Agree	Total Respondents	Mean Score
			1	2	3	4		
1	2	3	4	5	6	7	8	9
1	**Violence**	Violence between Lebanon and Israel is missing because of UNIFIL effective steps	0	17	201	19	237	3.01
2		Violence against peacekeepers after 2007 has declined	5	12	211	9	237	2.95
3		Peacekeepers are not specifically targeted except as opportunity targets	8	12	205	12	237	2.93
4	**De-mining**	Humanitarian De-mining is one of the major tasks of UNIFIL	5	11	200	21	237	3

1	2	3	4	5	6	7	8	9
5	**Conflict management mechanism**	Most effective is the use and effectiveness of tripartite meetings	29	100	62	46	237	2.53
6		Use of office of the HoM/FC to negotiate with Higher Authorities in Lebanon and Israel	4	37	126	70	237	3.11
7		Liaison and coordination section of Force HQ	1	14	88	134	237	3.5
8		Quick response and control of incidents by peacekeepers	3	14	38	182	237	3.68
9		Marking of the BL must be expedited to resolve issues	41	41	150	5	237	2.5
10	**Presence of militias in South Lebanon**	Much against the UN Resolution, the Hezbollah will always be present in South Lebanon due to ethnicity	7	3	209	18	237	3
11		The Hezbollah is too strong for the LAF to disarm	2	10	216	9	237	2.98
12	**Capacity building of LAF**	LAF has become a well-trained and capable organisation	6	8	206	17	237	3.01
13		LAF has been able to take only partial control of the security of South Lebanon	8	15	189	25	237	2.97
14		The LAF has been able to take full control of the security of South Lebanon	4	39	175	19	237	2.88
15		The LAF is still not in a position to defend Lebanon from another external aggression	0	2	217	18	237	3.07
16		The LAF has proved its capability to stand up to most of the internal threats excluding the Hezbollah	8	10	194	25	237	3
17	**Relationship with the local population**	The relationship between UNIFIL and the local population is excellent	1	6	190	40	237	3.14
18		UNIFIL's respect for local culture and tradition shapes its relationship with the local population	22	19	187	9	237	3.09

1	2	3	4	5	6	7	8	9
19		The financial contribution by UNIFIL/TCCs in improving the livelihood of the local population helps in building a good relationship with the local populace	2	45	122	68	237	3.08
20		UNIFIL's relationship with the local population varies with the contingent's nationality	0	19	216	2	237	2.93
21		The relationship of the local population with the contingents of non-Western nations is better than with the contingents of Western nations	0	10	208	19	237	3.04
22		The local population obstructs the movement of UNIFIL peacekeepers when there is a lack of respect for local culture and tradition	13	10	192	22	237	2.94
23		The local population obstructs the movement of UNIFIL peacekeepers when there is aggressive and unfriendly behaviour by UNIFIL	6	9	212	10	237	2.95
24		The local population obstructs the movement of UNIFIL peacekeepers when there is suspicion about UNIFIL's underlying motives	1	4	196	36	237	3.13
25		The frequency of such obstructions has reduced over the past few years	2	4	206	25	237	3.07
26	**Mandate**	UNIFIL (part of the mandate for which UNIFIL is solely responsible) has been able to implement/enforce its mandate	53	58	125	1	237	2.31
27	**The organizational structure of UNIFIL for mandate implementation**	The effectiveness of UNIFIL is due to its robust military structure	1	5	196	35	237	3.12
28		The effectiveness of UNIFIL is due to the political influence of TCCs from Europe	11	8	191	27	237	2.99

1	2	3	4	5	6	7	8	9
29		Despite differences creating operational synergy (interoperability) amongst the TCCs of Western and non-Western nations is easier	8	13	191	25	237	2.98
30	**Rules of Engagement**	RoE provides adequate flexibility to the peacekeepers to use force when necessary	6	11	200	20	237	2.99
31		RoE provides only restraining measures to avoid unnecessary use of force	1	73	78	85	237	3.04
32		RoE is being used as an excuse to avoid the use of force (even when necessary) by some contingents because of the presence of national caveats	13	44	123	57	237	2.95
33		RoE is being used as an excuse to avoid the use of force (even when necessary) by some contingents out of fear of retaliation by those against whom force is used	6	17	189	25	237	2.98

Responses from UNIFIL Contingents on Role of Military in Peacekeeping: Part B

Sl. No.	*Sub-Construct or Item*	*Strongly Disagree*	*Dis-agree*	*Neutral*	*Agree*	*Strongly Agree*	*Total Respondents*	*Mean Score on the sheets*
		1	2	3	4	5		
1	Participation in combat operation is an important military task	9	25	34	74	95	237	3.93
2	One achieves more by negotiation rather than the use of force	0	4	41	89	103	237	4.23
3	During a mission, one must be clear as to who is in command and control	0	6	44	89	98	237	4.18
4	The military task is to contribute to peace in a forceful way	0	20	52	62	103	237	4.05
5	Prefer the use of a kinder approach rather than force	3	8	50	72	104	237	4.12
6	The military task is to destroy the enemies of the peace process	6	14	42	79	96	237	4.03
7	In a mission, fighting an enemy is the priority	4	11	52	87	83	237	3.99
8	In a mission reconstruction is the main task of a force	5	12	50	79	91	237	4.01
9	As soldiers, one must help all sides and all people	5	15	56	81	80	237	3.91
10	In a mission, one achieves more by threatening rather than communicating	9	19	49	77	83	237	3.87
11	Good contacts with all parties are very important	6	16	58	80	77	237	3.87
12	The military task is to use force against anyone who disturbs the peace	5	18	56	77	81	237	3.89
13	Military force must be tough against the local forces rather than accommodating	7	21	48	89	72	237	3.84
14	Fighting is a priority role in a mission and other tasks come later	16	14	51	74	82	237	3.81
15	Military deployment is to help locals	8	18	53	62	96	237	3.93
16	For the non-cooperating party, one must negotiate and use force as a last resort	3	10	53	94	77	237	3.98
17	Military is deployed to fight	3	21	54	76	83	237	3.91
18	Military force must cooperate with all sides in a mission area	4	21	50	82	80	237	3.9
19	Reconstruction is the most important task and not fighting	2	15	50	89	81	237	3.98
20	The military must mediate between the parties	7	4	38	99	89	237	4.09

APPENDIX F
SUMMARY OF KEY GOALS AND EXTENT OF PROGRESS

Key Goals	*Sub-Goals*	*Key Questions*	*Extent of Progress*
1. Restoration of peace and security.	(a) Violence between Israel and Lebanon.	(a) Has the violence between Israel and Lebanon reduced?	(i) Except for occasional incidents along the BL, there has been no conflict since 2006. (ii) Gradual decrease in IDF and LAF face-offs. (iii) No cross-border events except for BL violations by Lebanese armed hunters.
	(b) Violence against peacekeepers.	(b) Has violence against peace-keepers reduced?	Substantial reduction—only five incidents between 2006 and 2012. No incidents after 2012.
	(c) Humanitarian de-mining.	(c.1) What have been the activities around and response to humanitarian de-mining?	With a substantial amount of cluster bombs/unexploded ordnance (UXO) destroyed, there is a reduction in civilian casualties because of landmines. This activity has been lauded by the local Lebanese population as one of the most important contributions of UNIFIL.
		(c.2) Has Israel handed over the maps to Lebanon?	Maps have been handed over.
Overall Assessment of Goal 1			With no major conflict and no cross-border events for a long period, a remarkable reduction in violence against peace-keepers and reasonable progress in humanitarian de-mining, UNIFIL has made visible success in fulfilling Goal 1.
2. Creating conditions for the prevention of resumption of hostilities between Lebanon and Israel.	(a) Mechanism is available for the prevention of hostilities.	(a.1) How have the available mechanisms helped in the prevention of resumption of hostilities?	Engagement by the HoM/FC, periodical Tripartite meetings, coordination by UNIFIL Liaison and Coordination teams, engagement by Civil Affairs Officers and immediate response by quick reaction teams have helped to mitigate the chances of even small incidents getting out of control. Tripartite meetings have been considered as the most effective mechanism. Such meetings were held even during the 2006 war.

Key Goals	*Sub-Goals*	*Key Questions*	*Extent of Progress*
	(b) Conflict management.	(b.1) Has UNIFIL contributed to the prevention of conflict from expanding geographically?	Remaining updated with the developing security situation in the area of operations, UNIFIL was able to pre-empt and help de-escalation of crises. Thereby, UNIFIL has prevented the state of conflict from expanding geographically.
Overall Assessment of Goal 2.			By remaining engaged with Israel and Lebanon at the strategic, operational, and tactical levels, UNIFIL has been able to help in creating conditions for the prevention of recurrence of major conflicts. UNIFIL has achieved significant success in achieving Goal 2
3. Ensuring South Lebanon is free of armed personnel, assets, and weapons other than that with the Lebanese government and the UNIFIL.	(a) Prevent the presence of Lebanese and non-Lebanese militias other than the Government of Lebanon and UNIFIL in South Lebanon.	(a.1) Are there unauthorised armed personnel in South Lebanon? (a.2) Are the measures to ensure assistance provided by UNIFIL for the removal of this armed personnel effective?	(a.1) There are still unauthorised armed personnel in South Lebanon. (a.2) UNIFIL assistance to the LAF is effective. But the LAF is not capable of removing the Hezbollah from South Lebanon because of the Hezbollah's support base in South Lebanon and being part of the government.
Overall Assessment of Goal 3.			With better cooperation from the LAF and improved training, UNIFIL has learnt to navigate the complex political and security landscape of South Lebanon. However, there are still unauthorised armed personnel in South Lebanon. Despite the challenges of the presence of unauthorised armed groups, UNIFIL could not be deterred from implementing its mandated tasks and achieved a reasonable degree of success.
4. Assistance to LAF in fulfill-ing its security responsibilities.	(a) Resolving disputes of occupied areas.	(a.1) Have Lebanon and Israel resolved their major disagreements? (a.2) Has the marking of the BL helped in resolving disputes?	Except for ironing out differences in marking the BL, no occupied area has been vacated yet. With progress made in BL marking, the frequency of accidental crossing of the BL has reduced. But since no marking has taken place in the disputed areas, the underlying disputes have not been resolved.

Key Goals	*Sub-Goals*	*Key Questions*	*Extent of Progress*
	(b) Capability building of LAF.	(b.1) Has the capability of the LAF to fulfil its responsibilities grown?	(i) With regular joint training, the LAF's professional skill has improved substantially. Large areas in South Lebanon except the Hezbollah-dominated areas are in control of the LAF. Progress of deployment has slowed down because of the commitment to quell internal disturbances and guard the Lebanese Syrian border during the Syrian war. (ii) The LAF is not capable of acting against the Hezbollah either directly or indirectly.
		(b.2) Is there freedom of movement for locals and UNIFIL in the AO? What are the reasons for the restriction of movement and does the pattern of restrictions on movement vary from contingent to contingent?	(b.2) (i) Restrictions on freedom of movement continues and there is an increase in the number of incidents. (ii) Reasons for restrictions on freedom of movement: • Armed UNIFIL patrols in heavy vehicles driving at high speed are disliked. • Photography in area of operation. • Lack of sensitivity to local culture and tradition. (iii) Contingents from Western nations are generally considered arrogant but contingents from Asian regions find better acceptability.
		(b.3) Has the LAF's cooperation with UNIFIL improved? Has UNIFIL helped the LAF to get external financial assistance?	(b.3) (i) With regular interaction at different levels and the exchange of officers, cooperation between UNIFIL and LAF has been reasonably good. The operational response from the LAF to UNIFIL, however, has been selective and not adequate. (ii) UNIFIL lobbied with the international community for US$ 500,000 assistance for the purchase of military equipment. Progress not known. Israel, however, lobbies against assistance to the LAF.

Key Goals	*Sub-Goals*	*Key Questions*	*Extent of Progress*
Overall Assessment of Goal 4.			The standard of professional skill of the LAF to take on the responsibility of security of South Lebanon has significantly enhanced. However, because of its involvement in internal disturbances throughout Lebanon, as well as political compulsion (facing the challenges of the Hezbollah), the LAF has not been able to exercise full control over the whole of South Lebanon. Therefore, UNIFIL has been able to achieve only partial success in Goal 4.
5. Ensure support from the local population.	(a) Good relations and support from the local population.	(a.1) Does the local population support UNIFIL? (a.2) Are there social ills created by peacekeepers?	UNIFIL's acceptability amongst the local population is quite good and has been able to achieve credibility and local legitimacy. Such support, however, is based on UNIFIL's contribution to developmental activities and peacekeepers respecting local sensitivity. No case of any social ills
Overall Assessment of Goal 5.			Until now, the local population supports UNIFIL. However, population support largely depends on the general attitude and conduct of the peacekeepers. The restriction on freedom of movement continues. The pattern of such restriction is influenced by the degree of sensitivity of the peacekeepers towards local culture and tradition. UNIFIL so far has been able to achieve significant success in Goal 5. However, there is a need to work for continued support from the local population.
6. Maintain the operational effectiveness of the mission.	(a) Clear and achievable mission mandate.	(a.1) Is the mission mandate clear and achievable? (a.2) Is the mission operationally prepared to effectively execute the mandated tasks?	The mandate is by and large clear and achievable except for disarming the Hezbollah. (a.2) (i) Peacekeepers are well trained and well equipped; their awareness of the mission, local culture and tradition and other sensitivities are of a high order; and support to the military contingents from the respective nations is good.

Key Goals	*Sub-Goals*	*Key Questions*	*Extent of Progress*
			(ii) With the reduction in budgetary support, the reduced strength of force negatively impacts its operational effectiveness.
		(a.3) Is there adequate support from the parties to the conflict to the mission for mandate implementation?	(a.3) (i) Political support from the IDF to UNIFIL for mandate implementation is extremely good but it criticises UNIFIL for not disarming the Hezbollah. (ii) Cooperation from Lebanon to resolve pending disputes and investigation of incidents by the mission is good except for incidents related to the Hezbollah.
	(b) Organisational structure for mandate implementation.	(b.1) How is the multinational force structure responding and adapting to challenges?	(i) Multinational force structure is an indication of the political commitment of the larger section of the international community to bring peace and stability between Israel and Lebanon. (ii) Cultural diversity and interoperability challenges amongst the contingents (operational ethos, training, and equipment) are overcome by regular on-the-job training.
		(b.2) Are the RoEs adequate to meet the operational needs of the mission?	(i) RoEs are adequate. But implementation is affected depending on the respective national directive on RoEs. (ii) Most of the contingents are shy of using force fearing military retaliation by the Hezbollah and the likely political backlash.

Key Goals	*Sub-Goals*	*Key Questions*	*Extent of Progress*
Overall Assessment of Goal 6.			The mandate is relatively clear. Despite the interoperability challenges of the multinational force, UNIFIL is militarily capable of implementing the mission mandate. However, geopolitical compulsions of the TCCs make it difficult for UNIFIL to enforce the mandate. The robust multinational structure is only symbolic. The Mission's resolve can be tested only when there is a direct attack on the peacekeepers by the Hezbollah or in a possible next major conflict between Lebanon and Israel.The major stakeholders including Israel and the local population of Lebanon are doubtful about UNIFIL's ability to fulfil Goal 6.
7. Credibility and Local Legitimacy	Adherence to principles of peacekeeping and people-centric operational activities.	(a.1) Is the operation credible in the eyes of the parties to the conflict and the local population? (a.2) Has the operation found local legitimacy?	(a.1) No negative feedback; the population supports UNIFIL. Israel, however, is sceptical of UNIFIL's achievements. (a.2). The absence of a full-fledged conflict is the presence of negative peace, a step in the direction of positive peace, and UNIFIL's achievement to obtain local legitimacy.
Overall Assessment of Goal 7.			UNIFIL has been able to effectively contribute towards a prolonged negative peace and earn credibility and local cooperation. UNIFIL's achievement in fulfilling Goal 7 has been creditable.

BIBLIOGRAPHY

Ahmad, Aisha. "Agenda for Peace or Budget for War? Evaluating the Economic Impact of International Intervention in Somalia." *International Journal* 67, no. 2(Spring 2012): 313–31, http://www.jstor.org/stable/23266009

Aksu, Esref. " The UN in the Congo conflict: ONUC" in The United Nations, intra-state peacekeeping and normative change (Manchester, England: Manchester University Press, 2018).

Alao, Abiodun; Mackinlay, John; and Olonisakin, Funmi. "Regional Peacekeeping after the Cold War." *Peacekeepers, Politicians and Warlords: The Liberian Peace Process*. Tokyo: United Nations University, 1999.

"A Peace Deal for South Sudan is Signed. Will it Last?" *The New York Times*, June 27, 2018. https://www.nytimes.com/2018/06/27/world/africa/south-sudan-peace-deal.html.

Ahre, John. "The Peace Process in the DRC: A transformation quagmire." *Accords*, 6 December 2012. http://www.accord.org.za/publication/peace-process-drc/.

Annan, Kofi. "Podium: Impartiality Does Not Mean Neutrality." *Independent*, January 22, 1999. https://www.independent.co.uk/arts-entertainment/podium-impartiality-does-not-mean-neutrality-1075401.html.

Aoun, Elena., ed. *The United Nations Interim Force in Lebanon: Multiple Perspectives on a Multinational Peace Operation*. Brussels: Peter Lang, 2018.

Aoun, Elena. "The European Involvement in Post 2006 UNIFIL: The Art of the Possible." In *The United Nations Interim Force in Lebanon, Multiple Perspectives on a Multinational Peace Operation*, edited by Elena Aoun. Brussels: Peter Lang, 2018.

Asquith, Herbert Henry. *The genesis of the war.* London: Cassell & Company, 1972. *International Security and Peacebuilding*, edited by Bah, Abu Bakarr. New Delhi: Knowledge World, 2017.

"Assessing the Effectiveness of the United Nations Mission in South Sudan/ UNMISS." *EPON Report* no. 2 (2019), 91. https://effectivepeaceops.net/unmiss/.

"Assessing the Effectiveness of the United Nations Mission in the DRC/ MONUC–MONUSCO." *EPON Report* no. 3 (2019). https://effectivepeaceops.net/wp-content/uploads/2019/06/EPON-MONUSCO-LowRes.pdf

"Assessing the Effectiveness of the United Nations Mission in Mali/MINUSMA." *EPON Report* no. 4, 2019. https://effectivepeaceops.net/wp-content/uploads/2019/05/EPON-MINUSMA-Report-Exec-Summary.pdf.

Autesserre, Séverine. "The Crisis of Peacekeeping: Why the UN Can't End Wars." *Foreign Affairs,* January/February 2019:101-116. https://www.foreignaffairs.com/articles/2018-12-11/crisis-peacekeeping.

Autesserre, Severine. "The Trouble with Congo: How Local Disputes Fuel Regional Conflicts." *Foreign Affairs,* 87, no. 3 (May-June 2008): 94-110, https://www.jstor.org/stable/20032653

Autesserre, Severine. *The Trouble with Congo: Local Violence and the Failure of International Peacekeeping.* New York: Cambridge University Press, 2010.

Avni, Benny. "UN failure is leading to another Lebanon war." *New York Post,* August 29, 2017. https://nypostcom.cdn.ampproject.org/c/nypost.com/2017/08/29/un-failure-is-leading-to-another-lebanon-war/amp.

Azhari Timour. "Analysis: The politics behind the Lebanon-Israel border talks." *Al Jazeera,* October 12, 2020, last updated October 14, 2020, https://www.aljazeera.com/news/2020/10/12/analysis-the-politics-of-the-lebanon-israel-border-talks

Ballard, John R. "A Regional Recipe for Success: Multinational Peace Operations in East Timor". In *Military Cooperation Multinational Peace Operations: Managing Cultural Diversity and Crisis Response,* edited by Soeters, Joseph, and Phillippe Manigart. New York: Routledge, 2008.

BBC News. "Lebanon: Why the country is in crisis." August 5, 2020. https://www.bbc.com/news/world-middle-east-5339010

Bardalai, A. K. *Changing Security Scenario: Implications for UN Peacekeeping.* New Delhi: Knowledge World for United Service Institution of India, 2006.

Bardalai, A. K. "UNIFIL: The many challenges of successful peacekeeping." *Journal of Defence Studies* 10, no. 3 (2016): 65-80.

Bardalai, A. K. "UNPKO and Military Contributions: Challenges and Opportunities for Asia-Pacific Governments." *Journal of the United Service Institution of India* CXLVII, no. 607 (2017): 26-34.

Barnett, Michael N. and Finnemore, Martha, "Implementation in Practice: The Use of Force to Protect Civilians in United Nations Peacekeeping." *International Organizations,* 53, no. 4 (Autumn 1994)

Bartuseviciene, Ilona; and Sakalyte, Evelina. "Organisational Assessment: Effectiveness vs. Efficiency." *Social Transformation in Contemporary Society* 1 (2013): 45–53.

Bara, Corinne; and Hultman, Lisa. "Just Different Hats? Comparing UN and Non-UN Peacekeeping." *International Peacekeeping* 27, no.3 (2020): 341-368, DOI:10.1080/13533312.2020.1737023

Barnett, N. Michael and Finnemore, Martha. "The Politics, Power and Pathologies of International Organisations, *International Organisations* 53, no. 4 (1994): 699-732.

Bazzi, Mohammad. Lebanon's Shadow Government. *Foreign Affairs* (2009, 11 September 2009). http://www.foreignaffairs.com.

Bellamy, Alex J. and Williams Paul. "Peace Operations and Global Order." *International Peacekeeping (Special Issue)* 11, no. 1 (2004).

Bellamy, Alex J.; Williams, Paul; and Griffin, Stuart. *Understanding Peacekeeping*. (Oxford: Polity Press, 2004).

Bentler, P.M.; and Chou, C.H., "Practical issues in structural modelling". *Sociological Methods & Research*, 16 (1987): 78-117.

Bergman, Ronen. "Hezbollah 3.0: How Israel's No. 1 Enemy is Preparing for the Next Lebanon War," 2015. http://www.ynetnews.com/articles/

Best, J.W.; and Kahn, J.V. *Research in Education* 10. New Jersey: Pearson Education Inc, 2011.

Biden, Joseph R. Jr. "Why America Must Lead Again: Rescuing U.S. Foreign Policy After Trump." *Foreign Affairs*, March/April 2020. https://www.foreignaffairs.com/articles/united-states/2020-01-23/why-america-must-lead-again

Biger, Gideon. "The Boundaries of Israel-Palestine Past, Present and Future: A Critical Geographical View." In *Israel Studies* 13: 68-93, edited by Troen, S. Ilan. Bloomington: USA, Indiana University Press, 2008.

Bingham, Richard D. and Clairee, Felbinger L. *Evaluation in Practice: A Methodological Approach*, 2nd Edition. New York: Seven Bridges, 2002.

Blandford, Nicholas. "Why peace is prevailing, for now, in South Lebanon", *The Christian Science Monitor*. Retrieved January 14, 2017, from http://www.csmonitor.com/World/Middle-East/2016/0823/Why-peace-is-prevailing-for-now-in-south-Lebanon.

Blandford, Nicholas. "Seven Villages: Origins and Implications." https://now.mmedia.me/Library/Files/EnglishDocumentation/Other%20Documents/The_Seven_Villages-paper-final2.pdf.

Blocq D. "Western soldiers and the protection of local civilians in UN peacekeeping operations: Is a nationalist orientation in the armed forces hindering our preparedness to fight?" *Armed Forces & Society* 36(2) (2010): 290-309.

Bratt, Duan. "Assessing the Success of UN PKO." *International Peacekeeping* 3, no.4 (1996): 66-81.

Bratt, Duan. "Explaining PKO: The UN in Internal Conflicts." *International Peacekeeping* 4, no. 3 (1997): 45-70.

Bratt, Duane. "Explaining Peacekeeping Performance: The UN in Internal Conflict." International Peacekeeping 4, no. 3 (2007): 45-70.

Bode, Ingvild and Karlsurd, John. "Implementation in Practice: The Use of force to Protect civilians in United Nations peacekeeping." *European Journal of International Relations*, 25, no. 2 (2019):458-485, doi:10.1177/135406611879 6540

Bohl, Ryan. "A New Brand of Nationalism Takes Root in the Middle East." *Stratfor,* September 4, 2020, https://worldview.stratfor.com/article/new-brand-nationalism-takes-root-middle-east

Booth, Wayne; C. Colombo, G. Gregory, and Joseph M. Williams. *The Craft of Research.* Chicago: The University of Chicago Press, 2008.

Boniecki, Kurt A. and Thomas W Britt. "Prejudice and the Peacekeeper". In *Psychology of the Peacekeepers: Lessons from the Field.* Edited by Thomas W. Britt and Amy B. Alder. Westport: Praeger, 2003.

Bosco, David. "The Multilateralist: The UN's troubled Lebanon peacekeepers." *Foreign Policy,* March 25, 2013. https://foreign policy.com/2013/03/25/the-uns-troubled-lebanon-peacekeepers/

Bourgeois, Hanna. "All Necessary Means' to Protect Civilians: The Interpretation and Implementation of UN Security Council Mandates Authorising the Protection of Civilians." *Journal of International Peacekeeping,* 24, no. 1-2 (2020

Bove, Vincenzo; Ruffa, Chiara and Ruggeri, Andrea. Composing Peace: Mission Composition in UN Peacekeeping. New York: Oxford University Press, 2020.

Bove, Vincenzo, and Andrea Ruggeri. "Peacekeeping Effectiveness and Blue Helmets' Distance from Locals." *Journal of Conflict Resolution* 63, no. 7 (August 2019): 1630–55. https://doi.org/10.1177/0022002719826115.

Bowden, J. "Reflections on the phenomenographic research process". In *Doing Developmental Phenomenography* (Qualitative Research Methods Series), edited by J Bowden and P. Green, Melbourne: RMIT University Press, 2005.

Browne, Edward Moxon. *A Future for Peacekeeping.* London: Macmillan Press, 1998.

Britt, Tomas W. and Amy B. Adler. *The Psychology of the Peacekeepers: Lessons from the Field,* Westport: Praeger Publishers, 2003.

Bryant, Nick. "UN: Seventy years of Changing World." *BBC News,* September 20, 2015. http://www.bbc.com/news/world-us-canada-34310354.

Burns, Arthur Lee. and Heathcote, Nina. *Peacekeeping by UN Forces.* London: Pall Mall Press, 1963.

Cameron, Kim S. "Effectiveness as Paradox: Consensus and Conflict in Conceptions of Organizational Effectiveness." *Management Science* 32, no. 5 (1986): 539-553.

Carvalho, Benjamin de. and Coning, Cedric de. "Rising Power and Future of Peacekeeping and Peace Building."*Norwegian Resource Centre Report* (November 14, 2013). http://peacebuilding.no

Catignani, Sergio, ed. *Israel and Hezbollah: An asymmetric conflict in historical and comparative perspective*. New York: Routledge, 2010.

Cervenak, Christine M. "Lessons of the Past: Experiences in Peace Operations." In *Peace Operations: Developing in American Strategy*. Edited by Antonia Handler Chayes and George T. Raach. Washington DC: National Defence University Press, 1995.

Chayes, Antonia Hanler and George T. Raach. *Peace Operations: Developing an American Strategy*. Washington: National Institute of University Press, 1995.

Chesterman, Simon. and Franck, Thomas M. "Leadership in Peace Operations: A Secretary-General or a General." In *The Management of Peacekeeping*, edited by Julian Junk, Francesco Mancini, Wolfgang Seibel and Till Blume (London: Lynne Rienner Publishers, 2017), 292–98.

Chiyuki, Aoi; Coning, Cedric de; and Thakur, Ramesh. "Unintended consequences, complex peace operations and peacebuilding systems." In *Unintended Consequences of* PKO, edited by Aoi Chiyuki, Cedric de Coning and Ramesh Thakur, 1-10. Tokyo/New York/Paris: United Nations University, 2007.

Chrarah, Nasser. "Terrorist Groups Exploit Palestinians in South Lebanon." September 2013. *Al-Monitor*. http://www.al-monitor.com/pulse/originals/2013/09/lebanon-ain-hilweh-takfiri-groups-influence.html.

Christianson, Scott. "The Origins of the World War I Agreement that Carved up the Middle East: How Great Britain and France secretly negotiated the Sykes-Picot Agreement." November 2015. http://www.smithsonianmag.com/history/sykes-picot-agreement.

Christianson, Scott. 100 *Documents That Changed the World: Magna Carta to Wikileaks*. Batsford Ltd., 2015.

Cimino, Matthieu. and Farhat, Nadim. "Lebanese Perceptions of the UNIFIL: Views from the South." In *The United Nations Interim Force in Lebanon: Multiple Perspectives on a Multinational Peace Operation*. Edited by Elena Aoun, 81-113. Brussels: Peter Lang, 2018.

Cluster Munitions Monitor 2014. February 15, 2017. On the Issues http://www.the-monitor.org/.

Connaughton, Richard. "Rwanda-Tropical Nazism." *Military Intervention and Peacekeeping: The Reality*. Hampshire, England: Ashgate, 2001.

Coning, Cedric de. "Civil-military coordination and complex peacebuilding systems." In *Civil-Military Cooperation in Post-Conflict Operations: Emerging theory and practice*, edited by Christopher Ankersen, London/New York: Routledge, 2008.

Coning, Cedric de. "Is stabilization the new normal? Implications of stabilization mandates for the use of force in UN peace operations." In *The Use of Force in UN Peacekeeping (1st ed.)* ed. Peter Nadin (London: Routledge, 2018).

Coning Cedric de. "Adaptive Peace Operations: Navigating the Complexity of Influencing Societal Change Without Causing Harm." *International Peacekeeping*, 27, no.5 (2020): 836-858. DOI: 10.1080/13533312.2020. 1797500

Coning, Cedric de. and Brusset, Emery. "Towards a Comprehensive Results-based Reporting and Performance Assessment.' *Norwegian Institute of International Affairs (NUPI) Report*, no. 4 (2018). https://reliefweb.int/sites/reliefweb.int/files/resources/NUPI_Report_4_Towards%2Ba%2BComprehensive%2BRes.pdf.

CNN Politics. "Abraham Accords." Last modified September 15, 2020. https://edition.cnn.com/2020/09/15/politics/israel-uae-abraham-accords-documents/index.html.

Cook, Steven A. "The End of Hope in the Middle East". *Foreign Policy*, September 5, 2020, https://foreignpolicy.com/2020/09/05/middle-east-end-hope-recovery-yemen-lebanon/

Cooper, D. and Schindler, P. *Business research methods* (10th edn.). New York: McGraw-Hill/Irwin, 2008.

Cox, Katherine E. "Beyond Self-Defence: United Nations PKO & and the Use of Force." *Denver Journal of International Law and Policy*, 27 (1999), 271:239-273.

Curran, David. "Muddling on through? Cosmopolitan Peacekeeping and Protection of Civilians." *International Peacekeeping* 24, no. 1 (2017) :63-85.

Dallaire, Romeo. *Shake Hands with the Devil*. Cambridge: Da Capo Press, 2003.

Daher, Marianne; Carré, David; Jaramillo Andrea; Olivares, Himmble; and Tomicic, Alemka. "Experience and Meaning in Qualitative Research: A Conceptual Review and a Methodological Device Proposal." *Forum: Qualitative Social Research* 18, no. 3, Art. 9 (September 2017).

Daniel, Donald C. F. and Bradd C. Hayes. *Beyond Traditional Peacekeeping*. London: Macmillan, 1995.

Daniel, Donald C. F.; Williams, Paul D.; and Smith, Adam C. "Deploying Combined Teams: Lessons Learned from Operational Partnership in UN Peacekeeping." *Providing for Peacekeeping* (12). August 2015. International Peace Institute Report. www.ipinst.org.

Davison, Roderic H. "Review 'From Paris to Sèvres: The Partition of the Ottoman Empire at the Peace Conference of 1919-1920." *Slavic Review* 34, no. 1 (1975):186-187.

Day, Adam and Hunt, Charles T. "Distractions, Distortions and Dilemmas: The Externalities of Protecting Civilians in United Nations Peacekeeping." Civil Wars (2021), DOI: 10.1080/13698249.2022.1995680

Deal Sarto and Raffaella A. *Israel Under Siege: The Politics of Insecurity and the Rise of the Israeli Neo-Revisionist Right*. Washington DC: Georgetown University Press, 2017.

Diehl, Paul. *International Peacekeeping*. Baltimore: The Johns Hopkins University Press, 1993.

Diehl, Paul and Alexandru Balas. "The Success and Failure of Peace Operations." *Peace Operations.* Cambridge: Polity, 2014.

Diehl, Paul F. and Daniel Druckman. *Evaluating Peace Operations.* New Delhi: Viva Books in arrangement with Lynne Rienner, 2011.

Diehl, Paul F. *International Peacekeeping: With a new epilogue on Somalia, Bosnia and Cambodia.* (Baltimore: Johns Hopkins Press, 1993).

Doyle, Michael W. and Sambanis, Nicholas. Making War and Building Peace: United Nations Peace Operations. Princeton: Princeton University Press, 2006.

Druckman, Daniel and Paul Stern. "Perspectives on Evaluating PKO." *International Journal of Peace Studies* 4, no. 1 (1999):79-86.

Egozi, Arie. "Israel asks Trump to Withhold TOWs, Drones from Lebanese Military Aid." *Breaking Defence* (December 3, 2019). https://breakingdefense.com/2019/12/israel-asks-trump-to-withhold-tows-drones-from-lebanese-military-aid/

Eisenberg, Laura Zittrain "Do Good Fences Make Good Neighbors? Israel and Lebanon After the Withdrawal." *Middle East Review of International Affairs* 4, no. 3 (2000)

Eisenberg, Laurie Zittrain. "From benign to malign Israeli Lebanese relations, 1948-78." In *Israel and Hezbollah: An asymmetric conflict in historical and comparative perspective,* edited by Clive Jones and Sergio Catignani. New York: Routledge, 2010.

Eisenkot, Gadi. "Northern Command Chief: No Interest in Launching Another Confrontation." In "Learning to Deter", Daniel Sobelman, *International Security* 41, no. 3 (winter 2016/17): 151-195.

Eisenhardt, Kathleen M. "Building from Case Study Research," *The Academy of Management Review* 14, no. 4 (October 1989): 532-550.

Elron, Efrat. "The Interplay between the Transnational and Multinational: Intercultural Integrating Mechanism in UN peace operations." In *Military Cooperation in Multinational Peace Operations: Managing cultural diversity and crisis response.* Edited by Joseph Soeters and Philippe Manigart. London: Routledge, 2008.

Elron, Efrat. "UNIFIL II, Israel, Lebanon, The United Nations and the International Community: New and Renewed Partnerships and Implications for Mission Effectiveness." In *Cultural Challenges in Military Operations.* Edited by Cees M. Coops and Tibor Szvircsev Tresch, (NATO Defence College, 2007), 90-108, https://www.jstor.org/stable/resrep10333.

El-Khadem, Samir. *The War of Surprises and Deceptions.* (Beirut: Arab Institute of East and West Studies, 2008).

Essens Ad, Vogelaar; Erhan Tanercan; and Donna Winslow., eds *The Human in Command: Peace Support Operations.* Amsterdam: Mets & Schilt, 2001.

Fetner, Gerald L. *Immersed in Great Affairs: Allan Nevins and the Heroic Age of American History*. Albany: State University of New York Press, 2004.

Fetherston, A. B. *Towards a Theory of United Nations Peacekeeping*. Palgrave Macmillan Press: UK, 1994.

Findlay, Trevor. "The Use of Force in UN Peace Operations." *SIPRI*. Stockholm: Oxford University Press, 2002.

Fisk, Robert. *Pity the Nation: The Abduction of Lebanon*. New York: Thunder's Mouth Press/Nation's Books, 2002.

Foot, Rosemary. "The Responsibility to Protect (R2P) and Its Evolution: Beijing's Influence on Norm Creation in Humanitarian Areas." *St Antony's International Review* 6, no. 2 (2011): 47–66. http://www.jstor.org/stable/26226764

Ford, Timothy. "Determining Success in Peace Operations." In *Challenges of Peace Operations: into the 21st Century Concluding Report 1997-2002*. Stockholm: Elanders Gotab, 2002.

Fortna, Virginia Page. "Does Peacekeeping Keep Peace? International Intervention and the Duration of Peace After Civil War." *International Studies Quarterly* 48, no.2 (2004): 269–292, https://doi.org/10.1111/j.0020-8833.2004.00301

Fraser, Trudy. "Peacekeeping and Rule of Law: Challenges posed by Intervention Brigades and other Coercive designation in support of the Protection of Civilians." In *Perspective on Peacekeeping and Atrocity Prevention: Expanding Stakeholders and Regional Arrangement*, edited by David Curran, Trudy Frazer, Larry Winter Roeder Jr., and Robert Zuber, 59-87. New York/Dordrecht/London: Springer, 2015.

Friesendorf, Cornelius. "Military cultures in peace and stability operations: Afghanistan and Lebanon." *International Peacekeeping* 26, no. 2 (2019): 244-247, DOI: 10.1080/13533312.2018.1561187

Fromkin, David. *A Peace to End All Peace: The Fall of the Ottoman Empire and the Creation of the Modern Middle East*. New York: Holt Paperbacks, 1989.

Gavin, Michelle D. "Kabila Will Not Stand in Elections, but Will Congo Really Change?" *Council on Foreign Relations*, August 15, 2018. https://www.cfr.org/blog/kabila-will-not-stand-elections-will-congo-really-change

Ghali, Butros Butros. *An Agenda for Peace*, A/47/277-S/24111. New York: The United Nations, 1992.

Gibbs, David N. "Is Peacekeeping a New Form of Imperialism?" *International Peacekeeping* 4, no. 1 (Spring 1997): 122–28.

Ginty, Roger Mac and Richmond, Oliver P. "The Local Turn in Peace Building: a critical agenda for peace." *The Third World Quarterly* 34, no. 5 (2013): 763-783, https://doi.org/10.1080/01436597.2013.800750

Good, Carter V. *Introduction to Educational Research.* New York: Appleton-Century-Crofts, 1959.

Gordon, Stuart. "Unintended consequences of Civil-Military Cooperation in Peace Operations." In *Unintended Consequences in Peacekeeping Operations.* Edited by Chiyuki Aoi, Cedric de Conning and Ramesh Thakur. Tokyo/New York/Paris: United Nations University Press, 2007.

Goulart, Fernando Rodrigues. "Blue Helmets, Armed Groups, and Peace at Stake: Does Combat Motivation Matter for Robust Peacekeeping to Succeed?" *International Peacekeeping* (2020), DOI: 10.1080/13533312.2020.1827950

Goulding, Marrack. *Peacemonger.* London: The Johns Hopkins University Press, 2003.

Goulding, Marrack. "The Evolution of United Nations Peacekeeping." *International Affairs* 69, no. 3 (1993), 453.

Goldstein, Joshua S. *Winning the War on War: The Decline of Armed Conflict Worldwide.* London: Penguin Books Ltd., 2012.

Golafshani, N. "Understanding reliability and validity in qualitative research." *The Qualitative Report* 8, no. 4 (2003) 2003:597-607. http://www.nova.edu/ssss/QR/QR8-4/golafshani.pdf.

Gowan, Richard. "Diplomatic Fallout: For UN and Europe, a Peacekeeping Crisis in Lebanon." *World Political Review*, 2013.

gov.ie. "Review of the 113th Infantry Battalion Leaving for Service with UNIFIL." Last modified October 8, 2019. https://www.gov.ie/en/speech/08fd43-review-of-the-113th-infantry-battalion-leaving-for-service-with-unif/,

Griffith, James. "Survey Research in Military Settings." In *Routledge Handbook of Research Methods in Military Studies.* Edited by Joseph Soeters, Patricia M. Shields and Sebastiaan. Rietjens. New York: Routledge, 2014.

Guehenno, Jean-Marie. *The Fog of Peace*, Washington: Brookings Institution, 2015. Goldstein, Joshua S. *Winning the War on War: The Decline of Armed Conflict Worldwide.* London: Penguin Books Ltd., 2012.

Guitta, Olivier. "France and Hizbullah: The End of the Affair." *U.S.-Europe Analysis Series*, November 2005. https://www.brookings.edu/wp-content/uploads/2016/06/guitta20051103.pdf

Hair, J.F.; W.C. Black, B.J. Babin and R.E. Anderson. *Multivariate Data Analysis.* Edinburgh Gate, Harlow: Pearson Education, 2014.

Hammond, Grant T. "The Perils of Peacekeeping for the US: Relearning Lessons from Beirut to Bosnia." In *A Future for Peacekeeping.* Edited by Edward Moxon-Browne, 74–75. London: Macmillan Press, 1998.

Helmreich, Paul C. (1986) *From Paris to Sèvres: The Partition of the Ottoman Empire at the Peace Conference of 1919-1920.* Ohio: Ohio University Press, 1986.

Howard, Lise Morje. *UN Peacekeeping in Civil War.* Cambridge: Cambridge University Press, 2008.

Howard, Lise Morje and Stark, Alexandra. "How Civil Wars End: The International System, Norms, and the Role of External Actors." *International Security* 42, no. 3 (Winter 2017/18): 127–171.

Howard, Lise Morje and Dayal, Anjali Kaushlesh. "The Use of Force in UN Peacekeeping." *International Organisation* 72, no. 1 (Winter 2018): 71-103, https://doi.org/10.1017/S0020818317000431.

Howard, Lise Morje. "Peacekeeping, Peace Enforcement, and UN Reform." *Georgetown Journal of International Affairs*16, no. 2 (2015): 6-13, http://www.jstor.org/stable/43773690.

Howard, Lise Morje. *Power in Peacekeeping*. New York: Cambridge University Press, 2019.

Humphreys, Andrew; Lara Dunston and Terry Carter. *Lonely Planet Syria & Lebanon*. Footscray. Victoria: Lonely Planet Publications, 2004.

Human Rights Watch Report. "The Fall of Srebrenica and the Failure of UN Peacekeeping Bosnia and Herzegovina." October 1995. https://www.hrw.org/sites/default/files/reports/bosnia1095web.pdf.

Hunt, Charles T. "All necessary means to what end? The unintended consequences of the 'robust turn' in UN Peace Operations." *International Peacekeeping* 24, no. 1 (2017) :108-131.

Ingresson, Tony. *The Politics of Combat: The Political and Strategic Impact of Tactical-Level Subcultures, 1939-1995.*, 2016. Lund University. http://lup.lub.lu.se/record/8871111.

International Peace Institute "Prioritizing and Sequencing Peacekeeping Mandates: The Case of MINUSMA." May 31, 2018. https://www.ipinst.org/2018/05/prioritizing-and-sequencing-peacekeeping-mandates-the-case-of-minusma.

Israel Ministry of Foreign Affairs. Last modified 2018. https://mfa.gov.il/MFA/ForeignPolicy/MFADocuments/Yearbook1/Pages/THE%20ARMISTICE%20AGREEMENTS.aspx.

Jacobson, Tomas W. "UN Peacekeeping: Few Successes, Many Failures, Inherent Flaws." *International Diplomacy & Public Policy Centre*, LLC, Colorado (March–April 2017). www.IDPPCENTER.com

Jett, Dennis C. *Why Peacekeeping Fails*. New York: Palgrave, 2001.

Jews Virtual Library. "Immigration to Israel: British Restrictions on Jewish Immigration to Palestine." Accessed October 8, 2020, https://www.jewishvirtuallibrary.org/british-restrictions-on-jewish-immigration-to-palestine.

Jones, M. L. "Using software to analyse qualitative data." *Malaysian Journal of Qualitative Research* 1, no. 1(2007): 64-76.

Jones, Bruce; and Hart, Andrew. "Keeping Middle East Peace?" International Peacekeeping 15, no. 1 (2008), 112:102-117.

Julian, Rachel; and Gasser, Russell. "Soldiers, civilians and peacekeeping – evidence and false assumptions." *International Peacekeeping*, 26, no. 1 (2019): 22-54. https://doi.org/10.1080/13533312.2018.1503933.

Junk, Julian; Francesco Mancini, Wolfgang Seibel and Till Blume., ed. *The Management of Peacekeeping*. London: Lynne Reinner Publishers, 2017.

Johansen, R.C. "U.N. Peacekeeping: How Should We Measure Success?" *Mershon International Studies Review* 38, no. 2 (1994):307-310.

Kalyvas, Stathis N. *The Logic of Violence in Civil War.* New York: Cambridge University Press, 2006.

Karam, Zeina. *Associated Press*, April 20, 2017.

Karlsrud, John; and Smith, A. C. "Europe's Return to UN Peacekeeping? Lessons from Mali." *Providing for Peacekeeping Report*, no. 11 (International Peace Institute, July 2015). http://www.ipinst.org.

Karlsrud, John and Oksamytna, Kseniya. "Norms and Practices in UN Peacekeeping: Evolution and Contestation." *International Peacekeeping*, 26, no.3 (2019), 253-254, DOI:10.1080/13533312.2019.1600637

Karlsrud, John. "Special Representatives of the Secretary-General as Norm Arbitrators? Understanding Bottom-up Authority in UN Peacekeeping." *Global Governance*, no.19(2013)

Kathman, Jacob. "Personal composition and member state contributions to United Nations peacekeeping operations." In "The known knowns and known unknowns of peacekeeping data," *International Peacekeeping* 24, no. 1 (2017):1-62. Edited by G. Clayton, DOI: 10.1080/13533312.2016.1226768

Kaufman, Asher (2010) "From Litani to Beirut – Israel's invasions of Lebanon 1978-85: causes and consequences." In *Israel and Hezbollah: An asymmetric conflict in historical and comparative perspective.* Edited by Clive, Jones and Sergio, Catignani. New York: Routledge, 2010.

Kedar, Lt Col (retd) Mordechai. "Why Do the Arabs Hate the Palestinians?" *The Begin-Sadat Centre for Strategic Studies*, September 24, 2020, https://besacenter.org/perspectives-papers/do-arabs-hate-palestinians/

Kenkel, Kai Michael. "Five generations of peace operations: from the "thin BL" to "painting a country blue." *Revista Brasleira de Politica International* 56, no. 1 (2013), Institute of Brasileira de Relacoes Internacionais, http://dx.doi.org/10.1590/S0034-73292013000100007.

Keinon, Herb. (2006, August 21) "Annan to give UNIFIL 'teeth'." *Jerusalem Post*, August 21, 2006, national edition.

"Khartoum Declaration of Agreement Between Parties of the Conflict in South Sudan." https://igad.int/programs/115-south-sudan-office/1874-khartoum-declaration-of-agreement-between-parties-of-the-conflict-in-south-sudan,

Khazen, Wadith el. "The Litani river of Lebanon and the desire of Israel to obtain additional water sources." Khazen.org The Information Newspaper, News, History, Community and Blogs. December 15, 2001. https://www.khazen.org/index.php/archive/92-de-khazen-members/cheikh-wadih-el-khazen/97-blank-78510489.

Khashan, Hilal. "The Middle East Alliance," *Geopolitical Futures*, September 22, 2020, https://geopoliticalfutures.com/the-new-middle-east-alliance/

King, Antony. "Defining Command." *Command: The Twenty-First Century General* (Cambridge: Cambridge University Press, 2019)

Knight, Andy. "Civil-Military Cooperation and human security." In *Civil-Military Cooperation in Post-Conflict Operations: Emerging theory and practice*, edited by Christopher Ankersen, 15-30. London/New York: Routledge, 2008.

Kochhar, M.R. *United Nations Peacekeeping and Operations in Somalia*. Gurgaon: Dipika Kochhar, 2000.

Koops, Joachim A.; Thierry Tardy and Paul D. Williams., eds *The Oxford Handbook of United Nations PKO*. Oxford: Oxford University Press, 2015.

Konrad, Mike. "The White Paper of 1939." *The American Thinker*, June 2, 2013. http://www.americanthinker.com/articles/2013/06/the_white_paper_of_1939. html.

Koss, Maren. "Flexible Resistance: How Hezbollah and Hamas Are Mending Ties." *Carnegie Middle East Centre*, July 11, 2018. https://carnegie-mec.org/2018/07/11/flexible-resistance-how-hezbollah-and-hamas-are-mending-ties-pub-76782

Koul, Luka Biong Deng. "Lessons form a Decade of South Sudanese Statehood." *Peacebuilding, Regions and Power*, Prio Blogs, July 11, 2021, https://blogs.prio.org/2021/07/lessons-from-a-decade-of-south-sudanese-statehood/

Kneissl, Karin. "An Analysis on UNIFIL Three Years after: How and until when will the "interim" continue?" November 2009. *Friedrich Ebert Stiftung*. http://library.fes.de/pdf-files/bueros/beirut/07161.pdf.

Kondoch, Boris. *International Peacekeeping*. Hampshire: Ashgate, 2007.

Kumalo, Liezelle. "South Sudan can learn from Liberia's road to peace." *ISS*, September 3, 2018. https://issafrica.org/iss-today/south-sudan-can-learn-from-liberias-road-to-peace?utm_source=BenchmarkEmail&utm_campaign=ISS_Today&utm_medium=email.

Labuda, Patryk I. "UN Peacekeeping as intervention by invitation: host-state consent and the use of force in Security Council-mandated stabilisation operations." *Journal on the Use of Force and International Law*, 7, no. 2 (2020): 329

Laurence, Marion. "An Impartial Force? Normative Ambiguity and Practice Change in UN Peace Operations." *International Peacekeeping*, 26, no.3 (January 2019), 258: 256-280, DOI:10.1080/13533312.2018.1517027

Lawrence, Tony. "Estonia has announced that it will shortly discontinue its deployment of peacekeepers to the UNIFIL mission in Lebanon." *International Centre for Defence and Security*, https://icds.ee/estonia-leaves-unifil/, last modified October 8, 2018.

Lawrence, Tony; Jermalavicius, Tomas; and Bulakh, Anna. "Soldiers for Peace: Estonia, Finland and Ireland in UNIFIL." *ICDS Report*, December 2016.

"Missions of the Lebanese Army." On the Issues. https://www.lebarmy.gov.lb/en/content/mission-lebanese-army.

Lipson, Michael. "A 'Garbage Model' of UN Peacekeeping." *Global Governance* 13, no. 1 (2007): 79-97.

Lipson, Michael. "Peacekeeping: Organised Hypocrisy." Paper prepared for the Workshop on Peacekeeping and Politics, Columbia University, October 17-18, 2002.

Lipson, Michael. 'Peacekeeping reform: managing change in an Organized Anarchy', *Journal of Intervention and Statebuilding* 6, no. 3 (2012): 279-298.

Lipner, Michele and Livingstone, Ann. "Impact Evaluations and Assessment of UN Peace Operations: What is the State of the Art?" *Challenges Forum Occasional Paper* no. 6 (2015). Sweden: Taberg Media Group AB, Laholm.

Luthans, Fred. "Successful vs. Effective Real Managers," *The Academy of Management Executive* (1987), no. 2 (May 1988): 127-132, http://www.jstor.org/stable/4164814?origin=JSTOR-pdf

Lynch, Colum. "UN Peacekeeping More Assertive, Creating Risk for Civilians." *Washington Post*, 15 August 2005

Mackinlay, John. *The Peacekeepers: An Assessment of PKO at the Arab-Israeli Interface.* London: Unwin Hyman, 1989.

Macmillan, Cham. (October 2019): 1-7, https://doi.org/10.1007/978-3-030-11795-5_20-1

Makdisi, Karim "The UNIFIL Peacekeeping Mandate: Kicking the Southern Lebanon Can Down the Road." *Pass Blue*, September 3, 2020, https://www.passblue.com/2020/09/03/the-unifil-peacekeeping-mandate-kicking-the-southern-lebanon-can-down-the-road/

Malhotra, N. K. and Dash, S. *Marketing research: An applied orientation* (6th edn.). New Delhi: Dorling Kindersley Pvt. Ltd., 2011.

Mamiya, Ralph. "Protection of Civilians and Political Strategies." *International Peace Institute Issue Brief*, May 2018. https://www.ipinst. org/2018/05/protection-of-civilians-and-political-strategies.

M. Lesch, Ann. and Tschirgi, Dan. *Origins and Development of the Arab Israeli Conflict*. West Port, Connecticut: Greenwood Press, 1998.

Mathias, Blake D. and Smith, Anne D. "Autobiographies in organizational research: using leaders' life stories in a triangulated research design." *Organizational Research Methods* 19, no. 2 (2016): 204-230.

Marton, Ference. and Booth, Shirley. *Learning and Awareness*. New Jersey: Lawrence Erlbaum Associates, 1997.

MacQueen, Norrie. *Peacekeeping and the International System*. London: Routledge, 2006.

Matthews, Joseph R. 'Assessing Organisational Effectiveness: The Role of Performance Measures.' *The Library Quarterly* 8, no. 1 (2011): 83–110.

Malito, Debora Valentina. "Neutral in Favour of Whom? The UN Intervention in Somalia and Somaliland Peace Process." *International Peacekeeping* 24, no. 2 (April 2017), 359: 280–303.

Mahmoud, Youssef. "Whatever Future Holds for Peace Operations, Peacebuilding must be more Local and Plural," IPI Global Observatory, September 25, 2020, https://theglobalobservatory.org/2020/09/whatever-future-holds-peace-operations-peacebuilding-must-be-more-local-plural/

Makdisi, Karim "Reconsidering the struggle over UNIFIL in Southern Lebanon," *Journal of Palestine Studies* 43, no.2 (February 2014): 24-41, https://doi.org/10.1525/jps.2014.43.2.24

Meiske, Maline and Ruggeri, Andrea. "Peacekeeping as a Tool of Foreign Policy," *Oxford Research Encyclopedias, Politics,* September 26. 2017, https://doi.org/10.1093/acrefore/9780190228637.013.462

Menkhaus, Ken. "Measuring Impact: Issues and Dilemmas." *Occasional Paper Series* Geneva: Inter Peace, 2004.

Mermin, Jonathan. "Television News and American Intervention in Somalia: The Myth of a Media-driven Foreign Policy." *Political Science Quarterly* 112, no. 3 (Autumn 1997): 385–403. https://www.jstor.org/stable/2657563.

Maxwell, J.A. *Qualitative research design: An interactive approach* (3rd ed.). Thousand Oaks, CA: Sage, 2007.

Meulen, Jan van der and Soeters, Joseph. "Introduction." In *Cultural Diversity in Armed Forces: An international comparison*. Edited by Jan van der Meulen and Joseph Soeters, 1-14. New York: Routledge, 2007

Middle East Monitor. "Hezbollah, Amal oppose Lebanon border talks with Israel." October 15, 2020, https://www.middleeastmonitor.com/20201014-hezbollah-amal-oppose-lebanon-border-talks-with-israel/

Mitchell, George E. "The Construct of Organizational Effectiveness: Perspectives from Leaders of International Non profits in the United States." *Non profit and Voluntary Sector Quarterly* 42, no. 2 (2013): 324-345.

Mor, Ben D. and Zeev Maoz. *Bound by Struggle: The Strategic Evolution of Enduring International Rivalries*. University of Michigan Press, 2002.

Masters, Jonathan, and Laub Zachary. "Hezbollah." January 3, 2014. Council on Foreign Relations., https://www.cfr.org/backgrounder/hezbollah.

Murphy, Ray. *UN Peacekeeping in Lebanon, Somalia and Kosovo. Operational and legal issues in practice*. (New York: 2007): 13-47

Murphy, Ray. "UN Peacekeeping in Lebanon and the use of force." *International Peacekeeping*, 6 no. 2 (1999): 38-63, DOI: 10.1080/13533319908413771

Nasarallah, Sayed. "Hezbollah Stronger, Gold will Always Remain Gold." Speech, Beirut, March 29, 2014. Al Manar. http://archive.almanar. com.lb/english/article.php?id=143208. http://archive.almanar.com.lb/english/article.php?id=255297.

Nasu, Hitoshi. "The Responsibility to React? Lessons from the Security Council's Response to the Southern Lebanon Crisis of 2006." *International Peacekeeping* 14, no. 3 (2007): 339-352.

Nayyar, V. K. *Winning of the Peace*. New Delhi: Sumit Enterprise, 2014.

Newby, Vanessa Frances. *Peacekeeping in South Lebanon: Credibility and Local Cooperation*. New York: Syracuse, 2018

Newby, Vanessa Frances. "Power, politics and perception: the impact of foreign policy on civilian–peacekeeper relations." *Third World Quarterly*, DOI: 10.1080/01436597.2017.1334542.

Newby, Vanessa Frances. "Positive hybridity? Unpacking UN security sector reform in South Lebanon." *Contemporary Politics*." 23, no.2 (2016):156-174.

Newby, Vanessa Frances. "Walk the Line: An investigation of the Micro-Processes of a UN Peacekeeping Mission." *Working Paper* 34 (2016):1-24.

Newby, Vanessa Frances. "Playing with Fire: Understanding the Sunni-Shiite Sectarian Lifecycle." *Griffith Asia Quarterly* 1, no. 2/3 (2013): 77-105.

Newby, Vanessa F. "Between the carrot and the stick: Mapping the role of credibility in peace operation." (Unpublished article)

Newby, Vanessa Frances. "The Pieces that Make the Peace: Micro-Processes of International Security." *International Peacekeeping* 23, no. 1 (2016): 133-157.

Newman, Edward and Oliver Richmond. *Challenges to Peacebuilding: Managing Spoilers During Conflict Resolution*. Tokyo: United Nations University Press, 2006.

Newman, Edward and Albrecht Schnabel. "Recovering from Civil Conflict: Reconciliation, Peace and Development." *International Peacekeeping Special Issue* 9, no. 2 (2002).

Nishikida, Aiko. "Palestinians from Seven Villages: their legal status and social conditions." *Koyoto Bulletin of Islamic Area Studies* 3, no. 1 (2009): 220-231.

Nisan, Mordechai. *The Conscience of Lebanon: A Political Biography of Etienne Sakr (Abu-Arz)*. London, New York: Routledge, 2003.

Noe, Nicholas. *Voice of Hezbollah: statements of Sayyed Hassan Nasrallah*. London: Verso, 2007.

Novosseloff, Alexandra. "United Nations Interim Force in Lebanon (UNIFIL I)." In *The Oxford Handbook of United Nations PKO*. Edited by Koops Joachim A., Norrie Macqueen, Thierry Tardy and Paul D. Williams. Oxford: Oxford University, 2015.

Novosseloff, Alexandra (2015). "Expanded United Nations Interim Force in Lebanon (UNIFIL II)." In *The Oxford Handbook of United Nations PKO*. Edited by Koops Joachim A., Norrie Macqueen, Thierry Tardy and Paul D. Williams. Oxford: Oxford University, 2015.

Novosseloff, Alexandra. "Can We make UN Peacekeeping Great Again?" *Global Peace Operations Review*, May 9, 2017. http://peaceoperations review.org/thematic-essays/can-we-make-un-peacekeeping-great-again.

Ottaway, Marina and Amr Hamzawy. "The Comprehensive Peace Agreement." January 4, 2011. *Carnegie Endowment for International Peace*. http://carnegieendowment.org/2011/01/04/comprehensive-peace-agreemen-pub-4223.

Parasuraman, A., Zeithaml, V. and Berry, L. L. "SERVQUAL: A Multiple-item Scale for Measuring Consumer Perceptions of Service Quality." *Journal of Retailing* 62, no. 1 (1998): 12–40.

Parker, James. *A History of Palestine from 135 AD to Modern Times*. Victor Gollancz: London, 1949.

Pepra, Kofi Nasia. *UN Robust Peacekeeping: Civilian Protection in Violent Civil Wars*. New York: Palgrave Macmillan, 2014.

Peter, Mateja. "Between Doctrine and Practice: The UN Peacekeeping Dilemma." *Global Governance* 21 (2015): 351-370.

Peterson, Scott. "Bloody Monday." In *Me Against my Brother: At War in Somalia, Sudan and Rwanda*. New York/London: Routledge, 2000.

Phyllis, Bennis. *Calling the Shots: How Washington Dominates Today's U.N.* New York: Olive Branch Press, 1996, 272.

Porter, Henry. "Days of Shame." *The Guardian*, November 17, 1995. https://www.theguardian.com/theguardian/1999/nov/17/features11.

Power, Samantha. "Come Back to UN Peacekeeping." http://www.undispatch.com

Pushkina, Darya. "A Recipe for Success? Ingredients of a Successful PKO." *International Peacekeeping* 13, no. 2 (2006):133-149.

Pushkina, Darya, Siewert, Markus B. and Wolff, Stefan. "Mission (im)possible? UN military peacekeeping operations in civil wars." *European Journal of International Relations*, 28, no. 1 (2022): 158-86. https://doi.org/10.1177%2F13540661211046602

Pouligny, Beatrice. *Peace Operations Seen from Below: UN Missions and Local People*. London: C. Hurst & Co. Publishers, 2006.

Powles, Anna; Negar Partow and Nick Nelson. *United Nations Peacekeeping Challenges: The Importance of the Integrated Approach*. Burlington, USA: Ashgate, 2015.

Questions Relating to the Situation in the Republic of Congo (Leopoldville)," https://www.un.org/depts/dhl/dag/docs/congo60.pdf

Rahman, Abdul. "Beirut blasts intensify the economic and political crisis in Lebanon," *Peoples Dispatch*, August 5, 2020. https://peoplesdispatch. org/ 2020/08/08/beirut-blasts-intensify-economic-and-political-crisis-in-lebanon/.

Raab, Jorg and Soeters, Joseph. "Peace Operations as Temporary Network Organisations." In *The Management of Peacekeeping*. Edited by Julian Junk, Francesco Mancini, Wolfgang Seibel and Till Blume. London: Lynne Rienner Publishers, 2017.

Ratner, Steven R. *The New UN Peacekeeping: Building Peace in Lands of Conflict after the Cold War*. New York: St Martin Press, 1995.

Razza, Namie Di. "What to Expect for the Future of Protection in UN Peace Operations." *IPI Global Observatory*, September 24, 2020. https:// theglobalobservatory.org/2020/09/what-to-expect-for-future-of-protection-in-un-peace-operations/

Rhoads, Emily Paddon. "Putting Human Rights up Front: Implications for Impartiality and the Politics of UN Peacekeeping." *International Peacekeeping*, 26, no. 3 (January 2019): 281-301, DOI:10.1080/13533312.2018.1561184

Rhoads, E.P. and Laurence, M. "Peace Operations, Principles, and Doctrine," In *The Palgrave Encyclopaedia of Peace and Conflict Studies*. Edited by Richmond O. and Visoka G., Palgrave

Richmond, Oliver P. "UN Peace Operations and Dilemmas of Peacebuilding Consensus." *International Peacekeeping* 11, no. 1 (March 2004): 83-101, DOI: 10.1080/1353331042000228403

Richmond, Oliver P. "The dilemmas of a hybrid peace: Negative or positive?" *Cooperation and Conflict* 50, no.1 (2015): 50-68. DOI:10.1177/001083671453 7 053

Rietjens, Sebastian, Joseph Soeters and William Klumper. "Measuring the Immeasurable? The Effect-Based Approach in Comprehensive Peace Operations." *International Journal of Public Administration* 35, no. 5 (2011): 329-338.

Rietjens, Sebastian and Ruffa, Chiara. "Understanding Coherence in UN Peacekeeping: A Conceptual Framework." *International Peacekeeping* 26, no. 4 (March 3, 2019), 402:383-407. https://doi.org/10.1080/13533312. 2019. 1596742.

Rikhye, Indar. *The Politics and Practice of United Nations Peacekeeping: Past, Present and Future*. (Toronto: Canadian International Peacekeeping Centre, 2000).

Rikhye, Indar. *The Theory and Practice of Peacekeeping*. (London: C. Hurst & Company, 1984).

Rikhye, Indar. *Military Adviser to the Secretary-General: UN Peacekeeping and Congo Crisis*. New York: St. Martin Press, 1993.

Rikhye, Indar Jit and K. Skjelsbaek, eds *The United Nations Peacekeeping: Results,*

Limitations and Prospects: The Lessons of 40 Years of Experience. London: Macmillan, 1996.

Rikhye, Indar Jit. "The United Nations Operation in the Congo: Peacekeeping, Peacemaking and Peacebuilding." In *Beyond Traditional Peacekeeping*. Edited by Donald C. F Daniel and Bradd C. Hayes. London: Macmillan, 1995, 207–27.

Rissler, Grant E. and Shields, Patricia M. "Positive Peace—A Necessary Touchstone for Public Administration." *Administrative Theory & Praxis* 41, no. 1 (2019): 60-78. https://doi.org/10.1080/10841806.2018.1479549.

Rodt, Annemarie Peen. "Successful Conflict Management by Military Means." *Ethnopolitics* 11, no. 4 (2012): 376-391.

Rose, Caroline D. "Not Quite a Lebanese-Israeli Entente," *Geopolitical Future*, October 19, 2020, https://geopoliticalfutures.com/not-quite-a-lebanese-israeli-entente/

Rubenberg, Cheryl A. *Israel and the American National Interest: A Critical Examination*. Illinois: University of Illinois Press, 1989.

Rubenberg, Cheryl A. *The Palestinians: A search of a Just Peace*. London: Lynne Rienner Publishers, 2003.

Rubinstein, Robert A. *Peacekeeping Under Fire: Culture and Intervention*. London: Paradigm Publishers, 2008.

Ruffa, Chiara. *Military Culture in Peace and Stability Operations: Afghanistan and Lebanon*. Philadelphia, Pennsylvania: University of Pennsylvania Press, 2018

Ruffa, Chiara. "What Peacekeepers Think and Do: An Exploratory Study of French, Ghanaian, Italian, and South Korean Armies in the United Nations Interim Force in Lebanon." *Armed Forces & Society* 40, no. 2 (2014): 199-225.

Ruffa, Chiara. "Military Cultures and Force Employment in Peace Operations." *Security Studies* 26, no. 3 (2017): 399-422.

Ruffa, Chiara and Pascal Vennesson. "Fighting and Helping? A Historical-Institutionalist Explanation of NGO–Military Relations." *Security Studies* 23, no. 3 (2014): 582-621.

Ruffa, Chiara. "French and Italian Units in Lebanon." *Military Cultures in Peace and Stability Operations: Afghanistan and Lebanon*,100-130. Philadelphia: University of Pennsylvania Press, 2019.

Ruffa, Chiara. "What Peacekeepers Think and Do: An Exploratory Study of French, Ghanaian, Italian, and South Korean Armies in the United Nations Interim Force in Lebanon." Armed Forces & Society 2014, 40(2) 199-225

Salvatore, Jessica Di and Ruggeri, Andrea. "Effectiveness of Peacekeeping Operations." *Contentious Politics and Political Violence, World Politics* (September 2017):1-32,

Salamey, Imad. *The Government and Politics of Lebanon*. New York: Routledge, 2013.

Sabrow, Sophia. "Local Perceptions of The Legitimacy of Peace Operations by the UN, Regional Organizations and the Individual States—A Case Study of The Mali Conflict", *International Peacekeeping* 24, no. 1 (2017):159-186.

Salvatore, Jessica Di. "Obstacle to Peace? Ethnic Geography and Effectiveness of peacekeeping" *British Journal of Political Science, 50,* no.3 (2020): 1089-1109, doi:10.1017/S0007123418000200

Sambanis, Nicholas. "Short–and Long–Term Effects of United Nations Peace Operations." The World Bank Economic Review 22, no. 1 (2008): 9-12.

Sanderson, John "The Cambodian Experience: A Success Story Still?" In *United Nations Peacekeeping Operations: Ad hoc Missions, Permanent Engagement.* Edited by Ramesh Thakur and Albrecht Schnabel. Tokyo/New York/Paris: The United Nations University, 2001,155–166.

Sandler, Todd. "International Peacekeeping Operations: Burden Sharing and Effectiveness." *Journal of Conflict Resolution* 61, no. 9 (2017):1875-1897, DOI: 10.1177/0022002717708601

Schmid Alex P. and Albert J. Jongman. *Political Terrorism: A New Guide to Actors, Authors, Concepts, Data Bases, Theories & Literature.* London: Transaction Publishers, 2005.

Seiple, Chris. *The US Military/NGO Relationship in Humanitarian Intervention.* Carlisle Barracks. PA: US Army Peacekeeping Institute, 1996.

Sherman, Jack. "With Peacekeeping Budget Approved, More Contentious Negotiations Lie Ahead." *IPI Global Observatory*, July 13, 2018. https://theglobalobservatory.org/2018/07/peacekeeping-budget-approved-contentious-negotiations ahead/

Shields, Patricia M. and Donald S. Travis. "Innovations in Warfare Strategy: Achieving Organisational Flexibility Through Ambidexterity." *Parameters* 47, no. 2 (2017): 65-76.

Shields, Patricia M. "Limits of Negative Peace, Faces of Positive Peace." *Parameters: Journal of the US Army War College* 47 (2017): 5-12.

Shields, Patricia M. and Nandini Rangarajan. *A Playbook for Research Methods: Integrating Conceptual Frameworks and Project Management.* New Forum Press, 2013. https://now.mmedia.me/Library/files.

Shields, Patricia M. "Jane Addams: Peace Activist and Peace Theorist." In *Jane Addams: Progressive Pioneer of Peace, Philosophy, Sociology, Social Work and Public Administration.* Texas: Springer International Publishing, 2017, 31-42.

Shields, Patricia M. and Joseph Soeters. "Peaceweaving: Jane Addams, Positive Peace, and Public Administration." *The American Review of Public Administration* 47, no. 3 (April 2017): 323–39. https://doi.org/10.1177/0275074015589629.

Sigri, Usal and Ufuk, Basar. "An Analysis of Assessment of PKO." *The Korean Journal of Defence Analysis* 26, no. 3 (2014): 389-406.

Sicker, Martin. *Reshaping Palestine: From Muhammad Ali to the British Mandate, 1831-1922*. Westport: Praeger Publishers, 1999.

Sirriyeh, Hussain. "The Emergence of Hezbollah and the Beginning of Resistance, 1982-85". In *An Asymmetric Conflict in Historical and Comparative Perspective*, edited by Jones, Clive and Catignani Sergio. Oxon: Routledge, 2010.

Sitkowski, Andrzej. *Peacekeeping: Myth and Reality*. London: Praeger Security International, 2006.

Skogmo, Bjorn. *UNIFIL: International Peacekeeping in Lebanon, 1978-1988*. Colorado: Lynne Rienner, 1989, 9.

Smith, Charles D. *Palestine and the Arab Israeli Conflict: A History with Documents*. Bedford/St. Martin's: Boston, 2004.

Sobelman, Daniel. "Learning to Deter: Deterrence Failure and Success in the Israel-Hezbollah Conflict, 2006-16." *International Security* 41, no. 3 (Winter 2016/17): 151-169.

Soeters, Joseph and Philippe Manigrat, ed. *Military Cooperation in Multinational Peace Operations: Managing cultural diversity and crisis response*. New York: Routledge, 2008.

Soeters, Joseph and Jan van der Meulen, ed. *Cultural Diversity in the Armed Forces: An international comparison*. New York: Routledge, 2007.

Soeters, Joseph. *Sociology and Military Studies. Classical and Current Foundations*. New York/London: Routledge, 2018.

Soeters, Joseph. *Management and Military Studies. Classical and Current Foundations*. New York/London, 2020.

Spink Lauren and Wells Matt. 'Under Fire: The July 2016 Violence in Juba and UN Response', October 5, 2016, Center for Civilians in Conflict, https://civiliansinconflict.org/publications/research/fire-july-2016-violence-juba-un-response

Spound, Daniel Levine. "Ugandan and Congolese Troops Are Conducting Joint Operations: What Could that Mean for MONUSCO?", *IPI Global Observatory*, December 20, 2021. https://theglobalobservatory.org/2021/12/ugandan-congolese-troops-joint-operations-monusco/

Stamnes, Eli. "Critical Security Studies and the United Nations Preventive Deployment in Macedonia." *International Peacekeeping* 11, no. 1 (2002):161-181.

Stewart, Lt Col., Bob. *Broken Lives: A personal view of the Bosnian Conflict*. London: Harper Collins, 1994.

Stern, Nehemia; Ben-Shalom, Uzi; Gold, Niv; Berger, Corinne; Antonovsky, Avishai; and Peleg, Dvir. "Tunnel Operations in the Israel Defense Forces: Adapting the Warrior Ethos to Post-Heroic Conflict." *Armed Forces & Society* (June 2020):1-21. https://doi.org/10.1177/0095327X20924040.

Stine, Robert and Foster, Dean. *Statistics for Business: Decision making and analysis* (2nd edn.). Pennsylvania: Pearson New International Edition, 2012.

Susan, Sach. "Weak Mandates Stall Lebanon Peacekeepers." *The Christian Science Monitor.* August 26, 2006. https://www.csmonitor.com/2006/0823/p01s03-wome.html.

Susser, Asher. "Fifty Years since the Six-Day War." *The Rusi Journal* 162, no. 3 (2017): 40-48.

Tardy, Thierry. "A Critique of Robust Peacekeeping in Contemporary Peace Operations", *International Peacekeeping* 18, no. 2 (2011): 152-167, DOI: 10.1080/13533312.2011.546089.

Tardy, Thierry. 'Emerging Powers and Peacekeeping: An Unlikely Normative Clash', GCSP Policy Paper, 2012–13. http://www.operationspaix.net,

Thakur, Ramesh and Edward Newman. *New Millennium, new perspective: The United Nations, Security and Governance.* (Tokyo: The United Nations University, 2000).

Thakur, Ramesh and Albrecht Schnabel. *United Nations PKO: Ad hoc missions, permanent engagement.* Tokyo: The United Nations University, 2001.

Thomas, David C.; Elron, Efrat; Stahl, Gunter; Ekelund, Bjorn Z; Ravlin, Elizabeth C.; Luc Cerdin, Jean; Poelmans, Steven; Brislin, Richard; Pekerti, Andre; Aycan, Zeynep; Maznevski, Martha; Au, Kevin; and Mila B. Lazarova. "Cultural Intelligence: Domain and Assessment" *International Journal of Cross-Cultural Management* 8, no. 123 (August 2008). DOI:10.1177/1470595808091787.

Toameh, Khaled Abu. "The Palestinians: Refugee Camps or Terrorist Bases?" *Gatestone Institute International Policy Council.* July 21, 2016. https://www.gatestoneinstitute.org/8511/palestinians-refugee-camps.

Tripodi, Paolo. "Soldiers' moral responsibility in peace support operations." *International Journal on World Peace* XXV, no. 1 (2008): 11-29.

Tripodi, Paolo. "When Peacekeepers Fail Thousands are going to Die. The ETO in Rwanda: A Story of Deception." *Small Wars and Insurgencies* 17, no. 2 (2006): 221-236.

Tripodi, Paolo. "Peacekeepers, Moral Autonomy and the Use of Force." *Journal of Military Ethics* 5, no. 3 (2006):14-232.

"UNDER FIRE: The July 2016 Violence in Juba and UN Response." *Centre for Civilians in Conflict,* 2016, www.civiliansinconflict.org

UN Department of Peace Operations. "The Protection of Civilians in United Nations Peacekeeping." *The,* Ref. 2019.17. November 1, 2019.

UN Department of Peace Operations. http://www.un.org/en/peacekeeping/operations/early.shtml

United Nations, "Questions Relating to the Situation in the Republic of Congo (Leopoldville)," https://www.un.org/depts/dhl/dag/docs/congo60.pdf

United Nations. "An Agenda for Peace." *Report of the Secretary-General*, A/47/277-S/24111. June 17, 1992.

UN Department of Public Information. Charter of the United Nations. New York: UN Department of Public Information, 1945.

UN. *United Nations PKO: Principles and guidelines.* New York: UN Department of Public Information, 2008.

United Nations, "Policy: The Protection of Civilians in United Nations Peacekeeping," November 2019, https://peacekeeping.un.org/sites/default/files/poc_policy_2019.pdf

United Nations Political Missions. *Report of the Secretary-General.* https://peaceoperationsreview.org/wp-content/uploads/2015/07/united_nations_report_secretary_general.pdf

UN Department of Peace Operations. Peacekeeping Operations Fact Sheet. March 31, 2020. https://peacekeeping.un.org/sites/default/files/pk_factsheet_3_20_english.pdf.

UN Security Council. *Report of the Secretary-General on the Implementation of Security Council Resolution 340 (1973)*, S/11052/Rev.1. October 27, 1973.

UN Department of Peacekeeping Operations. *UN Handbook on United Nations multidimensional PKO.* New York: Peacekeeping Best Practice Unit, 2003.

UN General Assembly Security Council. *Report of The Independent High-Level Panel on Peace Operations*, A/70/95–S/2015/446. June 17, 2015.

UN General Assembly. *Report of the Panel on United Nations Peace Operations A/55/305-S/2000/809*, August 21, 2000.

UN Department of Peace Operations. UNIFIL Background. https://unifil.unmissions.org/unifil-background.

UN General Assembly Security Council. *Agenda for Peace*, A/47/277–S/24111. June 17, 1992.

UN General Assembly. *Report of the Panel on United Nations Peace Operations*, A/55/305-S/2000/809. August 21, 2000.

UN General Assembly and Security Council. *High-Level Independent Panel Report*, A/70/95–S/2015/446. June 17, 2015.

UN General Assembly Security Council. *Comprehensive Review of The Whole Question of Peacekeeping Operations in all their Aspects A/55/305–S/2000/809*, August 21, 2000.

UN General Assembly. *Report of the Panel on United Nations Peace Operations*, A/55/305-S/2000/809. August 21, 2000.

UN General Assembly. *Report of the Special Committee on Peacekeeping Operations and its Working Group, Official Records Fifty-ninth Session Supplement No. 19 A/59/19/Rev.1*, January 31–February 25 and April 4-8, 2005.

UN General Assembly. *Approved resources for peacekeeping operations for the period from 1 July 2019 to 30 June 2020*, A/C.5/73/21. July 3, 2019.

UNGeneral Assembly. *Approved resources for peacekeeping operations for the period from 1 July 2018 to 30 June 2019*, A/C.5/72/25. July 5, 2018.

UN General Assembly. *Report of the Special Committee on Peacekeeping Operations, Official Records Seventy-Fifth Session Supplement No 19* A/75/19, 15 February-12 March 2021

UN Department of Peace Operations. "How We are Funded." https://peacekeeping.un.org/en/how-we-are-funded;

UN General Assembly. *Implementation of General Assembly resolutions*, 55/235 and 55/236, A/73/350/Add.1. December 24, 2018

UN Office of Internal Oversight Services (OIOS). https://oios.un.org/what-we-inspect-evaluate.

UN Office of Internal Oversight Services (OIOS). Inspection and Evaluation Division (IED), OIOS-IED, *Inspection and Evaluation Manual*. New York: September 2014. https://oios.un.org/sites/oios.un.org/files/images/oios-ied_manual.pdf.

UN Security Council. Situation in South Sudan, S/2019/722. September 10, 2019.

UN Office of Rule of Law and Security Institutions of the United Nations Department of Peacekeeping Operations. Planning Toolkit. https://peacekeeping.un.org/sites/default/files/planning_toolkit_web_version_0.pdf.

UN Department of Peace Operations. Background. https://unifil.unmissions.org/unifil-background.

UN Department of Peace Operations. UNIFIL Troop Contributing Countries. https://unifil.unmissions.org/unifil-troop-contributing-countries

UN General Assembly. *Report of the Panel on United Nations Peace Operations*, A/55/305-S/2000/809. August 21, 2000.

UN Department of Peacekeeping Operations and Department of Field Operations. *A New Partnership Agenda: Charting a New Horizon for UN Peacekeeping*. July 2009.

UN Peace Operations. MINUSMA Factsheet.https://peacekeeping.un.org/en/mission/minusma,

UN Security Council. *Eleventh report of the Secretary-General on the implementation of Security Council resolution 1701 (2006)*, S/2009/566. November 2, 2009.

UN Security Council. *Report of the Secretary-General on the implementation of Security Council resolution 1701 (2006)*, S/2015/147. February 27, 2015.

UN, UNIFIL. Military Strategic Concept of Operations for UNIFIL. 001/06, September 11, 2006.

UN. UNIFIL Maritime Task Force. https://unifil.unmissions.org/unifil-maritime-task-force

UN Security Council. *Report of the UN Secretary-General on the Implementation of Security Council Resolution 1701 (2006)*, S/2013/381. June 26, 2013.

UN Security Council. *Report of the UN Secretary-General on the Implementation of Security Council Resolution 1701 (2006)*, S/2017/201. March 8, 2017.

UN Security Council. United Nations Interim Forces in Lebanon, *Report of the UN Secretary-General*, S/2020/473. June 1, 2020.

UN Security Council. *Eleventh report of the Secretary-General on the implementation of Security Council resolution 1701 (2006)*, S/2009/566. November 2, 2009.

UN Security Council. *Report of the Secretary-General on the implementation of Security Council resolution 1701 (2006)*, S/2017/59. July 11, 2017.

UN Security Council. *Report of the Secretary-General on the implementation of Security Council resolution 1701 (2006)*, S/2019/237. March 14, 2019.

UN Security Council. *Report of the Secretary-General on the implementation of Security Council resolution 1701 (2006)*, S/2018/210. March 8, 2018.

UN Security Council. *Report of the Secretary-General on the implementation of Security Council resolution 1701 (2006)*, S/2018/210. March 8, 2018.

UN Security Council. *Report of the Secretary-General on the implementation of Security Council resolution 1701 (2006)*, S/2008/425. June 27, 2008.

UN Security Council. *Progress report of the Secretary-General on Ethiopia and Eritrea*, S/2001/1194. December 13, 2001.

UN Department of Safety and Security. https://www.un.org/en/safety-and-security

UN, *The Blue Helmets: A Review of United Nations Peacekeeping*. New York: United Nations, 1996.

UN Security Council. *Report of the Secretary-General on the implementation of Security Council resolution 1701 (2006)*, S/2015/147. February 27, 2015.

UN Security Council. *Report of the Secretary-General on the implementation of Security Council resolution 1701 (2006)*, S/2006/670. August 18, 2006.

UN Security Council. *Report of the Secretary-General on the implementation of Security Council resolution 1701 (2006)*, S/2022/556. July 14, 2022.

UN General Assembly. Press Releases, GA/11927, June 30, 2017; GA/AB/4287. July 5, 2028.

UN General Assembly. Resolution A/RES/1000 (ES-I). November 5, 1956.

UN General Assembly. *Approved resources for peacekeeping operations for the period from 1 July 2019 to 30 June 2020*, A/C.5/73/21. July 3, 2019.

United Nations Interim Force in Lebanon. *Report of the Secretary-General*, S/2020/473. June 1, 2020.

UN Department of Peace Operations. The UNSG's Remarks to The Security Council on The Covid-19 Pandemic, April 10, 2020. https://peacekeeping.un.org/en/unsgs-remarks-to-security-council-covid-19-pandemic.

UN Department of Peace Operations, The Protection of Civilians in United Nations Peacekeeping. *The UN Department of Peace Operations*, Ref. 2019.17. November 1, 2019.

UN Security Council. United Nations Interim Force in Lebanon, *Report of the Secretary-General*, S/2020/473. June 1, 2020.

The UN *Security Council Resolutions*: S/RES/143, July 14,1960; S/RES/145, July 22,1960; S/RES/146, August 9,1960; S/RES/161, February 21, 1961; S/RES/169, November 24, 1961.

United Nations. *Security Council Resolutions*: S/RES/143, S/RES/145, S/RES/146, S/RES/161, S/RES/169, S/1978/425, S/1978/426, S/897/1994, S/2001/394, S/2006/670, S/1701/2006, S/2007/392, S/2007/641, S/2008/135, S/2008/425, S/2008/715, S/2009/119, S/2009/330, S/2009/566, S/2010/105, S/2010/352, S/2010/565, S/2011/91, S/2011/406, S/2011/715, S/2012/124, S/2012/502, S/2012/837, S/2013/381, S/2013/650, S/2014/130, S/2014/438, S/2014/784, S/2015/147, S/2015/475, S/2015/837, S/2016/189, S/2016/572, S/2016/931, S/2017/201, S/2017/591, S/2017/964, S/2018/210, S/2018/703, S/2018/1029, S/2019/237, S/2019/574, S/2019/889, S/2020/195, S/PV.8349, S/RES/2436, S/RES/ 819, S/RES/824, S/RES/836, S/RES/844, S/RES/2485, S/2022/556.

United Nations. *Summary Study of the Experience Derived from the Establishment and Operation of the Force: Report of the Secretary-General*, A/3943. October 9, 1958.

US Ministry of Foreign Affairs. https://history.state.gov/milestones/1945-1952/arab-israeli-war.

US Central Intelligence Agency. "Lebanon: Refugees and internally displaced persons." *The CIA World Factbook*. Skyhorse Publishing, 2006.

US Department of State, Bureau of Near Eastern Affairs. "Background Note: Syria", October 2005.www.state.gov.

Van der, Lijn Jair "Success and failure of UN peacekeeping in UNMIS in Sudan." *Journal of International Peacekeeping* 14, no. 1-2 (2010): 27-59.

Walter, Barbara F.; Howard, Lise Morje; and Fortna, Virginia Page. "The Extraordinary Relationship between Peacekeeping and Peace." *British Journal of Political Science* (2020): 1-18, doi:10.1017/S000712342000023X

Wallis, Tim. "Nonviolent Peace force" *Civilian Peacekeeping. Oxford Encyclopaedia of Peace, 2020.*

Wells, Matt. "How UN Peacekeepers failed in South Sudan". CNN, June 25, 2016. http://edition.cnn.com/2016/06/24/opinions/south-sudan-peacekeeping-failures-matt-wells/.

Weiss, Thomas G. "Peace Operations and Humanitarian Interventions." In *The Oxford Handbook of United Nations PKO*. Edited by Koops, Joachim A.; Norrie Macqueen, Thierry Tardy and Paul D. Williams. Oxford: Oxford University, 2015.

Weiss, Thomas G. and Kuele, Giovanna. "The Global South and UN Peace Operations." *E International Relations* February 3, 2019. https://www.e-ir.info/2019/02/03/the-global-south-and-un-peace-operations/

Whalan, Jeni. "The Local Legitimacy of Peacekeepers." *Journal of Intervention and Statebuilding*, 11, no. 3 (2017): 306-320, https://doi.org/10.1080/17502977.2017.1353756.

Whalan, Jeni. "Power, Legitimacy, and their relationship." In *How Peace Operations Work: Power, Legitimacy and Effectiveness* (Oxford: Oxford University, 2013), 55.

Willard, Emily. *Rwanda: The Failure of Arusha Peace Accords*. National Security Archive Electronic Briefing Book No. 469, 21 May 1994. https://nsarchive2.gwu.edu/NSAEBB/NSAEBB469/

Williams, Paul D. *Enhancing US Support for Peace Operations in Africa*. Council Special Report no. 73 (May 25, 2015), 3.

Williams, Paul D. "The R2P, Protection of Civilians, and UN Peacekeeping Operations." Alex J. Bellamy and Tim Dunne, eds *The Oxford Handbook of the Responsibility to Protect*. Oxford university Press, 2016. 524-544.

Wolf, E.J.; Harrington, K.M.; Clark, S.L.; and Miller, M.W. "Sample size requirements for structural equation models: An evaluation of power, bias, and solution propriety." *Educational and Psychological Measurement* 73, no. 6 (2013): 913-934.

Woodhouse, Tom and Ramsbotham. *Peacekeeping and Conflict Resolution*. (London: Frank Cass, 2000). http://openaccess.uoc.edu/webapps/o2/bitstream/10609/50481/2/United%20Nations%20and% 20peace%20 operations_Unit1_The%20United% 20Nations%2C%20armed%20 conflict%20and%20peacekeeping.pdf.

Woodhouse, Andreu Solà-Martín Tom. "The United Nations, armed conflict and peacekeeping." Universitat Oberta de Catalunya.

Woznack, Devon. "Institutionalization in the Palestinian Refugee Camps of Lebanon." *Anthós* 6, no. 1, Article 12 (2014). http://pdxscholar.library.pdx.edu/anthos/vol6/iss1/12/.

Yamashita, Hikaru. "Impartial Use of Force in United Nations Peacekeeping." *International Peacekeeping*, 15, no. 5 (November 2008)

Yawanarajah, Nita and Julian Ouellet. "Peace Agreements." In *Beyond Intractability*. Edited by Guy Burgess and Heidi Burgess. University of Colorado, September 2003. https://www.beyondintractability.org/essay/structuring_peace_agree

Yukin, Eugene. "UNIFIL's Mandate and Rules of Engagement." *Middle East Policy and Security*, 2009. https://www.aub.edu.lb/ifi/ifi_saj/Documents/saj2009/unifil_mandate_rules_of_engagement_yukin.pdf.

Zartman, William and J. Lewis Rasmussen. *Peacemaking in International Conflict: Methods & Techniques*. Washington: United States Institute of Peace, 2011.

Zikmund, W.G.; Babin, B.J.; Carr, J.C.; Adhikari, A.; and Griffin, M. *Business Research Methods: A South-Asian Perspective* (8th edn.). Delhi: Cengage Learning India Pvt. Ltd., 2016.

Index

*

ABOUT THE AUTHOR

Major General (Dr) Apurba Kumar Bardalai is a veteran of the Indian Army and a graduate of the Defence Services Staff College, Wellington (India). During his service in the army, he held various command and staff assignments at different levels including the command of an infantry division. He was also the Commandant of the Indian Military Training Team in Bhutan from October 2011 to January 2014. Earlier, he served as a Military Observer in the United Nations Verification Mission in Angola in 1991-92. He was awarded the Ministry of External Affairs Fellowship at the United Services Institution of India for the year 2003-2005 for his research on "Changing Global Security: Its implications for UN Peacekeeping Operations." He also served in Lebanon as the Deputy Head of the Mission and Deputy Force Commander of UNIFIL from 2008 to 2010. The author holds a Ph.D. from Tilburg University, the Netherlands, for his research on *United Nations Interim Force in Lebanon: Assessment and Way Forward.*

Contact: *tonybardalai@gmail.com*